# The Logics of Healthcare

The Professional's Guide to Health Systems Science

# The Logics of Healthcare

## The Professional's Guide to Health Systems Science

Paul Lillrank

**CRC Press**
Taylor & Francis Group
Boca Raton London New York

CRC Press is an imprint of the
Taylor & Francis Group, an **informa** business

A PRODUCTIVITY PRESS BOOK

CRC Press
Taylor & Francis Group
6000 Broken Sound Parkway NW, Suite 300
Boca Raton, FL 33487-2742

© 2018 by Taylor & Francis Group, LLC
CRC Press is an imprint of Taylor & Francis Group, an Informa business

---

**Library of Congress Cataloging-in-Publication Data**

---

Names: Lillrank, Paul, 1955- author.
Title: The logics of healthcare : the professional's guide to health systems science / Paul Lillrank.
Description: Boca Raton : Taylor & Francis, 2018. | Includes index.
Identifiers: LCCN 2017039161| ISBN 9781138626249 (pbk. : alk. paper) | ISBN 9780815379324 (hardback : alk. paper) | ISBN 9781315229423 (ebook)
Subjects: | MESH: Delivery of Health Care | Health Services | Models, Theoretical | Outcome and Process Assessment (Health Care)
Classification: LCC RA425 | NLM W 84.1 | DDC 362.1--dc23
LC record available at https://lccn.loc.gov/2017039161

---

Visit the Taylor & Francis Web site at
http://www.taylorandfrancis.com

and the CRC Press Web site at
http://www.crcpress.com

# Contents

# Preface

Like many colleagues in operations management, I was drawn to study healthcare for very personal reasons. Well into my forties, I encountered my first serious medical incident.

There I was, lying in a bed at the clinic for infectious diseases at Helsinki University Hospital. It was the best days of the short Nordic summer; I should have been at the beach with my kids. My journey as a patient originated a few weeks before Christmas with a routine appendicitis going bad. I got severe back pain, had to take fistfuls of painkillers, and had to walk with crutches. The docs didn't connect the dots. It took six months to find the cause, a bacterial infection in soft tissues. Taken together, everything that was investigated, said, and prescribed could have easily been done within a week. Causes were unclear, and worst of all, no one was in charge. I made the rounds between specialists, labs, and imaging. Between each service encounter, I waited a week or more.

This was a Nordic welfare state with socialist medicine. Sure, I paid only a nominal fee for each service encounter, there was no hassle with insurers, and my personal finances were not ruined. But the lavishly funded welfare state chose to waste resources on poor processes while having one of its solid taxpayers, a man in his best years and a father of four, wasting away months in pain and uncertainty as a decaying piece of inventory lost in a maze. At the infection clinic, watching the IV bag lazily empty antibiotics into my circulation, in a flash of insight, wires connected, lights came on, and I had my eureka moment. Yes, I am inventory, work in process, no, a patient in process!

I had spent the two previous decades in operations management, the scientific study of production systems. I am not an engineer; my academic home base is social sciences. After graduating from Helsinki University in the early 1980s, I was one of the hundreds of doctoral students trekking to Japan to find the secrets of the emerging industrial superpower. In 1988, I defended my dissertation on quality management in Japanese industry and then made a stint at the Boston Consulting Group working with the then novel idea of "time-based competition." I returned to academia at the Stockholm School of Economics and, from there, to my current chair in quality and service management at Aalto University in Helsinki.[1] For several years, I have regularly been teaching at the Indian Institute of Technology in Kharagpur, West Bengal.

Operations management has wrestled with the question of how to reduce inventory and shorten cycle times. Actionable knowledge and effective methods have been developed. Why couldn't these be applied to health services? When I got on my feet again, I wrote an article about the management of time in healthcare and got it published in the journal of the Finnish Medical Association. The phone started ringing. I got a grant to explore the subject further and hired a research assistant. More funding poured in and bright postgraduate students showed up, wanting to get involved. We established an institute and called it Healthcare Engineering, Management, and Architecture. Work kept coming, and in due course, the consulting outfit Nordic Healthcare Group was spun off. Since then, it has grown to be the largest boutique consultancy focused on health and welfare services in the country.

In the early nineties, the thought of applying industrial management methods to healthcare was a novelty. I recall a surgeon's conference where I was invited to speak. I asked the audience about their processes. They were confused and amused: "Look, professor, we do not do processes; we help sick people."

I come from a family with several medical doctors. I worked my way through college with odd jobs at hospitals and detox centers. I know docs are only humans. Some have a knack for jokes that other humans find outright perverse. But I was convinced that medical professionals do their best. If they run jumbled processes and waste patients' time, it must be because they do not know any better. They are not educated about processes, inventories, control methods, and supply chains. My team and I took it as our mission to tell them how. We did a swath of detailed studies, mapped processes, involved teams, and came up with new process designs. Some improvements stuck and took performance to new levels; others were flashes in the pan that quickly died out as things reverted back to normal. Even with proved, demonstrated, and measured effects, improvements remained local. The symptoms appeared at the patient process level, but the root causes must be somewhere else. We expanded the scope from processes into regional service systems and found them following the logic of retailing. Improved performance in one place caused bottlenecks elsewhere. In health services, as in any supply chain, there are system dynamic effects not visible to the naked eye.

The government Funding Agency for Innovation tasked Healthcare Engineering, Management, and Architecture to look into management innovations in healthcare. Innovation, strictly speaking, is something novel, repeatable, and beneficial both to the innovator and to key constituencies; imitation and investment do not count.

---

[1] Aalto University was formed in 2010 as the result of a merger of the Helsinki University of Technology (established in 1849), the Helsinki School of Economics (1905), and the Helsinki School of Art and Design (1871).

In Finland, about three-quarters of health services are produced by the public sector. There we found no innovations. Indeed, some of the regional health districts performed clearly better than others, although it was hard to put a finger on exactly what they did differently. In a country where all districts operated under a similar regulatory and financial regime, the difference between the best and the worst was incredibly high. The findings from a small homogeneous Nordic society were essentially the same as in the well-known Dartmouth studies by John Vennberg and others. There was no meaningful and systematic connection between demand and supply, needs and resource consumption. In the United States, the amount of money spent is higher, and in India, much lower, but similar structural problems are present at all levels of expense.

In the private sector, we found a handful of innovations; I will describe some later in this book. Despite obvious benefits, all were struggling to get traction. There was no stampede from other providers to copy and implement.

My trust in the good intentions of the medical profession got a beating. I still believe that the absolute majority of medical professionals mean well and work hard. There are data from patient satisfaction surveys to prove that people in general have good experiences from service encounters with caregivers, but not necessarily from dealing with the system. The same problems pop up in both tax and insurance-financed systems. As the Organisation for Economic Co-operation and Development economics department puts it,[2] "There is no health care system that performs systematically better in delivering cost-effective health care." It may thus be less the type of system that matters and more how it is managed. Both market-based and more centralized command-and-control systems show strengths and weaknesses.

There must be a peculiar logic of healthcare that beats easy explanation.

Healthcare is a fiercely contested area of public policy everywhere, a political Moby Dick with the power to frustrate both the mighty and the benevolent. But debate is not necessarily the same as dialogue. A conversation can't lead to shared understanding if the participants can't agree on basic vocabulary. Many key concepts, such as health, process, performance, quality, value, and outcomes, are fuzzy, contradictory, and overlapping. System theorist Stuart A. Kauffman has stated a very basic truth about the need for conceptual clarity: "Only what is clearly separated can be properly joined."[3] This is the mission of this book.

This book will not provide shovel-ready solutions. You will not find the two principles and the five action points to put in place next Monday. I have written this as a postgraduate-level textbook for readers with an interest in health systems science.

---

[2] OECD (Organisation for Economic Co-operation and Development). 2010. Health care systems: Getting more value for money. OECD Economics Department Policy Notes, No. 2. Paris: OECD. https://www.oecd.org/eco/growth/46508904.pdf

[3] Kaufman, S.A. 2008. *Reinventing the Sacred: A New View of Science, Reason, and Religion.* New York: Basic Books.

This emerging field needs to take a page from the book of engineering. Technologies, even those that deal with behavior, are based on knowledge. Knowledge of a subject is the answer to three questions: what is it, what can be known about it, and how it works. Research should generate such knowledge and test it in practice.

I have written this book with three types of readers in mind. Many postgraduate students in operations management are interested in healthcare. You know the basics of industrial dynamics, but have rudimentary understanding of health services, bar some personal experiences. To you, I intend to show that production principles can be applied, but when I say "applied," I really mean it. With all due respect to Toyota Motor Company and Lean healthcare, a hospital is not a factory, patients do not move on assembly lines, and an operating room is not a machining center.

The second group I have in mind is medical school students. Recently, I have met more and more of you as my home base, Aalto University School of Science, and the friendly neighborhood medical school of Helsinki University have found each other in a common vision. Medical students have acquired or are about to acquire domain knowledge in anatomy, physiology, and a plethora of pathologies. You have cut dead bodies and met real patients in real distress. But your training provides little understanding of the system that sends you to the front line.

The third group is the practitioners, administrators, and policy-makers in the field. You have read some books and attended seminars. You have embarked on quality journeys, described processes, and reduced waste. You have picked the low-hanging fruit and now ask, now what? I hope this book will provide a conceptual ladder to reach beyond the obvious.

# Acknowledgments

This book has been long in the making. I am most grateful to all my students, who have offered both inspiration and criticism; to all the medical practitioners, who have insisted on relevance; and to colleagues in academia, who have demanded rigor.

My students at Aalto, Johan Groop, and Tomi Malmström joined me in a series of brainstorming sessions to develop the original idea of demand–supply operating modes,[1] the conceptual underpinning of this book. I have learned a lot from the critical enthusiasm of Paulus Torkki, Anssi Mikola, Antti Peltokorpi, Karita Reijonsaari, Julia Venesmaa, Iiris Hörhammer, Katariina Silander, and An Chen.

The founding team of the Nordic Healthcare Group, Vesa Kämäräinen, Petri Parvinen, Virpi Kronström, and Jaakko Kujala, as well as the builders, Olli Tolkki, Vesa Komssi, Riikka-Leena Leskelä, and Petri Heikkilä, demonstrated that theories can be turned into technologies. At Helsinki University Hospital, Markku Mäkijärvi and Janne Aaltonen have been great sparring partners, and Juha Tuominen in the private sector.

My many visits to the Indian Institute of Technology in Kharagpur have opened my eyes to global health and the Lean solutions in developing countries. The Rajendra Mishra School of Engineering Entrepreneurship and its head, Professor Partha Pratim Das, have generously hosted me as a regular visitor. Discussions with assistant professor Ram Babu Roy and research scholars Sreekanth V K, Amrita, and Mohd. Zuhair and many others have stimulated my thinking greatly. V.K. Singh, with a distinguished career in military medicine and health policy, has been a good friend and excellent guide to the predicament of healthcare in the developing world.

In Japan, I learned a lot from Professor Michiko Moriyama of Hiroshima University, Professor Hironobu Matsushita of Tokyo University of Information Sciences, and Professor Hideyuki Kawaguchi of Seijo Gakuen University.

I am grateful to my employer, Aalto University School of Science, for granting me a sabbatical leave that made writing this book possible, as well as to the International House of Japan in Tokyo, which provided a relaxing environment for the tedious work.

---

[1] Lillrank, P., Groop, J., and Malmström, T. 2010. Demand and supply–based operating modes—A framework for analyzing health care service production. *Milbank Quarterly* 88:4, pp. 595–615.

# Author

**Paul Lillrank** has been a professor of quality and service management at Aalto University in Helsinki since 1994. He has served as the head of the Department of Industrial Engineering and Management for eight years and had been academic dean of the school's MBA program.

Paul Lillrank earned a PhD in social and political sciences from Helsinki University in 1988 after spending six years as a postgraduate student in Japan, where he researched quality management in Japanese industry. After graduating, he joined the Boston Consulting Group in Tokyo and later in Stockholm, returning to academia in 1992 as an affiliated professor at the European Institute of Japanese Studies at the Stockholm School of Economics. He has been a visiting professor at the University of Tokyo, has served as program director at the College des Ingenieurs in Paris, and teaches regularly at the Indian Institute of Technology, Kharagpur.

# Chapter 1

# Introduction

Health is a human capability that enables well-being, work, and happiness. Care is an essential good, like air, water, food, and shelter. Health, however, can't be had on a plate or consumed from a tap. While some determinants of health, such as nutrition and drugs, are tradable products, one man's health is not another's illness. Health is not a steady state. Constellations of health and illness, functioning, and disability come in all shades of gray, varying between groups, individuals, and different stages of life. Health is the outcome of several things. Some are known and predictable, such as toxins, infectious diseases, unhealthy behavior, and the inevitable frailty of old age. Others, such as the growth of cancer cells and the impact of the genome, are rift with unknowns. Still others are pure random happenstances, the tough luck of being in the wrong place at the wrong time to be hit by a truck or the cardiac attack that comes like a bolt out of the blue.

Safety and security in matters of health are fundamental concerns of societies. Governments can legitimately tax and regulate if they provide help in dire need. Human societies throw compassion, knowledge, and money against disease, trauma, and premature death. Modern medicine has increased the range of the curable and prompted communities to build health service production systems at considerable expense.

Despite best efforts, healthcare is a troubled sector everywhere. Nowhere does it work to the satisfaction of all constituencies, payers, patients, providers, and politicians. No matter the spending level, healthcare can't deliver to expectations in the same way most other industries can. We may scorn the travel and tourism sector for not having been able to offer vacations to Mars. Still, when confronted with the technical and financial obstacles of space travel, any sensible person knows to shut up. Demand accepts the limitations of supply. In healthcare, the demand–supply confrontation is not always amicable. People ask to be cured from conditions to which there is no cure and blame the system when it can't deliver. As patients seldom foot the whole bill, they don't care who pays and what it costs.

As any human endeavor, healthcare is a product of both design and evolution. As a production system, it can't violate the laws of physics, chemistry, and biology. As a social system, it is bound by norms, morality, and legislation. As a part of the pecuniary economy, it faces scarcity, trade-offs, and prioritization.

Receiving help in medical need is perceived as a universal human right. From this follows massive demand, to which the only viable solution is mass production. High-volume production must use division of labor, specialization, and standardization, from which follow fragmentation and organizational silos. Still, the core of healthcare, the transformation from illness to health, lies in the healing relationship between individuals. On the demand side, it calls for patient choice, empowerment, and individual care plans. The supply side is expected to respond with craft production, skilled professionals making items one at the time for individual customers. However, when resources are limited and everybody in need deserves something, nobody can get everything, including the full and undivided attention of a craftsman.

Medical professionals are motivated and educated for craft production. Managers are supposed to counter fragmentation by integration and connect silos with coordinated processes. Healthcare should produce diagnoses that integrate all relevant knowledge, turn them into care plans, and execute them as seamless patient journeys. Healthcare is struggling with conflicting logics, craft and mass production, patient preferences and medical expertise, and professionalism and managerialism. Healthcare has a demand problem, a supply problem, and a demand–supply matching problem.

## 1.1 Marginal Rate of Return and the Malthusian Trap

In the developing world, the scarcity of everything is the overriding concern. In poor countries like India, people die at roadsides for lack of simple basic care. When a poor country gets to invest in health services, results take off like a rocket.[1] Starting from a low base, increased health spending produces obvious gains in public health, which in turn translates into a larger and more productive labor force. The rich countries have been through all this.

### 1.1.1 Marginal Rate of Return

In terms of spending, the extreme end is the United States, with developing countries on the other end. In 2014, the United States spent 18% of its gross national product (GNP) on health, while India managed a paltry 4.7%, that is, $9403 versus $75 in current dollars per person per year.[2] The European Union average per capita expenditure was US$3613.

One of the best-known figures in health economics is the curve showing the relationship between health expenditure and public health expressed as life expectancy at birth.[3] When average spend per capita passes the $2000 per capita mark, the curve starts to flatten out. The connection between resources and effects weakens and eventually turns slightly negative. This is the marginal rate or return. The first unit of consumption brings happiness and joy, the second less so, and the third is not worth the money. Increased spending delivers a declining amount of utility and people stop consuming. The logic of the marginal rate of return does not hold in health services.

Will the demand for health services ever saturate? A healthy middle-aged person is inclined to think that no sensible person can wish to spend one extra minute at a hospital. Health services are not inherently pleasant; visits to the dentist are pure horror. Demand, however, is not only the number of people seeking help, but the number of health problems and the corresponding volume of care episodes. A rather small minority consumes the lion's part of all services. In the United States, the top 1% ranked by their healthcare expenses accounted for more than a fifth of the total expenditure, and the top 5% for half of it. Overall, the sickest half of the population accounted for 97.3%, while the other half consumed only 2.7% of care.[4] Demand is not evenly distributed across populations; it can keep growing while the average health of the average person improves.

Despite the high and rising expenditure, the rich world is marred by a sense of scarcity. There is never enough; more could always be spent. Healthcare is in a Malthusian trap.[5] Reverend Thomas Malthus (1766–1834), one of the great classical economists, described the pervasive logic of scarcity in preindustrial societies. Good fortunes can increase a society's food resources. Abundance will lead to population growth. With more mouths to feed, the per capita food supply retires back to its original level. Any increase in supply is consumed by an equal increase in demand. No matter the absolute amount of food, populations constantly balance at the edge of starvation.

In the United Kingdom, the National Health Service (NHS) offers its services free of charge at the point of care. Between the years 2000 and 2010, it got a budget increase of about 50%.[6] That did next to nothing to reduce queues. No matter how much money politicians fork over, the service constantly claims it is underfunded. Every year, there is a winter of discontent. The same phenomenon is visible at emergency departments everywhere. Queues are long and some patients leave without being seen. Increasing capacity has little effect on queue length because as soon as patients realize that waiting times are reasonable, the arrival rate increases, which adds to the queue again.

The original Malthusian trap of food production was sprung by overwhelming force: the enormous productivity increase following the Industrial Revolution. Starvation was overcome and eventually turned into surplus and gluttony. Many great social thinkers, from Karl Marx to Lord Beveridge,[7] the founder of the British welfare state, and John Maynard Keynes,[8] the most influential economist of the 20th century, believed that when basic needs are fulfilled and daily life is no longer a survival game, the marginal rate of return effect will kick in. People will stop consuming and turn their interest toward leisure and noble pursuits in the realms of social life, fine arts, and spirituality. However, so far there is no evidence, beyond some fringe groups, that demand would saturate. Reverend Malthus would have been shocked to know that obesity is now a more serious health problem than malnourishment in the world, with the exception of sub-Saharan Africa.[9] The health service providers who constantly ask for more are not willing to estimate a spending level at which demand for care would saturate.

### 1.1.2 Cuckoo Effect

A nation may, through its elected representatives, decide to spend its wealth on health services rather than on defense, education, or railroads. It would be an allocative decision based on preferences and acknowledged trade-offs. Why not? Healthcare is a good industry. It does not pollute much. It offers a lot of employment opportunities at all skill levels.

Health expenditure, however, does not increase as a chain of rational decisions and carefully weighted choices between alternative good things. The public wants to have its cake and eat it too. Costs keep growing stealthily below the radar. Public providers on annual fixed budgets use up all their means by mid-October. Then, they turn to politicians and ask for more under thinly veiled threats to refuse service and cause political mayhem. Private providers order more diagnostic examinations and clinical interventions and expect to get paid regardless of accomplished health value. Insurers hike their rates; politicians increase taxes or cut budgets elsewhere.

Health expenditure in the rich world has for decades been growing faster than economic output.[3] The ratio of healthcare expenditure has grown in relation to everything else, the GNP, total government outlays, and household consumption. Healthcare becomes the cuckoo chick that expands at the expense of others and kicks many a noble pursuit out of the nest.

What can't go on must stop. It can be a calamitous fiscal breakdown or a slow decay in increments small enough to elude perception and resolute political action.

Lionel Shriver uses the liberties of a fiction writer to paint such a picture in her dystopian novel *The Mandibles*.[10,11] The Mandibles are a wealthy family in New York. The story starts in 2029 with a cyber-attack and a fiscal crisis. Organized oldies of the "me generation" have an iron grip of politics. While schools, public order, electricity, and sanitation slowly collapse, the only things that remain standing are inflation-adjusted Medicare and Social Security, consuming 80% of federal and local budgets. The fortune of the Mandibles descends from comfortable upper middle class to paupers and eventually to unpaid farm labor.

Catastrophe scenarios are not part of polite conversations. Alarmism may lead to ill-founded political moves. Nevertheless, the Malthusian trap and the cuckoo effect are real to anybody who bothers to pay attention to the public policy debate and look at the numbers. Cost inflation has many causes but no silver bullet solution.

## 1.2 Demand-side Cost Drivers

Increased life expectancy and public health are the supreme human welfare achievements of market capitalism, rules-based orderly societies, and the rational tradition of the Enlightenment. But success can have unintended consequences.

### 1.2.1 Old Normal

From the year zero to 1700 productivity, the relation between input and output hardly grew at all and the per capita economic output remained flat. In the mid-19th century, after a long and torturous start, the wealth created by industrial capitalism started to trickle down to the masses. While the figures vary by country, region, and social class, by and large the average person in the rich world now has a material standard of living that is up to 30 times higher than it was when Marx and Engels published the *Communist Manifesto* in 1848.[12]

Better nutrition and sanitation reduced the burden of infectious diseases and malnutrition. In the leading industrial nation, the United Kingdom, life expectancy started to pick up in the mid-19th century from the long-term historical average of around 40. By the start of World War II, it had climbed to 60, in 1955 it reached 70, and it has continued to the current 80+.[13]

The years from 1948 to 1973 were an exceptional period in human history. Now is nostalgically known as the Golden Decades or the Old Normal.[14] Several factors contributed to the rapid growth and equitable spread of wealth in Western societies. World War II caused damage that had to be repaired. It eliminated old elites and installed democracy and participation. Populations were young with few dependents (the demographic dividend). Technological advances turned into mass-produced items (automobiles, airplanes, white goods, and consumer electronics) that created new industries with well-paid jobs. Western countries had a monopoly on the institutions of capitalism, functioning markets, good governance, rule of law, and professional management. The Old Normal was also a period of rapid and revolutionary innovations in medicine.

### 1.2.2 Old Normal of Clinical Medicine

During most of its history, Western medicine, as described by David Wootton in *Bad Medicine*,[15] did more harm than good. That was neither for malicious intent nor for lack of effort. The premodern world had no scientifically sound theories about the human body and its diseases that could have led to technologies, that is, effective therapies. The turning point came in the late 19th century. More than 200 years of tinkering with microscopes finally led to the microbe theory of disease and a practical technology when Joseph Lister, in 1875, performed the first antiseptic surgical operation. It took about 70 more years before modern medicine could deliver life-saving interventions.

Clinical medicine went from victory to victory in the battle against the Grim Reaper. James Le Fanu[16] has summed the major innovations as the 12 definitive moments:

1. Penicillin
2. Cortisone
3. Connection between smoking and lung cancer
4. Chlorpromazine (reduces the effects of psychosis)
5. Polio vaccination and intensive care
6. Open heart surgery
7. Hip and knee joint replacement surgery
8. Kidney transplantations
9. Stroke prevention
10. Childhood cancer cures
11. Test-tube babies
12. Discovery of the helicobacter, the cause of peptic ulcer

The results were overwhelming enough to prompt rapid diffusion. For penicillin, no clinical trials or regulatory approvals were even thought of.

During the third quarter of the 20th century, clinical medicine accomplished what engineering had done a century earlier with steam engines, dynamite, steel-hulled ships, and the telegraph. It delivered marvels that made the miracles of saints look paltry in comparison.

Postwar economic growth led to massive public health programs and the welfare state. Healthcare became a universal human right, and theory-based therapies were within the reach of everybody. In 1839, the then richest man in Europe, Nathan Rothschild, died at the age of 59 from a staphylococcus inflammation on his lower back. The man who could buy everything died of a routine infection easily cured today for anyone who could find his way to a doctor, even a pharmacy.[17]

A quarter of a century of marvelous growth created expectations of ever-continuing progress. The genie was out of the bottle and refused to go back when the world changed.

### 1.2.3 New Normal

The Golden Decades came to an abrupt stop in October 1973 with the first oil crisis. It caused economic turmoil and political insecurity and brought a new awareness of the limits of growth and doubt in continuing progress. The oil crisis was a seminal event but not a root cause. For reasons that have caused much controversy among economists, the productivity growth rate stalled and has since not recovered, except for a brief jump in the early 1990s with the internet boom. The collapse of communism, the euphoria of the "end of history",[18,19] and the marvel of the internet and smartphones have masked the secular trend of sluggish productivity growth.

Every political measure on both the right and the left has been tried to no avail. For the time being, the New Normal is here to stay.

The simple explanation is that the Old Normal was an exception.[20] Some of the growth drivers were not replicable. Women can be liberated from the kitchen to the workplace only once, education opportunities eventually reach the limits of ability, technologies mature, and baby boomers grow old. Infrastructure, such as water and sewage, can be built once; then, it is there as a continuous source of value but not as an engine of growth. To illustrate, *The Economist* put on its January 12, 2013, cover an image of Rodin's famous statue "The Thinker," seated on a toilet, pondering, "Will we ever innovate anything this useful again?" Western economies have reached an innovation frontier not easily penetrated. The New Normal means it is back to ordinary economics, with long-term growth rates at best around 1% or 2%.[21] It is not enough to sustain the appetite of the healthcare cuckoo.

## *1.2.4 Collateral Damage and Unintended Consequences*

Healthcare is a victim of the economic success of capitalism and its own accomplishments. When people no longer died like flies of infectious diseases and compound fractures, mortality was reduced and life expectancy grew. Many survived their disease debut, the cardiovascular and cancer incidents that previously took away people in their early fifties. But every success sows the seeds of its own undoing. A menace crept upon health services, frailty, and the reduced mental functioning that comes with advanced age.

Populations have been aging slowly and steadily since the 18th century. It is not the state of affairs as such but the rate of change that creates problems.

With reduced mortality, morbidity changes shape. The bulk of demand has shifted from accidents and infections to noncommunicable diseases (NCDs), many related to lifestyles and old age. Simultaneously, capitalist opulence had a devastating impact on work ethics, communities, families, and health behavior.[22] Mechanization reduced hard toil and long walks, while more than enough calories were consumed. Smoking, indeed, has been reduced due to persistent campaigning. Other public health methods appear toothless against obesity, sedentary lifestyles, substance abuse, diabetes, depression, dementia, and the multitude of ailments that come with old age.

> A few years ago, I was interviewing managers at a big, brand-new hospital in New Delhi, India. I spent some time in the arrival area looking around and watching the crowd. Something felt out of place. It was not the lavish décor or the electronic signboards. It struck me that there were people of all ages. In similar places in the Nordic countries and Japan, you see only old people. The few young patients are brought in through the ambulance entrance. When I shared this observation with doctors at Helsinki University Hospital, I was promptly informed that at their internal medicine wards the patients' average age is 73.

## 1.3 Supply-side Cost Drivers

Where there is demand, there is supply. If money is no objection, service providers happily offer the best and most expensive of everything in facilities, devices, pharmaceuticals, and labor. In the United States, the world cost leader, the overall growth rate of expenditure has come down since the economic crisis of 2007. However, it still outpaces by a wide margin both economic growth and inflation and is bound to continue doing so.[23]

Incidentally, as the Old Normal turned into the New Normal, the medical innovation spigot turned itself off. Since the discovery of the helicobacter in 1976, there have been mostly incremental improvements at the margin. Medical innovations cluster around rare diseases and deliver cures that are extremely costly. Obviously, they are of great help to the concerned individuals, but the public health impact is negligible. Nothing like the 12 definitive moments has emerged to deal with diabetes, dementia, and depression.

New dramatic cures are hard to come by, but new diseases are easy to innovate. Medicalization is a process by which human conditions and troubles are defined and treated as medical issues. Particularly in "culturally transmitted diseases," such as mild depressions, supply creates demand.[24]

The supply side has not been too keen on containing costs. In all developed countries, healthcare is financed through third-party payment systems, voluntary or regulated insurance, national insurance schemes, or taxation. The third-party financiers, insurers, and governments pay providers through global budgets, fee-for-service, capitation, or combinations thereof. None provide proper incentives for what has become commonplace in competitive industries, improved quality, variety, and availability at reduced prices. Where incentives are not properly aligned, process improvement faces an uphill battle.

## 1.4 Demand–Supply Imbalance

Despite increased resources, healthcare as a whole appears to be ill-equipped to deal with the big issues, changes from short-course acute treatments with definitive ends to ailments that build up slowly and do not go away. The supply side is still geared to the episodic, urgent, and dramatic, while the average older and weaker patients demand long-term, low-intensity care. As Samuel Shem puts it in his satirical novel *The House of God*, "The cardiac team successfully prevented a timely and peaceful death".[25]

In the twilight zone between the Old and the New Normal, all health service systems in the rich world suffer from similar problems. The public debate in the United States has been fierce and the criticism devastating. It appears that nobody is willing to stand up to defend the current order; still not much is happening. The European debate has been more muted. Many U.S. commentators speak lyrically about the benefits of European universal access, tax finance, and government control. On the ground, it is the harsh prose of regional politics, professional interests, and cheap brownie points that rule the day.

In system and spending terms, the United States and the United Kingdom are the two extremes. The United States does not have a healthcare system. It is a jumbled agglomeration of all types of financial models, out-of-pocket, private insurance, managed insurance, national insurance, and the Veterans Affairs as an organizational island of tax-financed socialist medicine.[26] In the United Kingdom, everything is paid by taxes; there are no fees at the point of care. The United States spends 18% of its GNP, the United Kingdom half of that. Measured on health outcomes, both cluster near the bottom of the Organisation for Economic Co-operation and Development (OECD) countries.[27] When two very different systems exhibit similar problems, the root cause must be something other than administration and finance.

### *1.4.1 Failures of Reliability*

A service system that deals with life-and-death issues is supposed to apply the tools and technologies of high-reliability organizations. Railroads, airlines, and nuclear power plants have been through a long and torturous road of learning how to deal with risks.[28]

In the years 2000 and 2001, the Institute of Medicine Committee on Quality of Health Care in America published two exhaustive reports on healthcare: *To Err Is Human* and *Crossing the Quality Chasm*.[29] They estimated that as many as 98,000 people per year die from medical errors, more than the figure from workplace injuries. Add the financial cost to the human tragedy, and medical error rises to the top ranks of urgent public problems. Both reports emphasized that the problem is due more to error-prone institutional systems than to mistakes by individual healthcare workers. A great deal of effort has been spent to remedy the problem, particularly under the leadership of the Institute for Healthcare Improvement (IHI) and its founder, Donald M. Berwick.[30] While methodologies have been developed, it appears that they diffuse painstakingly slowly. Many countries do not even collect statistics on medical errors and adverse events. The causes are many and diverse. A common threat is that healthcare does not face the same kind of institutional pressure as other hazardous industries.

### *1.4.2 Overcare and Undercare*

The Scylla and the Charybdis[31] of modern healthcare are the simultaneity of undercare and overcare.[32] The devil is doing too little too late, and the blue sea is doing too much too soon. Undercare is obvious in poor countries and where economic access to care is limited. However, in universal access health systems at a given resource level, some patients get too little care, making them increasingly worse, while others get too much with the same outcome.

Overcare and undercare are the compound effect of two misalignments. Sometimes, the level of specialty is too low and the patient can't be helped, while at other times it is too high and wastes resources that could have done better elsewhere. Treatment can start too late in relation to an episode of illness. Care becomes more costly and complicated than that with a timely starting point. On the contrary, getting worried too early tends to lead to overdiagnosis and overcare.

Simultaneous overcare and undercare do not have a corollary in other industries. Manufacturing has no such problems. If a product is too costly to make in relation to its perceived worth, or it carries significant risk to the users, markets and regulators restore balance. In healthcare, markets and regulators are inside the system; indeed, they are essential parts of it. There are valid reasons why free competitive markets rarely work their magic in healthcare. When the brutal logic of demand and supply, the efficient monitoring of effort and outcome, and the mechanism of the marginal rate of return can't be used, somebody has to make the allocative decisions. Markets can't work and governments don't know what to do. That is a predicament.

### 1.4.3  Primary Care Comes Second

While there is growing demand for low-intensity, long-term care, specialist care and dramatic interventions still take the lion's share of budgets. This has been known for some time. In 1976, the World Health Organization (WHO) published the Alma-Ata Declaration, in which it proclaimed the priority of primary care. It is politically correct accepted wisdom. But when it comes to allocative decisions, nothing much changes. Specialized care keeps growing while primary care languishes.[33]

It is not only the policy-makers that are to blame. The general public and policy makers have by and large bought the conception of heroic medicine. The super-surgeon who can remove a life-threatening brain tumor is better paid than the primary care doctor who struggles with the endless stream of strep throats and irritated bowels. It is inevitable that markets reward the super-specialists. The tragedy of the tax-financed and publicly administered healthcare in the Nordic countries is that the governments do not use their power to go against the market.

### 1.4.4  Quality of Death

The mismatch between demand and supply is most grotesque in care at the end of life. According to a survey conducted by the Economist Intelligence Unit,[34] there is a huge gap between what people want from end-of-life care and what they are likely to get. Representative samples of people in four large countries with differing demographics, religious traditions, and levels of development (America, Brazil, Italy, and Japan) were asked a set of questions about dying and end-of-life care.

In all four countries, the majority of people said they hoped to die at home. But fewer said they expected to do so—and even fewer said that their deceased loved ones had. Apart from in Brazil, only small shares said that extending life as long as possible was more important than dying without pain, discomfort, and stress. That wish is increasingly unlikely to be granted.[35]

## 1.4.5 Craft and Mass Production

In operations management terms, the predicament of healthcare is the continuous wrestling match between craft and mass production, the need to meet every patient as an individual while being able to produce high-volume care for the masses. In this respect, healthcare struggles with the same predicament as education. The best education ever was when Socrates taught Plato, and when King Philip II of Macedon hired Aristotle to groom his son Alexander for greatness. However, education could be brought to the masses only through Prussian-style high-volume rote learning. Ever since, education has struggled with the predicament of craft and mass.[36]

Craft production at a doctor's office is appropriate for general practice and minor ailments, such as routine dental care. For specialist care, it is hardly feasible. A family doctor can't follow a patient on a complicated journey through highly specialized diagnostics and interventions. Dedicating a whole team of specialists for uninterrupted care for every patient is too costly. The solution has been to follow the example of industry and build health factories.

Mass production exploits the classical productivity drivers, division of labor, specialization, and standardization. Patients must be selected and segmented to fit medical specialties. To ensure quality and reliability, variability must be reduced by strict standards. Patients have to wait between steps. This leads to the nasty side effects of fragmentation, depersonalization, and waiting. They should be countered by integration and coordination. Somebody must integrate the specialized fragments of knowledge into a whole diagnostic picture; the standardized tasks must be coordinated into smooth flows. Manufacturers have devised methods, such as multifunctional product development teams, mass customization, modularization, enterprise resource planning (ERP) systems, kanban control, and supply chain management. Health service producers are still struggling to find corresponding mechanisms.

Industrial management methods, such as Lean and the theory of constraints (TOC), have accomplished much good. There is a large literature on the subject presenting detailed methodologies, tools, and cases.[37] There are wonderful stories of successful quality journeys spearheaded by charismatic leaders. The evidence for Lean tends to accumulate at a few successful players that appear and reappear in the textbooks: Mayo Clinic, Cleveland Clinic, Intermountain, Kaiser Permanente, Thelda Care, and the two famous Indian hospitals: Narayana Hrudayalaya in Bangalore and Aravind Eye Clinic in Tamil Nadu. On aggregate, not much is happening, at least not anything comparable to the impact Lean production has had in the automobile and consumer electronics industries. For a broad impact, management can't rely on extraordinary individuals. Operations management is successful when it develops methods that any reasonably competent and diligent manager can use.

It is not obvious that the factory should be a role model for the hospital. Despite a lot of hype in the 1990s, the factory was not a good role model even for software development.[38] Health services are partly craft, partly mass. The healing relationships are between individuals. But they need to be accomplished in huge volumes, reliably, and at affordable cost. This is the challenge of health service production.

### 1.4.6 Back to the Future

In a twist of historical irony, clinical medicine is back to the future. After a few glorious decades of progress, the medical professions again find themselves in situations where, to the majority of patients, they can't ensure health, but only deliver help. They can reduce pain, offer comfort, and, as Voltaire in the 18th century famously quipped, entertain the patient while nature has its way.

## 1.5 What to Do?

The megatrends that I have briefly sketched are scary. Policy-makers would be wise to develop a plan for how to adjust health service systems to affordable levels of spending. The larger-than-life mission of health service research is to develop insights, theories, and tools that are needed to avoid a hard landing. Indeed, a great deal of effort has been put into devising ways to deal with the predicament of healthcare. The approaches can roughly be divided into two pairs: keep spending versus stop spending, and use government force versus mobilize market forces.

### 1.5.1 Keep Spending

If people want health services, and they can afford them, what's the problem? Increase taxes, if you must. Let the cuckoo chick grow. If the other birds in the nest perish, that is, well, Darwinism. If enough resources are thrown on health services, at some point the Malthusian trap will be sprung, demand will saturate, and the health market will finally reach equilibrium. Many respected professionals[39] subscribe to this idea.

A subset of the spending option is the technology vision. With technical innovations in devices, pharmaceuticals and clinical interventions outcomes can be improved. When there is a pill for every ill, a cure for every disease, healthcare can finally deliver to demand and be worth the expense. The research community, obviously, subscribes to this idea.

## 1.5.2 Freeze Spending

The opposite view is to just stop spending. Policy-makers should make priorities, establish limits, and declare a moratorium on growth. In health systems controlled by governments, this could, technically speaking, be done by a stroke of a pen. Tax-financed systems consume exactly the amount of resources that politicians allocate, not a penny more, not a penny less. A government could simply say, "Look, folks, we can't spend this much on one cuckoo chick. Let's go back to the budget we had, say, in 2006. Not a bad year, no health catastrophes, but then we spent a fifth less than today. If we could do it then, we can do it now. When the economy picks up, there will be room for growth again."

Under ordinary circumstances, no democratic government would dare such a move. There are, however, extraordinary circumstances where draconian means have been used. A case in point is Greece. The austerity measures that were put in place by the creditors meant severe cuts in health services. The effects have been ugly. It appears that there is no orderly retreat from high to low spending, no way to just go back to what was an acceptable situation 10 years ago.[40]

The austerity option has two subsets. The administrative vision is known as New Public Management (NPM). Initiated under the Thatcher government in the United Kingdom, it arose as a response to the enormous growth of public services. Its noble objective was that health services should apply methods of business administration, clear objectives, numerical measurements, key performance indicators, and executive bonuses. Such straightforward control mechanisms, however, do not work well in professional work where key decisions are made at the operative level. NPM creates cadres of administrators with incentives to micromanage. For obvious reasons, the medical professions are militantly opposed, which indeed tends to hamper implementation.[41]

The production efficiency vision points at slack in the system. Between one-third and half of what is done in healthcare is estimated to be wasteful and not contribute to health; at times, it is even harmful.[30] The OECD estimates that by improving efficiency, public spending savings would be large, approaching 2% of the gross domestic product (GDP) on average in the OECD countries.[3]

If waste could be removed through Lean healthcare, evidence-based medicine, and justified prioritization, then there would be both resources and results. Spending could be frozen or reduced without anybody noticing. The trouble, however, is the same as with advertising. The industry knows half of the money is wasted, but nobody knows which half. Excuse the pun, but in health service systems, it is not easy to tell fat from muscle.

## 1.5.3 Government Power

Governments are involved in healthcare in all advanced societies. Free markets where patients pay out of pocket and prices are set by supply and demand in open competition exist only in some developing countries, and at fringes not covered by third-party financiers, such as cosmetic surgery. A solution would be to increase government powers. In the United States, a part of the opinion sees this as socialist medicine with death panels; others look to Europe for smart governmental solutions.

Socialist planned economies have been disasters wherever tried. But even conservatives admit that in some specific areas, such as space exploration and military hardware, they were quite efficient. Central planning can work in complicated capital goods, where negotiations are conducted between highly qualified engineering PhDs on both the buyer and the seller sides. In consumer markets, such as food and clothing, economic planners have never worked out how to match demand and supply. It is no coincidence that in the Nordic countries, where governments are in control of healthcare, specialist care in urgent matters is highly effective, while consumer healthcare is a constant source of public discontent.

From a European perspective, increasing government power does not look like an attractive solution. Politicians already have it but are reluctant or incapable of using it wisely. Governments are involved in healthcare in three ways. Governments provide financing through taxes, through national health insurance systems, or by regulating the health insurance industry. Second, governments use their powers to regulate how medicine is practiced by setting standards for professional accreditation, approving new pharmaceuticals and devices, and weeding out bad behavior. Third, governments, both central and local, can run health service production organizations, hospitals and health centers, as public bureaucracies. The first two tasks are not seriously challenged anywhere. The third, should governments engage in production, is hotly debated in the Nordic countries.

The bureaucratic government is one of the most significant innovations of Western civilization.[42] It replaced nepotism, corruption, and direct violence in the affairs of the state. Like fire, power is a good servant but a bad master. It has to be contained by rules. Such are the chain of command and reporting relationships, professional, salaried bureaucrats who are selected and advance on merit only, and due procedure and a paper trail for everything. A bureaucracy has a fixed annual budget. Bribes are not allowed; instead, there are fixed administrative fees (stamp tax). A bureaucrat is supposed to treat every citizen equally by applying the proper rules. To provide individual treatment to some is corruption. Bureaucrats must be protected against public ire; they can be sued or reprimanded only for procedural errors. It goes without saying that the principles of bureaucracy are easily corrupted. Nevertheless, an organization designed as a bureaucracy is ill-suited to deal with customer demand. Individual needs can't be accommodated if there is no corresponding rule. Fixed budgets can't respond to fluctuations in demand. Bureaucrats can't be rewarded by bonuses. A bureaucracy responds to its political masters and can be judged only in how strictly it follows rules, not by the outcomes of its actions. If a public bureaucracy is set to deliver consumer products and services, it will inevitably fail. A bureaucracy works effectively and is the proper organizational form only in issues that are of general interest, such as infrastructure, safety, and security, and/or those where consumers can't make informed choices. The bureaucratic organization is eminently suited to some health tasks, such as massive emergencies, pandemics, and vaccination programs, where the individual must submit to the public good.

Governments do not need to administer command economies or run hospitals as state bureaucracies. They can use their power to engage and direct market forces.

## *1.5.4 Market Forces*

Free and unfettered markets do not work in healthcare for many valid reasons. Fee markets are rare even in other sectors of modern economies. Virtually every commercial activity is subject to some rules set by authorities. In the Nordic countries, you can't even sell cold lemonade without permission. Indeed, no markets beyond simple barter trade can be sustained without a third party that sets rules and enforces them. All markets are quasi-markets, to some extent designed by regulators.

Markets work wonders. The power of incentives is well established both theoretically and empirically. Most people most of the time do things that they perceive to be beneficial to themselves and their communities, and avoid things that bring harm. Financiers and customers can structure incentives.

The basic financial flows are those that go from a third-party financier, insurer, or government to a care-providing organization. They can be structured in four ways: global fixed budgets, fee-for-service (pay for procedure), capitation (a membership fee that entitles the member to a set of services), and value-based care where providers are paid for accomplished health outcomes.

The logic of a quasi-market is that an authority defines what are the good things that providers should do, measures those things, and then pays for documented performance. The problem lies in definition and measurement. In healthcare, it is not obvious that more is better. Various pay-for-performance schemes typically end up supporting some kind of behavior that may not be beneficial for the whole.

The most promising line of thought is value-based healthcare (VBHC). Developed by Michael Porter and colleagues,[43] it puts forth the simple principle that health service producers should be paid by accomplished health outcomes at the patient level over a full cycle of care. Observe that the term *value* here is not an absolute but a relation, the difference between benefit and sacrifice, between what you get and what you pay. Outcome is the medical condition of a patient measured as clinical indicators, functioning, and experience at a certain point of time, typically after a cycle of care.

The principle is obvious and appealing. It is, indeed, the same as in the urban legend of the Chinese emperor and his doctors. As long as the emperor was well, the doctors were lavishly compensated. When the emperor got ill, the doctors did not receive pay. If the emperor died, the doctors promptly lost their heads.

VBHC is still a theory struggling to find its practice among several problems of defining and measuring outcomes and linking them to what was done at what expense. This is the area where advances in information and communication technology (ICT) carry a lot of promise.

Payers can use quasi-markets to put top-down pressure on providers.[44] Empowered patients can generate bottom-up pressure. After all, a customer is the economic agent who decides which provider gets paid for what. If people would pay out of pocket, or rather out of a Singapore-style publicly administered health savings account, they would become consumers keenly aware of cost and quality. On the contrary, markets would make people face the consequences of their choices. Those who don't pay attention toward their health will have to face karma or rely on a sparsely knitted governmental safety net.

Patients have not been able to leverage their power as customers for valid reasons. If a medical need is urgent, there is no time to engage in bargaining. Information asymmetry means that the doctor knows more than the patient about diseases and cures, and can use this as an advantage. Another area where ICT can have leverage is changing the doctor–patient role relation. As Eric Topol puts it, the most harrowing words a patient used to hear were, "The doctor will see you now." In the coming world of empowered patients who can shop around, Topol believes the tables will be turned. The doctor will wish to hear the words, "The patient will see you now"; that is, finally there will be a billable piece of work to do.[45]

Wearable devices, real-time monitoring, telemedicine, assisted self-service, and appointments over a web camera will increase patient choice. As usual, technology enthusiasts and early adopters tend to overestimate the short-term consequences and underestimate the long-term ones. Nevertheless, there is a real possibility that in some types of medical problems, patients can acquire enough information, knowledge, and judgment to break the traditional information asymmetry and behave like any reasonably rational consumer in the health service market.

All these suggested solutions and visions carry an element of truth. They make sense one by one, but turn muddy when confronted with the complexities of the real world.

## 1.6 Mission of This Book

The predicament of healthcare is real. It is present in the many technical dilemmas, such as overcare versus undercare, craft versus mass, and specialization versus integration, as well as in the wicked problems of priorities and allocations. Decision-makers need all the help they can get from innovators and the academic community.

### 1.6.1 Health Systems Science

This book is a contribution to the emerging discipline of health systems science (HSS). In 2008, the IHI proposed the Triple Aim as a compact set of objectives. Health service systems should simultaneously improve the individual experience of care, improve the overall health of populations, and reduce the per capita costs of care. In 2013, the American Medical Association (AMA) launched an initiative labeled "health systems science." It aims to bring together various strands of management and policy sciences into a coherent framework on how healthcare is delivered, how healthcare professionals work together, and how the health system should get its acts together in pursuit of the Triple Aim.[46]

The education system that gives access to membership in the medical professions has traditionally been standing on two legs, the biomedical basic sciences describing the human body and its functioning, and the practical clinical medicine of diagnostics and interventions. The AMA says a third leg is needed. It should be a system view that considers the totality of the pursuit of health. It should bring together the professional logic of the doctor, the commercial view of the patient, and politicians' concerns of fiscal sustainability into a managerial framework.

A system view works in two ways. It provides a holistic big picture; it also makes it possible to look at system parts and components at the microlevel. A system view is like an elevator that allows an observer to move between the whole and its parts without getting lost. The system view prompts attention to contexts. Each system level in a vertical hierarchy follows its own rules. What works on the macrolevel is not necessarily applicable on the microlevel; this is the tragedy of NPM. What works in assembly manufacturing is not always applicable in personal services.

### 1.6.2 Healthcare Is Not One

The suggested solutions to the predicament of healthcare share a common assumption. Healthcare is envisioned as one industry, with one set of problems that affect all its parts equally. Consequently, there is a search for a universal solution that could be implemented for everything with equal force and effect.

The mission of this book is to challenge the sloppy holistic vision of healthcare as one industry with one logic. Healthcare needs a coherent way to dissect the system into managerially meaningful parts. I make the argument that healthcare is cluster, or rather a multiverse of several activities, each with distinctive business models and managerial logics. All deal with medical issues, but face different types of demand to which they deploy different solutions. Some of them, particularly emergency services, are clearly identifiable. Some others do not have physical embodiments; they appear as overlapping logics of operation. To this effect, I will present the demand and supply–based operating logic (DSO).[47] It is a conceptual construct that segments healthcare into seven different types. The analytical cutting edge is demand and supply constellations, the relation between what needs to be done and what can be done. The seven DSO categories are emergency, prevention, one visit, electives, cure, care, and projects.

The predicament of healthcare looks less confusing when examining each DSO separately. Here are a few examples.

Emergency services are designed to deal with urgent and severe medical issues. Even a die-hard conservative will admit that to help people in life-threatening distress is a job suited for government, like external security (military) and internal safety (law enforcement). On the long-term aggregate level, the volume of emergency cases is predictable, but not hour by hour at specific sites. There must be resources on standby. Therefore, a global budget is an appropriate financial instrument.

Prevention deals with subclinical elevated risk. When successful, something that could have happened does not happen. It is an area where more spending is justified. However, the behavioral technologies used are not very effective; success is highly dependent on the motivation and engagement of both the caregiver and patient. Both parties should have skin in the game. Therefore, some kind of outcome value-based financial system would be appropriate.

One visit refers to medical cases that are neither urgent nor severe, such as filling a dental cavity, doing a regular medical checkup, or treating a routine infection. The services are predictable and can be selected from a menu and sold at fixed prices. Out-of-pocket payment and competitive markets can be used.

Electives are single procedures that are performed on schedule on preselected and prepared patients. They are the part of healthcare that most closely resembles an automobile assembly plant. Production efficiency following the principles of Lean management is eminently applicable. Fee-for-service and bundled payment can be used.

Cure means complex cases where the care process can't be planned in advance from end to end. It is typical for complex cancer and multimorbidities. Processes are explorative; clinical decisions need to be adjusted as experience accumulates. Cure resembles new product development. It takes teamwork, rich information, and continuous adjustment. Financial arrangements are by necessity complex.

Care is for cases that are chronic or terminal; there is no expected positive end point. Care is managed like building maintenance. The objective is to arrest decline by monitoring and regular therapies. As costs are predictable, regular payment schedules are usable.

Projects are complex undertakings involving several specialized caregivers. They can build on what is known about supply chain management and contracting.

The DSOs are systems within a system. In a similar vein, healthcare is a system within the service sector, which is bound by the general principles of production, which is founded on the basics of purposeful action in human societies.

## 1.7  Organization of This Book

The organization of this book is illustrated in Figure 1.1. To understand the logics of healthcare, it must be seen as part of the artificial world, human societies and institutions that have partly evolved through social evolution, partly been constructed as purposeful action. A specific type of purposeful action is production, the acts of transforming something of less value into something of higher value. The extreme type of production is the high-volume factory. Services are production where providers and customers collaborate to accomplish state changes in material and immaterial entities, such as repairing buildings, transporting people, and providing experiences. Healthcare is a service that provides help in medical problems. There are several issues that are similar to all health services. The DSO logics offer a sharper view based on different demand–supply constellations.

Different logics can be seen as layers. A particular instance, say a patient case, a process, the organization of a clinic, or the configuration of a regional health service system, rests on the foundations of logic. They are purposeful action; they submit to the general logic of production and to the particulars of services, consider the specifics of health issues, and need to adapt to what needs to be done and what can be done. Depending on the situation, different logics have different impacts. As an analogy, think of human behavior. There is a base layer of biology embedded in the genome. Then come early experiences, socialization within a group, education, and awareness of situations. All are at play with varying forces in singular instances.

In Chapter 2, I explore the basics of purposeful action and some methodological issues. Logic is the result of sensemaking. It comes in chunks of logic, concepts, principles, and mechanisms that help make sense of things, but do not have the power to explain or predict with precision. Healthcare is a purposeful activity with social, technological, and economic constraints. Technologies build on ontology, the conception of the nature of things; epistemology, the effort to measure and evaluate; and dynamics, the understanding of how things work. Purposeful action depends on three basic constraints an actor faces: Do you know what to do? Can you do it? Do you want to do it?

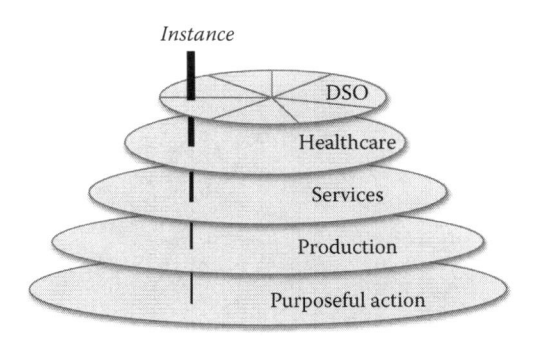

**Figure 1.1  Organization of this book.**

In Chapter 3, I describe the general logic of transformations and transactions, production and trade. All production systems are founded on one or several production functions, bundles of technologies that accomplish transformations in the entities operated on. The production function is organized as flows, processes, and systems. This is basic operations management, of which I have selected some core principles that appear in their most pure form in mass manufacturing but are general to all types of production and bear relevance to healthcare.

In Chapter 4, I build on Chapter 3 and describe how the general principles of production get amended in services. Services are collaborations where producers and customers agree on mutual rights and responsibilities in order to accomplish a state change. All services have to deal with issues that are central to healthcare, individual customer contact, immaterial explorative flows, and the distinction between what is done and how it is done.

Chapter 5 is about the characteristics of health services in general. They follow the logic of production and that of services, but have to deal with issues that are not common elsewhere. Demand comes in various types; some is urgent and some can wait. Health services have two products, to enable health and to provide help. Healthcare has four types of production functions or healing effects: the natural history of disease, the placebo effect, theory-backed therapies, and behavioral changes. They are seldom deterministic. From this follows the difference between output and outcome. The former is what is done to a patient, and the latter what happens to a patient's medical condition. The measurement and evaluation of these is the principal problem that stands in the way of VBHC.

Chapter 6 presents the DSO and how the seven DSO types are derived. A DSO is a constellation of demand and supply, what needs to be done, and what can be done.

In the final chapter, I explore some implications and possibilities that the DSO construct may open up.

## Notes

1. Novignon et al. (2012).
2. World Health Organization Global Health Expenditure database. http://data.worldbank.org/indicator/SH.XPD.TOTL.ZS.
3. OECD (2010).
4. Cohen (2014).
5. For a discussion on the Malthusian trap, see Clark (2007).
6. https://www.kingsfund.org.uk/blog/2016/05/how-does-this-years-nhs-budget-compare-historically.
7. Abel-Smith (1992).
8. Keynes (1963) expressed this vision in his famous 1930 essay, "Economic Possibilities for Our Grandchildren."
9. Global Burden of Disease Report (2010).
10. Shriver (2016).

11. For a nonfiction analysis of collapse scenarios, see Orlov (2013) and Olson (1984).
12. The standard source for long-term growth indicators is Maddison (2007). For discussion about the impact of the Industrial Revolution or bourgeois revolution, see McCloskey (2010), Mokyr (2017), and Piketty (2015). Long-term productivity has been analyzed by Gordon (2016).
13. For a detailed discussion of life expectancy, see Fogel (2004).
14. The term *New Normal* was introduced by U.S. economist Tyler Cowen in 2010 (Cowen 2010). In the period 1950–1970, the average annual per capita increase in economic output for the world was 2.8%, for Europe 3.8%, for America 1.9%, for Africa 2.1%, and for Asia 3.5%. Their corresponding figures for the period 1990–2012 were, respectively, 2.5%, 1.9%, 1.5%, 1.4%, and 3.8% (Piketty 2015; Table 21c).
15. Wootton (2006).
16. James Le Fanu (2011).
17. Landes (1999).
18. Fukuyama (1992).
19. Fukuyama has been much misunderstood. His original thesis was that history, as the struggle between liberal democracy and totalitarianism for the double price of wealth and freedom, had come to an end. History as a chain of events obviously continues.
20. Levinson (2016).
21. Piketty (2015).
22. The question of what are the social consequences of prosperity has been studied by Offer (2007) and Murray (2013).
23. Pwc. Medical cost trend: Behind the numbers 2017. https://www.pwc.com/us/en/healthcare/publications/pdf/pwc-hri-medical-cost-trend-2017.pdf.
24. Greenberg (2010).
25. Shem (1978).
26. Reid (2016).
27. OECD Health at a Glance 2016. For the argument, see Niemietz (2016).
28. Perrow (1999).
29. Institute of Medicine (1999, 2001).
30. Berwick (2014).
31. Scylla and Charybdis are sea monsters in Greek mythology. Being between them is having to choose between two evils.
32. Brownlee (2007) and Welch et al. (2011).
33. WHO (2008).
34. *The Economist*, April 29, 2017.
35. For a thoughtful discussion on end-of-life care, see Gawande (2014).
36. The struggle to solve the craft–mass predicament through technology is vividly described in Toyama (2015).
37. For academic reviews, see, for example, de Souza (2009), Mazzocato et al. (2010), and Arlbjørn and Freytag (2013). For handbooks, consider Jackson (2011), Aherne and Whelton (2010), and Albanese et al. (2014).
38. Cusumano (1990).
39. See, for example, the highly readable memoirs of Henry Marsh, a neurosurgeon, and Stephen Westaby, a cardiac surgeon. Both have made their careers within the UK National Health Service (NHS). Both suggest that the problems of care can be solved by increasing taxes and spending (Marsh 2014, Westaby 2017). For a contradictory

view of an equally accomplished oncologist in the United States, see Brawley (2011). His recipe is to stop overcare and reduce waste.

40. This is a phenomenon called hysteresis or, more specifically, elasticity limit. It is originally from materials science. If you bend a steel rod slightly and then release it, it will bounce back. If you apply force beyond a point, it will not return to its original shape. Something is broken. In labor economics, hysteresis signifies the observation that people who have suffered long bouts of unemployment are no longer employable, even when opportunities arise. In a similar vein, a retreat in healthcare spending would not be an orderly retreat to the situation just a few years back (see Stuckler and Basu 2013).

41. Simonet (2011).

42. The classical work on bureaucracy is Weber (1978).

43. Porter and Teisberg (2006) and Porter and Guth (2012).

44. In the United States and elsewhere, employers who carry a substantial burden of health costs have started putting pressure on providers (see Torinus 2014).

45. Topol (2015).

46. Skochelak and Hawkings (2017).

47. The original version of the DSO model was presented in Lillrank et al. (2010).

*Chapter 2*

# The Logic of Purposeful Action in the Artificial World

## 2.1 Logic and Sensemaking

There are several books with the title *The Logic of XYZ*.[1] Paul Sandori has written one named *The Logic of Machines and Structures*.[2] Renaissance scientists identified the six classical simple machines: lever, wheel and axle, pulley, inclined plane, wedge, and screw. They are mechanical devices that change the direction or magnitude of a force. Each represents a chunk of logic found in nature. They are the building blocks of which more complicated mechanical compound machines, such as the bicycle, are built.

Take another. Mancur Olson's *The Logic of Collective Action* (1971) is a slim volume with dense analysis. It seeks to explain several puzzling social phenomena, such as the rise of elites and oligarchies, power struggles, interest groups, and labor market machinations, and in another book of Olson,[3,4] the fall of the Soviet Union. Olson postulates a simple logic. Small groups are easier to organize than large groups. For example, the orange farmers in Florida are few enough to know each other and become aware of their common interests. They can organize a powerful lobby to get regulatory benefits, such as entry barriers. The resulting higher prices and restricted supply hurt the orange-consuming public, a very large group. It is not aware of its interest; orange eating is not a solid base for group identity. The damage per consumer is negligible; therefore, nobody bothers to fight. The logic of collective action explains how small, well-organized interest groups can exploit large unorganized groups.

### 2.1.1 Chunks of Logic and Variability

The logic of machines and the logic of collective action can be analyzed using the classical tools of the scientific method. Ontology asks what is it, epistemology ponders what can be known about it, and dynamics explicates how it works. Taken together, these three are knowledge: you know what it is, you can observe its states, and you have an idea of cause and effect. The wheel and axle consist of a wheel attached to a smaller axle with a hinge or bearing (ontology). These two parts can be observed to rotate (epistemology). A force is transferred from one to the other; a small force applied to the periphery of the large wheel can move a larger load attached to the axle (dynamics). With this knowledge, technologies can be developed, such as a wheelbarrow, wagon, windlass, and water wheel. Collective action is founded on the communication, purpose, and social organization of small groups. Knowing this, some people organize interest groups and lobbies.

The simple machines are phenomena found in nature; collective action takes place in human societies. Both nature and society are too complex to study in their totality. The scientific method reduces them to a manageable size and makes simplifying assumptions. Isaac Newton (1643–1727) discovered the three laws of motion: inertia, momentum, and reaction. They are universally true chunks of logic. However, he had to create a mental image of objects with single mass points moving in a vacuum. These conditions are seldom true in the real world, where friction and air resistance affect motion. Nevertheless, simple machines and the laws of motion can be assumed to be real, true, and effective even when they appear in contexts with several other complementary or contradictory forces in play. The logic of collective action can be observed to work in some situations; in some others, it doesn't. It is not a law of nature that would compel every small group to become a predator. But it helps make sense of what is going on and identify machinations that would remain obscure without this piece of insight.

Natural sciences can identify mechanisms and combine them as technologies that work predictably. A bicycle is a frame that puts several simple machines to work. Societies do not work that way. The history of ideas of society has been a quest for the fundamental logic of everything, the ring that rules them all. None has lasted. Even specific sectors of society, such as the economy, have been hard to capture with one logic, be it the struggle between labor and capital, aggregate demand, or the money supply. In want of a general theory of everything, we will have to make do with midrange theories[5] and chunks[6] of logic. One such is the Laffer curve, which depicts the relation between tax rate and tax revenue.[7] If the tax rate is 0%, there will be zero revenue. However, if the rate is 100%, revenue will also be zero, because people stop working or find ways to evade taxes. The rate that brings in the maximum revenue must be somewhere in between. The impact of a change in tax rate can be estimated in specific situations, but there is no formula to calculate it exactly in advance, because unknown factors affect people's behavior.

The Laffer curve makes sense, but it does not stand on a knowledge base that would enable exact predictions and fail-proof policy interventions.

Let me give another example. Assume you want to grasp the logic of travel. After the particularities of land, sea, air, and rail have been cleaned away, travel is defined by three factors: distance, time, and speed. If you know two, you can calculate the third. Their relations are true by definition; that is, they are tautologies. Nevertheless, knowing this, you can't reliably and accurately predict your arrival time. The trouble is that there is variability in all factors. Roads may be blocked and the assumed distance does not hold. Traffic may be congested, reducing speed. Travel is subject to unknown amounts and types of variability. While the logic is clear, real, and true, knowledge of it does not yet give you control, because the chunk of logic is at work in the real world, not in a vacuum where all other things are equal. Societies and economies are open systems where all potent influences can't be known and manipulated. The world is full of variability. Modern factories make utmost efforts to reduce it. Production is arranged within buildings, protected behind barbed wire, and isolated with passcodes and air locks. Nevertheless, variability is there.

In management, there are several chunks of logic. An influential one, to which I will return later, is called Little's law. It establishes the relations between cycle time, inventory, and throughput, that is, the time it takes to accomplish a series of tasks, how much stuff is in the pipeline, and how much comes out. If you know two, you can calculate the third. Like travel, this chunk of logic is tautologically true and makes perfect sense. It tells something important of how production works, but even in factories, variability frustrates precision.

### 2.1.2 Articulated Logic

Chunks of logic are expressed as concepts, abstract ideas representing the fundamental characteristics of what they represent. The nature of concepts has been debated since the ancient Greeks. The two principal schools are the nominalists and the realists. Take, as an example, the concept "bird." Have you ever seen a bird? No, you haven't, says the nominalist. You might have observed sparrows, seagulls, and pigeons, but not a bird, since it is just a name, a concept for a class of animals with feathered wings. Yes, you might have seen, with your mind's eye, the true idea of a bird, the realist would counter. What you see are only imperfect shadows of the real thing. If the debate sounds esoteric, take a more current issue. Have you ever seen a "market"? No, you haven't. The only things you can observe are transactions between buyers and sellers, which you then might arbitrarily aggregate into the markets of sport utility vehicles, currency swap obligations, lactose-free milk, or comic books. Yet, some people talk about markets as if they had a life of their own, behaviors, such as going up and down, or mental properties, such as nervosity and greed.

The sufficient answer is that concepts are useful as handles of reality. If we could only observe and talk about transactions, we would miss the forest for the trees.

A market is made out of transactions, a forest consists of trees, and a patient population includes people with medical problems. The abstract concept helps to see features that are barely visible in single instances. At the conceptual level, different forces can be identified. The behavior of others affects the decisions of buyers and sellers. A tree has different system dynamics than a forest. A patient population cannot be inferred from a single individual.

A particularly useful conceptual tool is the Weberian *ideal type* developed by the German sociologist Max Weber.[8] An ideal type is a conceptual artifact that elicits the most central features of a phenomenon. It is not meant to refer to perfect things, moral ideals, or statistical averages. Using the word *ideal*, Max Weber referred to the world of ideas or mental images, not to perfection.

The perfect market is an ideal type. Economists have built a conceptual construct that fulfills the criteria of a perfectly functioning market. The market would be thick and liquid, meaning that there were enough well-endowed buyers and sellers so that no individual could have an outsized impact on the whole. Buyers and sellers would have perfect information about the objects of transactions that would have to be in homogeneous products that would perfectly substitute for each other. Both parties would be perfectly rational in pursuing their utility. Anybody wanting to enter a market could do it without thresholds or friction, while any failure would vanish into the night without much ado.

Perfect markets do not exist in the real world; neither are they perfect in the sense that markets would solve all problems. Real markets are social constructs, rule-governed practices like marriage and family. A perfect marriage can be envisioned, but it would be hard to find an example. All real-world social systems have imperfections and are subject to variability. But without the idea of a perfect market, or a perfect marriage, or for that matter, perfect health, the imperfections cannot be identified and acted on. Thus, an ideal type provides a benchmark, a mental anchor to which the observable reality can be compared.

Several interlinked concepts make a construct. It can be an artificial creation, an ideal type like the perfect market that exists in an observer's mind, but not in the external reality. A physical construct is a physical representation of an object, which maintains general relationships between its constituent aspects, such as a model airplane or a globe. A hypothetical construct is an explanatory variable, which is not directly observable. For example, intelligence is used to explain phenomena in psychology, but it is not directly observable. A battery of tests can reveal only fragments, such as numerical or spatial intelligence. The underlying core intelligence, called the g-factor,[9] is a construct. In history, the Middle Ages is a construct that is used to delineate a historical period in Europe using some central concepts, such as feudalism, lack of economic progress, and the dominance of organized religion. For some purposes, it is useful; for others, it is a mental obstacle.

Concepts and constructs are cognitive tools that work like lenses. When you understand the concept of market, you see what you didn't see a minute ago. If you take the trouble to learn about intelligence, the world will look different.

In management, several conceptual lenses have been introduced; for example, *muda* is Japanese for waste.[10] Reducing or eliminating it is a central task of Lean production. The concept itself is a derivative from the concepts value and value-adding activities. There is no waste without value; there can be no useless things if there is no purpose. *Muda* follows from the insight that while a process is supposed to produce something valuable, everything that is done in the process is not contributing.

*Transaction cost economics* (TCE) is founded on the insight that all transactions are costly, as they require search, selection, contracting, and monitoring. When a company ponders should it make a component itself or buy it from an external supplier, it should calculate the costs of external transactions and compare them with the costs of internal administration.[11]

*Tacit knowledge* is a phenomenon explicated by knowledge management.[12] It draws attention to the fact that there is important knowledge that is not explicated and documented, but nevertheless needs to be managed.

Conceptual tools as lenses may enlarge or minimize, include or exclude. They may show sharply something while obscuring something else. If you focus on the social, you might miss the personal and vice versa. Multiple lenses provide a kaleidoscopic vision.

Constructs can be turned into dynamic models and testable hypotheses if they imply a prediction: if you do A, then B will happen with predictability *p*.

### 2.1.3 Chunks of Logic Build Intuition

Practicing managers do not necessarily have the time and skill to twist and test every chunk of logic. But it is important to be aware of them. Logic chunks do not connect as perfect and predictable general theories, but they integrate into the intuition of a manager.[13] While logic chunks do not necessarily provide instructions of what to do, they frequently tell where to look for answers and what should definitely not be done. If Little's law is part of your intuition, you know better than trying to increase throughput by reducing inventory. A great deal of the practice of medicine is based on clinical intuition made of innumerable chunks of logic.

## 2.2 Artificial World

Science is the ultimate sensemaking tool of mankind. The natural sciences have made great progress in expanding our understanding of the universe and in providing the knowledge foundation for useful technologies. So far, the scientific study of humans and their societies has not been equally successful. Following Herbert Simon's classical work *The Sciences of the Artificial* (1996), the scientific endeavor can be divided into four sectors.

## 2.2.1 Sectors of Science

### Sciences of Mind and Nature

First, there are the sciences of the mind: mathematics, formal logic, and theoretical philosophy. The founders of the Enlightenment in the seventeenth and eighteenth centuries[14] postulated reason as a universal human capability hardwired into our brains. Every properly educated individual is equally capable of seeing that 2 + 2 = 4, and that if Socrates is a man and all men are philosophers, Socrates must be a philosopher. Basic reasoning is the same in all cultures and circumstances.

Second, there are the sciences that build on observations of nature, the world out there, where it is as it is. There has been an ongoing debate on whether there really is a "world out there" and not just a reflection of the "world in here" in the mind of the perceiver. This is one of the controversies to which there is no solution[15]. For practical purposes, it suffices to say that if the world appears similar to any observer, and repeats its regularities tirelessly to any experimenter, it is there.

### Art and Humanities

The third sector is art and humanities.[16] Ideas and works of art are subject to learned commentary. English literature is about reading, understanding, dissecting, contextualizing, and commenting on great works of literature. A master's degree in literature may help, but it does not qualify one to become a successful fiction writer. Business administration is an elaborated analysis on the behavior of successful corporations. It helps to have an MBA, but it does not guarantee success as a CEO. Before the advent of modern medicine, healthcare was commentary on diseases. Doctors well versed in philosophy and theology speculated on medical conditions while nature had its course. The hard work of cutting into flesh was outsourced to barbers and military medics.

### Science of the Artificial

The fourth sector is the science of the artificial world of societies, institutions, and organizations created but not designed by humans. Natural languages are human accomplishments, but nobody ever designed them. Societies have sometimes been built to plan, but they have not necessarily turned out as intended. Society is partly built on purpose, partly evolved.

Human action takes place within and shapes the artificial world. Some of it is play where the activity itself is the end. Some is evolutionary without explicated purpose, reactions to stimuli, going with the flow. While people have limited visions and limited rationality, there nevertheless are purposes. Purposeful action—what people do for a living and for the greater good—has a purpose other than itself. It happens in, and is affected and constrained by, the various systems of the artificial world.

Logic has two components, cause and purpose. The former is what preoccupies the natural sciences. Gravity, structural mechanics, and other laws of nature form the latticework of the orderly physical universe out there. But causal explanations have a limited reach into the world of humans. I did what I did because I had to, or because I wanted to, or a combination of both. Individuals, groups, and organizations are not only reactors, mechanically responding to outer forces. Humans are *actors* that have behaviors. An actor with the capability of setting priorities and making decisions has the capability of *agency* and is called an *agent*. An agent that can observe itself and its surroundings and change accordingly is an *adaptive agent*.[17] The logic needed to cover adaptive agents should include both causes and purposes.

There is a discrepancy between individual actions and their aggregated consequences.[18] Society is not the simple sum of individual intentions, as a forest is not just the sum of the trees. Different system levels exhibit different behaviors. Some behaviors are under cognitive control; others are subject to structural influences not easily detected. The artificial world is not part of nature; neither is it beyond, separate, or independent from nature. Herbert Simon[19] put it elegantly:

> So too we must be careful about equating "biological" with "natural." A forest may be a phenomenon of nature; a farm certainly is not. The very species upon which we depend for our food, our corn and our cattle are artifacts of our ingenuity. A plowed field is no more part of nature than an asphalted street and no less.
>
> These examples set the terms of our problem, for those things we call artifacts are not apart from nature. They have no dispensation to ignore or violate natural law. At the same time they are adapted to human goals and purposes. They are what they are in order to satisfy our desire to fly or to eat well. As our aims change, so too do our artifacts and vice versa.
>
> If science is to encompass these objects and phenomena in which human purpose as well as natural law are embodied, it must have means for relating these two disparate components.
>
> But you will have to understand me as using "artificial" in as neutral a sense as possible, as meaning man-made as opposed to natural.

The artificial world can be studied using methods from natural sciences and mathematics. That is social science. But the artificial world is not governed by precise mechanisms that could be replicated, tested, and turned into technologies that social engineers might use. Social forces do not repeat themselves with the same regularity as natural forces. Nevertheless, the artificial world has some regularity, an anatomy that can be expressed as a latticework of systems of various kinds.

## 2.2.2 Structures of the Artificial World

### Systems

System is a very basic conceptualization. System is both a way to think—to be systematic—and a focus of inquiry. The Greek origin of the noun *system* is *sustema*, meaning "a composite whole."

The term *system* has many definitions promulgated by various schools of thought.[20] There is system science, systemic thinking, and systemic approaches. A frugal definition includes the following:

- A system has boundaries. Something that floats all over and penetrates everything can't be a system.
- There are two or more distinct elements or components within the boundary.
- There are some interactions between the components that make it more than the static sum of its parts.
- A system connects to other systems through interfaces.

An important aspect of system thinking is the idea of system levels from micro to macro. A leaf is a system that is part of a tree, which is a part of a forest, which is a part of a landscape. A leaf is a system composed of cells, molecules, and atoms. The human body is a system that consists of several organ systems, such as the cardiovascular, which is composed of the organs, heart, lungs, arteries and veins, and blood, which are composed of tissues that are made of cells. A small system is a component of a larger one. Each system level has a logic of its own.

System levels are units of analysis. Missing the forest for the trees is a cardinal sin. Reductionism is the idea that every complex phenomenon can be fully explained by analyzing its simplest, most basic mechanisms. Its opposite is holism (also spelled wholism), the idea that different parts are all interconnected and cannot be understood without understanding the entire whole. Reductionism and holism are extreme positions that bring simplicity, but not clarity. The middle ground takes more effort. It is to dissect systems into components, understand what they are and how they work, then put them together again as a synthesis, and then connect to the next higher system level.

### Institutions

In all societies, there are jobs to be done. Every person is born. Pregnancy and delivery are issues that must be taken care of in some way. Out of this necessity arises the institution that deals with maternity, childbirth, and infant care. The young must be nurtured and turned into functional members of society. They have to learn perception, language, rules, and roles guiding interactions between people, and acquire technologies, knowledge, and skill. This is the institution of education. People need to move; there is the institution of transport. People must eat; there are arrangements for the production, distribution, safety, and aesthetics of food. Most fundamentally, all societies need to devise ways to make and enforce rules, solve conflicts, and determine who deserves what. This is politics and administration.

Institutional theory[21] deals with the deep and resilient aspects of society. It considers the processes by which rules, norms, and routines become established as authoritative guidelines for social behavior. Daron Acemoglu and James A. Robinson[22] argue that the wealth and poverty of nations can be explained by how different societies get their key institutions in order. Nations with inclusive institutions offering space for many to participate tend to prosper, while those with exclusive institutions controlled by small elites tend to fail.

The most pertinent feature of an institution is that it is not a single structure; therefore, no single agent can control all of it. All kinds of players participate. In matters of how to raise a child, there are plentiful actors who wish to get involved, not only parents and relatives but also peer groups, media, suppliers of baby food and toys, educators, agitators, and government agencies. During human history, totalitarian regimes have made attempts to take control over institutions.[23] Most often, they have ended in failure. Society as a set of institutions has its own ways.

Health and illness are pressing human considerations. There is an institution for them. It includes health-related values, perceptions and norms, health service production, technological infrastructure, finance, and regulation. The institutional view is important to frame health service production as a part of something bigger. It is the technical element of the broader institutional arrangements around the human mind and body.

Organizations, such as hospitals, are the easily identifiable elements of institutions. Organizations have names, borders made out of membership, hierarchies of power and position, tasks, and accomplishments. Organizations are socio-techno-economic machines within which people do things.

## Instance and Context

On the microlevel, the artificial world consists of individual persons and issues. These are called instances. Production systems deal with instances. An unfinished car moving along an assembly line and an individual patient going through cancer treatment are instances of the respective production systems. Technically speaking, they are *flow units*, an individual product, person, or case that flows through a system while something is done to it.

Context is the immediate environment where the instance is located, a station at the assembly line, an examination room. One instance in one context is a situation. Situations are created when an instance and a context adjust to each other. The adjustment is called *setup*. It is a term used in operations management to depict the task of adjusting machines for a production run. The requirements of the instance and the resources available in the context are aligned. In healthcare, the basic situation, the molecule of the healthcare system, is the service encounter where a patient interacts with a healer. The setup is the various discussions, inquiries, examinations, and analyses by which the situation is made sense of and action prepared.

As depicted in the upper left corner of Figure 2.1, one instance in one context can be studied to find the logic of this particular situation. When a patient moves from one encounter to another, from the doctor's office to the lab, the pharmacy, or the operating room, the instance remains the same, but the context, and thereby the situation, changes. A string of situations are a service process. Several such processes can be bundled together to find a common pattern and describe regularities. One context with several instances allows quantitative case studies. A singular context, such as an emergency department, can be analyzed by classifying and counting instances, for example, arriving patients, to find patterns of arrival times, volumes, and primary complaints.

### Situations and Structures

If you ask somebody, "What is the best thing to do?" the answer tends to be, "It depends on the situation." Used in this way, *situation* is a conversation killer. The prudent follow-up question should be, "Sure, but what is the situation?" Or, "What kinds of situations are there?"

A perennial problem in social science is the relation between the individual and the context.[24] Contingency theory[25] is a stream of thought saying that most things depend on the context. Situations are the combination of context and instance. Both can to a variable degree be unique or usual. There are very few situations lost in space, bearing no resemblance to anything that anybody has ever experienced. Societies maintain themselves and produce stability by generating similar contexts and typical situations.[26] Service processes are made out of formatted situations.

In social sciences, there is a broad intellectual tradition called structuralism.[27] It postulates that elements of human culture and behavior must be understood in terms of their relationship to larger, overarching structures, such as Western

|  | One context | Several contexts |
|---|---|---|
| One instance | Situation<br>Single case study<br>Ethnography<br>*Service encounter* | One agent through<br>   contexts and situations<br>Narratives<br>*Service episode* |
| Several instances | Several agents in same context.<br>Quantitative case study<br>*Repetitive processes* | Quantitative cross-case<br>*Complex process*<br>*Project* |

**Figure 2.1    Instance and context.**

civilization, capitalism, and the bureaucratic state. Structuralism is the macroapproach to the artificial world, while instances, contexts, and situations are the microperspective. Both are necessary, but neither is sufficient. Looking at structures only is the holistic fallacy where individuals are reduced to pawns in a game. A pure microapproach leads to the reductionist fallacy, the view that everything can be explained by the basic building blocks, the world as movements of material, the human body as an agglomeration of cells, or the economy as the sum of trades by rational actors. The system view has it that the world is made out of layers of systems and subsystems, each with a logic of its own. A simple and useful system view is to distinguish between architecture, design, and setup.

## Architecture, Design, and Setup

Architecture here means permanent structures that are the result of major resource allocations. While nothing in the artificial world is really permanent, architecture can't be changed without adding or eliminating something substantial. Buildings are architectures set in stone, concrete, and steel. In politics, a constitution is architecture protected by a cumbersome procedure. Production architectures follow from the logic of technology. A shipyard has an architecture that differs from that of a factory producing sneakers. A passenger car has an architecture based on four wheels and a compact chassis, which differentiates it from two- and three-wheeled motor vehicles.

Design means how components and tasks are organized within an architecture. Designs have stability, but rearrangements can be made with some effort. Passenger cars can be styled for different customer segments. Restaurants have three basic designs: buffets from where customers pick different foods, a counter where orders are taken and delivered, and seating and service at the table. Organizational change is about changing processes, that is, designs of how things are done.

Setup happens when an instance approaches a context, such as when a customer expresses interest in buying. The context has its architecture and design. Within these limits, customers can choose and bargain. Car buyers can compose individual sets of colors and options; in restaurants, customers compose their meals by choosing from the menu; in the doctor's office, the patient explains the problem. Situations can be constructed by selecting from what is available and adjusting as appropriate.

Architecture, design, and setup are hierarchical system layers. The base determines the limits of what can be done at the top. Buildings are defined by load-bearing walls and stairwells. Within them, curtain walls and furniture can be designed in various configurations. If you have a party, you can set up your room by moving tables and chairs.

## 2.2.3 System Layers and Logics

In the artificial world, systems do not necessarily have sharp boundaries. Several systems impact purposeful action. In industrial psychology and sociology, there is a long tradition of research into sociotechnical systems.[28] Where humans are involved, there are psychological and social forces in motion. The social system defines a person's role in various settings, as family member, employee, citizen, customer, or passenger. Technology both commands and restricts. Economics is present when choices have to be made under scarcity; the cake can't be both kept and consumed. The artificial world can be sliced in many ways; for the sake of argument, I boil them down to these basic three: the social, the technical, and the economic system.[29]

> System perspectives are often illustrated with the ancient Indian parable of the blind men and an elephant. It is a story of a group of blind men who have never come across an elephant before. They learn and conceptualize what the elephant is like by touching it. Each blind man feels a different part of the elephant body, but only one part, such as the side or the tusk. They then describe the elephant based on their experience. Their descriptions are obviously in complete disagreement, they suspect that the other person is dishonest, and they come to blows. The moral of the parable is that humans have a tendency to project their partial experiences as the whole truth and ignore other people's experiences.

The social, technical, and economic are systems with different logics. They overlap and can be visualized, as in Figure 2.2, as layers that impact both the context and the instance. As an illustration, consider the following situation. A patient meets a doctor. An instance walks into a context, and the two make it a situation. The social system influences the beliefs, fears, and hopes of the patient. They are imprinted by earlier experiences of self and significant others. Both parties have expectations on what a proper patient–doctor relationship should be, influenced by accepted conceptions of authority and expertise. The technological system is there as knowledge acquired through education and skills developed through training. There are protocols, codified best practices, devices, and pharmaceuticals. The technology system defines what can be known about the patient's medical condition and what can be done to help. The economic system lurks in the background. The doctor expects to be paid for his efforts, as do all those who have delivered equipment and supplies. An insurance company or a government bureaucracy has established rules about costing and pricing. Everything that is technically possible is not economically affordable. Some benefits must be contrasted to costs.

Many moral dilemmas arise from conflicts between the social, technical, and economic. For example, technology has made it possible to screen unborn fetuses for genetic disorders. What used to be left for fate and providence is now subject to agonizing choice. A baby with severe handicaps puts economic strain on both the family and health finances. Social norms may forbid abortion. The three layers create a conflict that is not easily solved.

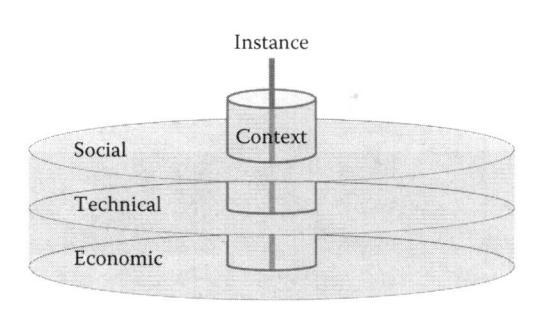

**Figure 2.2  System layers.**

## 2.2.4 Social Logic

The social world includes a myriad of things. I keep them together, for simplicity. The social world consists of individual and interpersonal behavior. It includes spirituality, the mind, and rationality. There are also issues that go beyond one person, such as group behavior, roles, status, hierarchies, and organizations as supraindividual artificial creations. Being human is to be social and to have a history. In short, the social describes what makes people human, warts and all.

Behavioral economics[30] has discovered several ways people make decisions. They are chunks of logic called heuristics, patterns of reasoning people apply when they try to make sense of situations. One such example is that people tend to put more emotional value on risk than on rewards. A dollar lost gives a three times more intense emotion than a dollar gained. Risk aversion is not rational in the sense of calculative maximization of gain, but given the logic of emotional intensity, it makes sense to pursue mental balance. Regret is, indeed, a very strong emotion that in many cases surpasses greed. Behavior that appears stupid from an economic perspective can make perfect sense from a psychological perspective. The logic of loss and regret helps explain why people are not more entrepreneurial and tend to resist organizational change. You know what you have and can imagine how it would feel to lose it, but you can't know for sure what you might get instead.

### Models of Individual Behavior

Take any major controversy about society; in the end, it boils down to two divides: Are people pieces or players? Is society held together by power or by cooperation?[31] In other words, are humans reactors that respond to structures, power, and instincts, or are they adaptive agents who shape their own worlds?

If most humans are only pawns in a game, the power of the game master determines all moves. If people are players, it is natural to assume that they get into dealings with each other and seek to better their situation through cooperation.

The power models tend to have an idea of an original model, a paradise, protocommunism, or matriarchal order that lays out the blueprint of what is good for you. Human history is conceptualized as the story of the fall. The dark side, evil forces, sin, ownership, or patriarchy destroyed paradise. Countervailing power, a messiah, a revolutionary elite, is called to restore the original order.

The cooperation model does not postulate original states but the slow evolution of man. History is driven by the evolution of cooperation in successively larger spheres, from families to clans, kingdoms, and empires. People tend to be both lazy and curious. If they can find ways to improve their situations by cooperating with others, they will do it. Cooperation, however, is not easy. There is always the risk of free riding. Societies that can figure out social arrangements to deal with destructive opportunism can enlarge the sphere of cooperation, amass more resources, build larger structures, and conquer the world.[32] Over the past two centuries, the view of man has undergone a long megatrend that has shifted to favor the view of humans as actors rather than reactors.

> When the capitalist market economy got into full gear in the mid-nineteenth century, it built colossal structures. Corporations hired armies of laborers and staffed their offices with organization men in gray flannel suits. The fragmented fiefdoms of Europe were integrated into nation-states. The power of governments increased. News media and universal schooling drove out local dialects and ancient customs and engineered national identities. Simultaneously, science and technology performed magnificent feats, compared to which the miracles of saints looked paltry. Ships could be built of material that did not rot, and the power of fire could be harnessed to make them sail against the wind. Tunnels could be dug through solid mountains and insurmountable rivers spanned with bridges of iron. Men and women could be placed in their assigned slots and made to jump on command. Economists pitched in by building models on the assumption that everybody is a rational maximizer and an economic man. Structure ruled. The individual was nothing more than an ant in a hill reacting in a predetermined way to stimuli given by the structure.
>
> The reactor model of human behavior reached its pinnacle during the World Wars. Then came time for reckoning. The dominance of structure and rationality was attacked on many fronts. One of the first was that of Herbert Simon (1947). He challenged the view that humans are rational maximizers by simply arguing that it is beyond the capacity of the brain. Even in structured situations, such as a game of chess, people cannot comprehend more than a few moves ahead. Making investment decisions under uncertainty is more challenging. Instead of maximizing, people satisfice, set up personal aspiration levels, and are content with good enough. In *A Behavioral Theory of the Firm*, Cyert and March (1963) demonstrated that corporations are not

homogeneous structures with one will and intention. Rather, they are messy coalitions of conflicting interests.

The ultimatum game, the empirical centerpiece of behavioral economics, dealt a body blow to the economic man. Simplified, the setup is as follows. You are the experimenter and you have two subjects, Ann and Bob. The deal is you will give $100 to Ann on the condition that she shares the money with Bob. Ann can decide how much she will keep for herself and how much she shares. But Bob is given the power of ultimatum. If he does not approve the sharing, neither Ann nor Bob gets anything. You, the experimenter, take the money back. For the calculating mind of the economic man, $1 is more than $0. So if Bob is a rational maximizer, he should accept any deal that gives him even a pittance. But countless repetitions of the experiment in a multitude of settings have shown that this is not how the Bobs of this world reason. The typical cutoff point is between 60/40 and 70/30. Something other than rational maximization of gain is at play. What that something is has been subject to much theorizing. It could be s sense of justice, or an aversion to being taken for a ride and being treated as a doormat. Be that as it may, the idea of rational maximization has taken a beating.

Jensen[33] has summarized the agency-based view as the resourceful, evaluative, maximizing model (REMM). It has four postulates:

1. Individuals are resourceful. They are creative and respond to changes in their environment and do what they feel is in the best interests of their own and those they care for, and avoid things that may do harm. This is the central tenant to the view of humans as adaptive agents.
2. Individuals are evaluators. They care about everything within their range of perception.
3. Individuals' wants are unlimited. There is no point of perfect satiation. The human mind always prowls for something new and better.
4. Individuals are maximizers. Given the limits of what is attainable, people want the highest combined utility. That is, people consider the relation between effort and result and are willing to make trade-offs and substitutions. Thus, maximization is not necessarily a simple-minded drive to maximize one thing, such as money or power, but to get the best deals given the pros and cons, the risk and the payoff, the effort and the outcome.[34]

## Human Relations

The social world is not only about individuals. People seek confirmation; adaptive agents adapt to the behavior of others. If something unexpected happens, a person collapses at a train station or a stock market crashes, people look not only at the object but also to other people's behavior for clues. Sensemaking is a social act.

Within the social sciences, there is a school of thought labeled constructivism. Its basic tenet is the Thomas theorem:[35] "If men define situations as real, they are real in their consequences." Action is guided by subjective perceptions and how a situation is interpreted. It does not matter whether there is an objectively correct or verifiable interpretation. If you think there is a grave danger to your health, you act accordingly.

Radical constructivism claims that almost everything is socially constructed. Human societies can make whatever arrangements they like. Families and family roles, gender, authority relations, and trading patterns can be formed without restrictions, if there is a sufficient political will.

When taken to the extremes, constructivism, like many other streams of thought, approaches the lunatic fringe. But there is an important take-home message for healthcare. People do not react to reality as it is—or as a natural scientist would have it. People react to reality as they perceive it, right or wrong. In this sense, illness and health are social constructs.

## 2.2.5 Technical Logic

Following Brian Arthur,[36] I use the word *technology* in a meaning broader than moonshots, robots, or nanomaterial. There are behavioral technologies used to alter behavior. Preventive medicine uses them a lot. It is well known that junk food and a sedentary lifestyle lead to the metabolic condition, a witches' brew of hypertension, bad cholesterol, poor respiration, abdominal fat, weak muscles, and brittle bones. Behaviors need to be changed. How is that to be done, as everybody knows it is not easy? It takes some behavioral technology.

Technology means a systematic and purposeful attempt to accomplish something based on knowledge about the underlying phenomena, be they natural, mental, physiological, or social. Technology builds on knowledge. It comes in three parts: ontology (what is it?), dynamics (how does it work?), and epistemology (what can be known about it?). When you know what something is, how much there is of it, and how it works, you have knowledge about it. With knowledge, technologies can be developed. Technology in its basic form is, if you do A, then B will follow with probability $p$ (Figure 2.3).[37]

### Ontology and Dynamics

Ontology is the area of philosophy that inquires to the essence of things: What can be said to exist? What is real? In medical contexts, ontology is akin to anatomy, the study of the structure of the human body. Over the course of history, structural elements, such as organs, tissues, and cells, have been discovered, labeled, and classified.

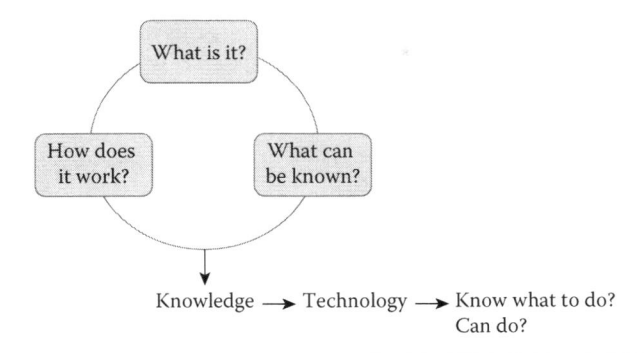

**Figure 2.3 Knowledge and technology.**

In a medical context, dynamics is akin to physiology, the study of the functioning of the body in terms of physiological systems and processes, such as the blood circulation and neural connections between the brain and muscles. Combining anatomy and physiology gives the conception of organ systems, such as the cardiovascular system that describes how the heart pumps blood through arteries to all parts of the body, transfers through minuscule capillaries to the veins, and flows back to the heart, to be pushed to the lungs for cleaning and oxygenation, and then all over again.

## Epistemology

Epistemology is the area of philosophy that inquires into what can be known, and how things can be measured. While ontology (anatomy) is about putting name tags on things, and dynamics (physiology) is about modeling relations and changes, epistemology is about quantities.[38] It is about finding the true value of a clinical indicator and steers clear of measurement errors, biases, and false representation. Ontology asks what is real; epistemology asks what is true.

A few centuries ago, the ontological inquiry into the nature of things came up with a phenomenon called temperature. A body can be hot or cold. Without physics, it was not possible to get any deeper. Casual observers can distinguish between hot and cold, the sophisticates between hot and piping hot. The epistemological question was, Can the varieties of temperature be measured somehow? The Swedish astronomer Anders Celsius (1701–1744) found a way to operationalize temperature by using a proxy, the states of water at different temperatures. Somewhat arbitrarily, and in conflict with Daniel Fahrenheit (1686–1736), he drew a line at the point where water freezes solid, and another where it turns to steam. He assumed that the phenomenon is linear and drew a scale from 0 to 100. By using other proxies, such as mercury, a measurement instrument, the thermometer was born.

States of things can be measured in absolute and relative terms. Absolute measures can be used when a context is standardized to the extent that different instances are reliably commeasurable. Think of sports. Track and field—running, jumping, and throwing—are performed in a standardized field with controlled equipment and exact measures. Therefore, there can be world and Olympic records. Running in the open, such as a road marathon, is not a standard context. Even less so is orienteering, a group of sports that require navigational skills using a map and compass to get from point to point in diverse and unfamiliar terrain. There can be no absolute and comparable readings between contests. The same is true for games, such as soccer and tennis. Performance is winning games against opponents. Victories are quantified as ranking in the leagues.

A similar distinction exists in productive activities. Some performance elements can be measured absolutely against standards, for example, the error rate in high-volume chip manufacturing, where zero defect is a relevant objective. In most other areas, it is about competing in a nonstandard field for the top position ahead of others.

While the absolute and the relative are easily distinguished, the quantitative and the qualitative are less so. As illustrated in Figure 2.4, qualitative measures can be relative, such as in a beauty contest, where the contestants are rank ordered. There is no universally accepted ontology of beauty based on which quantitative measures could be obtained. It produces numbers, the first, the second, and the third, but there is no way of telling the distance between the winner and the runners-up. Semiquantitative measures are used in sports where a panel of judges compare each performance to an idea model of, say, the perfect triple Lutz in figure skating or the spotless reverse two-and-a-half somersault dive.

Measurement is to describe things using measures, numbers that signify quantities or positions. Evaluation is to pass judgment. How good is good? How bad is bad? Is a result satisfactory, or do we need to take corrective action? Descriptive statistics present numbers; analytical statistics explore the relations between numbers.

A company makes a net profit of 1 million. That is a number produced by the accounting system. Assume the number is true. But is 1 million a good or a bad result? To know that, comparisons with other numbers must be made to produce evaluative ratios. How much was it in relation to total sales (return on sales [ROS])? What was the amount of net assets used (return on net assets [RONA])? Are those figures good or bad compared with the figures of the previous 5 years? Are they in line with the figures of other companies in the industry? Are they up to what owners and investors expect?

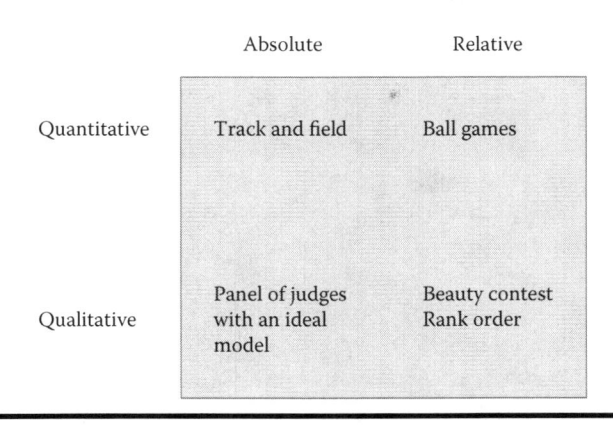

|  | Absolute | Relative |
|---|---|---|
| Quantitative | Track and field | Ball games |
| Qualitative | Panel of judges with an ideal model | Beauty contest Rank order |

**Figure 2.4   Absolute and relative, quantitative and qualitative measures.**

A single piece of measurement lost in space is a factoid. It may or may not be a true representation of the factual condition. But without context and comparison, it only looks like a fact. Evaluation is about giving meaning to facts.[39]

In competitive markets, the chief performance evaluator is the customer, the economic agent who chooses, pays, and uses. To the extent that there is choice, and people pay with money they can freely use, customers are the ultimate arbitrators of performance. In nonmarket contexts, such as public service, professional standards of conduct are established and peer reviews employed.

## *Technology*

Technology means the exploitation of a phenomenon and its known dynamics for some purpose.[36] One such phenomenon is that certain carbohydrates tend to explode when ignited. This is harnessed in the technology called the internal combustion engine. In human societies, a well-known phenomenon is that people tend to react to incentives, be they economic, social, or linked to a sense of purpose. Management exploits this through compensation systems, recognition, and corporate cultures.

Technologies that are based on knowledge about physical phenomena are physical technologies, such as engineering. Biology is the foundation of clinical medicine. Technologies that draw on knowledge about behavior are behavioral technologies. Different technologies give different levels of control. Theories of the natural world are to a large extent quantifiable and deterministic; theories of the artificial world are mostly soft, lacking the predictive power of hard science.

The purpose of science is to develop better theories; the purpose of practice is to put them in use as better technologies. The history of medicine is the interplay of theories and therapies. As sharper distinctions between anatomical entities and physiological processes and their pathologies were developed, and the results of interventions put to test, more effective therapies were developed. Technologies are designed to achieve purposes. Herbert Simon[19] puts it neatly:

> Engineers are not the only professional designers. Everyone designs who devises courses of action aimed at changing existing situations into preferred ones. The intellectual activity that produces material artifacts is no different fundamentally from the one that prescribes remedies for a sick patient or the one that devises a new sales plan for a company or a social welfare policy for a state. Design, so construed, is the core of all professional training; it is the principal mark that distinguishes the professions from the sciences. Schools of engineering, as well as schools of architecture, business, education, law, and medicine, are all centrally concerned with the process of design.

The interplay between theory and technology moves in both directions. The sequence from basic to applied science to applications is elegant but rare. A more common one is that technology develops in generations. New versions run into obstacles that require sharper theories to penetrate and thereby create the known unknowns for scientists to explore. Technologies can evolve based on observations and experience without little or no understanding about the underlying dynamics.

> A case in point is the history of the steam engine. The first workable "engine of fire" was built by Thomas Newcomb in 1711. While big, clumsy, and dangerous, it succeeded in its intended purpose to drive pumps to drain mine shafts. Thomas Watts introduced an improved version in 1765. Both of these gentlemen were illiterate but handy blacksmiths. Even with the best contemporary natural science, they would not have been able to look inside the black box of nature to know what they were doing. They just tinkered their way through trial and error and built machines that worked in practice but not in theory. A century later, Sadi Carnot and Lord Kelvin opened the box. The laws of thermodynamics finally made it possible to scientifically explain what technology had accomplished. When the underlying phenomena became captured by mathematical formula, technical development could move from tinkering to calculation.[40]

## Management Technologies

Management is a purposeful activity. It strives to organize things that will not happen spontaneously through evolution or collective action. It needs technologies based on theories of how the world works. One such example is double-entry bookkeeping. It can be said to be one of the greatest innovations of Western civilization.

Without it, the management of large enterprises would not have been possible. It paved the way to limited liability corporations, commercial credit, the market economy, and modern prosperity.

> Luca Pacioli, a contemporary and a friend of Leonardo da Vinci, invented double-entry bookkeeping. While some of the principles have appeared earlier and elsewhere, Pacioli was the first to codify the system in his mathematics textbook *Summa de arithmetica, geometria, proportioni et proportionalità*, published in Venice in 1494. It is still used in a form close to the original. The model has had staying power. The conceptualization was powerful at the root, and consistent from there up.
>
> The empirical reality is that in a business venture, money comes and goes. Imagine you run a small business, say, a bakery. Customers come in and leave money in your till. You have to pay for supplies, salaries, rents, and invest in equipment. It can become messy. Pacioli create order by giving clear definitions of basic elements, income, outlay, debit, credit, assets, and liabilities. All transactions must be recorded in ledgers. Then come the system dynamics. Your business is a system with boundaries and interfaces. Money comes in only through certain channels. There is no good fairy miraculously leaving cash under the pillow. Neither should there be any outlays that are not recorded.
>
> The system demands that every entry to an account requires a corresponding and opposite entry to a different account. One account will be debited because it receives value, and the other account will be credited because it has been given value.
>
> Recording of a debit amount and an equal credit amount results in total debits being equal to total credits in the general ledger. If the accounting entries are recorded without error, the aggregate balance of all accounts having debit balances will be equal to the aggregate balance of all accounts having credit balances. In the case of an error, each debit and credit can be traced back to a journal and transaction source document, thus preserving an audit trail. The accounting equation Equity = Assets − Liabilities serves as an error detection tool. If at any point the sum of debits for all accounts does not equal the corresponding sum of credits for all accounts, an error has occurred.
>
> A business is a microcosm of the orderly universe. Double-entry bookkeeping is both a description and a tool to manage it. In any business at any time, money has been coming, staying, and going. It took a systematic mind to find the logic and devise a method of how to exploit it.[41]

Management technologies do not have the mechanisms and machinery of engineering technologies. Very few management technologies have, like double-entry bookkeeping, a clear structure and demonstrated dynamics. The scientific foundation of management technologies is weak. But it is painstakingly emerging through a cloud of unclear language. "Profit" might be sufficiently clear, but only if you take the trouble to define it exactly, for example, as "earnings before interests, tax, depreciation, and amortization" (EBITDA). "Productivity" is reasonably straightforward as the relation between input and output, but it still requires the clarification, whether it is the input of labor, capital, or both that is counted. In healthcare, there is still a lot of confusion about what is disease, illness, or abnormality. Healthcare, as well as management, abounds with massively unclear ontologies.

Ontological exercises are sometime dismissed as "mere semantics," an endless squabble about the meaning of words. But there is no such thing as mere semantics. If speaker A uses a word that listener B understands differently, there can be no meaningful conversation, even less shared understanding. The literature on social sciences is to a large extent unproductive cacophony, as the participants can't agree on semantics, that is, a common ontology and the proper words to describe it. When starting out with a scientific inquiry that is meant to be more than mere empirical description, or an organizational change that is supposed to be more than mere cosmetics, it is advisable to spend sufficient time and effort in laying the foundations of ontology, dynamics, and epistemology.

## 2.2.6 Economic Logic

The economic world is a subset of the social; there is no economy beyond the social world. However, the economy highlights some aspects of human existence that are important enough to have their own headline.

The simplest definition of economy is "the process or system by which goods and services are produced, sold, and bought in a country or region."[42] A more sophisticated definition of the economic world is founded on the undisputable fact that resources are scarce. If anybody could get anything at any time, there would be no need for economics. Even for those who have it all, the scarcity of time, location, and attention is unavoidable. Eternal life cannot be bought. You can't physically be in two places simultaneously; neither can you give your full attention to more than one thing at a time.

### Allocation of Resources According to Preference and Utility

Resources, including time, must be allocated following some logic. Allocation means choice between alternatives. There are trade-offs: you cannot have your cake and eat it too. Allocations and trade-offs are painful; therefore, many wish to avoid and ignore the economic logic.

In order to choose, there must be some kind of preferences, a way to tell the bad from the good, and the best from the average. Economists assume that people have values that reveal themselves as preferences, although economists do not see it as their task to tell what they are or what they should be.[43] To this end, economists use the term *utility*. It is like an empty vessel; you can fill it with whatever you wish. But you can't wish that vessel away by claiming that people do not pursue their interests, however defined, or that the utilities are exactly the same for everybody.

The measurement of utility is tricky. The easiest way is to use money. However, as behavioral economics has demonstrated, money is not the only currency. People evaluate things using many heuristics, such as justice, fairness, status, loyalty, authority, and purity.[44] Further, individual preferences play out in situations that are socially constructed. A detached bystander and those involved may interpret situations differently. The quantification of utility, as I will discuss later, is a major preoccupation in the evaluation of quality of life, health outcomes, and value-based care.

In marketing and operations management, a convenient shorthand for utility is "job-to-be-done".[45] A job is the progress that a person is trying to make in a particular circumstance. Progress is movement toward a goal or an aspiration through various means.

## Values and Economic Value

Values, in a moral sense, mean what people think as the most ultimately worthy. The buck stops at values; they are not subject to opportunism and horse trading. There are people, now and during human history, who have been willing to sacrifice their own and others' lives and property for some ultimate values, such as freedom, faith, or purity. For most people, most of the time values are tradable. Every man has his price.

In the health policy debate, the naïve argument that human life is a value that cannot be calculated in money appears frequently. But when pressed on the subject, nobody in his or her right mind would be willing to submit the whole national health budget to save one life, while leaving everybody else without care for a year. There is a price to human life that can be calculated by revealed preferences, for example, how much people are willing to pay to mitigate avoidable risks.[46]

Obviously, there is no price if somebody else pays and bears the burden. When such moral hazards are removed and people have to personally face both sides of a trade-off, values pretty quickly get organized as preferences.

The word *values* is confusingly similar to the word *value*. In the economic world, value, more specifically, *economic value*, means the difference between what you give and what you get in a transaction.[47] You give your time and get a salary; you pay a dollar and get a pint of milk. As an employer, you part with money and get labor; as a shopkeeper, you let go of your inventory and get revenue in the tiller. If the benefit is greater than the sacrifice, the economic value is positive. More technically, economic value is the sum of the buyer's and the seller's surpluses. As a buyer, the milk is worth more to you than a dollar; to the seller, the dollar is worth more than the milk that is sacrificed in the trade.

Economic value is a relation between give and get. The get part could be called "worth." If something is worth the effort, it means the worth is larger than the effort. Spending the effort means that value is created. This is the logic behind value-based care. Health outcomes should be worth more than the amount of dollars spent.

The word *value* is used in many imprecise and contradictory ways, as are many other concepts, such as quality, efficiency, and profit. For clarity, I will use the term *economic value* when I mean the relation between giving and getting.

The economic layer highlights a basic constellation. There are resources we have and things we want. Since we can't have it all at the same time in the same place, we have to choose. Choices are guided by preferences; something carries more utility than something else. When choices involve two or more parties, there are transactions. The activity involved in setting up a transaction is called bargaining.

## 2.2.7 Layers and Multiverse

A perennial problem in social science is how to deal with layers of reality. One situation, like a patient visiting a doctor, can be interpreted as a social encounter of people with differing positions of authority, a service event where technologies are applied to change a state, an economic transaction between a service provider and her customer, or on the wacky side, a case of capitalism exerting control of bodies.[48] All can arguably be real and true. Doctoral students, after having settled on a topic to study, will have to spend substantial effort in defining their perspective and approach: which layers are studied, which are considered crucial. Sometimes getting the research questions right takes more time than answering them. The layers of logic that define different social realities are like a multiverse, parallel universes between which an inquisitive mind can travel.[49]

How to understand and deal with a social multiverse has been a central theme during my academic career.

### Japan: Improvement as a Parallel Reality

After graduating with a master's degree in social sciences in the early 1980s, I became interested in Japan. There was more than the samurai warrior to attract interest in the Far East. Sensible people[50] promoted the view that Japan had invented a new paradigm of political economy that combined traditional Confucian values with hypercompetitive capitalism. I was one of the hundreds of Western PhD candidates who trekked east to figure out the secrets of the emerging economic superpower.

My topic was the then famous quality control (QC) circle movement. After 6 years of research, language studies, and immersion in the local culture, I presented my thesis. The QC circle is a parallel hybrid organization that exploits the dynamics of the informal organization to achieve quality and productivity goals set by the formal organization.[51]

A particularly puzzling issue in understanding the QC circle was the claim that it is a "voluntary" activity, *jishusei* in Japanese. Having said that, managers added that everybody is obliged to participate. That just didn't make sense. I pestered professors and QC managers, who had trouble understanding my concern. What's the problem with everybody participating in a voluntary activity?

One of my case companies was Fuji Heavy Industries. I visited their truck manufacturing plant in western Tokyo. I put my question to the sympathetic QC manager. He admitted having never thought about that, but invited me to follow him to the shop floor to have a look at *jishusei* in action.

The plant had three parallel assembly lines where medium-sized trucks were finished by one team each. The teams also doubled as QC circles. Between the assembly lines, each had a resting place, a small hut like a barrack used at construction sites. "This is where they do the *jishusei*," the manager said, taking me inside one of the huts. There was a table with teapots and newspapers, some statistical charts on the wall, a few quality manuals on a shelf, and an aquarium. There was no door. Instead, above the entrance there was a *shimenawa*, a rope thick in the middle, usually seen at the entrance of Shinto shrines. As a religious symbol, it marks the border between the profane and the sacred.

At that moment, I saw the light. *Jishusei* is not a question of the freedom to participate in or abstain from workshop activities. It means that the QC circle, when in session, is a socially distinct space, a *ba*,[52] where the constraints of the corporate hierarchy and the seniority rule do not apply. A junior is free to criticize a senior, which would not be accepted in other circumstances. The QC circle is a hybrid organization, a mixture of formal task orientation (quality improvement) and the social roles found in the workplace, an informal organization. The social world of industry is a multiverse of parallel realities.

## The Airline as a Cultural Multiverse

In the mid-1990s, I got involved with the Finnish national airline, Finnair. The aftermath of the First Gulf War sent fuel prices up and airline revenue down. The carrier needed to beef up its service quality. Bowing to contemporary management fads, the CEO bought the idea of the service chain. Everything should be aligned to the customer journey, from reservation and booking to check-in, in-flight experience, and arrival. All personnel groups were obliged to participate in training courses on customer centricity. It did not go down well. Ground service and flight attendants got the message, while others, such as pilots, mechanics, and ramp controllers, did not see the point, as they rarely saw a customer. They insisted that their jobs were safety and security, accomplished by knowledge of technology and adherence to protocol. The training program disintegrated when pilots and technical personnel dropped out. The chief operating officer (COO) asked my team to find out why.

We spent time at the airport, in the back office, cargo areas, and catering lines, trying to make sense of the logic of production. A view emerged. We labeled it product–process cultures (PPCs). They were neatly separated by one chunk of logic: What is the worst possible outcome of one single error incident?[53]

The first PPC is safety. The worst possible single accident would be a fully loaded wide-body aircraft failing in takeoff and crashing into a nearby shopping center at rush hour. The company would not survive such a loss of life, property, and reputation. Consequently, anything pertinent to safety is ruled by the logic of safety. As the literature on high-reliability organizations[54] has detailed, that means humorless adherence to protocol and checklists, continuous vigilance to potential risk factors, and thorough analysis of every near-miss. Certain engineering types find this exciting.

The second PPC is punctuality. A delayed or canceled flight means cost and trouble. Those caused by external events, such as air traffic congestion or bad weather, hit all competitors. Internal causes are the multitude of tasks that have to be accomplished before takeoff. The aircraft must be fueled, cleaned, and cleared; the crew must be at their positions, sufficiently rested; and passengers and cargo must be loaded. A mapping exercise produced a list of more than 100 mission-critical elements. The damage caused by a delay may be substantial, but not catastrophic. Punctuality is negotiable. An aircraft may be asked to wait for connecting passengers, because the cost of rerouting them would be larger than that of the delay. Consequently, the ground crew in charge of punctuality will routinely do what is a cardinal sin to the safety people: establish priorities and negotiate trade-offs.

The third PPC is personal service. A process can be designed and standardized. However, good personal service includes attention to particular needs, the capability to solve problems, such as when a sudden jolt of turbulence lands the contents of a double espresso in the wrong place. Personal service has the capability to impact experiences. If an incident is handled nicely, the passenger may walk off the plane in a better mood than if nothing had happened. A quality incident can have a negative or positive impact, depending on how it is managed.

The final PPC is industrial mass production: logistics, catering, and luggage handling. They are ruled by the logic of discrete-piece disconnected flow, staffing, scheduling, and statistical process control. Single errors, such as a lost suitcase, may not be substantial, but they have a nasty tendency to add up.

The take-home message from this study was that an organization consists of overlapping realities, not easily visible to the naked eye of the casual observer. The logic of action does not neatly follow occupational personnel categories. Situations change and different situations are ruled by different rules. Some people walk in and out of such situations daily; others spend their whole working life in one PPC. A complex organization is a multiverse of parallel realities. This is true also in healthcare.

## 2.3 Purposeful Action and Its Constraints

The purpose of business is to make money. Since this could mean shortsighted opportunism, thoughtful people add, "Now and in the future." As this could as well describe what the Mafia does, another waiver is added: "Following the laws and moral rules of the land." Japanese industrialists would feel compelled to add, "… and by answering to the needs of people and being of service to society."[55]

Purposeful activity is a struggle between the jobs that should be done and various socio-techno-economic constraints, and variability.

## 2.3.1 Causes and Purposes

Aristotle[56] postulated four types of causes: material, effective, formal, and ideal. Take an object, say, a knife. What caused it? There must be material substance. Some force has had an effect on it to give it a form that represents an idea in the mind of the person who conceived and made it. The material and the effective cause can be described in terms of physics. The form and the idea are purposes.

Aristotle promoted the idea of practical wisdom (*pronesis*). It covers both ends and means. Simple wisdom has ends, but not means. It is easily spotted in idealistic posturing. Means without ends equals the simple cleverness of the cunning maverick.

In economic terms, purpose is an instance of utility, that is, anything that people find valuable and worth an effort: needs, wants, desires, and jobs to be done. Purposes are endless and egoistic, like the infantile omnipotence of newborns; give me the best of everything right now, right here. Therefore, a central aspect in the study of purposeful action is to look at constraints. Herbert Simon[19] puts it nicely:

> What a person cannot do he or she will not do, no matter how strong the urge to do it. In the face of real-world complexity, the business firm turns to procedures that find good enough answers to questions whose best answers are unknowable.

To achieve a purpose, there must be resources, capabilities, technologies, and organizations. Resources are not; they become. People in Texas and the Middle East were sitting on masses of rotten and compacted hydrocarbons considered rather a nuisance than a resource until the Industrial Revolution brought the internal combustion engine and turned oil into an essential resource.

To exploit resources requires capabilities. Capability can be manual dexterity, cognitive ability to figure things out, or social skills to engage and exchange with others. Capability allows functioning in the pursuit of things considered important.[57] Actors with purpose and means are agents endowed with agency. But no agent is omnipotent; purposes do not materialize spontaneously. Agents are impacted by contexts, structures, the consequences of their own actions, other people and their actions, historical legacies, rule systems, shared institutions, common perceptions, technologies, and economic trade-offs. Taken together, all such things can be compacted into two concepts, variability and decay.

## 2.3.2 *Variability and Decay*

The Cheshire Cat said to Alice in Wonderland, "If you do not know where you are going, any road will take you there."[58] If you do something without a purpose, there is no risk of making a mistake. If you aim at a purpose, everything will not go as planned every time. The world is a struggle between order and chaos. The technical term for chaos is variability. Variability is the phenomenon that sometime lays the best plans into ashes. Variability is what makes the military man conclude that no strategy will survive the first contact with the enemy.

At the most abstract level, variability is nonuniformity of a class of entities, more colloquially, deviations from the planned, the things that do not go as expected.[59] Variability shows up as a lack of consistency or fixed pattern; it is the liability to vary, change, and fluctuate. In statistics, variability is measured by how spread out or closely clustered a set of data is. It is the extent to which data points in a data set diverge from the average, as well as the extent to which these data points differ from each other. There are four commonly used measures of variability: range, mean, variance, and standard deviation.

Like the Roman god Janus, variability has two faces. In the biosphere, variability is the creative energy of evolution. The blind variability of mutations can lead to robust outcomes, because time is of no concern, and neither are all the trillions of losers left dead by the wayside. The artificial world is found on imposed order. The driving forces are ideas and purposes, created, designed, and constructed artifacts. To accomplish them, variability must be fought.

In production, variability comes in many shapes. Customers place orders when they please. Suppliers may deliver wrong parts in wrong volumes at wrong times to a wrong place. To replace the "wrongs" with "rights" requires control. In the artificial world, most things are standardized and predictable. Creativity can appear at the top of things only if the base is standardized. Without a standard way to write music and play instruments, there could be no Mozart.

Control is management: planning, organizing, scheduling, monitoring results, making adjustments, making improvements, and learning. Resources and capabilities must be controlled to the beat of the inherent variability and randomness of things. Many people do not like the idea of control and rebel against standards. Sure, the bureaucratic state imposes many meaningless controls. However, most of the controls and standards are embedded in the artificial world and taken for granted. A perceptive traveler in the developing world will soon become aware of the importance of embedded standards when traffic pours all over roads, the charger does not fit into the electric socket, and tap water is not potable. The importance of order, control, and standards becomes visible only when they break down.[60]

A subset of variability is decay. It means decline from a state that is designed to be sound and prosperous. As Paul Simon put it in a song, "Everything put together sooner or later falls apart."[61] As control weakens, things fall into ruin.

With age, buildings and bodies decline in appearance, strength, and vigor. Structures, designs, and setups do not remain in their initial conditions. Inevitable decline is postponed by the area of management called maintenance. Its primary measure is sustainability and the life cycles of things.

## 2.3.3 Know, Can, Want

A useful shorthand for the behavioral prerequisites of purposeful action comes from the psychology of work.[62] To reach a purpose, an agent must clear these hurdles:

- Know what to do: Have an idea of what needs to be done in a context.
- Can do: Have the capabilities and the technical and economic resources to act.
- Want to do: Have the will and motivation to initiate and pursue.[63]

Social, technical, and economic systems constrain what people want, know, and can. These can be combined into a construct explicating the constraints of purposeful action, as summarized in Table 2.1.

People know what to do when something makes sense, when a technology is available and the utility that follows action can be envisioned.

What can be done is constrained by the social layer, morality, rules, norms, and laws. For centuries, Western doctors were not allowed to look inside the human body, as religious sensibilities thought of it as a vandal act on the temple of the soul. Today abortion and euthanasia are hotly contested subjects of what is socially acceptable. Technology constrains the doable. So far, there is no technology

**Table 2.1   Constraints of Purposeful Action**

|  | *Socio* | *Techno* | *Economic* |
|---|---|---|---|
| Know what to do | Assessment of situations<br>*What is its logic?* | Diagnostics<br>Dynamics<br>*Will it work?* | Utility<br>Purpose<br>*What for?* |
| Can do | Legitimacy<br>Collaboration<br>*What is socially acceptable?* | Resources, capabilities<br>Production function<br>*What is doable?* | Economic resources<br>Allocations<br>*What is affordable?* |
| Want to do | Social incentives<br>Obligations<br>Taboos<br>*Am I encouraged or prohibited?* | Risk<br><br>*Dare I do it?* | Economic incentives<br><br>*What's in it for me?* |

to cure diabetes. The technically possible is not always economically affordable, a fact that becomes painfully clear in developing countries.

An agent may know what to do and be able to do it, but still not do it because of lack of want and motivation. A pertinent mystery of healthcare quality assurance is that, in the case of patient safety, the technology (hand sanitation) is there, the economic and social utility is calculable, and there are no moral objections against hand hygiene, but still people fail to wash their hands at the peril of their patients.

### 2.3.4 Demand and Supply

The world of purposeful action can be described as two pairs, as in Figure 2.5. You want something, whatever you prefer and desire in your situation. That is your job to be done. When it is done, utility is created. To realistically want something, you have to have something. Call it resources, your accumulated capital, your skills and capabilities, social relations, justifiable claims on other people, or citizen's rights. There must be some reasonable balance between what you want and what you have. Wildly unrealistic expectations are a shortcut to unhappiness.

To get something you, can produce it yourself, that is, transform something into something else. Very few people are self-sufficient or self-reliant. If you can't make it alone, you can engage in a transaction, use your resources to buy it, or convince somebody to help. Transformations and transactions, production and trade are linked, unless you are Robinson Crusoe on a lonely island.

From this emerges a conceptual construct, the basic building block of the logic of production, services, and healthcare: the demand–supply constellation, the dynamic relation between what needs to be done and what can be done.

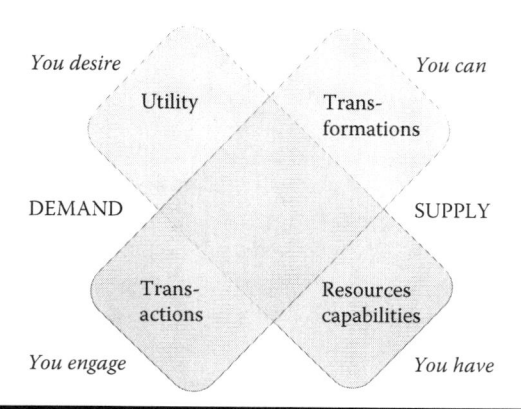

**Figure 2.5   Components of purposeful action.**

## Notes

1. As a sample, consider the following:
   *The Logic of Scientific Discovery*—Karl Popper
   *The Logic of Failure*—Dietrich Dornier
   *The Logic of Human Destiny*—Robert Wright
   *The Logic of Faith*—St. Thomas of Aquinas
   *The Logic of the Heart*—James R. Peters
   *The Logic of Life*—Tim Hartford
   *The Logic of Political Survival*—Bruce Bueno de Mesquita
   *The Logics of Madness*—Samuel Resnik
2. Sandori (1982).
3. Olson (2000).
4. The Soviet system sought to isolate individuals at all levels of the state and party hierarchy and make them dependent on their superiors and loyal to the supreme ruler at the apex. Eventually, people at the same level of the hierarchy found each other. They turned into small interest groups that could conspire against higher-ups and exploit subordinates. This led to serious organizational dysfunction, which contributed to the collapse.
5. Dani Rodrick (2015) has suggested that economists should give up the pursuit of general theories and focus on the midrange.
6. *Chunk* as a noun means a thick, solid piece of something—a significant amount of something. As a verb, *to chunk* means to divide something into chunks. In psychology and linguistic analysis, *to chunk* means to group together connected items or words so that they can be stored or processed as single concepts. *Chunk* thus has the dual meaning of divide and connect, analysis and synthesis.
7. Laffer (2004).
8. Weber (1949).
9. The g-factor was proposed by the British psychologist C.E. Spearman (1904). It has since been studied and elaborated significantly.
10. Ishikawa (1985).
11. The idea of transaction costs was developed by Ronald Coase (1937) and expanded by Oliver Williamson (1985).
12. Nonaka and Takeuchi (1995).
13. This point has been made by Hopp and Spearman (2011).
14. Gottlieb (2016).
15. Makari (2015).
16. In the Anglo-Saxon world, there is a rather sharp distinction between sciences and arts and humanities. In Continental Europe, this distinction is not prominent.
17. Axelrod (1997).
18. Shelling (2006).
19. Simon (1996).
20. For an overview of system thinking, see Jackson (2000) and Jolly (2015).
21. The classical text on institutional theory is DiMaggio and Powell (1983).
22. Acemoglu and Robinson (2012).
23. The explicit objective of totalitarians, such as Lenin, Mussolini, and Hitler, was to use the state to take full control over all institutions of society under corporatism. For a view on the role of modern corporatism, see Phelps (2011), especially Chapter 6: "The Third Way: Corporatism Right and Left."

24. Ross and Nisbett (2011).
25. Contingency theory claims that there is no one best way to organize a corporation, to lead a company, or to make decisions. The optimal course of action is contingent (dependent) on the situation. See Morgan (2007) and Lawrence and Lorsch (1967).
26. Structuration and socialization refer to the mechanisms by which societies re-create themselves every day (Giddens 1984).
27. Clarke (1981).
28. Hackman and Oldham (1980) and Pava (1983).
29. There are several schemes in the system science literature. For example, Harold Linstone uses three perspectives: technical, organizational, and personal (quoted in Jolly 2015). Nelson and Stolterman (2012) add to this list political, economic, ethical, and spiritual.
30. For recent advances in behavioral economics, see Thaler (2015), Kahneman (2011), and Ariely (2008). Important classical contributions are Simon (1982) and Kahneman and Tversky (1979).
31. LeGrand (2003).
32. Bowles and Gintis (2011).
33. Jensen (1998).
34. For rhetoric purposes, Jensen contrasts REMM with four other models. These are more caricatures than ideal types. As they tend to pop up in debates on healthcare, they are worth noting. (1) The economic man: Humans are short-run money maximizers. They are only concerned with money. They are not willing to trade money for other things, such as human development or happiness. (2) The sociological or social victim: Humans are a product of their environment. They are conformists whose behavior is determined by tradition, customs, and power. Lacking agency, humans are victims of structures and therefore not responsible or accountable for their decisions. As victims, they can only demand mercy and charity. (3) The political perfect agent: Humans are seen as infallible agents seeking to maximize the public good rather than their own welfare. This view is often behind government officials and medical professionals who are supposed to only be concerned with the overall good. (4) The altruist: Humans gain utility from helping others. People select a cause and work for the attainment of that goal without seeking personal winning.
35. The Thomas theorem was formulated in 1928 by William Isaac Thomas and Dorothy Swaine Thomas. The theorem has been applied and discussed at length in Berger and Luckman (1966).
36. Arthur (2009).
37. Gerring (2012) and Niiniluoto (2002).
38. Epistemology has another dimension, the question of which are valid sources of knowledge. Over human history, there have been various competing epistemologies. The defining feature of a traditional society is a belief in tradition as the primary source of knowledge. The people of the book believe everything a human being needs to know can be found in Scripture. The Renaissance and Enlightenment proclaimed observations and reason as the primary, if not the only, acceptable epistemology. The Romantic counterrevolution posted feelings, authenticity, and national spirit as equally infallible. In modern medicine, the randomized controlled trial (RCT) is the epistemological gold standard.

39. The quality of information as the extent to which a receiver captures the meaning of a sender. It can be expressed as $M = f(D, C)$, meaning is a function of data and context. See Lillrank (2003a).
40. The build, evaluate, theorize, justify sequence has been described in March and Smith (1995).
41. Gleeson-White (2011).
42. www.merriam-webster.com/dictionary/economy.
43. This is a source of much controversy. Classical economics postulates the economic man, the self-interested maximizer of economic utility measurable as money. This, however, was never meant to be a normative statement of how people should behave. It is a simplifying assumption made in order to make economic modeling possible. A person or an organization can be a rational maximizer in only one or a few ways. Human beings can be irrational in an infinite number of ways. Early economic theory simply did not have the tools to deal with irrationality. See Beinhocker (2007).
44. For types of moral reasoning, see Haidt (2012).
45. Christensen et al. (2016) and Ulwick (2005).
46. There is a vast literature on the trade-offs people are willing to make. A special case is the additional wages that must be paid to induce people to work in riskier occupations. Based on these observations, the "value of a statistical life" can be calculated. Currently, the value of a statistical life ranges from $6 million at the U.S. Department of Transportation to $7.9 million at the Food and Drug Administration and $9.1 million at the Environmental Protection Agency (Goodman et al. 2011).
47. Zeithaml (1988).
48. For a review of perspectives, see Lupton (2012).
49. The idea of a social multiverse can be traced back to the Canadian sociologist Erwing Goffman (1955). He argued that when we interact with others, we enter a stage and take on the role of an actor presenting a character to an audience. Social interaction is the performance of various identities that change depending on context.
50. Vogel (1979).
51. An expanded version of my thesis is Lillrank and Kano (1989).
52. The idea of *ba*, as a specifically defined social situation, has been described in Nonaka and Takeuchi (1995). In Japanese, *ba* with the prefix *gen* is *genba*, literally "the real place," the shop floor, or where the rubber meets the road.
53. Lillrank and Kostama (2001).
54. Weick and Sutcliffe (2007).
55. As an example, see the book by the founder of Matsushita Electric/Panasonic (Matsushita 1986).
56. Aristotle's *Nicomachean Ethics* is available at http://www.virtuescience.com/nicomachean-ethics.html. *Pronesis* could also be translated as *prudence* or *mindfulness*.
57. Nobel laureate Amartya Sen (2001) has emphasized that in development economics, capability enhancement is more important than material handouts.
58. *Alice's Adventures in Wonderland* is an 1865 fantasy novel written by English mathematician Charles Lutwidge Dodgson under the pseudonym Lewis Carroll. This line is not in the Alice in Wonderland books. It is a summary of the following exchange:
    "Would you tell me, please, which way I ought to go from here"?
    "That depends a good deal on where you want to get to," said the Cat.
    "I don't much care where—," said Alice.

"Then it doesn't matter which way you go," said the Cat.

"—so long as I get SOMEWHERE," Alice added as an explanation.

"Oh, you're sure to do that," said the Cat, "if you only walk long enough."

59. Hopp and Spearman (2011).
60. People brought up in affluent and orderly societies tend to have an unjustified and ignorant aversion to standards and control. It becomes apparent at a first visit to a developing country where order and standards are lacking. This point has been made by Banerjee and Duflo (2011).
61. This is a line in the song "Everything Put Together Falls Apart" on the *Paul Simon* album (1971).
62. Hackman and Oldham (1980).
63. These three constraints can be derived from Aristotle's four causes. Can do is to have the material and tools (effective cause), know what to do is the formal cause, and want to do is the ideal cause.

# Chapter 3

# The Logic of Production

## 3.1 Production Function and Types of Transformations

The production function is a classical economic concept. It depicts the transformer that changes the factors of production, land, capital, and labor into guns, butter, cloth, or whatever is demanded. Economists treat the production function as a black box; they are usually not interested in its innards. For operations management, it is the central focus of inquiry.[1]

The most ancient production function is collection, capture, and extraction of something that exists out there in the natural world. Fruits and seeds don't run away, so they can be found and collected. Animals escape pursuers, they need to be captured by hunters, trappers, or fishermen. Minerals are dug out from mines, trees are cut down, and stone is laboriously extracted from quarries.

The Neolithic Revolution introduced the production functions of cultivation and animal husbandry. Natural processes, such as the growth of edible plants, are enhanced by selective breeding and supported by weeding and watering. Animals are fed and slaughtered.

Chemical reactions and biological processes can be harnessed. The most basic is oxygenation through fire and heat treatment. Chemical substances and catalysts do their work in oil refineries and petrochemical plants. Microbes churn away in dairies and turn milk into cheese.

Subtractive fabrication is at work when Michelangelo takes off some shavings from a block of marble and the statue of David is presented to the world. A blacksmith pounds on steel and turns it into a blade. Blank pieces of stone, wood, and metal can be given shapes that somebody dreamed up. The most elegant definition of manufacturing is by H.J. Warnecke[2]: "Manufacturing is the application of controlled energy to matter in order to realize an idea."

Additive fabrication happens when layers of material are added to a core or a form. Candle manufacturing is an early example. Recently, three-dimensional printing, building parts by adding layers of molecules, has made great advances.

Assembly is to put prefabricated pieces together to create a product made of several different parts. It is called discrete manufacturing if the parts and the end product are individual pieces. This is in contrast to continuous flow manufacturing, such as paper mills, where both the components and the end product are substances divisible to the molecular level. If the pieces to be assembled are not prefabricated but shaped individually at the site, such as the traditional way of building homes and ships, production is called construction.

The production function is the technology or the bundle of technologies that bring together the four Aristotelian causes, the material cause (raw material), the effective cause (processing), the formal cause (design), and the ideal cause (intended utility). The first two are equal to production technologies, the tools, machines, pipelines, chemical reactions, and other contraptions that transform material into products. The formal and the ideal causes are product technologies, the shafts, valves, electric circuitry, and panels from which products are designed. Consequently, production includes two basic steps: you plan something and then you do it. Technology puts constraints on what can be produced but does not limit human imagination. Charles Babbage dreamed up the computer, but his technology, which relied on steam and brass valves, did not suffice to make his vision come true. In some cases, planning and doing merge into explorative design work; you try something out, see how it fits in, adjust, judge, and move to the next step. In some other cases, plans are painstakingly made to the smallest detail and then implemented by a contract manufacturer. As illustrated in Figure 3.1, the production function is organized as production processes, which are then managed, measured, and improved.

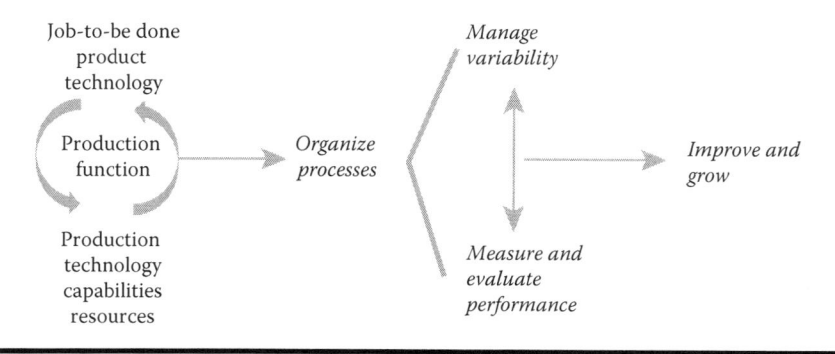

**Figure 3.1  The production function is organized.**

# 3.2 Product Technology: Differentiation, Variety, and Integration

As a customer with some money to spend in a competitive market with a lot to offer, you are the ultimate evaluator. How do you think when you encounter a product on sale?

## 3.2.1 Differentiation and Price

You ask what is it? What could it do to me? How can I use it to improve my life and do the things that I want? Why should I pick this one? Can I believe it is built without errors and delivered as promised? All this is in management parlance called differentiation, the qualitative nonprice issues that differentiate one product from another.[3] Differentiation builds on technology and design, the qualitative characteristics that make products stand out in relation to current competitors and previous generations of products.

Differentiation and price are the fundamental questions of matching demand and supply. Is the expected utility of owning and using a product higher than the certain disutility of parting with your money, and giving up all the other possible things you could have spent it on?

Price is not in direct relation to production cost. There is a whole jungle of market forces that affect the final selling price. Nevertheless, production cost puts a floor under price; selling below cost is not sustainable. Price is related to the efficiency of a production system.

## 3.2.2 Product Attributes

Differentiation comes as four attributes: functionality, performance, grade, and style.

*Functionality* is the idea of a product, what it can do or what can be done with it to what effect. Functionality is the embodiment of utility and purpose. For example, the functionality of a knife is its ability to cut. As cuts can be applied to a variety of materials and purposes, a knife is multifunctional. A corkscrew similarly has the function of penetrating material, but its design allows it to specialize in narrow objects and stick in position.

*Performance* is the technical solution to a given functionality. A knife can be made of stone, bronze, or high-grade steel. Laser knives have the same functionality but employ a different technology. Functionality signifies what is done, while performance denotes how well it is done.

*Grade* means different levels of the same functionality and performance. A knife can be long or short, but it is still a knife. Printing paper comes in grades, measured as grams per square meter. Grades are developed to specific customer segments and corresponding requirements. Different grades typically have different production costs. High-grade steel is expensive to make; thick paper consumes more material. If you pay more, you get a better grade.

*Style*[4] means alternatives within one functionality, performance, and grade, such as shapes, colors, or ornaments. A knife can have handles of different color and texture. There is no right or wrong for styles; some prefer dark and others blond.

### 3.2.3 Integration

Complex products, such as a smartphone, have several functionalities, each based on different technologies embedded in components, such as a processor, memory, radio, sensor, and touch-sensitive screen. *Product integration* means the act of combining various technologies into a functioning and esthetically pleasant whole. Each element needs to contribute but also submit to the demands of the whole. Integration means trade-offs; all individual components can't have maximal performance.

In healthcare, diagnostics is integration. Various information components from anamneses, examinations, laboratories, and imagining are brought together and merged into a shared understanding of the situation.[5] I discuss this further in Chapter 5.

### 3.2.4 Product Variety

Functionality, performance, grade, and style can be combined in innumerable ways as designs. They can be expressed in terms ranging from the you-know-it-when-you-see-it innate characteristics to the more mundane strength, weight, power, durability, ease of use, aesthetic pleasure, and capability to impress others.[6] The totality of different items on offer is *variety*.

Variety should not be confused with *variability*, nonuniformity of a class of entities or random deviations from the expected, or *variation*, measurable deviation from a given target.

In systems theory, variety denotes the total number of distinct states of a system. In markets, variety is the set of choices available to a consumer.[7] Large variety means there is something for every purse and purpose.

Product variety corresponds to demand variety. People have varying needs and desires. Markets are the institutional devices to match the variety of demand and the variety of supply. One of the major impacts of the Internet is improved matching. Instead of making do with the one-size-fits-all products of the local store, customers can browse the endless listings offered by e-commerce operators and find the best match.[8]

### 3.2.5 Industrial Quality

In everyday language, functionality, performance, grade, and style are called quality. In its broadest sense, quality is linked to customer satisfaction; quality is whatever makes you happy. This, however, is imprecise and has led to much confusion.

Quality in its core industrial meaning is conformance to requirements: how accurately an idea of a product was realized. When a component or a final product is done, it is compared with requirements, say, dimensions, color, or chemical compositions, to see whether it conforms with or deviates from specifications.

Product variety is designed; product quality is a matter of execution. Design requires imagination, command of technologies, understanding of customers, and risk taking. Execution is about conformity, exact targets, and risk minimization. Customers choose between designed varieties, but avoid faulty products. The success of a design can be known only after markets have made their judgments. Conformance to specifications can be measured right away. Combining two phenomena with radically different ontologies and epistemologies into one word is confusing. But the word *quality* is widely used and can't be abolished. A solution is to call the design issues *big quality*, and the execution and control issues *small quality*.[9] I will return to this later in the chapter.

# 3.3 Production Systems

The arrow kills the deer. The chisel takes out shavings from a piece of marble. But the production functions can't work alone. They need to be structured as production systems. As any systems, they have ontologies (what are they?) and epistemologies (what can be known, measured, and evaluated?).

Production systems have two sides. One is to analyze and break down jobs into their constituent parts to find the most efficient way to perform them. This is division of labor, specialization, and standardization. The other is to join parts into wholes and build them in a certain order. This is integration of product designs and coordination of production processes.

## 3.3.1 Specialization and Coordination

The original type of production was craft. A craftsman, supported by a few apprentices, produced by hand every utensil, tool, or piece of clothing one at a time. The customer specified what was needed and how much it could cost. Each component had to be individually joined to the others. Craft production limits what can be produced in which volumes and at what cost.

### Division of Labor and Specialization

Adam Smith (1723–1790), the father of classical economics, described the organizational changes of the Industrial Revolution. In *The Wealth of Nations*, published in 1776, he identified the basic chunks of logic as division of labor, specialization, and standardization.[10]

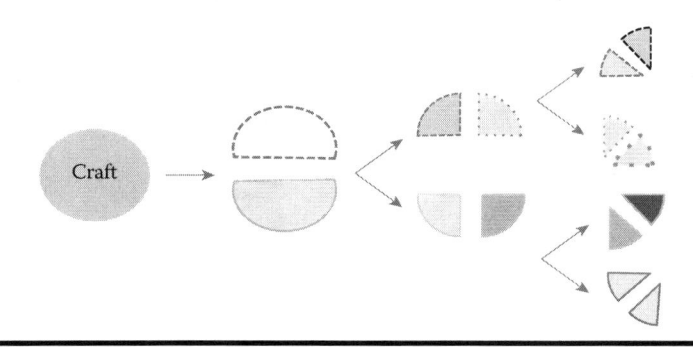

**Figure 3.2   Division of labor.**

The division of labor, as illustrated in Figure 3.2, means that a full job to be done is divided into two tasks, from one craftsman to two. The division continues further and further into smaller and more specialized tasks.

As labor gets divided, one worker gets one piece of work to do. It may be a few movements taking a few seconds, such as shoveling coal into an oven, tightening bolts, or moving pieces from one rack to another. The range of skills required per person shrinks. A worker can specialize in certain types of jobs, learn to do them better, and achieve mastery. This is known as the learning curve. Eventually, a best way to do things is found. Then it can be standardized and performed in a similar way every time. Standard work methods can be documented and taught.

## Standardization and Experimentation

From standardization followed a great new opportunity. The artificial world of production could now, like nature, be subject to systematic experimentation. If things are done differently each time, results obviously differ. It is hard to find a pattern in the relation between what was done and what was achieved. Knowledge does not accumulate, and learning remains slow. When a task is performed in the same way, every time work reaches a stable state. Performance data can be collected. Then something in the standard is changed and a similar data set is collected. Comparison will tell if the new way is better than the old. This made it possible to apply statistics and the experimental method to improve industrial production.

## Interchangeable Part

A century after Adam Smith, standardization accumulated into a breakthrough known as the interchangeable part. It was long in the making, but the person most dramatically associated with it is Eli Whitney (1765–1825), an innovator and an arms manufacturer. After the American independence, he received enormous orders of muskets for the army, but was at a loss for how to supply the required volumes.[11]

A musket is made of a lock, stock, and barrel. The lock and the trigger are an assembly of about half a dozen metal parts made by casting metal in a mold. The process was inaccurate to the extent that before assembly, a skilled craftsman had to perform a laborious setup. Each part varied in its own way, and had to be first fitted and then assembled one at a time. Each musket was an individual instance of a basic design.

As a result of numerous small innovations in casting and machining, the parts could be made to precision. An assembler could pick any part from a bin containing a production run (batch) of that part, put it together with another type of part from another bin, and they would fit without fitting. Variation of parts was reduced; all parts in a batch were identical. The time and trouble of setup and fitting could be reduced, and assembly became standard work. This principle has continued working wonders all the way to the Toyota Production System.

The interchangeable part led to two major developments. Standard work with known movements and time consumption could be organized as a process connecting several workstations, each doing their own part of the job. Henry Ford (1863–1947) and the moving assembly line brought this principle to its fruition. Second, the craft shop was divided into component manufacturing and assembly. Organizations became subject to the division of labor. A whole factory could be dedicated to produce just one part. This has in due course led to the modern global supply chains.

### 3.3.2 Production Processes as Coordination Devices

Design integrates products; management coordinates production. Division of labor breaks jobs into tasks that produce parts of a whole job to be done. Due to specialization and standardization, each is produced with increasing efficiency. But they must be joined together. Production processes are the coordination mechanisms to do that.

At the most generic level, *process* means anything that changes in time and space. Such a general term can be used for anything from the peace process in the Middle East to the process of getting up from the bed in the morning. Processes can emerge through random evolution or collective action with no one in charge. Here, however, focus is on processes that have been established for the purpose of getting jobs done repeatedly. Production processes are real and can be observed. In a factory, you can see how a part moves, changes shape, and stops in a holding area. However, some abstract concepts are needed to grasp the logic of a production process and its elements. Production processes have the following characteristics:

- A production process has a *purpose* that can be expressed as the utility achieved by *transformations*.
- A production process employs a *production function*, a combination of technologies, resources, and capabilities.

- The entity to be transformed is the *flow unit*.
- Transformations are accomplished at *workstations* that process flow units and perform tasks.
- A production process combines several tasks into a *flow* of connected steps with a beginning and an end.
- A production process is *formalized* in a physical layout, in documents, or in memory so that it can be *repeated*.
- Production processes have the generic characteristics of *systems*: several entities that interact within a *boundary*. They are nested as different system levels from the microscopic (processing) to the macroscopic (supply chains).

### 3.3.3 Process Elements and Functioning

Like the human body, a production system has parts (heart), which perform tasks (pump blood) in measurable ways (blood pressure). The structure and functioning of production processes are illustrated in Figure 3.3. Table 3.1 adds the relevant measurements. In short, a workstation is the resource that does a transformation. It receives parts and materials from inventory and is set up to perform a task to a flow unit. When done, a workstation hands the flow unit over to the next workstation (step) and the flow unit moves as a flow between workstations and inventories. When a flow unit has completed its journey, it is counted as one unit of throughput and moved to a stock of finished goods and then made available to customers. Now we will discuss the key concepts in more detail.

### Workstation

A workstation is the place or the facility where tasks are performed, a person, a team, a machine, a computer program, or combinations thereof. A workstation is usually stationary, like the smithy where metal is forged, or a station at an assembly line. It can be mobile, such as a repairman with his tools or a doctor with her bag. A workstation is equipped with fixed resources and equipment. There is capital invested in them, and they carry capital costs. A workstation gets job orders from a previous workstation in the line, or from a scheduling system. It gets parts, such as nuts and bolts; consumables, such as glue and paint; and disposables, such as latex gloves from parts inventories. If workers are on fixed salaries, labor is fixed cost; if they are paid by the piece, labor is variable cost.

### Tasks

Workstations perform tasks. Tasks are combinations of *activities*, the smallest product of division of labor and specialization. The early pioneers of operations management, Frank and Lillian Gilbreth[12] identified 18 basic activities or movements and

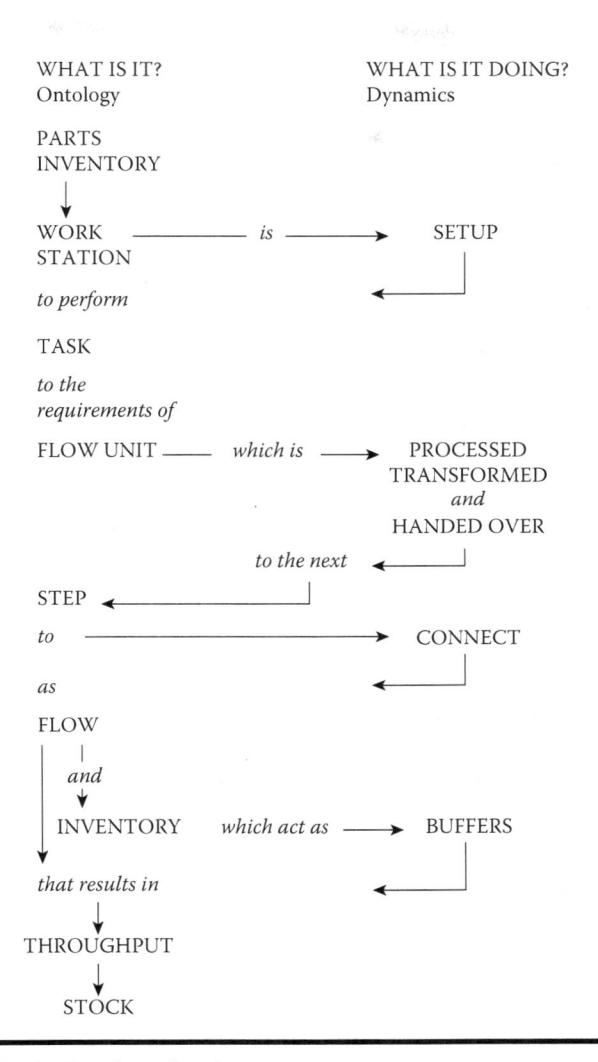

**Figure 3.3** The logic of production.

called them Therblig (*Gilbreth* in reverse, with the *th* transposed). These included receiving, grasping, moving, holding, releasing, searching, and selecting. The proper way to perform an activity is a skill. Drawing a blood sample is an activity where a hollow needle is inserted in an aorta and the vacuum generated by a syringe is utilized. In modern activity-based costing (ABC),[13] activity is the smallest unit that can be assigned a cost. Activities do not have a stand-alone value; piercing an artery alone is of no use.

From a management perspective, the smallest meaningful unit of analysis is a *task,* also called *processing.* It is a set of activities performed by one workstation. While activities usually do not have a stand-alone value, tasks are accomplishments. A needle

**Table 3.1  Elements of Production**

| Element | What Is It? | What Can Be Known? |
|---|---|---|
| Workstation | A resource that performs a task | Capacity utilization<br>Fixed cost (tools and equipment) |
| Task | Transformation<br>Processing | Duration<br>Resource consumption, variable cost<br>Conformance to specifications |
| Flow unit | The entity to be transformed | State at a point in time<br>Movements |
| Setup | Preparing a workstation and/or a flow unit for processing | Duration<br>Cost |
| Step | A task that is connected to and coordinated with other tasks | In–out connections |
| Handover | The movement or moving of a flow unit between steps | Control information |
| Flow | The route or journey of a flow unit | Beginning, end, number of steps<br>Alternative routes |
| Inventory (WIP) | Flow units within a process, being processed, or waiting to be processed | Volume<br>Cost |
| Cycle time | The time it takes for a flow unit to move through certain steps | Time |
| Batch | A set of flow units moving together | Batch size |
| Throughput | Completed flow units | Production volume per time unit |

inserted in an artery is an activity that combines with others, such as greeting the patient, checking identity, applying a tourniquet, finding an artery, sealing blood in a container, adding a disinfectant and surgical tape, printing a label, and sending the vial to a lab, to create the task of collecting an arterial blood sample for diagnostic purposes.

Tasks can be performed in many ways using different technologies. Tasks are measured by duration (processing time), the amount of resources used, and conformance to specifications. Some people and machines are more capable and accurate than others. Tasks are constrained by available skills and technologies.

## Flow Unit

It takes two to a task, the operator and the object of operations. In assembly manufacturing, flow units are discrete parts. In process industries, such as petrochemicals and brewing, the flow unit is the batch of material in a container or in a pipeline. The flow unit is a more general concept and can also be applied to services. In healthcare, a patient is a flow unit.[14]

The flow unit makes a journey from task to task. The end point is the finished goods inventory. From there, a new journey starts as the product life cycle, which ends with decommissioning, scrapping, and recycling. The starting point is less clear. In shipbuilding, it is when the keel is laid, and in discrete manufacturing, when material is released from material storage. In assembly, manufacturing parts lose their individual status as flow units when they are joined with others to become subassemblies. Reversely, in disassembly, such as taking apart used computers for recycling, a separated component becomes a flow unit.

Discrete flow units can move alone or in groups called batches. In some situations, batches are efficient. For example, if a piece has to be moved by a forklift, and the forklift can take 10 pieces, it may wait for all 10 to accumulate before making a move. The downside is that flow units have to wait for the batch to fill up.

## Setup

Setup means the activities and tasks required to prepare a workstation or several of them to process a flow unit. For workstations, the setup typically implies the adjustment of tools and jigs and ordering of materials. For flows, the setup includes routing, which route should this flow unit, or batch of them, take from workstation to workstation. If the flow units are identical and processed in the same way, the setup is done once; thereafter, processing is repeated. If the flow units are different, each requires its own setup, which takes time, effort, and information. Processing requires setup, but as such, setup does not have stand-alone value. The faster the better; to standardize and automate setups is preferable. In a surgical theatre, setup includes all the tasks that must be done before processing starts with the first incision. The room must be ready; the patient must be cleaned, anesthetized, and put into position. As will be discussed in Chapter 4, in services setup plays a crucial role.

## Step

A task connected with other tasks it is called *step*. Taking a blood sample is a step of a diagnostic process. As illustrated in Figure 3.4, a step is a task performed by a workstation with input and output connectors. A step is initiated by demand,

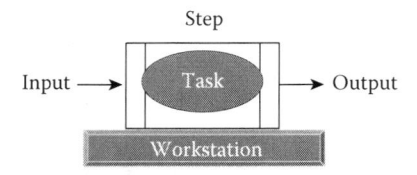

**Figure 3.4  A step in a process.**

an order, a request, or a scheduled event to process a flow unit and deliver it to the next step. When a task is part of a process, it becomes a step.

The distinction between tasks and steps is also the distinction between professionalism and managerialism. Professionals are focused on performing tasks in the best possible way, while managers are interested in how steps connect as flows.

## Handover

A *handover* happens when a flow unit is handed over to the next step. On moving assembly lines, the flow unit keeps moving at a steady phase; the handover happens when it slips over to the next workstation. In disconnected flows, the flow unit is handed over to an inventory to wait for its turn.

Handovers can be initiated in two ways, push and pull. In the push type, each workstation or process follows a master schedule and pushes its output down the line. In the pull type, each workstation requests, that is, makes an internal order for flow units. This is the *kanban* system made famous by Toyota. Its origin is in the supermarket. An empty shelf, or more exactly, a shelf with only the items left defined as a replenishment number (almost empty), calls to be filled.

In healthcare, both push and pull are used. When a surgical intervention is completed, the team pushes the patient to the postanesthesia care unit (PACU), which sees to it that the patient wakes up from anesthesia, and then proceeds with a handover to the surgical ward, where another team takes over. A doctor can pull patients from a queue or a waiting list.

In factories with limited product variety, the handover is usually instant and unproblematic. When a flow unit shows up, the workstation knows what to do. With increased variety, the handover must contain information; what is this flow unit and what should be done to it?

## Flow and Sequence

A *flow* is made out of several connected steps through which a flow unit is routed on its journey from start to finish.

Connected tasks are performed in an order, a *sequence*. It can be a critical path with a fixed order (first A, then B, then C). It can be variable (first A, then C or B, then D) or parallel (first A, then B and C, then D). In some situations, the sequence is obvious—question before answer, diagnosis before treatment—whereas in some others, such as explorative surgery, the sequence can't be set in advance. To determine the sequence is *routing*: Where is the flow unit supposed to go? To allocate time and resources is *scheduling*: When should it be there, and what resources should be ready to meet it?

## Inventory and Stock

A process uses resources. The resources have to be made available before a task can be performed. *Inventory* is a resource available before it can be used. While waiting, it may gather dust, rust, get lost, or become obsolete. Unfinished flow units have to be stashed away in storage units and documented so that they can be found when needed.

In an ideal world, there would be no inventory. Flow units and parts would appear instantly to be worked on without delay. If, say, a fire breaks out and help is needed, a fire engine would be just around the corner. In the real world, such synchrony is seldom possible. Flow units have to wait for their turn.

*Stock* is the inventory of finished goods, also called finished goods inventory. It holds products that can be shipped and sold to customers.

## Repetition and Journey

The difference between steps and flows highlights two important perspectives to production processes. To the workstation, process means the repetition of the same step. To the flow, process means the journey of a flow unit from beginning to end, as illustrated in Figure 3.5. Imagine you stand at a workstation watching flow units pass by. Alternatively, you can hitch a ride with a flow unit and

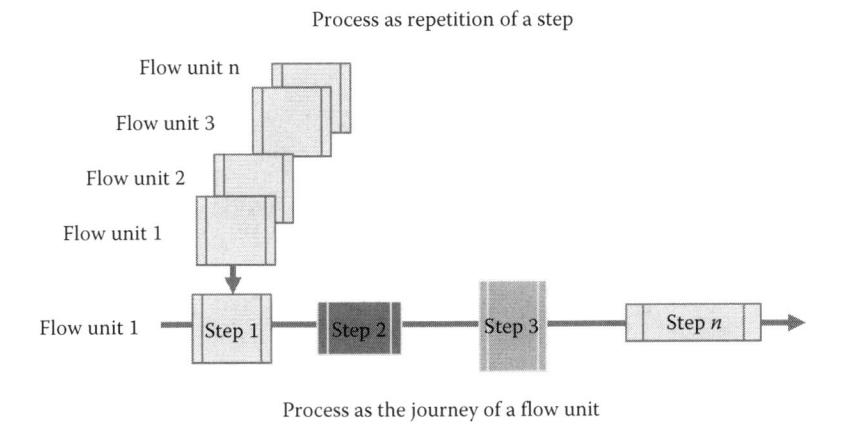

**Figure 3.5   Process as flow and repetition.**

watch all the new components being attached. A process can be experienced like a river. Sit by the shore and watch the river flow, or get on a raft and watch the scenery glide by.

These two perspectives are frequently confused in the management literature. *Process as repetition* is constrained by the production function, that is, the technologies employed at a workstation. The technology level puts an upper limit on what and how much can be done. In volume production, tasks are repetitions defined by one setup; therefore, all the tools and techniques of standardization and statistical process control (SPC) are available. A workstation only requires that resources are available, the lights are on, and flow units keep coming for processing without delay. *Process as flow* combines the efforts of several workstations. The flow unit is on a journey, and journeys require routes and navigation. The management and improvement of processes as repetition and processes as flows require different management tools and thinking.

### 3.3.4 Process Measurements

The elements of production processes have characteristics that can be observed and measured, as summarized in Table 3.1. The most important measurements are discussed in the following sections.

### Capacity Utilization

*Utilization* describes the fraction of total time a workstation is operating. As illustrated in Figure 3.6, a workstation, and by aggregation a process, has a theoretical maximum capacity bounded by physical limits. There are practical limits as well, such as working hours, which are restricted by legislation and the extra cost of overtime. Under normal conditions, scheduled downtime, such as maintenance and lunch breaks, must be deducted to get the amount of *usable capacity*. Further, unscheduled stoppages or downtime due to tool breaks and machine failures are deducted to give the *available capacity*. If a workstation has nothing to do because there are no flow units waiting to be processed, capacity stands *idle*.

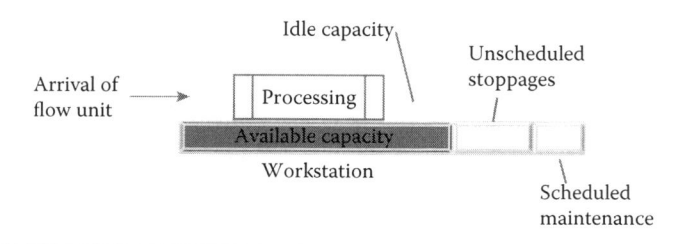

**Figure 3.6 Capacity utilization.**

Scheduled and nonscheduled stoppages, measured as downtime, are an issue of management policies, work time allocation and maintenance, and the care of equipment. Idle time is an issue of flow management. Utilization, or the capacity utilization rate (CUR), is the actual processing capacity as a percent of available capacity.[15] The better the CUR, the cheaper the unit cost, as there are no idle resources costing money while doing nothing. Utilization is an indicator of how well coordination is managed.

## Time

In production, everything takes time. As time passes, costs accumulate and resources deplete. Therefore, time is a good proxy measure for almost everything. The time measures are

- Processing time is the time it takes a workstation to perform a task.
- Idle time is the time a workstation waits for flow units.
- Cycle time (CT) is the time it takes for a flow unit, or a batch of them, to go through a process, that is, a sequence of steps.
- Throughput time is the total time for a flow unit to move from the beginning to the end point.

*Flow efficiency* is the general descriptor of how swiftly flow units move through their journey. The primary objective is a swift and even flow.[16]

## Work-in-Process Inventory and Cycle Time

Inventory can roughly be divided into two: that of parts and materials, and that of unfinished flow units. The latter is called work-in-process (WIP) inventory. It consists of the flow units that are processed at a workstation, as well as those that wait for their turns. Inventory thus can be described in two ways: how many flow units are within the system, and how long does it take for a flow unit to pass through. The time measure is CT.

Inventory is a necessary evil; it has a downside and an upside. Inventory costs money. Materials, energy, and labor have been consumed, but an unfinished flow unit can't be sold. Workers and suppliers must be paid regularly even though customers haven't yet paid their bills. A manufacturer must finance the inventory through working capital. If capital is scarce and interest rates for short-term borrowing are high, the cost of keeping a lot of inventory becomes a serious concern. On the other hand, inventory acts as a buffer, a kind of shock absorber between steps. If inventory is low, a workstation may have to stay idle for want of flow units to process. That hampers utilization and increases cost. Inventory management is therefore a central part of daily management.

## Throughput

Throughput is the volume of production, flow units that are finished and put into a finished goods inventory, or delivered right away to customers. Throughput is thus calculated as the number of finished products in a period of time, hour, day, week, or month.

## Stock Level

Stock is the buffer between market demand and production. To have a lot of products in stock is an insurance against stock-outs and back orders, the unfortunate situation where there is a customer ready and willing to pay but right now there is nothing to offer. Stock, as any inventory, is costly to keep. It may become obsolete, go out of fashion, and have to be sold at a discount or scrapped. There is a trade-off between stock level and order fulfillment. It is serious in high-price items, such as luxury cars or machine tools; in cheap items, such as nuts, bolts, and pieces of bended metal, it is less so. The trade-off can be managed by selecting the proper operating mode. Make to stock (MTS) is to estimate the average demand and the optimal stock level, that is, the minimum stock level that guarantees order fulfillment, and then make just enough to maintain the optimal level. Its opposite is make to order (MTO); production starts only when a customer order has been secured.

### 3.3.5 Process Architectures

The journey of the flow unit goes through workstations and WIP inventory points. It can be configured as variants of five ideal-type architectures: project, job shop, disconnected (batch) flow, connected flow, and continuous flow. These are process architectures that depend on product and production technologies. Oceangoing ships, automobiles, iron nails, and fermented milk are different products and produced in different ways. Different types of products require different types of processes, as illustrated in the classical product–process matrix.[17] A variant adapted to the terminology of this book is given in Figure 3.7.

Process architectures are answers to three questions. First, is there one flow unit or are there several. Second, what moves? Is it the flow unit or the workstation? Third, if the flow unit moves, is the flow continuous or are there interruptions? The five production system architectures are derived from these elements.

## Project

Projects are big undertakings to build complex products. While production processes, by definition, involve repetition and regularity, projects are undertakings that deliver unique individual results. There is only one flow unit at a time. It is a unique design, although it can make use of standard components. There typically is

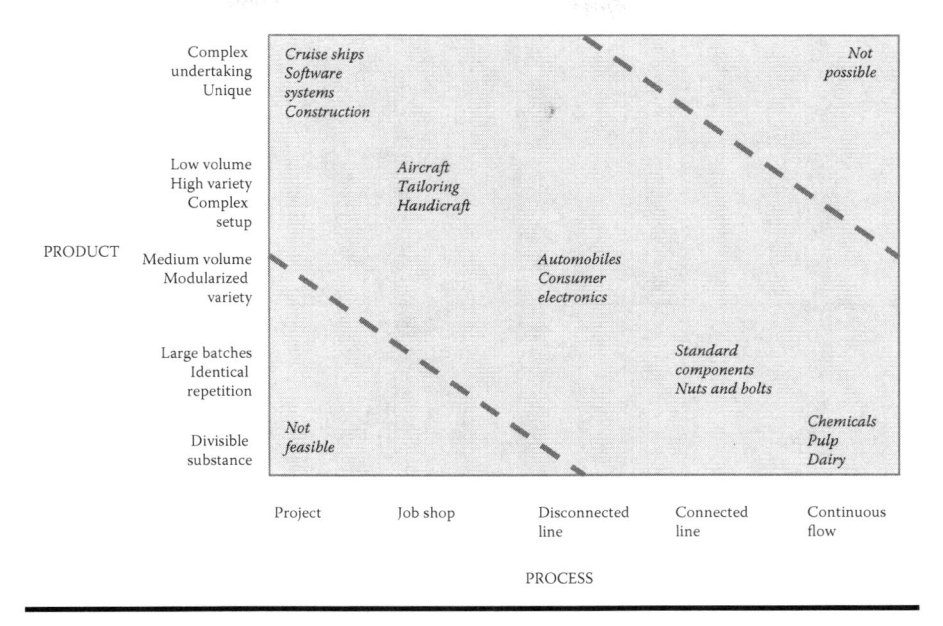

**Figure 3.7    Product–process matrix.**

a project organization composed of several independent parties that come together for that specific project under a project manager. Projects have a budget, time-line, and task to accomplish. Buildings, ships, satellites, and software are typically produced as projects.

## Job Shop

In a job shop, the flow unit is stationary or moves only within the shop. Think of a blacksmith in his smithy. A piece of steel is heated, forged with a hammer, heated again, hardened in cold water, grinded, and polished. The job shop is one workstation, which may have several tools and workbenches, such as an anvil, an oven, and a grinding wheel. There are not that many flow units inside. The same actor performs different tasks; division of labor and specialization within the shop are not taken very far. A job shop produces items in low volumes and does not make exact copies; while the products can be similar, they are not iden-tical. They can be complex, such as a custom-built piece of industrial machinery or a samurai sword. The dividing line between projects and job shops is not sharp. The main differentiators are size and organization. A job shop typically is made out of one or several craftsmen, while projects have specific project organizations.

The job shop is typically the connecting junction of many part flows, as illus-trated in Figure 3.8. It is also called jumbled flow.

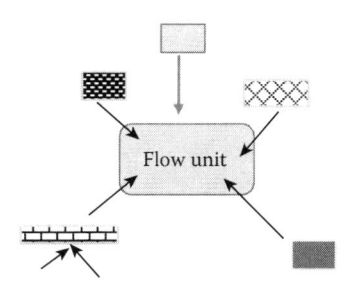

**Figure 3.8  Job shop.**

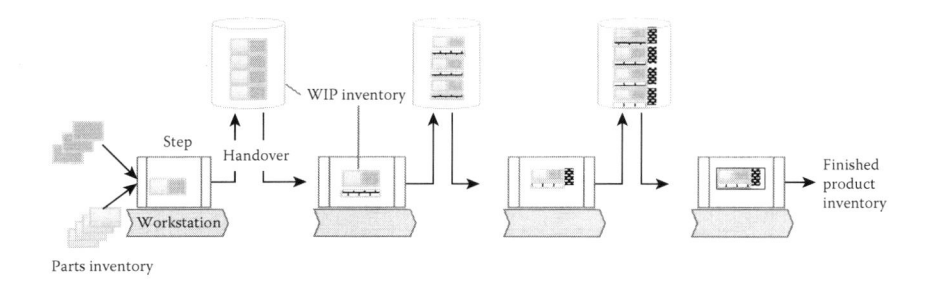

**Figure 3.9  Disconnected line.**

## Disconnected Line

A disconnected line (Figure 3.9) is used for low- or medium-volume multiple products that may share some components. The defining characteristic is that the flow unit takes a break after each step before it moves to the next workstation. Thus, the disconnected line has flow units in WIP inventory. In contrast to the job shop, the flow units move between different specialized workstations. The flow units can move to the inventory and out from there one by one, or be transported between workstations in batches. Thus, the central management problems with disconnected lines are how flow units are routed, that is, how the journey is laid out, and how to deal with inventory.

## Connected Line

The connected line (Figure 3.10) is the gold standard of efficiency. It moves flow units without interruptions. The moving assembly line, the device made famous by Henry Ford and Charlie Chaplin, is a connected line. Despite its role in the public imagination of the factory, connected lines are not that common. The problem is that a connected line requires a tremendous level of standardization and near-perfect synchrony. It is ill-suited to handle large product variety, and it is sensitive to variability. In the automotive industry, connected flows are typically used only for final assembly.

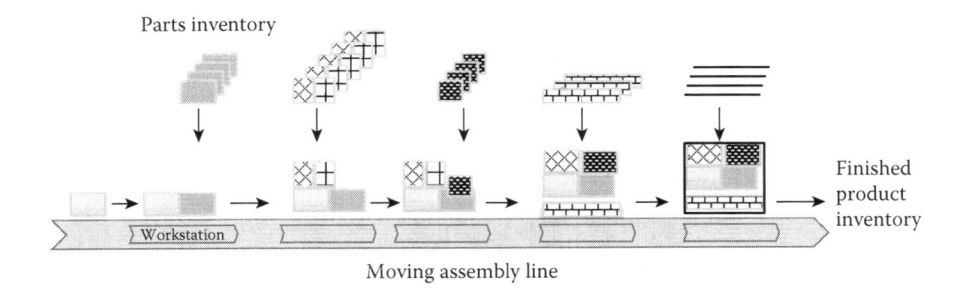

**Figure 3.10 Connected line.**

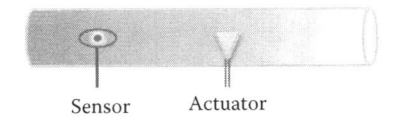

**Figure 3.11 Continuous flow.**

## Continuous Flow

Continuous flow processes are used for products that are not discrete parts, but rather materials that simmer in a tank or move through a pipeline. They are used for high-volume commodities, such as pulp, petrochemicals, and beer. The material, and the flow, turns from continuous to discrete when a batch is separated in containers, which happens in bottling plants, where connected lines are used.

Batches are set up according to various recipes, that is, product designs. In a brewery, the material is left to chemical and biological processes. Whisky matures in sherry-flavored oak casks on its own without a producer doing anything. In such processes, there are no steps or waste, except the 2% of the whisky evaporating through the oak. Distillers fondly call it the angel's share. Some flows require continuous monitoring and interventions, such as changing temperature, adding and subtracting elements, or various actuators to shake or stir the concoction (Figure 3.11).

## Architecture and Design

Products and technologies determine the five basic production architectures. Architectures can't be changed on a whim. However, within limits, flows can be designed in various ways. As the connected flow is the most efficient, there has been experimentation to move production toward this architecture. Not all attempts have been successful. Boeing announced in 2007 that it would produce its new 777 aircraft on a moving assembly line instead of the traditional job shop. After repeated failures and mounting losses, the attempt was abandoned without much ado. Planes are not cars. The number of components that need to be brought together to make an automobile are counted in the thousands; a wide-body aircraft has a million of them. A car can come off the assembly line every 45 seconds; an aircraft takes 3 days. A line that moves 1.8 inches per hour is not necessarily connected.[18]

## Cross-functional Processes and Supply Chains

The discussion so far has been about production sites and what happens within them. A producing organization is not only factories. Important things happen before and after; factories are connected. The units of analysis above the factory must be considered.

The *cross-functional process*, also known as *business process*, appeared as a unit of analysis with observations of production flows that were complicated and delayed as they crossed administrative borders. A border stands between different organizational units, each with their own processes. In a manufacturing company that makes custom-engineered products, the process typically starts with sales, which has generated a customer order. The order is the flow unit. It is first examined, acknowledged, and registered by the order handling unit. Then it is handed over to engineering, where customer-specific adjustments are made and components ordered from suppliers. From there, it goes to manufacturing, and continues to shipping and gets on its way to the customer, perhaps accompanied by a maintenance contract. The flow unit is the same, while each process has its own logic; some are manufacturing and others are service processes. Each border crossing requires some paperwork, referrals, and reports.[19]

The cross-functional process highlights that production processes are not only transformations but also coordinating devices. There is more to production than only manufacturing. Process management is not only a struggle against production risks. Various process owners get involved in interdepartmental rivalries and corporate politics. While handovers within a process may cause some problems, they are a significantly bigger issue between processes that belong to different organizational units.

With cross-functional processes, conflicts between process managers are bound to happen. If two process managers can't agree, they can kick the problem upstairs until it lands on the desk of an executive who is the superior of both. Within a hierarchy, conflicts can be solved by administrative fiat; that is, an executive has the power of office and the legitimate right to make decisions.

In modern manufacturing, a large number of processes are outsourced to independent suppliers. This creates a macroextension of the production process, the *supply chain*, supply star, or supply network, depending on how the flows are configured. Downstream, a supply chain typically has an integrator, or an original equipment manufacturer (OEM), the company that owns the brand and sells to end users. The suppliers are autonomous legal entities. One legal entity does not have administrative fiat over another. The relations between supply chain members are regulated with contracts. As supply chain members usually are in different locations and even on different continents, management of the relations requires contracting, the setting up of rules of engagement in legally binding documents. As member companies can have different objectives, strategies, cost positions, and profit objectives, supply chain management becomes a complex undertaking.[20]

Another extension is the *business ecosystem*. While a chain or a network is made of connected nodes that trade with each other, an ecosystem, on top of that, includes players that impact each other without having formal relations. For example, the design, manufacture, distribution, and use of bike helmets have an impact on what kind of skull fractures enter the trauma clinic. The helmet producers, however, do not trade with emergency departments. In this respect, ecosystems resemble institutions; nobody is in charge of all of it.

## Function and Process as Design Principles

Within a given architecture, organizations can be designed in various ways. The two fundamental design options are the functional and the process-based organization. A functional organization is based on the logic of specialization and capacity utilization. A process-based organization is designed around the central flows, the journeys of flow units through the whole system. In healthcare, this is a central theme: Should a hospital be organized around clinical specialties or clinical pathways, that is, patient journeys?

Organizations are consequences of division of labor and specialization. From this comes the principle of putting specialists of the same feather in the same room. Like with like. The functional principle when applied in factories means that similar machines are grouped together, lathes in one corner and drills in another. In a company that both designs and builds automobiles, the functional principle groups technologies in specific organizational units. All brake specialists are in the brake department. This has the benefit of increasing creative interactions between specialists. They recognize and respect the super-specialists and are willing to assign authority to the most accomplished. The functional organization can produce technical wonders. However, it tends to ignore what happens to the hapless flow unit. In the mind of the brake specialist, an automobile is all brakes. Functions battle each other for resources and influence; no one wants to submit to the whole. But customers ask for integrated designs where all components join properly and work together. It takes a hierarchy to bang the specialist in order. This is why technology companies, such as Apple, have brutal hierarchies.[21]

The mechanism is the same as in production processes. Without a hard-nosed owner of the whole flow, the workstations do not necessarily pay attention to proper handovers. They put their stuff in the out bin and think they are done. Focus on functions creates jumbled flows.

A solution is to apply a process-based organizational design. The flow unit is put in the center, and everything is aligned around it. In the automotive industry, this was taken to the extreme by appointing powerful product managers.[22]

They had the overall responsibility of one model, from beginning to end, and had all necessary resources under their command. In a process-based organization, reporting relationships and information flows are aligned with the process, thus eliminating administrative obstacles to the flow. Flow efficiency rules over resource efficiency.

But there is a downside to process-based architectures. The highly specialized functional units are split. The brake experts are allocated out to serve under various product managers. Cutting-edge technology development, as well as professional authority, takes hits. In a huge organization, such as Toyota Motor Company, each product–process can have enough volume to keep the specialists busy and funded. In smaller organizations, the capacity of a super-specialist may not be sufficiently used in serving only one process. If there is not sufficient volume, the process-based organization can't maintain sufficient capacity utilization and turns into a cost problem.

A compromise is that our brake specialist divides her time between the function and a process. This is an organizational design called the matrix organization. The $X$ axis of the matrix is functions, and the $Y$ axis processes. Each cell in the matrix reports both to a function head and to a process manager. But nobody is happy serving two masters. Conflicts arise; allocations of time and focus have to be made. Matrix organizations are notoriously difficult to manage.[23] This is one more reason for the emergence of the supply chain. Let organizations focus on what they do best, and then let them trade with each other.

## 3.4 Production Dynamics and Management

Anatomy gives a view of the basic elements (organs and tissues) of the human body and how they are structured. On top of that, there is an interest to know how they work alone and together. That is physiology. In production, the same is true. Production systems have elements that can be identified. The elements behave in certain ways. The behaviors can be observed, measured, and evaluated. Regular behaviors can be explicated as dynamics.

Every product, material, and machine has its particular dynamic. That vast body of knowledge is not touched here. Of interest are the generic dynamic relations between the basic elements of production.

### 3.4.1 Productivity

Productivity in its simplest form is the relation between inputs and outputs, resource consumption and the utility of accomplishments. It is an aggregate measure that applies best to industries and national economies. Production systems use more detailed measures.

The input–output relation at a point in time does not tell very much; productivity is used to track changes. When productivity increases, more can be had for less; when productivity decreases, it takes more to get less. If productivity is constant, an economy can grow only if resources, such as land, labor, natural resources, and capital, are deployed in increasing volumes. When more resources can't be had, the only growth engine is productivity. When existing resources are managed more efficiently, output increases without a corresponding increase in input.

The ontology of productivity is clear, but the epistemology is difficult. Input is the totality of the resources spent. The most important are labor and capital. Therefore, labor and capital productivity are calculated separately, and combined into total factor productivity (TFP).

Output is the total volume of throughput. It can be measured as revenue, the total amount of money received from customers. The problem is, how well does price represent what was accomplished? In many industries, technology, quality, user friendliness, and other key indicators have improved tremendously, while prices have fallen. A clunky dot matrix printer used to cost several times more in constant dollars than the modern quiet and clean laser printer. Prices won't reflect the difference. Output requires qualitative performance measures. Thereby productivity is divided into two categories. Quality-adjusted productivity accounts for qualitative differences, while nonadjusted, or quantitative, productivity measures the output in dollar terms.[24]

Operations management takes products and technologies as givens at a point in time. The challenge is to figure out better ways to organize the elements of production and manage them to increase productivity.

## 3.4.2 Variability and Quality Control

A central element of all purposeful activities is the presence of variability, the lack of pattern or predictability in events. When production systems have been designed, daily management is about dealing with variability, to find it, avoid it, amend it, and ensure against it.

### Risk and Uncertainty

Risk is variability contained within a set of known outcomes. A coin can land as heads or tails. Rolling a dice produces an outcome that is one of six possible. Assuming the dice is not loaded, each outcome has the same probability. Probabilities can be derived logically, as with the coin and the dice. Some others, such as getting killed in a road accident, can be estimated from historical data. Murphy's law says that if something can go wrong, it will go wrong. But most things don't go wrong in an infinite number of ways. Failure mode and effect analysis (FMEA) is a methodology for finding Murphy. Risk is the probability of something happening multiplied by the effect.

Uncertainty means a situation where the outcomes, as well as their probabilities, are not known. It may be because of lack of knowledge and experience, or because the world in this respect does not follow a predictable pattern. Keynesian economics is based on the notion of fundamental uncertainty, which is not just a reflection of deficiencies in our cognitive faculties. The economic world is an open system. Surprises happen.

## Types of Variability

Factories reduce variability by placing production inside buildings surrounded by fences and guarded by passcodes. Division of labor, specialization, and standardization are tools to contain and control variability.

Variability can be divided into external and internal. In a market economy, customers buy what they want when they want in quantities that suit them. Such independent external demand is good news, as it indicates more sales. It may turn into bad news if products are not available and stocks are empty. External demand, however, does not hit production unannounced. Customer orders are translated into dependent internal demand, that is, work orders for workstations. Variations in external demand can be smoothened but not eliminated. A specialized producer rejects demand that does not fit.

Variability can also be planned or self-inflicted. The variety of products that a company offers for sale is intentional. High product variety means that the number of issues to keep track of is high. The devil is not only in the details; it lurks in the relations between details. Production systems can unintentionally create variability. Any deviation from target or missed deadline creates a cascade of variability within the system. Internal variability shows up as waiting time, excess inventory, or excess capacity. Other types of variability are unscheduled downtime, tool breaks, absenteeism, and malfunctioning.

## Variation

Variation, as the term is used in Statistical Process Control (SPC),[25] is the deviation from a given target. Variation appears when control and variability collide.

Designers set targets for products and specify dimensions, surfaces, weight, or material composition of products as numerical values. Variation can be expressed as the distance from the target. For example, if a designer says a metal shaft should be 2 mm in diameter, but an actual instance turns out as 2.01 mm, the distance is 0.01 mm. In this respect, variation, unlike variability, is normative. It is good to hit the target; it is bad to deviate from it. Targets are set with the purpose to control production and make things predictable.

Targets can be set by various levels of precision. If the target is 2 mm, a tolerance band, ±0.01, can be set. Any instance that comes within this range is accepted. The term *tolerance* indicates that the product will tolerate this amount of deviation and still function properly. In services, "zone of tolerance" indicates the level of abuse customers will accept without walking away.

## Common and Specific Causes of Variation

Variation has two principal causes, internal and external. Production processes exhibit random variation arising from "common causes." A process, when it operates in its normal state, regularly produces a number of outputs that deviate from target. They are internal causes inherent in the system design. Common causes are random and exhibit the statistical stability of random variables. Processes are said to be under statistical control when the number of deviations can be predicted. The process capability index is a statistical measure of the ability of a process to produce output within specification limits, that is, tolerances. This measurement is usually illustrated by a histogram (bar graph) showing the spread of results. Statistical control means that while variation is not eliminated, it is put into the cage of predictability.

Sometime processes are not under statistical control and behave unpredictably. That is a case of variation that arises from specific or "assignable causes," discrete events or external disturbances. Those may come from tool breaks, vibrations, operator errors, deformations in raw material, or other discrete events. Assignable causes are incidents that happen in space and time. They can be tracked down by asking why until the root cause is revealed and fixed.

Specific causes require local solutions, while common causes call for redesigning the system. Mixing up common and specific causes leads to serious organizational pathologies. If there is randomness in the system, local solutions, such as more effort and diligence, will not solve problems that arise from the very root design of the system.

> Edwards Deming, the American statistician who got fame for teaching quality control to the Japanese, made a highly educating and entertaining demonstration of the effects of common causes, the red bead experiment. There is a container holding 800 white and 200 red beads. Whites represent products that fulfill all the requirements of good quality, while the reds are defective, products that cannot be sold. The experiment subjects are asked to use a paddle with matching holes to scoop up a set of beads. The more whites, the better their performance, which is meticulously recorded on a production control chart. Subjects are exhorted to do their best. But it soon becomes clear that will and skill have nothing to do with the outcome. No matter what the subjects do, results are determined by randomness. As this sinks in, motivational hullabaloo appears utterly meaningless.[26]

Attempts to solve systemic problems with local solutions lead to tampering.[27] Operations are adjusted reactively with quick fixes and workarounds, which only make the problem worse. On the other hand, if the problem really is local but the solution is a system change, excessive bureaucracy is created. A typical example in professional organizations is a case where one individual misbehaves, say, the expense account on a business trip is used for booze and nightclubs. The sinner gets caught, but the administration does not have the guts to deal with the individual as an assignable cause. Instead, it is interpreted as a system problem that is corrected with more rules and restrictions on business travel, creating further layers of bureaucracy that may or may not solve the problem, but certainly make life difficult for both saints and sinners.

Causes or errors should be found for remedies to be effective. The problem is that examining one defective piece does not necessarily reveal the origin of the problem. If data is collected on relevant measures and put in a time series, statistical analysis can reveal whether the source of the problems is common or specific. Common causes show up with regularity, while specific causes announce themselves as trends or spikes. This methodology, SPC, was developed by Walter Shewhart,[28] popularized by Edwards Deming,[29] and further elaborated as Six Sigma. When the primary causes of deviations can be identified, analysis and corrective action can be focused.

Common and specific causes are not ontological certainties. They depend on information and knowledge. When a common cause is thoroughly dissected by Six Sigma statistical analysis, it may disintegrate into several specific and actionable causes.

With SPC, quality management acquired a theory-based technology to identify and act on quality problems. It reduced the costs and hassles of poor quality, enabled standardization, and improved economic performance. It became a technology that could reach beyond the obvious.

## Small q and Big Q

As illustrated in Figure 3.12, quality denotes a relation. The basic relation, conformance to specifications, technical quality, or *small q*, is that between *ex ante* given specifications and the accomplished output.

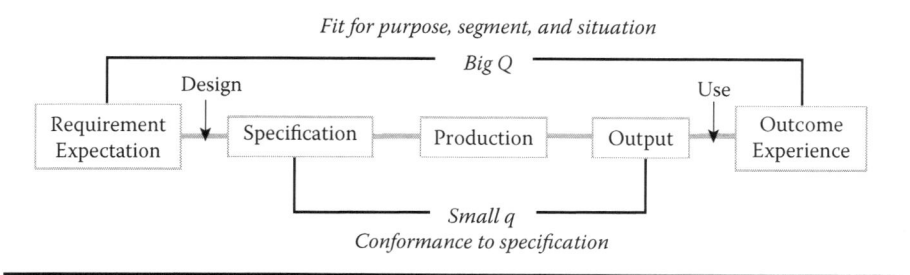

**Figure 3.12   Small q and big Q.**

The small q technology of SPC was the foundation of continuous improvement, which contributed to the rise of Japan as a manufacturing powerhouse. That happened in the post-WWII era, when most civilian products were both scarce and shoddy. Customers had little choice but take it or leave it. With increasing wealth, product variety expanded and customers got more choice. Making products exactly to engineering specifications was no longer sufficient as a success recipe. Facing the whims of the mighty consumer, producers had to enlarge their scope. This was the rise of Total Quality Management (TQM), and the *big Q*. Customer satisfaction became the rallying cry. Quality as management concept expanded from conformance to specifications to encompass functionality, performance, grade, and style.

While small q could rely on SPC as a powerful technology, big Q faced the same complexities and uncertainties inherent in product design and consumer marketing. There is very little solid theory on consumer behavior to enable precise prediction, which new features will succeed in the market. Figure 3.12 illustrates that big Q is a phenomenon that has a significantly different ontology than small q.

Small q is the relation between explicit, *ex ante* specifications and output. What should be done is known before it is done. Output is measured using the variables given in the specifications, and deviations can be calculated with accuracy. Big Q is the relation between two flimsy things: expectations and experiences. Customers may have expectations that are not realistic or informed. In many cases, customers have great trouble in defining and articulating exactly what they want. Market research struggles with translating expectations to requirements that could be incorporated in designs. When a product is ready and delivered, customers can experience it in many ways in a multitude of contexts. Products can be misused or abused. In other words, small q is an attempt to combat variability by focusing on specific targets one at the time. Big Q opens the floodgates of customer-introduced variability. The TQM movement tried to deal with such complexities by introducing decision-making aids, such as quality function deployment (QFD) and the House of Quality,[30] a matrix-based tool that aims at bringing together customer requirements and product features. Elegant as it is, it succumbs to the same constraint as any formal method. If customers can't articulate their requirements with sufficient precision, garbage goes in and garbage comes out. While TQM has faded into the woodwork, small q is alive and well under the Six Sigma banner.

## Cost of Poor Quality

Quality is usually promoted as a customer-oriented management approach. That is true; bad quality is customer abuse and will eventually show up as lost revenue. However, quality as conformance to requirements is not only a property of a flow unit or a batch of them. In a flow perspective, small q equals punctuality, conformance to schedule. With time variability, process coordination becomes difficult and requires buffers.

### 3.4.3 *Inventory and Buffers*

In a perfectly controlled production system, the flow unit would move without delay from workstation to workstation. Throughput time would be the sum of processing time. In the real world, this is seldom possible. In some cases, flow units must be gathered into batches to reduce transport and setup. Each flow unit will have to wait for the rest of its batch. Even when batches are not used, the ever-present variability requires buffer inventories to act as a suspension system.

### Little's Law

The relations between Work-in-process inventory, CT (the time a flow unit spends in the process), and throughput (the amount of flow units processed per day or week) are related by a neat chunk of logic known as Little's law. It was developed in a paper published in 1961 by John D.C. Little.[31] It states the relation between WIP, throughput volume (TH), and CT as WIP = TH × CT. This formula can be rearranged as CT = WIP/TH.

Little's law is general and tautological. The only restrictions are that it refers to long-term averages and the process must be stable; it does not apply when a process exhibits a systematic trend, such as steadily building up WIP inventory or anything that makes the process substantially different during the interval when data is collected.

Little's law can be used for many purposes. If any of the two measures are known, the third can be calculated. Suppose that a company bills on average $10,000 a day (TH) and that customers take 45 days on average to pay (CT). The total amount of accounts receivable (WIP) will be 10,000 × 45 = $450,000. Measuring CT directly can be difficult, as it would entail time-stamping each flow unit as it enters and leaves the system. Throughput is routinely tracked because it is related to revenue. WIP can be known through periodic counts. If averages of WIP and TH are known, CT = WIP/TH. In the above example, it would be 45 = 450,000/10,000.

The literature on Lean production calls for WIP reduction. Little's law indicates that WIP and CT reduction are two sides of the same coin. As long as TH remains constant, any reduction in WIP must be accompanied by a reduction in CT, and vice versa. The places where to look for speedier CT are where inventory is piling up.

Little's law can yet be written in a third form: TH = WIP/CT. Think of two systems with the same production function and TH. One has high WIP and long CT; the other has low WIP and short CT. Obviously, anybody would prefer the latter, as it is more efficient in converting WIP into throughput, that is, getting jobs done rapidly without flow units waiting as WIP inventory. This is the difference where management matters.

## Bottlenecks

Short CT requires that the output created by a workstation is available to the next station as needed, but not any sooner. The trouble is that some workstations may, for technical reasons, allocative decisions, or variability, have a different capacity than others. As illustrated in Figure 3.13, the weakest step in a flow is called a bottleneck. A chain is no stronger than its weakest link.[32]

A bottleneck is a workstation with a constraining capacity. It produces less per time unit than the stations before and/or after. Another definition of a bottleneck is that it is the workstation with the highest utilization. There is no idling, but it still can't keep up. In Figure 3.13, the performance of the weakest link (Step 2) determines the performance of the whole process. If Step 1 works harder and increases its volume, it only manages to create an even larger pile of inventory in front of the bottleneck (Step 2). Steps 3 to *n* are starved of flow units to work on and have idle capacity.

The obvious solution would be to allocate resources inside a process so that all steps produce a similar amount of output to balance the flow and eliminate bottlenecks. This is not easily done if there are several technologies with different performances, if the steps have different process capabilities, or if demand keeps shifting in volume, arrival rate, and type. From this follows that bottlenecks can move. Due to the vagaries of variability, today's champion workstation can be tomorrow's loser.[33]

## VUT Equation

Another chunk of logic explicates the relation between waiting time and utilization at a single workstation. CT is waiting time plus processing time. The fundamental cause of waiting in a queue is lack of coordination between arrivals and processing. If flow units could be synchronized to arrive when the workstation has finished with the previous flow unit, there would be no queuing. If there is variability in arrivals and/or processing time, queues build up.

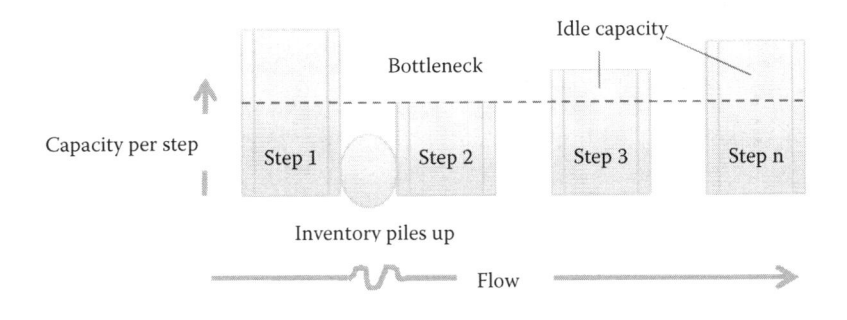

**Figure 3.13   A bottleneck in a process.**

The waiting time here is the time spent in a queue at a workstation. It is denoted WT. In its most general form, the VUT equation is written as WT = VUT.

V stands for a variability component that is a function of both arrival and process variability, that is, external and internal variability. U stands for utilization, that is, the time a workstation is not idle for lack of parts. T stands for average effective process time for one flow unit.

The components can be elaborated and calculated in several ways that are explained in textbooks[34] and not of further concern here. The important insight from the VUT equation is that variability and utilization interact. High variability is most damaging in situations with high utilization, that is, at bottlenecks. As utilization approaches 100%, waiting time due to queuing approaches infinity. This can happen in traffic. If a highway is utilized to full capacity and vehicles move bumper to bumper, a small disturbance will create a traffic jam with rapid ripple effects.

## Variability, Again

Little's law, bottlenecks, and the VUT equation are chunks of logic that reach beyond common sense. It would be sensible to assume that if everybody just worked a little bit harder, that is, workstation utilization would be higher, then there would be more throughput, less waiting, and lower cost. In an ideal world with no variability, this could be true to a limit. In the real world, when all workstations are fully loaded, any little glitch directly impacts the waiting time of all the flow units in line.

That brings back the questions of variability and quality. If nothing never goes wrong, WIP and CT both can go down. This is the core issue of standardization and small quality control.[35] Deviations affect not only the flow units, which eventually show up as customer-perceived quality problems, but the time it takes to process a step. If both steps and journeys can be standardized so that they always do the same things with the same output using the same resources for the same duration, a production system will approach perfect synchrony with optimal resource and flow efficiency.

The first and most fundamental lesson of production dynamics is to drive out variability through standardization and control. Where this can be done, production systems operate like clockwork. In the real world, and particularly so in personal services such as healthcare, this can't be done. To be more precise, even if it could be done, it would soon start to produce other ill effects, such as half-treated patients that require more appointments, that in due course would defeat the very purpose of the system. In an imperfect world, variability must be accepted and managed within the limits of the possible.

A way to standardize and manage time is to use takt time. It works like a metronome, the device novice players put on top of their pianos to help keep rhythm. Takt time calculation takes the expected throughput (number for completed flow units) per time unit (day), and uses it to divide the available time into takts. A takt is the standard time allowed for a step. Takt time is a normative framework that allows managers to see whether production is on schedule, falling behind, or getting ahead. Takt time is useful if the takt for each step is equal to or larger than processing time, if there is little variability in the processing time and handovers, and if the takts can be calculated for a process with several types of processing. If these conditions are not met, takt time becomes a straightjacket. In environments with high variability in demand, such as emergency departments, takt time can be used only in standardized and predictable subprocesses.[36]

This is the dilemma that operations management seeks to address: how to improve capacity utilization and CT, resource efficiency and flow efficiency simultaneously.

## Portfolio of Buffers

The standardization of steps is easier than the standardization of flows. The standardization of steps and processing can draw on technologies, such as precise tools, numerically controlled machines, automation, and robotics. As the precision of steps increases, flows become more predictable. With high variability in steps, journeys remain variable.

A buffer is a resource that acts as a shock absorber is a production system. Buffers can be of three types, or a combination of them: inventory of components and/or flow units, time, and excess capacity. Retails stores add inventory in anticipation of holiday seasons. Services can't be produced for inventory; therefore, either time or capacity has to be used. Airport security control may not be able to add capacity to meet demand; passengers will have to wait in a queue. There are cases where time can't deliberately be used as a buffer. Emergency and rescue services are founded on the mission of rapid response. Burning houses and bleeding people can't wait. If time and inventory are out of play, excess capacity is the only remaining buffer. A fire department can have vehicles, equipment, and personnel idling without being taken to task for poor productivity. Capacity utilization is not a concern if excess capacity is the only buffer at hand.

## Daily Management

The ever-present external and internal variability can be designed away only to a limit. Production systems require daily management to prevent decay into chaos. It is like steering a ship; even when the waters are calm, somebody has to be at the wheel.

Daily management is based on routine monitoring, preferably visualization of key performance indicators. Deviations from targets should be quickly identified and acted on. Buffers must be moved around. If the same problems keep coming up, the causes, assignable and common, need to be dug out and eliminated. Daily management and continuous improvement go together.

### 3.4.4 Setup and Handover

The unit cost of a product is determined by two basic factors: the cost of processing, including raw material, components, energy, facilities, equipment, and labor, and the costs associated with how production is organized. The first is external, determined by technology, or comes with the architecture; the second is an internal management issue.

The only element that transforms material to product is processing. It embodies the production function. If no major breakthroughs in technology and capital investment are in sight, processing is as it is. Inventories and buffers are used as shock absorbers, but their volume (WIP) and the associated time consumption (CT) are instruments that managers can play. Two other examples are setups and handovers.

### Setup and Repeat

Setup means the things that must be done to get a workstation going. In the conceptual terminology of Chapter 2, setup happens when an instance meets a context and some adjustments have to be made to create a situation.

When a setup is done, the process can be repeated in an identical fashion to produce a batch of identical, interchangeable parts. Assuming there are no unscheduled stoppages and the workstation is well supplied with material, capacity utilization can be high. The question then is, how many repetitions per one setup? The longer the production run, the less the setup cost is per part. If the setup costs $100 to do and 100 copies are made, the setup puts a $1 cost burden on each instance. If 1,000 copies are made in the same uninterrupted run, the burden is $0.1; if 10,000, it is $0.01; and so on. Obviously, this can't go on forever. Each order of parts has a cost, and there are costs of keeping inventory. Considering these, the optimal run length or lot size can be calculated.[37] This is one of the core mechanisms of economies of scale; the more you make, the cheaper it gets.

In early mass production, the factory was the physical embodiment of the setup. Ford Motor Company built the first fully integrated automotive production facility in Highland Park, Michigan, in 1908. It was a highly efficient engineering marvel. In total, more than 15 million cars were manufactured, reaching a rate of 9,000 to 10,000 cars a day in 1925. That was more than any other model of its day. The price was just $260 (about $3240 in 2016 dollars). The downside was it could produce only one product variety, the black T Ford, known as Tin Lizzie. When in 1927 Henry Ford bowed to market pressure and introduced the new A model, production had to be shut down for several months to retool and set up the entire production system for the new model.

If setup is expensive, variety has to succumb to volume and price. If variety is not a concern, as with standard components, such as nuts and bolts, a very large lot can follow one setup. For end products, customers will have to do with what is available at mass production prices; alternatively, they can go for custom-built Lamborghinis and pay through the nose.

The question to ask is, why on earth do we have to spend so much on setup? This was the stroke of genius behind the Toyota Production System. Setups can be improved by making them standard procedures. Setup does not have to be embedded into the very architecture of a factory if machines, workstations, and processes can be made flexible.

An automobile requires a number of sheet metal parts stamped into form to make bonnets, doors, tail fins, and other surface parts. The form is produced by a die attached to a stamping machine that with great force presses the die against a piece of cold-rolled steel plate. The dies are heavy. They need to be aligned and trimmed just right to produce error-free parts. Setting up a machine used to take at least a full working day. With a bit of tinkering, Taichi Ohno and Shigeo Shingo, who later became Toyota management gurus, succeeded in cutting down the setup time to less than 10 minutes. This was the now famous single-minute exchange of die (SMED), the management technology that became one of the cornerstones of Lean production.[38]

As the cost of the setup goes down, so does the optimal lot size. When the setup cost approaches zero, the optimal lot size approaches one. This means, in theory, that fully individual products could be built at the same cost as mass-produced ones. In personal services where the lot size per definition is one person, setup becomes a central concern.

### 3.4.5 *Production Process and Value Chain*

The technologies bundled into a production function do the transformations. They need processes and organizations to support. An arrow without a bow and a chisel without a hammer accomplish nothing much. The archer needs the support of a band of hunters to drive the deer within range. The sculptor needs scaffolding to reach the proper spot with his chisel. More support can always be added. As organizations grow, the fundamental production function disappears from sight behind layers of administration. In military parlance, the distance from "tooth to tail" depicts the number of support personnel one combat soldier requires to function properly. At some stage, the point of diminishing return is reached and more accomplishes less.

Process describes everything that is done. But all of it does not contribute. This is a core insight of Lean production. How then do we distinguish the activities that create value, that is, put something in the "what you get" side of the give–get constellation of economic value.

The simple answer comes with the value chain concept, also known as the value stream.[39] It denotes the tasks that must be done for value to be created. A value chain, by definition, includes only tasks that are mission critical to the final purpose.

The difference between the value chain and the process is waste. The Lean production literature uses the Japanese language term *muda* to denote all the things that consume resources but do not contribute to value. Lean teaches that *muda* should relentlessly be identified and eliminated.

Some types of *muda* are easier to identify than others. Many workplaces are in disarray with a lot of *muda* in plain sight. Quality errors are clearly *muda*. Searching for misplaced tools or documents does not create value. Putting workplaces in order and designating a place for every tool and document is picking low-hanging fruit. When that is done, *muda* is no longer visible. Sharper definitions are needed.

Waste is per definition the opposite of value; it can't be known without knowing value. In the Lean literature, the ontology of value is what the customer appreciates and is willing to pay for. The corresponding epistemologies must be total sales, pricing power, customer satisfaction, and customer loyalty. Then the dynamics; what makes people choose certain products over others, enjoy using them, and stay loyal to a brand? As I have discussed, in a market customer choice is founded on price in relation to differentiation, the nonprice issues of product attributes (functionality, performance, grade, and style) and delivery (availability at the right place and time). Attributes are designed before production. A factory is not supposed to alter product designs. Moreover, customer value is not easily itemized down to each of the 30,000 parts of an automobile. Many products are packages of functions. Thus, the conception of value anchored in customer preferences is not helpful at a production site. What production can do is to make error-free copies as efficiently as possible to enable low prices, and take out variability to improve small quality and delivery precision.

Strictly speaking, value is added only in transformations, that is, when a flow unit is processed. However, a production system is not only the production function; organizational scaffolding is needed. Processing can't be done if the workstation is not set up properly and the flow unit is not present. Buffer inventories can be eliminated only if all variability is eliminated and the whole system works in perfect synchrony. It does not make sense to say that setup, handover, and buffers do not contribute to value.

And what about a company cafeteria? While not adding value directly to the end product, it is good for business, as starving workers are prone to errors and a cafeteria can be a meeting place for creative ideas. To deal with this, the concept of *business value* has been introduced.[40] It signifies activities that are necessary contributions to running a business. But from here starts a slippery slope of second, third, and *n*th order contributions. Every last administrative clerk will testify that not a pebble can be removed from the bureaucratic levee without opening it up to a flood of chaos. Back to square one.

To say that CT is value-adding time plus non-value-adding time is to say not much. It is a tautology. As Hopp and Spearman[41] sarcastically note, it is like saying that all people in the world are either Hillary Clinton or not Hillary Clinton. The confusion here goes back to ontology, the imprecise way of confusing value with worth. Economic value is the relation between what you give and what you get. Economic value can be increased by reducing price, which in turn requires reduced costs of production. The task thus becomes to reduce cost without compromising something valuable. The problem with value and *muda* can be solved by the following concepts.

In production, everything that is done involves some giving; raw materials, energy, and paid labor time are consumed. The sacrifice can be divided into two parts. The first is embedded in processing. The second is process design and management within the constraints of architecture. As Little's law shows, the same throughput can be achieved with different combinations of CT and WIP inventory. There can be two production systems, both with the same technology and production volume, but one has short waiting times and low inventory, while the other keeps flow units waiting as work in progress. The difference is management.

The value chain is a simplification. *Muda* is best left to describe the obvious waste. A more useful distinction can be made between processing and management. The former depends on technologies and capabilities. Investing in better technologies and training can improve it. Management is about designing and adjusting processes: how to do setups, handovers, routing, and scheduling, and how to manage buffers and bottlenecks. Setup and inventory management are not *muda* to be eliminated, but tasks that can be performed with high or low efficiency. In healthcare, this shows up as the distinction between clinical interventions and patient journeys. There is a limit to how fast a surgeon can operate. If a workstation is driven to the limits, errors are bound to happen. If the journey of the flow unit is swift and even, everybody will be happy.

## 3.5 Volume, Variety, and Cost

If you can do it once and it looks good, can you repeat it a thousand times? A thousand copies cost less to make than a thousand individuals. This is the logic of industrial production. High-volume mass production makes goods available and affordable, but robs them of their individuality. The volume–variety dilemma arises from a simple human trait. If you lack something, you want it and then some more. When you have enough of it, you desire something different.

### 3.5.1 Economies of Scale

Economies of scale is a chunk of logic that describes mechanisms through which the volumes of large-scale production in some situations translate into lower cost per produced unit. The more you make, the cheaper it gets.

Scale means the size of the production system. It is related to the volume of production, but scale and volume imply different mechanisms. These are described in the operations management body of knowledge.[42]

The first is the above-mentioned mechanisms or division of labor, specialization, and standardization. They are not applicable in small job shops with a few craftsmen and large demand variety. They come into play only in large organizations.

Second, a large-scale organization can amass more resources and knowledge. If some expensive resources are indivisible, such as operating theatre (OTs) and diagnostic equipment, a large organization can ensure a higher CUR and reduce unit cost. Large hospitals can afford better, newer, or more specialized equipment than small ones, and offer better career options, specialization areas, and collegial support.

Third, to the extent that large scale leads to large volumes, fixed costs, like setup costs, can be spread over a larger number of produced units. This mechanism is particularly powerful in software. Assume you develop a set of software at the total production cost of $1 million. You sell it to one customer. Installation and training will cost, say, $100,000. Your production cost is $1.1 million. On top of that you put your margin, which together makes the price you ask the customer to pay. Now assume you get another customer. The customer-specific variable cost is still the $100,000 for installation and training. But the development cost can now be shared between two customers. Keep adding customers, and you can reduce the price to gain even more customers while you make money hand over fist. Development is a fixed cost akin to setup. Installation is a variable cost akin to repetition. As the burden of fixed cost is shared by an increasing number of customers, price will fall and approach the variable cost.

Fourth, in some industries scale has a technical definition. For physical reasons, blast furnaces have a minimum scale defined by energy efficiency, below which cost penalties are inevitable. This is also known as the container effect; the larger a container, the less surface area and packaging material to volume there is.

Fifth, the learning curve describes a situation where an individual becomes more proficient as the cumulative number of repetitions increases. A large organization can offer more chances to repeat the same procedure, thereby boosting the learning curve. The experience curve is essentially the same, but applies to a larger unit of analysis, such as a team or a plant, where learning includes better teamwork and coordination. The learning and experience curves are important in healthcare, particularly in routine or near-standard procedures, such as cataract surgery.

Sixth, scale can increase the volume of purchases and the ensuing bargaining power over suppliers. In a similar vein, a large establishment can command an important position in the regional economy and use its position to extract various benefits, that is, become too big to fail.

Economies of scale applies best to the production of one product on one product line. If several products are produced on the same line, calculations become complex. In such situations, another mechanism can be exploited. The term *economies of scope* is used to denote a situation where the same system can be used to produce different products more effectively than with a separate dedicated system. An example is air transport. If an aircraft can take both passengers and cargo, this is more efficient than having dedicated planes for each type of load.

Economies of scale is a complex conceptual construct subject to variability. It works well in some situations, and it will have negative effects in others. There is also diseconomies of scale. As an organization grows, the need for coordination and control increases. Larger scale requires layers of management and more formalized control, that is, bureaucracy. Economies of scale can produce several benefits. If unit cost reduction is the objective, the core mechanism is the relation of fixed and variable cost, setup and repetition. As we will see, in services where setups are individual, economies of scale is problematic.

### Upside and Downside

The upside of the Industrial Revolution, economies of scale, division of labor, specialization, standardization, and new technologies was first plenty, then opulence. The downside was fragmentation and meaninglessness, the state sociologists call alienation, the curse of industrial civilization. The independent craftsman and his professional identity were reduced to cogs in a big wheel. Design and execution were separated. Craft as the useful art disappeared from factories. Skilled fitters were no longer needed, as interchangeable parts were made to fit. When the setups were done, it was all repetition. Any Tom, Dick, and Harry fresh from immigration could take an assembly line job and quickly learn the required motions. This created the rift between competence and comprehension;[43] a worker can be fully competent in one or a few tasks without comprehending the meaningful whole.

The painful rift between the upside and the downside of industrial production methods is still present. Some call it the "contradiction of capitalism".[44] In truth, it is not a contradiction but a trade-off. Everybody covets value, wealth, and comfort. But their making takes effort and discipline. Variability and decay can't be beaten back by intuition and impulse. This trade-off is present in preventive medicine; there is a trade-off between a sedentary lifestyle and health.

### 3.5.2 Volume and Variety

The history of production can be told in terms of volume and variety, as summarized in Figure 3.14. The original position in preindustrial societies was scarcity of everything. In today's money, our ancestors had to do with $3 a day. It bought food, mostly cereals, and an occasional sliver of meat, one set of clothes, and a cot under a roof. In the eighteenth century, most people in western Europe were chronically malnourished; only the lucky 1% could eat to their heart's content.[45]

Production of whatever humans needed simply could not get the volumes. Tilling fields by hand tools, transporting stuff by oxen charts, and building tools one by one did not produce enough. The Industrial Revolution and the new

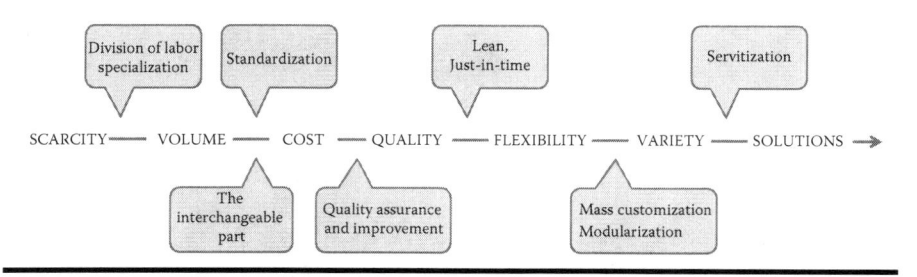

**Figure 3.14  Milestones in the history of production.**

socio-techno-economic organization of production and economies of scale solved the problems of want and volume.

Solutions tend to create new problems. When goods can be supplied in high volumes, the question turns to the demand side. Who can afford to buy them? Since the mid-nineteenth century, wages kept rising, but not yet at a pace that would have ensured mass demand. Prices had to go down, which called for more efficiency in production, sourcing, and distribution.

## Cost and Quality

Scientific management was the first systematic attempt to apply scientific thinking and measurements to production. The best-known proponent of the movement to put science in the factory is Frederic Winslow Taylor (1856–1915). His slim volume *The Principles of Scientific Management* was for decades the bible of factory managers and is considered one of the most important intellectual achievements of the twentieth century.[46] It is still worth reading. Taylor applied radical reductionism to the problems of efficiency. Division of labor, specialization, and standardization were driven to the extreme; every task was broken down to its smallest motions. As every motion takes time, an elegant basic building block was laid clear: motion–time. It is equivalent to the discovery of the cell as the building block of anatomy. Every motion could be studied to find out the most time-efficient way to do it.

Scientific management increased efficiency and prices could fall. With more demand, production systems expanded, became more complex, and as we have seen, invited variability. Every motion could not be performed every time in perfect conformance to specifications. Even if they could, they would not sum up as a perfectly effective process. Indeed, the concepts of systems and system layers were introduced only in the 1950s in the works of Ludwig von Bertalanffy (1901–1972), a biologist.[47]

The quality movement provided a response. Quality assurance and improvement (QA&I) brought variability under control, and volumes could continue to grow. Eventually, markets in the rich world began to saturate. More of the same was not enough. When basic needs are filled, people want not only more of the same but also better and different.

## Product Variety

New products with novel functions kept coming. Several major scientific break-throughs in physics and chemistry were made in the period between the mid-nineteenth century and the First World War. The 1930s, despite, or maybe because of, the economic crisis, was the most innovative decade on record. Basic science was turned into technologies. WWII further refined and expanded mass production. After the war, middle classes were offered a plethora of new affordable devices, the personal automobile, indoor plumbing, electricity, refrigeration and other white goods for the home, radio, color television, and hi-fi sound. Each of these offered new functionalities with a profound impact. Take refrigeration.[48] The home refrigerator changed the layout of kitchens and the daily habits of house-wives. The industry to produce them created hundreds of thousands of jobs. But that was only the visible top of it. Industrial applications produced the refrigerated railway car. Perishable meat could now be processed locally and transported over long distances. That was the end of the cowboy who drove live cattle to centralized slaughterhouses.

With a few exceptions—the Internet, the personal computer, and the mobile phone—very few products with entirely new functionalities have appeared for decades. As many observers have noted, on average, people's lives changed more during the period 1910–1960 than from 1960 to 2010.[49]

When volumes are saturated and little new functionality is at hand, what remain are performance, grade, and style. Every variety requires a sufficient customer base to utilize the effects of mass production. There are three solutions. The first, as we have seen, is founded on Lean production, the flexibility that comes when setups can be performed more efficiently and the optimal lot size goes down. Variety can proliferate without a stiff cost penalty.

The second solution is to increase the customer base for each variety. This is the commercial side of globalism. Production and distribution move goods, information, and people.[50] Production is constrained by the locations of factories and customers. Distance means transport costs. In the early phases of industrialization, production and markets were in the West, which consequently grew fabulously rich compared with the rest. When transport cost started to fall due to railroads and ocean shipping, markets could expand. Factories could be bigger and serve international markets.

The current phase of globalization started around 1990 with the advent of information and communication technologies (ICT) and the Internet. Product and production technologies are bundles of information embedded in designs, drawings, specifications, and manuals. Such information can be printed, distributed, read, and learned. But production is not only about designing and building a production system; it must be constantly managed, adjusted, fine-tuned, and improved against variability. Coordination takes some specific management skills that are not abundantly available. In the early 1990s, real-time communication over the Internet started to break down the information constraint and made the global supply chain possible.

A stroll through a shopping mall quickly reveals that product variety is not a pressing problem. When the world is a *de facto* single market, even the smallest sliver of variety can command huge volumes. In the industrial heartlands of southern China, highly specialized products, such as baby-sized pink rubber boots with Pokémon images, can be produced by the trainload. Global supply chains mask the basic dilemma of volume and variety. In some industries, particularly in services, distance matters, and with it the dilemma of volume and variety remains.

At some point, the proliferation of variety reaches a saturation point. People faced too many options with minor differences. Choice turns from a blessing to a curse. A solution is to provide solutions. In societies of abundance, people do not necessarily covet more products. People have jobs to do and tasks to accomplish, such as finding regular transport, having an exciting vacation, or refurbishing a kitchen. Being one's own integrator and coordinator is at times tedious. There is growing demand for solutions to get jobs done. This entails a combination of goods and services, a topic to which I will return in Chapter 4.

## Specialized, Integrated, and Modular Products

From the Fordian summit of mass production, operations management started a long slow trek back toward craft. But it could not turn back the clock to the world before the interchangeable part. How could mass production efficiency be combined with variety so that individual needs are fulfilled? An instance has to be stripped of its identity to become the interchangeable part of a standard process. Then it needs to be resurrected to become an individual again. The solutions require a conceptualization of products as general purpose, special purpose, multipurpose, modular, and platforms with apps.

A knife is general purpose; it can be used to cut, slice, slash, hack, rub, poke, and stab. The tool remains the same; it is just grasped and moved in different ways for different purposes. This is the "operating mode," the mobilization of a single resource for a variety of purposes. I discuss it in more detail in Chapter 6.

Think of yourself being at a Boy Scout camp and having just been assigned the job to peel a sack of potatoes for dinner. You can use your general-purpose knife. It will do the job, but not very well. The peels will vary in thickness, causing loss of valuable material. You will want to have a single-purpose specialized tool, a potato peeler. It is designed for only one thing. Productivity and quality increase mightily. Unfortunately, the single-purpose peeler is not good for much else. Next, you need to slice meat, cut vegetables, and open cans. If you have many tasks, you need a box with all kinds of different single-purpose tools. But it will be heavy to log around, and when you need it most, it will be somewhere else.

Then think of a Swiss Army knife. It may have up to 26 different special-purpose tools, all connected to a single frame. But none of the individual tools is very good as such. Competing for space on the frame, functionalities will be compromised. A sommelier in a fine dining restaurant would never use the corkscrew on a Swiss Army knife. Portability is its selling point. If you go hiking in the Himalayas, you might want to carry one.

Further, think of a 29-piece multibit ratcheting screwdriver set. It comes with metric and SAE drive sockets and hex, Phillips, and Torx bits that neatly plug into an ergonomically designed handle. The handle is a platform that allows several specialized modules to plug in one at a time without having to compete for space.

A module is a system within a system. It is a subassembly that is made out of several parts, while it is a part of a larger whole. A module has a boundary and standardized interfaces. Modules attach to each other, like Lego bricks, or to a common platform, such as printed circuits to a board. Standard modules can be produced in large volumes, but combined as individual designs.

A customer can choose between different alternative modules. Each will fit the whole in the same way without fitting. For example, an automobile has modules such as the engine, the power train, the electronic control system, and the braking system. A customer first chooses a platform, say, the Volvo 60 Series. The chassis comes in two modular types, sedan and wagon. Then the engine is chosen, diesel or gasoline, of different power ranges. The choice sequence goes on to colors, interior details, and music systems. Modularization creates an illusion of variety; the more modules, the more options and combinations.

The platform and app are the information technology (IT) equivalent of the screwdriver set—the revolutionary concept that made the smartphone. The operating system, iOS or Android, is the basic platform hosted in mass-produced handsets. Because the platform is standardized, various apps can be developed for a multitude of purposes. As of January 2017, 2.2 million apps were available in the App Store.[51] From this follows that there is virtually unlimited variety as to how a single phone can be configured. Before the smartphone, Nokia tried to solve the variety problem by producing a plethora of different handsets in all conceivable colors, materials, and shapes, while the basic functionality and performance were limited to the narrow options of the Symbian operating system. It didn't end well. Variety is more than curved plastics.

The smartphone platform must be standard and its integrity rigidly guarded through frequent updates. If the variety of platforms increases, total variety will go down. This was the situation with computer software before Windows. When every hardware maker had their own operating system, the market was fragmented, and there was little incentive for independent software houses to invest and develop small-volume application programs. With one or two global platforms, even obscure niche apps can be profitably launched. Variety requires standardized platforms.

# 3.6 The Logic of Transactions and the Business Model

Production and trade, supply and demand go together. Production without trade is self-sufficiency, the historical recipe for poverty. Trade without production is shuffling the same old deck of cards from hand to hand. Operations management textbooks are usually written under the assumption that if you can make it, they will buy it. In the real world, many markets are saturated; several industries have overcapacity. Management functions, operations, marketing, finance, and new product development must integrate their efforts. An elegant description of this is the business model.

## 3.6.1 Business Model Canvas

A business model is an abstract representation of how a company does business in a context. The model attempts to capture the relations between parts, marketing, sales, technology, production, and accounting. Management integration means that parts submit to the whole and the whole must find its place within a network and a wider ecosystem. Consequently, everything must be aligned to everything else.

A much used business model template is the Business Model Canvas (BMC). It was originally developed by the German management scholar Alex Osterwalder in his PhD thesis in 2004,[52] and has since expanded into numerous variants.[53] A version of the BMC, adapted to fit the terminology used in this book, is presented in Figure 3.15.

The left side of the BMC has been discussed in this chapter: how key activities are organized into flows, how resources are managed as capabilities and inventories,

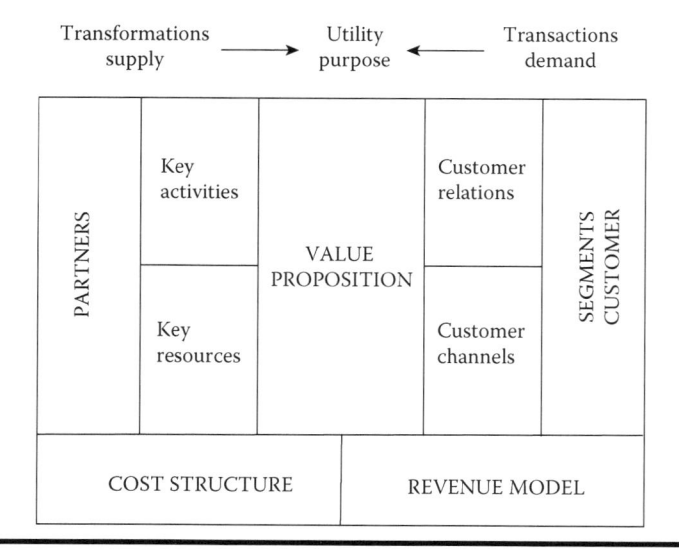

**Figure 3.15  Business model canvas.**

and how partners are organized into supply chains. The center, right, and bottom require some clarification.

## 3.6.2 Value and Exchange

Markets are social relations between buyers and sellers. Trading takes place in stock exchanges, market squares, and shopping malls. They are physical representations of the concept of market as a platform for exchange. It is made out of social norms that regulate the roles and actions of the parties.

### Value Proposition

Economics is said to be the "dismal science" practiced by people who "know the price of everything but the value of nothing."[54] The opposite would be a wealthy sentimentalist, who has vague notions of value, but scant ideas of the cost and effort of production, and is never compelled to examine the price tag on anything. This lame joke both contains a point and misses it. Price and economic value are related, but not identical. A more precise expression is value-in-exchange and value-in-use, a distinction that traces back to Adam Smith.

Value-in-use is the same as utility, something that increases human welfare by getting desirable things done. Value-in-exchange is the price that parties accept in a transaction. In an ideal world, there would be a consistent relation between these two. As a buyer, you never pay more than what your utility is worth; as a seller, you never sell for less than what the object of exchange is worth to the customer. When markets balance, prices reflect the true utility of everything and everybody is happy.

In the real world, buyers will have to make decisions with less than perfect information about value-in-use. Many products, for example, leather shoes, do not reveal true fit when tried on in a shop. It takes some use before value becomes apparent. In services, this is even more pronounced. At the point of exchange, a service does not yet exist. At best, it can be described as templates, process models, or features, and illustrated by proxies, such as pictures of facilities. Therefore, services can be sold only as value propositions.

### Imperfect Markets

The defining characteristic of a market is voluntary exchange. People enter markets at their will and engage in trade with others with the purpose of gain. If exchanges are not voluntary, there are no markets but various types of coercion, administrative acts, or robbery and plunder.[55]

The perfect market is an ideal type, real markets, as any other human endeavors, are subject to variability. There are opportunists and cheaters on both sides. To prevent such maladies from destroying markets, there must be rules and enforcement. Since conflicts involve both parties, none of them alone can be the arbitrator.

There must be a third party to enforce a code of conduct and have the power to shape justice. Typically, the third party is a ruler or a government. On a day-to-day basis, markets are self-regulating. In case of overwhelming variability (misconduct), markets will self-destruct, unless a third party maintains order. Markets can't handle negative externalities, damages that do not touch the trading partners but have an adverse effect of a third party. Monopolists can kidnap markets, and inside traders can manipulate prices. Therefore, most markets in advanced societies are regulated. In some cases, such as pharmaceuticals, the regulation is heavy-handed to the extent that it is not clear whether markets are at work anymore.

## Transaction Costs, Hierarchies, and Markets

Transformations consume resources and cause production costs. So do transactions. Marketing, selling, contracting, monitoring, follow-up, and learning are effortful activities that are not free and imply risks. The technical term is *transaction cost*. They play a significant role in how the world works, how production is organized, and how wealth is spread. There is a broad research area within economics and organization theory called transaction cost economics (TCE).[56]

Anybody considering establishing a production system confronts the make or buy question. Which components and tasks should I produce in my own organization? Which should I buy from others? If I buy, I will have to carry external transaction costs. If I do it myself, I will have internal transaction costs, the necessary administration and management of each task and component. Moreover, if I do it myself, can I afford the investment and get enough volume to keep costs down? An external supplier may have the specialization level and volumes that I can't match. On the other hand, if the task or component in question is critical for my differentiation, is it wise to use suppliers that also sell to my competitors?

Transaction costs, specialization, and differentiation form a logic chunk that impacts the make or buy decision. Make means control within my own hierarchical organization; buy means going to the market and establishing a supply chain. Transaction costs depend on information and risk. With Internet and global trade rules, transaction costs have come down, which explains why an increasing number of producers opt to buy.

## Bargaining

The relationship between the price paid and the utility acquired depends on the conditions of transactions, and thereby gets messed up by social, technical, and economic constraints. The technical term for the haggling that goes on in markets is *bargaining*.

Consumers in Western societies are accustomed to fixed prices. A bargain is the odd item you find at a department store sale. Bargaining is what you do during a tourist trip at an oriental bazaar and expect to be cheated. Bargaining, however, is broader than haggling. Bargaining takes place when you determine that the fixed price for that shirt is too high, keep your money, and walk away.

Bargaining is a phenomenon much studied in microeconomics. It happens in situations where both parties basically stand to win from a deal; both are better off if an agreement can be made. But the exact price and the terms of trade are not obviously clear. Assume you are about to sell your car. The absolute minimum price you are determined to get is $5000, not a dollar less. Obviously, you would like to get as much as possible. Somebody is interested in your vehicle. The absolute maximum price he is willing to pay, not a dollar more, is $7000. Within that range, the bargaining space, a deal is possible. Neither party has any interest in revealing their limits. All tricks of human persuasion can be mobilized in bargaining, as anybody who has visited used car dealerships will know. The more uncertainty there is about a deal, the more the value-in-exchange can divert from the value-in-use. This happens frequently in healthcare, where patients and insurance companies have no way of being sure what the actual outcomes and benefits of a procedure may be.

### 3.6.3 Segmentation and Customer Relations

The buyer and seller are participants in a transaction, the agents that execute a trade. Customer, supplier, and provider are broader roles.

### Segmentation

Segmentation is to divide a set of entities into subgroups, segments, according to some criteria, such as age, sex, residence, ethnic group, profession, or income level. A customer segment is in some relevant characteristic more homogeneous than the whole customer population, and thereby, variability of demand can be managed by offering segment-specific products.

### Chooser, Payer, and User

As illustrated in Figure 3.16, a customer is an economic agent, individual, or organization that has the capability to choose, pay, and use, that is, benefit from the utility of a purchased item.

Strictly speaking, an agent is a customer only when all three capabilities are present. There can be agents who are only choosers; somebody else pays and uses. If you have a teenage daughter, you may be familiar with the situation where your only role is to pay. Somebody who has only the role of user, such as unemployed welfare recipients, have to accept what others choose and pay.

An agent that chooses and pays is a purchaser that buys on behalf of others. Those who only pay and use but have no choice are subjects of a monopoly. An agent who chooses and uses but does not pay is a benefactor.

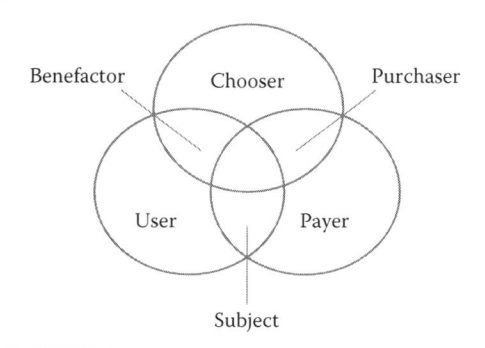

**Figure 3.16   Customer as chooser, payer, and user.**

Customer relations refers to the way a business communicates and interacts to gain and retain a loyal base of customers. The relationship involves marketing communications, sales support, technical assistance, and customer service.

### 3.6.4 Customer Channels and Distribution

Customer channels are the ways through which a producer reaches existing and prospective customers.

### Wholesale and Retail

In manufacturing, there is a clear distinction between production and distribution systems. As a product leaves the factory where it is built, it has an independent economic circulation through wholesale and retail channels, consumption, after-markets, and end-of-life (recycling and disposal) arrangements. The distribution of physical consumer goods follows the well-known patterns of wholesale and retail. When a manufacturer is done, the goods are shipped to various constellations of trading houses, wholesalers, distributors, and retailers, who take their cut, stack the stuff on shelves, and make them available to customers.

Distribution can be seen as an extension of manufacturing, as it channels the goods to the users. As a business, distribution, however, is a type of service, as it does not produce anything but changes in ownership. A minute ago, you owned $6000 in cash. Now you own a car.

### Delivery Point and Catchment Area

Delivery systems can be divided into two basic types. Facility-based systems are those where the customer is supposed to come to the seller's facility to pick up the goods. In field-based systems, the seller delivers the goods to a customer's location.

Facility-based delivery systems have a basic anatomy. Its parts are the delivery point, typically a store at a specific location; a catchment area, which means the geographical area where most customers come from; and the variety of items available.

Variety is measured as the number of stock-keeping units (SKUs) available at a point of delivery. A SKU is a distinct type of item for sale. Inventory is the quantity of each SKU at a point in time. Variety as the number of SKUs can be divided into two basic types: substitutes and nonsubstitutes. The former means the number of items with the same basic functionality but different performances, grades, and styles. If you shop for tomato ketchup, the superstore offers a couple dozen different ketchups that you can choose between, while the convenience store has only one. Nonsubstitute means if you shop for ketchup but it is out of stock, soy milk is not a substitute for it. Substitutes are choices between grades, while nonsubstitutes are choices between different functionalities. This abstraction is important in health service system design. If you hurt your wrist, you can seek help from a set of substitutes, a paramedic, a nurse, a general practitioner, an orthopedic, or a highly specialized hand surgeon. If you are looking for a health center at which to register your family, you look for the range of nonsubstitutes, the different clinical skill sets it can manage, such as maternity, dental, and pediatric care.

From these elements comes the dynamics of distribution. Each store has a catchment area. The distance between the store location and the average location of customers is location access. It can be expressed as distance and travel time. Another aspect of access is the time service is available, the opening hours of the store. Together, these are the average time–location access of a facility. Frequently purchased items, such as groceries, have small catchment areas, as customers tend to minimize the time and trouble of travel. The distribution of such items is access driven; convenience is a major competitive advantage. In retailing, this is exploited by convenience stores. They are located at places with heavy foot traffic and are open for business 24/7. While they typically charge significantly higher prices than larger stores and carry only a few thousand basic necessities, customers are willing to pay for convenience.

Rarely bought items, such as clothing and consumer electronics, have larger catchment areas. Easy access is traded off for variety. Big box retailers exploit it to the hilt. Large operators, such as Walmart supercenters, may have more than 140,000 different items in one store.[57] People are willing to travel from miles around to enjoy such material cornucopias.

In terms of variety, almost anything can be found at a superstore. However, for some customers and some products, the advantage comes from specialization. If you are really hooked on something, say, exotic tea, you will not be content with the couple of dozen run-of-the-mill varieties at the superstore. You happily beat your path to a specialist store. It sells only tea, a narrow range of nonsubstitute varieties, but a deep range of substitutes, teas of all conceivable qualities. In a specialty store, you can expect expert advice from staff that have a deep personal interest in the product, and can bring you the experiences of other customers, with whom they spend their days discussing the exclusive minutiae of the products. Shopping becomes an experience, compared with the dull routine of the superstore, where you are expected to read the labels, pick your choice, and head for the cash counter. The specialty store caters to nerds. They are few and far between; therefore, the catchment area of a specialty store is large, or they can be found only in big cities. Access must be poor. Specialty retailing is labor-intensive; therefore, it has to charge high prices.

A fourth category, the super cheap budget store, ignores everything else and goes for the customer segment for which cheap prices are the overriding objective.

The physiology of retailing produces four model solutions: the access-maximizing convenience store, the variety-maximizing superstore, the specialty-maximizing nerd shop, and the generic discounter, which is bad at everything except the price.

Access, variety, specialization, and average price form a quadrilemma, a four-factor optimization problem with no solution that would satisfy all needs. The retail trade has solved it by offering different channels to exploit each advantage. The man in the middle, the one that tries to sit on four chairs simultaneously, can offer only bad compromises. Specialized strategies give customers the opportunity to trade off one benefit for another. A trade-off implies real choice. A one-size-fits-all compromise takes it away.

## Notes

1. The terminology of operations management is not fully standardized. Here I follow the language of Hopp and Spearman (2011) and Hopp (2011). For a practical version of these, see Pound et al. (2014).
2. Warnecke (1993).
3. Porter (1980).
4. The term *style*, as I use it here, refers to the sensory characteristics, appearance, touch, and feel of a product. Design has broader meaning and includes choices related to all four attributes.
5. Lillrank (2012).
6. David Garvin (1986) gives the following list of perspectives on quality: transcendental (you know it when you see it), production quality (conformance to requirements), product features (functionality and grade), value (price–quality), competition (benchmarking), and customers (satisfaction). Lumping all good things under one concept makes it useless for analytical purposes. The transcendental aspect is discussed in Robert Pirsig's cult classic, *Zen and the Art of Motorcycle Maintenance* (1974), and its sequel, *Lila—An Inquiry into Morals* (1991).
7. Ashby (1956).
8. Roth (2015).
9. The terms *big quality* and *small quality* were coined by Joseph Juran (1988, p. 47). The confusion regarding big and small quality, however, remains. The conflicting ontology of quality explains why the quality movement has lost traction. For a discussion, see Lillrank (2003a, 2003b, 2015).

10. The original work is Smith (1776).
11. For historical accounts on the Industrial Revolution and the emergence of production systems, see Landes (2003) and Mokyr (2016).
12. Frank and Lillian Gilbreth (1912).
13. Cooper and Kaplan (1991).
14. Modig and Ålström (2012).
15. Vissers and Beech (2005).
16. *Swift and even flow* is a term launched by Schmenner and Swink (1998).
17. Hayes and Wheelwright (1979a, 1979b).
18. Pound, Edward S., Bell, Jeffrey H., and Spearman, Mark L. (2014) *Factory physics for managers*. New York: McGraw-Hill. p.22.
19. Davenport (1993) and Hammer and Champy (1993).
20. Lambert (2012) and Hopp (2011).
21. Isaacson (2014).
22. Hayes et al. (1988).
23. Davis and Lawrence (1978).
24. Qualitative measures sound more realistic from a customer perspective. However, as William Baumol (2012) has argued, to understand the cost crisis in healthcare, quantitative productivity must be used.
25. Mitra (2016) and Oakland (1999).
26. There are several variants and elaborations of the red bead experiment. See http://www.redbead.com/
27. In the context of process control, tampering means adjusting the process based on observations that are within the expected range of variation. Such adjustments make the process perform worse by increasing variation.
28. Shewhart (1931).
29. Deming (1986, 1993).
30. QFD is a method developed in Japan in the 1960s to connect customer requirements to engineering specifications using the House of Quality, a matrix tool. See Hauser and Clausing (1988).
31. The original paper that contains the mathematical proof of the law is Little (1961). For a discussion on the meaning and implications, see Hopp and Spearman (2011).
32. The bottleneck theory is more formally known as the theory of constraints (TOC). It was originally developed by Dr. Eli Goldratt (Goldratt and Cox 1984). It is one of the most influential business books ever. The TOC has since then been developed further, and added a number of sophisticated thinking tools. For TOC applications in healthcare, see Knight (2014) and Ronen and Pliskin (2006).
33. For a neat illustration, see the animation provided by Alex Knight, the author of *Pride and Joy*, at http://www.alex-knight.com/the-dice-game.
34. See Chapter 2 in Hopp and Spearman (2011).
35. The flow versus resource efficiency dilemma is explained in Modig and Ålström (2012).
36. For the use of takt time to manage simple processes in healthcare, such as vaccinations, see Kolker (2012).
37. Optimal production lot size determines the most economical amount to be ordered from a workstation or process. The economic order quantity (EOQ) is one of the classical production scheduling models developed by Ford W. Harris in 1913.
38. Womack et al. (1990), Shingo (1988), Ohno (1988), and Monden (1998).

39. *Value chain* and *value stream* are basically synonyms. A chain is made of separate links; therefore, value chain is appropriate for production with discrete steps and processes. *Stream* indicates a continuous flow.

40. Harrington (1991).

41. Hopp and Spearman (2011, p. 200).

42. Douma and Schreuder (2008) and Sloman et al. (2013).

43. For the difference between competence and comprehension in natural evolution, see Dennet (2017).

44. De Grauwe (2017).

45. Fogel (2004).

46. Taylor (1911).

47. Ludwig von Bertalanffy is recognized as the creator of the general system theory. For a summary of his work, see von Bertalanffy (2015).

48. Johnson (2014).

49. Florida (2002).

50. Richard Baldwin (2017) describes the impact of the three cascading constraints: transport of goods, information, and people. The movement of people remains a significant constraint.

51. https://www.statista.com/statistics/276623/number-of-apps-available-in-leading-app-stores/

52. Osterwalder (2004).

53. Osterwalder et al. (2010).

54. This phrase is generally attributed to Oscar Wilde, who was talking about cynics, not economists.

55. Critics of the market economy often argue that exchanges can't be truly voluntary for essential goods, that is, products and services that are necessary for survival, such as water, food, and healthcare. Such markets have special dynamics, as the buyers are desperate to close a deal at any cost. If there is insufficient supply in relation to demand, and the sellers can collude to avoid price competition, such markets can become destructive. This is frequently the case with famines. As Amartya Sen has argued (*1982*), no famines since the 1830s have been caused by insufficient supply, but rather by poor logistics and predatory hoarders. Nevertheless, there is a sharp line between voluntary and forced acts, regardless of consequences. Further, the definition of essential good is not clear and can be corrupted. Basically, it means the things necessary for staying alive. But it is easily corrupted to include whatever. In welfare societies, it can include items like foreign vacations and flat-panel televisions.

56. North (1992).

57. http://corporate.walmart.com/_news_/news-archive/2005/01/07/our-retail-divisions.

# Chapter 4

# The Logic of Services

## 4.1 Immaterial Utility and Integrated Resources

### 4.1.1 Services as Immaterial Utility

To serve others creates utility that does not take a material form. I scratch your back and you scratch mine; alone we are itching, and together we are well groomed. The origin of service is favors, acts, and deeds people do to each other, expecting the favor to be returned.

Services as a professional and commercial enterprise exploiting technologies and markets are rather recent. The early classical economists, including Adam Smith, did not see the immaterial as economically significant. Services do not circulate in the economy like goods do. After being enacted, they evaporate. Since services do not create permanent inputs to economic growth, how could they be of value? In those days, the majority of service workers were domestic servants. The employer–employee relation was embedded in tradition and authority, so what would be the need for service operations management?[1]

Services progressed on the professional and commercial frontiers. Professionalization means the introduction of technologies and production functions and specific ways of arranging them into processes. These are not within the skills of the average person, but must be learned through theoretical education and practical training. Those who undertake such trouble and become able to do things others can't expect to be paid for their efforts. This necessitates transactions in commercial markets for services. The two-way progress from favors to professional and commercial services is illustrated in Figure 4.1.

Commercialism can flourish without professionalism. That happens when help is hired. The payer could do the job, but rather spends his time doing something else. Gray and black markets are highly commercial but not professional.

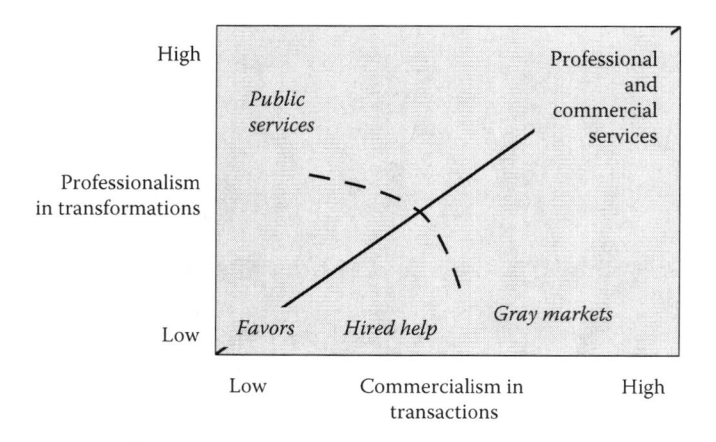

**Figure 4.1 Favors and services.**

Professionalism can expand without much commercialism. That happens in the tax-financed public sector, which does not sell services on a commercial basis but offers them as citizens' rights.

With increasing wealth, the service sector expanded. By the mid-twentieth century, it was close to a third of advanced economies and now is more than two-thirds.[2] Such a large chunk of economic activity needed concepts and constructs to enable purposeful management. A way of conceptualizing services developed within marketing. The novel ontology was that there are products without a physical form; services have immaterial commercial value. Services can't be owned, stolen, or returned, but they can be priced, sold, and bought. Services are produced as interactions between producer and customer, and can't be stored for later use. This line of thinking has been crystalized in the IHIP definition: services differ from physical products in that they are immaterial, heterogeneous, inseparable, and perishable.[3]

IHIP, however, did not make a clear conceptual cut across the large spectrum of services, from housecleaning to legal advice, from taxis to heart transplants. A dentist provides a service, but the pain of the drill is very much material. An automatic teller machine (ATM) ignores the heterogeneity of demand and provides a highly standardized service. Insurance claim processing does not require personal interaction. Vegetables and cut flowers are goods but also perishable. In some services, providers act on individuals (dentists). Some others work on facilities (cleaners), equipment (car repair), or data (diagnostics).[4] Some services are highly customized and use a lot of labor, while others are standardized and automated.[5] The diversity of the service spectrum led to endless and fruitless debates of what is service and what is product. Service marketing proposed a continuum. At the one end are pure services with no or little material content, such as psychotherapy and legal advice. At the other extreme are pure material goods, commodities such as Brent crude or grade A wheat. In between there are various combinations, services with added products and products with added services.[6]

The IHIP model is founded on the distinction between the materiality of goods and the immateriality of services. For service operations management, the useful notion is that immaterial services can't be produced in advance and stored in buffers, inventories, and warehouses. An airline can't operate airplanes and then sell flights off the rack. A surgeon can't operate if the patient is not present and prepared. As discussed in Chapter 3, inventory management is very central to the logic of production. Buffers are necessary, and they can be in only three forms: inventory, time, or excess capacity. From this follows that in services, the balancing act is between having excess capacity and keeping customers waiting. Inventory management in services is capacity and queue management.

### 4.1.2 Services as Involvement

The IHIP definition is based on the ontological conception of immaterial products. As this did not lead to sharp classifications, attention shifted to services as processes.[7] Service customers meet producers directly and get involved in production, while manufacturers' customers are not allowed to enter factory premises. In services, customers are present at the service sites, arguing and bargaining. Manufacturers collect customer data from sales records and surveys, to be aggregated, analyzed, and fed back to the development and design departments as averages and trends.

In services, the individual person is the instance that enters the service producer's context. The person turns into the flow unit and engages in bargaining about how the setup should be defined and the situation structured. Mass manufacturing isolated itself from customers with distribution systems and anonymized the instance into a standard batch of identical pieces. In services, every instance requires a setup.

The meaningful variable is the amount of time, data, and effort to perform the setup. The more complex a setup, the more interaction and involvement are needed. At the simple standard end, there are ATMs and automated web tools that accept only a few inputs in predetermined ranges: identify yourself, select from a menu, and press enter. At the complex end, there are iterative diagnostic processes trying to make sense of an unknown ailment. The nature and intensity of the customer contact become the variables around which services are classified.[8]

When the customer is involved in production, the material–immaterial distinction loses significance. Manufacturing is not all mass production. A machine shop or a shipyard builds individual products to the specifications of one customer; a tailor adjusts the double-breasted suit to hide the bulge of this particular gentleman. Thus, a defining element of services is to what extent and in which ways the customer and the producer interact in setup and production.[9]

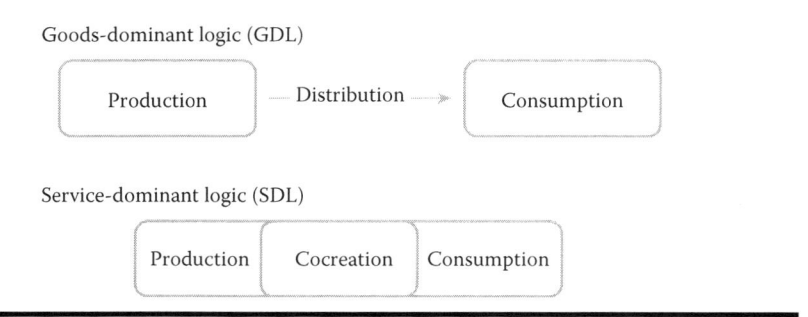

**Figure 4.2   GDL and SDL.**

Customer-centric thinking got a boost from the conceptual distinction between the traditional goods-dominant logic (GDL) and the new service-dominant logic (SDL).[10] The basic idea is illustrated in Figure 4.2. GDL is based on a worldview where production and consumption are separated. A production site can be located wherever it is profitable. Products are shipped to markets and distributed through various channels. Customers are assumed to recognize the value of a product when they touch it and consume it as they see fit. Marketing tries to capture and articulate needs and wants and communicate them to producers as best they can. Producers run the show along their own script. To the contrary, SDL is based on the conception that providers and customers jointly create value in a phase of production called cocreation of value. In services, the production function is a provider–customer joint accomplishment.

Further, GDL assumes that the act of production is a one-way street from an active resource to a passive object. In manufacturing, a piece of metal does not talk back to the lathe operator. It merely reacts following the laws of physics. The producer calls the shots; there is no bargaining about how the situation should be defined. GDL assumes that the customer is a reactor, while SDL assumes that the customer is an actor, an adaptive agent and a collaborator.

## *4.1.3 Services as Resource Integration*

As often happens in management research, a new conceptualization does not make the old one false. It just adds perspective and detail. IHIP and SDL are not contradictory but overlapping and mutually reinforcing. They have been combined into the resource integration (RI) model.[11]

Cocreation means that the producer's and the customer's resources are integrated to produce value. The IHIP categories apply differently to different aspects of what is integrated. The service transaction is immaterial, as services can be sold only as contractual promises of some future action. Heterogeneity applies to customer resources, as individuals have varying needs and requests. Inseparability appears in production where both parties must be present and participating.

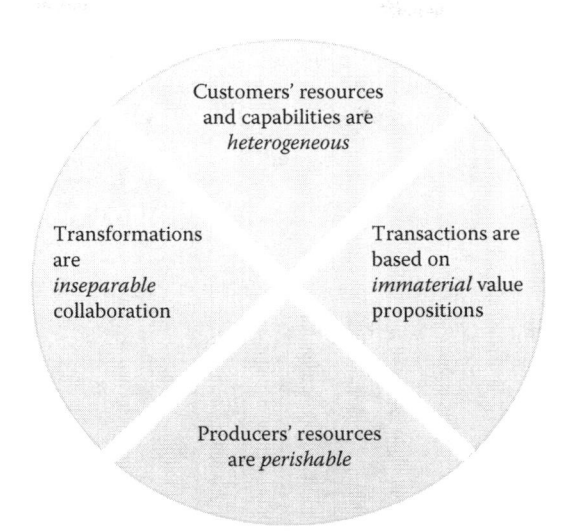

**Figure 4.3    RI model of services.**

Producer's resources are perishable. If no customer shows up, a producers' capacity is left unused and can't be stored for later use. The RI view elegantly combines IHIP and SDL, as illustrated in Figure 4.3.

What matters is to what extent a customer participates in the design and execution of production. While service producers bring skills and tools, customers bring jobs to be done and conceptions of utility that are worth paying for.

The IHIP, SDL, and RI models are founded in marketing. Marketing, by definition, is oriented toward customers.[12] The relative bargaining position of customers and providers can vary. In a seller's market, there is less supply than demand. The seller has the upper hand and can ask the customer to take it or leave it. A market with more supply than there are people willing to buy is called a buyer's market. In a buyer's market, sellers chase customers, promote them to kings, and pretend they are always right.

During the rapid growth decades after WWII, supply expanded in both quantity and variety. Increased volumes led to intense rivalry between sellers. Finding out the wants and whims of the omnipotent consumer became the primary occupation of marketing. When found out, producers were expected to bend backwards to fulfill needs. Consequently, the customer perspective has dominated over the producer perspective, and service marketing over service operations.

The SDL literature gives the impression that cocreation is collaboration between equals. However, not every market belongs to the buyer; sometimes the customer is wrong. The producer may not be able to do what is asked or does not feel the pressure to make the extra effort. During the past few decades, there has been less rivalry, as many markets have consolidated into a few global brands, thereby reducing customers' bargaining power. In countries with tax-financed and publicly administered healthcare, there is no market at all. There are no customers, only taxpayers and citizens with rights. In such circumstances, SDL and cocreation leave something unsaid. Alas, garbage collection is a service. But where is the customer and what exactly is cocreated and integrated? The ontology of service needs to be adjusted by examining the production function as collaborations of various types.

## 4.2 Production Function: Transformations in Services

In services, as in all productive activities, there must be a production function that transforms something into something else. It is arranged as processes and organizations.

### 4.2.1 Service Is State Change

The production function in services can be described as a bundle of technologies, interactions, and activities that change a state. A while ago, you had an aching tooth; now you don't. The hallway used to be shoddy; this morning it shines. You stand at a bus stop in the rain and wish you were home. A taxi appears and promises to change your geolocation. The utility of a service is founded in the difference between alternative states.[13]

Demand for service starts with a person finding herself in a situation that could be better. There is a need and a job to be done. There is a preferred state where she would like to be but can't get there on her own devices. The difference between the current and the preferred state is worthy enough of a fee. A budding entrepreneur sees a chance and offers a service. If it is successful, there will be repeats. A service business is created. Eventually, it stabilizes and evolves into a service system. In this respect, customers participate in defining the architecture and in designing the service. When service systems are established, the customer just needs to specify the details, that is, contribute to the setup. The producer operates the system.

A state change happens to an entity that already exists, a product, building, person, or group. Changing the state of an existing entity and creating a new entity are two different things. As very few things in this world are entirely novel, new also means identical or modified copies of an original. Services as state changes combined with the material–immaterial dimension produce the four types illustrated in Figure 4.4.

Manufacturing means that a new material entity is created, first as a new design, and then as copies. Immaterial things can be created and copied, that is, intellectual properties, such as pictures, music, software, and recipes.

Services are state changes in existing entities. If those are material goods, a service changes the state from dirty to spick and span (cleaning), from high to low risk of failure (maintenance), or from broken to functioning (repair). If the existing entity is immaterial, such as cognition, feelings, or health, the state

|  | Material | Immaterial |
|---|---|---|
| New entity designed or copied | *Manufactured goods* | *Intellectual property* |
| State change in existing entity | *Maintenance Upgrade Repair* | *Cognition Experience Behavior* |

**Figure 4.4   Services are state changes on material and immaterial entities.**

change can be from ignorant to knowledgeable, from bored to amused, or from sick to healthy.

Service production does not result in gadgets, but in changes in states, including states of gadgets. Such changes are effectuated by various technologies. Travel and transport is a service where the location of a person or a good is altered by transport technologies. They can broadly be categorized by those happening on land, on water, or in the air; by the energy form used (muscle, wind, or engines); by the carrying capacity (bulk or parcel); and by speed. Education is a service to change the mind and skill sets of students. Tourism generates utility by taking people to a pleasant (beach) or exciting (the Himalayas) places. Entertainment promises to create amusement to replace boredom. Insurance and security changes the status of an object from unprotected to protected. Professional services, such as law, medicine, engineering, and management consulting, provide expert advice to change clients' decision-making capabilities.

States and state changes come in three different types. First, there are permanent, irrevocable changes. If you are unfortunate enough to get appendicitis, a serious infection in the cul-de-sac of your intestines, and a surgeon removes your appendix, then, for the rest of your life, you are in a state described as a person without an appendix. Second, there are states that have a limited life cycle. You get yourself a smart haircut. It will be fine for a week or two, but eventually it will decay as your hair grows. A good meal keeps you going for several hours, but eventually the hunger pains will be there again. The third type is when a state change is limited and scheduled. It is a service episode with a set duration, such as 2 weeks at a beach resort. When the vacation is over, the state is back to normal.

## Processing in Services

Transformations are accomplished through processing, the "rubber meets the road" phase in manufacturing where a lathe removes shavings from a piece of metal and transforms its shape. Processing can be standardized if deterministic technologies are used; every activity in a given context leads to a predictable result. In mature manufacturing, the physics of the transformation from raw material to product is well known. Some services have simple "physics." If a vehicle moves at a known speed over a known distance, the arrival time can be calculated.

Many services do not have a scientific body of knowledge from which technologies can be developed. Like the steam engine, many services develop through trial and error. Behavioral sciences operate mostly with statistical probabilities, from which exact outcomes in singular situations can't be reliably predicted. Technologies, such as those employed in psychotherapy, cannot guarantee given outcomes in terms of permanently altered states. If verified and tested scientific knowledge is not available, production builds on experience and tradition.

## Customer as the Flow Unit

The description of processes in Chapter 3 bears the mark of the home base of modern operations management, the automobile assembly plant. The language is that of discrete manufacturing, where products are built stepwise in an assembly process. The flow units start as the smallest parts, nuts, bolts, and wires. They merge, continue the journey, and merge again and again to become throughput and inventory in the final stocking unit.

In process industries, such as petrochemicals, breweries, or dairies, the descriptive language is different. Chemical and biological reactions happen in vats, storage tanks, and pipes, where substances are subject to catalysts, pressure, and temperature and moved around by mixers, pumps, and valves. The flow unit is a production batch that is infinitely divisible down to the molecule. The flow unit becomes discrete when the material is packed, bottled, or canned.

In services, the descriptors again are different. In some services, the process has a clear physical manifestation. Think of an airport as a service theatre or a servicescape.[14] The passenger is the flow unit. She has to engage the ground crew in a tightly scripted and scheduled play. The system has a number of contact points, where the passenger is expected to collaborate, show travel documents and identification, comply when security searches for contraband, and line up to enter an aircraft. The flow unit remains the same. Its state has changed from somebody who enters the airport to somebody who is seated with belt fastened. While the functionality achieved is the same, the process can be designed in various ways. In Europe, if you carry only hand luggage, stay within the pass-free Schengen area, and check in on the Internet, there are two contact points, security and boarding. Getting on an intercontinental flight at Indira Gandhi International Airport in New Delhi takes eight contact points.

In professional services, such as law offices or consultancies, the language would again be different. The flow unit is a customer case. It has little, if any, physical manifestations. A process includes negotiations with clients, brainstorming sessions, data gathering, number crunching, document analysis, case team meetings, and PowerPoint presentations. When the files and folders are closed and the professionals go home for the night, the process is hibernating. The next morning, it is reactivated again.

In services, the flow unit can take three forms, the person (or group of them), the person's property, and the person's case. They can combine and separate in various ways. The flow unit entering an airport is a person with property, that is, heavy luggage. At check-in, the two separate and go their own ways, but maintain their identities and their connection manifested in a barcode identification tag. At the luggage carousel, the two join again. If the luggage is lost, a corrective process is set up to deal with the case of the lost luggage. The passenger may leave the scene and wait for the case to close. Services where a person is directly involved are called personal services. Others are not personal in the sense of ongoing human interaction, but individual in the sense that there is an owner of the property and the case.

The first defining characteristic of service is that economic value is a state change in relation to effort and cost. The second is that the flow unit is an individual person, a piece of property, or a case (Figure 4.5).

## 4.2.2 Differentiation and Variety in Services

The two strategic routes, competition through differentiation or price, are valid in services. Services have the attributes functionality, performance, grade, and style. Services are subject to the small q of deviation from given promises. The major

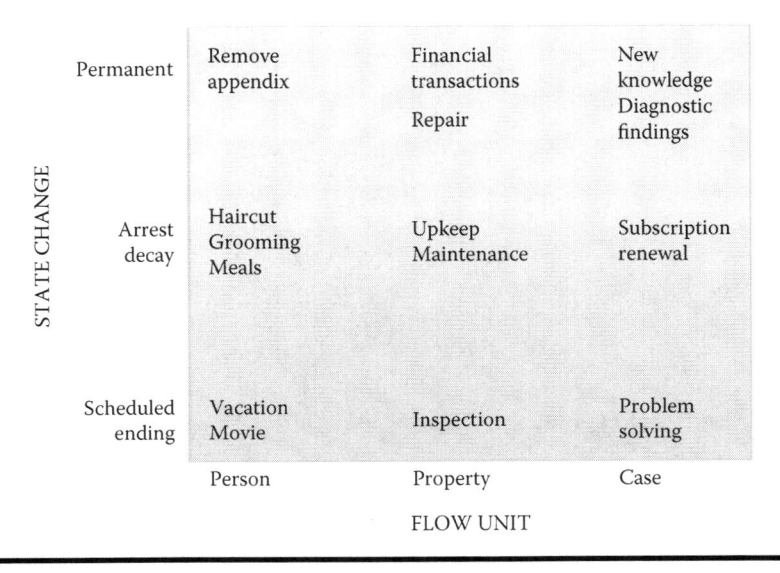

**Figure 4.5  State changes and flow units define services.**

difference is that in services, the perceived value is not only what was accomplished but also how it was done.

## The What and the How

In manufacturing, customers do not care much about how a product was built, what was the capacity utilization, cycle times, or inventory levels, as long as the product is built to specifications and delivered as promised. In services, the part of the process where customers participate is open and visible. How things are done is not easily separated from what is done.

What is done, the state change, equals the functionality of a service: Which state of affairs is changed to what? How large is the utility of the difference? The how is the performance of the process by which the state change is accomplished. In manufacturing, the principal measures of process dynamics are capacity utilization, cycle time, work in process (WIP), and throughput. In services, the time-related measures become important to the customer, the flow unit. Waiting to get access to a service is irritating and carries opportunity costs; the more pleasant things could have been done instead. Queuing inside a process as human WIP is even worse. The customer has already committed time and resources. If she walks away, everything invested so far is lost. In services, flow efficiency is directly related to the customers' economic value. Resource efficiency, that is, how effectively the producer uses resources to create throughput, is an issue only if it affects price.

Services come in grades, first, business, and economy classes. Hotels are graded with stars from one to five. The basic functionality is the same, safe transport and a place to sleep. The grade is typically marked by the service theatre, amenities and facilities, add-on services, and personal attention, that is, the time and effort spent on setup.

A process can be executed with a variety of styles, flexibility or rigidness, attentiveness or arrogance, empathy or rudeness, dignity or humiliation—all within the same functionality, performance, and grade. Obviously, there is a correlation between grade and style. Upmarket operators hire more qualified staff, and subject them to training and customer ratings. Still, there is a nonlinear relationship between these two. What do you prefer, a perfectly executed cure with rude bedside manners, or a treatment error by the most pleasant doctor on earth?

## Variety and Volume in Services

Services can be mass-produced. There is mass tourism, high-volume hotels, and Internet banking. Simply adding resources creates volume. Psychotherapy can be a high-volume industry if there is a therapist's office on every block, next to the Starbucks. But volume and economies of scale are not the same thing. Economies of scale is the dynamic effect by which the more that is produced, the cheaper it gets. To understand this, the peculiarities of service processes need to be explored.

# 4.3 Service Production Systems

In services, as in any purposeful action, the production function can't stand alone. It needs to be organized as systems with tasks, steps, flows, and inventories. Collaboration around the immaterial value of a state change requires some material scaffolding.

The general logic of production applies to services with some modifications. There are division of labor, specialization, and standardization. Integrated offerings and coordinated processes bring the ensuing fragmentation together. At the core of the service production function is collaboration. Providers and customer join forces and combine resources to accomplish the utility that lies in the difference between states. State changes are accomplished by one or several tasks linked as steps and connected as flows. The flow unit is a customer in person, her property, or a customer case. The flow unit can be stationary with workstations coming and going, or it can move between stationary workstations. There are service projects, job shops, disconnected flows, connected flows, and continuous flows. Processes with discrete steps have cycle time, WIP inventory, and throughput, and are subject to capacity utilization and the dynamics of buffer inventories. Services as state changes can't be stored, but the material resources needed for service processes can be accumulated.

## 4.3.1 Variability in Services

In services, the production process has a number of issues that make it different from factory processes. In services, as in manufacturing, variability is a concern. Factories are built and managed to keep variability to a minimum. In services, variability enters the production function in the shape of the customer. The IHIP definition of services postulates the H as heterogeneity. Service customers are discrete, individual entities. Even if a group of customers has perfectly identical needs and requests, there is variability that arises from inevitable natural causes. People vary in height, weight, age, experience, and capabilities.

In services, variability is amplified by inevitable decay. People grow older and bodies weaker; some get wise, and others cynical. Pieces of property are subject to wear and tear. The same customer a year later is not exactly the same person anymore, and neither is his car or his suitcase.

From customer-introduced variability[15] and the need to do individual setup follow that perfect mass production with connected lines is not possible in services. Every service step for every customer requires a setup. For a process made out of several steps (service episodes), it may be called the master setup, including routing and resource allocations (scheduling). In healthcare, a care plan equals a master setup for individual patients. Each step, such as taking samples in a lab, requires its own setup. When a step has been performed, there is a handover to the next. In personal services, the customer may do the handover and walk to the next step, from the lab, with results in hand, to see the doctor, or go home and return a week later to a scheduled appointment. From this follows that in services, all parts of the flow are not necessarily observable to the producer, which in turn further amplifies variability.

The key issues are setup, handover, and flow. But like in manufacturing, in services setups can be done in many ways and with variable efficiency.

## 4.3.2 Service Setup

In Chapter 3, I described how the behavior of the flow unit defines production architectures; is it stationary, moving in discrete steps, or moving as a continuous flow. In services, the defining issue is how a customer as a flow unit behaves in setups and handovers. This produces a complementary perspective on production architectures.

In manufacturing, setup means the activities that must be performed before a workstation can start processing. Tools, jigs, and supplies must be arranged properly. Unlike processing, setup is not determined by the physics of the production function; it is a managerial issue and can be performed in many ways.

Every flow unit that has individuality requires a setup. At minimum, the setup is a go/no-go acknowledgment that the particular flow unit complies with the requirements given in a master setup. Something that has never been done before requires elaborate setup. The more individuality, the more setup. If the flow unit is an adaptive agent, setup implies bargaining.

### Anatomy of the Setup

The anatomy of setup is illustrated in Figure 4.6. Demand (an instance) knocks on the door of a production facility (a context) and asks to be processed. The first contact point, the gatekeeper, must assess the input and make sense of it. What is

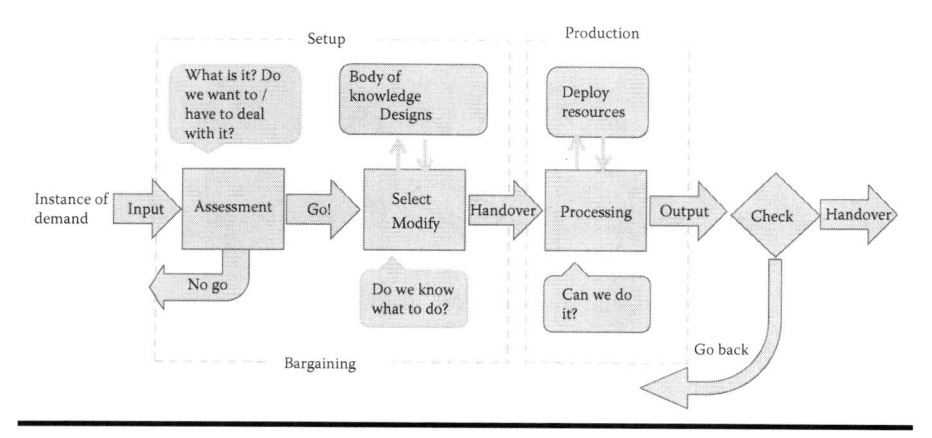

**Figure 4.6   Service setup.**

it? Does it belong here? Do we want to deal with it? Is it acceptable, authorized, and relevant? The gatekeeper produces a go/no-go decision. This is assessment.

If the gatekeeper says go, the instance turns into a flow unit, like a person entering an airport becoming a passenger, and a person accepted to an emergency clinic turning into a patient. If the flow unit does not have valid credentials or does not fit a given demand profile, it is turned away. Some bargaining at the entrance may ensue.

In the next phase, the flow unit is examined in more detail according to the basic demand–supply constellation. Demand, what the flow unit signals as a job to be done, is checked against what can be done given the available body of knowledge, resources, and capabilities. At airports, the boarding agent controls the validity of the ticket and the amount of hand luggage. In an emergency department, the checklist may be more complicated. The triage nurse observes chest pain and shortness of breath. The nurse knows this indicates cardiac arrest and that cardiopulmonary resuscitation must be started immediately. It has been done before, so there is a production function and a repository of process designs at hand. The workstation knows what to do. A template is selected and modified as needed. Once it is sufficiently clear what should be done, resources are assigned and processing can begin. When it is done, the result is checked and handed over to the next station. If the result is not satisfactory, the setup may have to be redone.

Assessment, selection, and modification together are the setup—the definition of the situation in terms of what needs to be done and what can be done. In services, where the flow unit is an adaptive agent, it participates in doing the setup and has a variable amount of resources, capabilities, and bargaining power to influence it.

The way setups are done can be used to divide processes into four types: standard, the fixed format, routine, and nonroutine processes.[16]

## Standard Process

A fully standardized process in manufacturing has one setup and several identical repetitions. Between the repetitions, the workstation only checks that the next flow unit fulfills given requirements. Semiautomated machines are designed to stop at a no-go. The process grinds to a halt and stays that way until corrective action is taken. Standard processes are like the proverbial square hole that accepts only square pegs.

In services, very few processes have an exact resemblance of industrial mass production. Near-standard processes can be used when the flow unit is property and the task is clearly defined, such as moving a suitcase into a specified cargo hold.

## Formatted Processes

The setup for a formatted process acknowledges some individuality of the flow units, but only within predetermined limits. The flow unit and the job to be done are described with a given set of variables with given ranges. There is no bargaining space; for the customer, the options are take it or leave it.

Consider an ATM. There is an interface with predefined input fields. You may interact with an ATM, but you are not allowed to bargain. The setup requires some fixed inputs from you, a valid card, your PIN code, and some defined choices from a menu—deposit or withdrawal, credit or debit account, sum, receipt yes or no? If you fail at any step, the service will not be executed. The assessment gatekeeper can identify only one type of acceptable input. Only your personal PIN is accepted; everything else is rejected. As for the sum to be withdrawn, the machine accepts only a range between the minimum and maximum allowed amount, given that you have a sufficient balance. The machine has the gatekeeping algorithms to make a go/no-go decision.

As long as customers, like those using banking services, are individuals, the setup can't be wholly eliminated. Formatted setup is akin to modularized products. The range of variety gives an illusion of personalization, while all defining variables and their allowed ranges are known. From this follow significant benefits. The service provider can be high volume at low cost by asking the customer to do the setup as self-service. ATMs do the processing, dispose cash, or make a bank transfer. In other self-services, such as buffet restaurants, the customer does the setup, choosing among a selection of dishes, and the processing, that is, picks up the food.

The mirror image of self-service is a service factory. The producer does most of the job, and the required interaction is minimal, for example, automated monthly payment systems. The customer signs up for a service and gives the parameters, and the producer executes the service following a script. In the Nordic countries, for most wage earners the tax office (assuming it can be called service) is a service factory. If you are salaried, have no income from capital, and have no specific deductibles, the system does your taxes and prepares a report. You can access it with your bank ID on the tax office's website or receive a paper copy. You don't even have to sign. A service factory operates following a master setup. Service steps are initiated not on demand but according to a schedule.

The Amazon Kindle bookshop is a combination of self-service and service factory. The system knows who I am, what I have browsed, dropped, and bought. It even knows how far I have read and with what speed. The system has a better memory than I do. If I attempt to buy a book that is already in my library, the system issues a kind warning. It knows my habits and preferences and can rather well predict what I might buy next.

## Routine Processes

Routine processes (Figure 4.7) refer to situations where the process is set up separately for each flow unit, but the options are not fully formatted. Each instance is somewhat unique, and the context has to be modified. The setup is open for some bargaining given the limits of what is available and what can be done. The gatekeeper

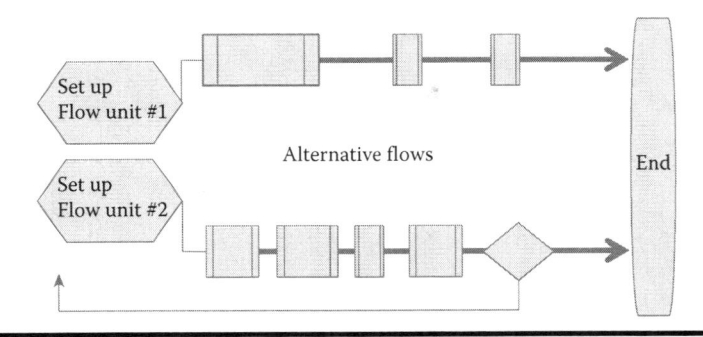

**Figure 4.7   Routine processes.**

can say go, no-go, or maybe. Routine processes employ predefined categories to classify inputs and select appropriate process designs from the rack. There are square, round, and triangular holes of many sizes for a variety of pegs. Routine processes are typical in healthcare where a process needs to be set up for each patient. However, many medical problems are well known and can be ascribed a known diagnosis and corresponding treatment. A routine process can be swift, if the assessment is easy; the algorithm can be picked from a repository; and processing is close to standard. The quality issue here is, was the assessment correct, did the setup consider everything relevant, and was the right action chosen? A service system employing routine processes can improve its efficiency by developing, designing, formatting, and classifying a large repertoire of processes. In other words, service systems can have inventories of ready-made process designs.

## Explorative Processes

If the setup is not clear and a suitable process design can't be swiftly found, some sensemaking, exploration, hypothesis building, and testing need to be done before it is time for action. Such situations are labeled nonroutine processes[17] or complex product systems,[18] and here explorative processes.

In an explorative process, the input is assessed as relevant and given a "go" by the gatekeeper. The "want to do" issue is clear, but "know what to do" is not. The flow unit can't be assigned to a predefined process design; it is unclear how the context should be adjusted. The situation requires exploration of the issues and iterative problem solving. As the contours clear, an explorative process evolves into a routine that eventually boils down to a few fixed-format or standard processes. As an example, think of arriving at the site of an accident. There are fire and smoke, screaming people, and mauled bodies. It is not obvious what it is. It could be an explosion, a vehicle accident, or a terrorist attack. It may take a while before a layperson can make sense of the situation. An experienced rescue service commander quickly sorts out the observations, recognizes patterns, gets an idea, and knows what to do. One man's chaos is another man's routine.

Explorative processes are not present in mass manufacturing. Everything to be done has been planned and laid out. Job shops have elements of exploration as craftsmen figure out how to build each individual product in the best way. Explorative processes are typical in research and development (R&D). A product idea may be realized by several alternative technical solutions. These are not known or even knowable[19] in advance. The only way to find out is to explore by building prototypes and testing them, or running simulations. From this follows and important distinction among processes: those that can be planned in every necessary detail from beginning to end, and those that can be planned only one or a few steps at a time. Professional services have more in common with R&D than with manufacturing. A lawyer usually can't be all that sure how a legal case will proceed, as much depends on the opposition and how a court interprets evidence and argumentation. Explorative processes are common in healthcare, as we will see in the next chapters.

## Agility

As in manufacturing, a service flow can include several phases with different process types. Basic parts, nuts, and bolts are made with connected flows, components with disconnected flows, and final assembly, again as connected flow.

In general, productivity increases as explorative processes are routinized, routines formatted, and formats simplified to the base essentials. Explorative processes consume a lot of resources. With systematic documentation, problem solving, and learning from experience, processes can be stabilized. Efficient trauma centers concentrate resources to the front-end activities, gatekeeping and setups that require a great deal of expertise and flexibility. Everything else is routinized or formatted into modules and components as far as possible. This is known as the agile principle.[20] It can, as in Figure 4.8, be illustrated with the shape of a broom or a trumpet.[21]

## Service–Process Matrix

Standard, formatted, routine, and explorative processes do not have sharp ontologies; the dividing lines are not clear. The defining dimension is a compound of two variables.

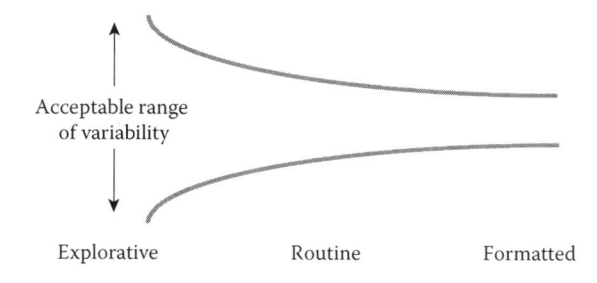

**Figure 4.8   From explorative to formatted process.**

The first variable is the variability of demand, the similarity–dissimilarity of the flow unit to be processed. Variability in demand is "out there," where all kinds of things happen. At one extreme is a flow unit that embodies uncertainty, maximal variability, something a gatekeeper has never seen before. On the other end is a flow unit that is like an interchangeable part, fully identical with a known description and similar to every other flow unit in a batch.

The second variable measures the extent to which a production system can protect its gate and reject some types of demand. Some services segment customers and clearly signal whom they serve for which requests. Customers can segment themselves. If you are on a budget, you know to avoid fine dining restaurants; if you are having a baby, you do not go to a care home. An appointment-only dental clinic is at the other end of the variable. It deals with a given range of dental problems. Those in need of psychotherapy are asked to go elsewhere. At the opposite extreme are services that society's last resource, "the buck stops here" services, if you wish. An emergency department is not supposed to reject anybody with an urgent and severe medical matter. The police and the coroner must at times handle jobs that no one else wants to touch. There is no bargaining with a dead body.

These two variables are compounded as the $Y$ axis in Figure 4.9. The $X$ axis is the above-discussed setup-based process types: explorative, routine, formatted, and standard. These together produce the product–process matrix equivalent for services.

A production process is designed and operated in order to achieve a purpose. In standard processes, the goal is clear. It is fully described in the *ex ante* specifications by which the process is run. A process produces exactly the results that it has been designed for, imperfections included. A formatted process gives a result that can be inferred from the setup. In routine processes, the objective is not that specific, and in explorative processes even less so. While standard and formatted processes are deterministic, routines and explorative processes have an element of equifinality; there are many paths to the same goal, or there are several alternative outcomes that accomplish a given purpose.

## Back Office and Front Office

Service operations have supply networks that prepare the material resources used in service production, such as facilities, equipment, consumables, and disposables. They are designed and managed similarly to any logistics, facilities management, and administrative system. This is the back office, the facility behind the front office or service theatre where frontline service providers meet customers.

The back office performs two types of tasks separated by the order penetration point (OPP). In logistics, it signifies the point where a product is assigned to a particular order or a customer.[22] The customer order and the flow of materials meet, and a product is assigned to an individual buyer. In retail stores, the OPP is at the cash register, which doubles as a powerful computer keeping track of both income and inventory. If a customer pays with a credit card and swipes a customer

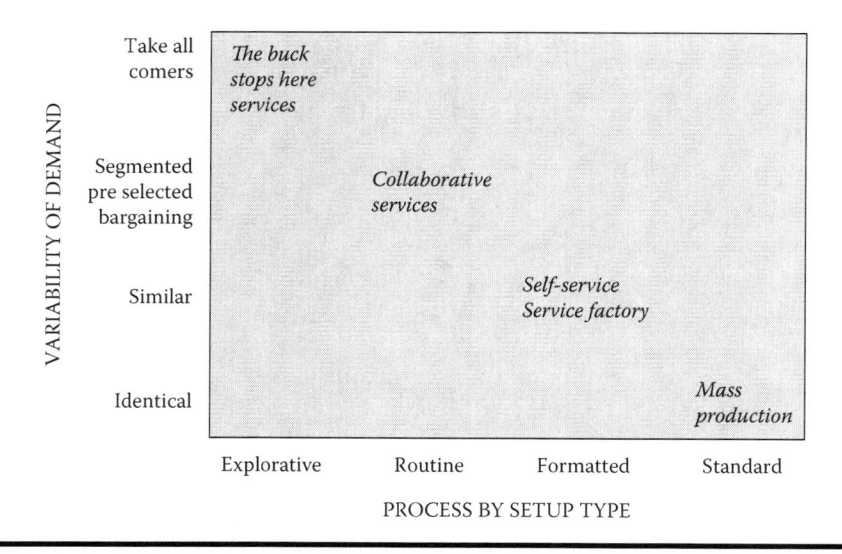

**Figure 4.9    Service–process matrix.**

loyalty card, the store will know exactly who bought what items within what basket of goods, when it happened, and how much was paid. The store will also know how much stuff is left on the shelves. This enables restocking with great precision. A well-managed store is neither out of stock nor left with unsellable goods.

Pre-OPP tasks can be managed by applying standard methods for estimating demand and allocating capacity. As illustrated in Figure 4.10, a hotel can predict demand for a season, allocate resources, and make pricing decisions. As prospective customers make reservations, the OPP is passed and demand turns individual. A setup is performed as customer-specific variations, such as the accommodation of late or early arrivals, accompanying minors, or auxiliary services. The producer–customer resource integration (RI) is initiated. When the customer arrives and checks in, a customer episode begins. It may consist of several contact points and encounters at the front desk, with the bell captain, and at breakfast. Consumption, that is, the actualization of value, however, is not entirely limited to the relationship, but to a network of players over which the hotel does not necessarily have influence. For a traveler, the value of hotel accommodation lies in what he or she can do while in town. That is why the three most important competitive advantages in the hotel industry are said to be location, location, and location.

A typical service production system includes three elements. The back office is where various preparations are done and supplies kept. Customers do not have insight or access. There is no individual collaboration before the OPP; therefore, that part of the back office can be run like a manufacturing plant. The back office also deals with customer-specific preparations using formatted or routine processes. The front office is the service theatre, a place where producers interact with customers.

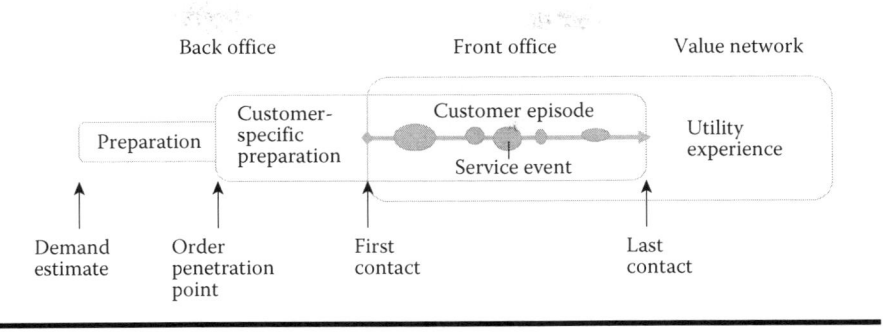

**Figure 4.10  Service system of a hotel.**

It requires routines, occasionally explorative processes. The value network, or the hinterland of services, is the context in which service value is experienced.

### 4.3.3 Service Handovers

In factories, a flow unit is handed over from one workstation to the next directly or through a stop at WIP inventory. In services, there are several types of handovers; a flow unit, person, property, and/or case cross borders. The crossings are difference in time, location, or resources. Like setups, handovers can be standardized; that is, the flow unit always goes to a predetermined location. Handovers can be formatted or routine if the next step is determined by an algorithm or deliberation. They may also be explorative if the next step is not obvious and requires some sensemaking.

#### Time, Location, and Resource Handovers

A time border is present in situations with one service provider (workstation), one flow unit, and several steps. A physiotherapist treats a patient in a sequence of several sessions (steps). The patient is supposed to show up at the right place at the right time. The therapist must check her notes and collect her thoughts before each session to connect what has been done with what will be done next.

A location border can be between physical workstations, such as the airport check-in, security, and boarding, or the operating room and the postanesthesia care unit (PACU) at a hospital.

A resource border can be between a stationary flow unit and mobile resources. A patient lies in a bed, while doctors and nurses come and go. The next may not know what the previous has said and done, if patient information is not handed over.

#### Self-administered and Automatic Handovers

In some services, providers leave the handover to the customer. Shopping malls do not carry customers from store to store. Airlines expect people to show up at the departure gate on time. Maps and signs are provided, but how people get there is their problem, unless there are specific arrangements for special assistance, as with children traveling alone.

The travel and tourism industry has developed two service types according to handovers. The all-inclusive package tour comes with handovers. The travel agency sees to it that tourists move from the starting point to the end point in a continuous flow. Buses take tourists from airport to hotel to attractions and back on a schedule. With Internet booking platforms, tourists can compose their own itinerary and hand themselves over from one step to the next. Service producers offer no handovers, only steps.

## Handover Is Information

In services, the handover requires information that is an input to the setup. It details the current status of the flow unit, what has been done already, what happened in the meantime, and what should be done next.

The proper execution of activities and tasks is a matter of professional knowledge and skill about the technologies of the relevant production functions. Running a process with multiple handovers is a management job. Managers do not have to be experts on tasks; their main concern is the flow and the in–out connections between steps. It takes coordination to see to it that the handovers are done properly and that the flow unit moves swiftly and without unnecessary delays. The next step needs to know the updated status of the flow unit, if there is anything beyond ordinary, and what needs to be done next. Sometimes this can be done by direct communication between actors; most often, it must be documented. In health services, referrals and medical records are commonly used handover tools.

Handovers are the weak links of processes. Handover failures, miscommunication, misunderstandings, delays, inappropriate responses, and omissions are process management problems. A process with several actors has, or should have, a process owner, a person who is in charge of the whole.

## Handovers Create Inventory

A handover that takes time creates WIP inventory. In services, the equivalent to WIP inventory is waiting time. For customers, a job shop or a connected flow would be ideal. The service would flow like a river—no interruptions, no comings and goings, and somebody is always in charge. But this is not always possible. Different tasks require different tools, skills, and locations.

> Research on the process of giving birth has found that the best way to reduce the mother's anxiety and improve the service experience is to have the same midwife stay during the whole process.[23] However, labor can take up to 36 hours. Midwives typical work in 8-hour shifts. Labor rules protecting employees from fatigue make it impossible to have a

continuous flow with one caregiver. Handovers between midwives are inevitable.

If a job to be done cannot be a connected flow, it must be coordinated as a disconnected flow with buffers. The management of handovers entails information systems and all the technicalities and formalities that reporting and documentation entail.

## 4.3.4 Customer Journey

In personal services, a production flow can be described as a customer journey. It proceeds as a sequence of steps connected by handovers. In manufacturing, the process map usually includes only producer's activities, since the flow units are not agents with behaviors of their own. The service blueprinting approach[24] includes customer activities, customer and front-office interactions, and back-office preparations. The swimming lane chart depicts each actor as a horizontal row. Figure 4.11 shows a journey of a case and a stationary customer. Assume you are on a business trip and you sit in your hotel room. You have to prepare a presentation for tomorrow, but hunger pain prevents you from thinking straight. You place an order to

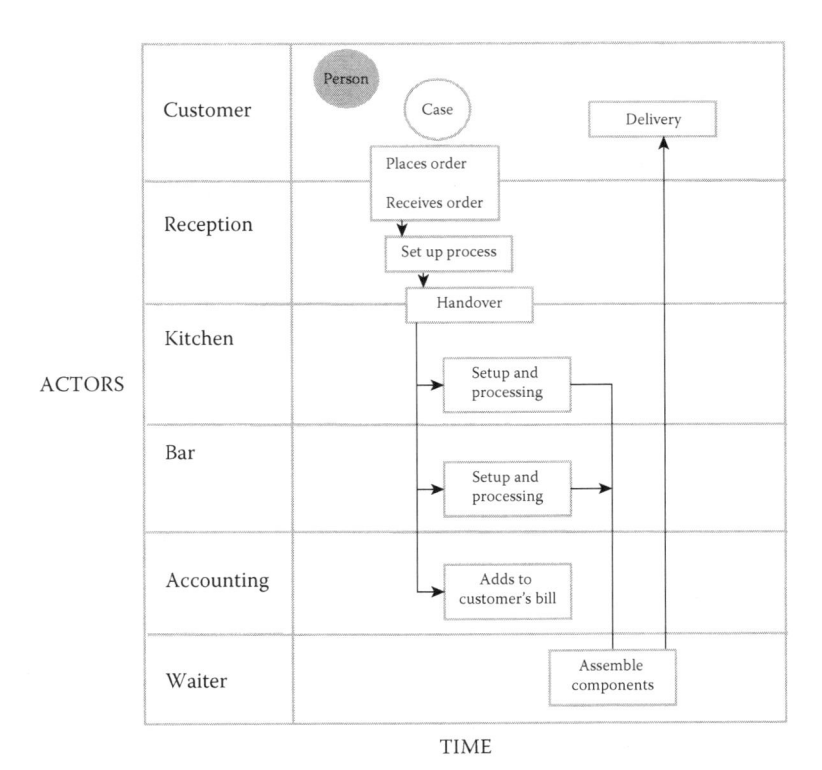

**Figure 4.11   Service blueprint.**

room service. The time you wait for delivery is valuable. Every minute lost waiting is a minute of lost work.

Customer demand is formulated as an order to the reception desk. There it is set up as three tasks: prepare the sandwich, get the beer, and add the items to the customer's bill. The kitchen does its own setup, activates a recipe, pulls materials, and processes the sandwich. The order is then completed with beer from the bar, and handed over to a waiter for delivery. The bill is added to the customer's room.

Now the same as an abstraction. The flow units are the person and the case. The two separate when the order is placed and reconnect at delivery. The customer is an adaptive agent who can define setups and bargain about details. The case is defined by the setup. When a customer in person is involved, production must be in the make-to-order (MTO) mode. Processing is done by workstations that hand over the case to the next station in a sequence. When the case connects with the person at delivery, the meal turns into the customer's property and its quality can be assessed.

When a case separates from a person, it becomes a flow unit that follows the same principles as in manufacturing. If the kitchen is busy, the order spends some minutes in a buffer of incoming orders. The flow can be connected if WIP inventory is low, that is, there are no or only a few orders in the pipeline. If several are coming in, the kitchen may have to use batch processing, that is, first do all the bread, then all the butter, then all the cheese, and finally deliver the whole batch.

From this follows that the value chain, or the value stream in services, is different from that in manufacturing. As a customer in person, you are not part of the flow of the case, nor are you fully disconnected.

## Value Stream

The distinction between value-added activities and *muda* has been used in services.[25] As I discussed in Chapter 3, the conceptualization is tautological and not very useful, except in obvious cases with low-hanging fruit. In services, it gets a different meaning.

The flow unit in services is a customer in person, a customer's property (luggage), or a customer case (an order). Suitcases and meals are not adaptive agents and can be processed as in a factory. The activities performed for a customer in person usually constitute disconnected service steps (contact points or service encounters), unless a service provider needs to be constantly present, such as in an intensive care unit (ICU). The value stream may be called a customer episode, the things a customer perceives and does when part of a service system, including waiting time. The value stream is a continuous flow of experience, occasionally maintained, adjusted, and amplified by service events. Technically speaking, the value stream in services is a combination of a disconnected line and a connected flow.

The what issues are settled at setup; the how issues are constantly present with varying intensity. For a bank customer, the contact points are important. Between them, the relation is on standby, passively providing a sense of security and the possibility to activate the relationship at will. For a home insurance customer, the less need for contact, the better.

The value stream has implications to service management. First, in manufacturing the value chain is practically identical with that in processing. The typical value stream map shows a production process as producer's activities. In services, the link between processing and the value stream is not obvious. Hotel customers create value together with the producer by making use of resources the producer has made available, such as the bar and the pool, but also on their own when they venture downtown for shopping. Service producers create conditions where customers can create value for themselves and with each other. From this follows that customer activities must be included in a service process description.

Second, WIP inventory and buffer management is not only an inventory cost but also a customer value issue. Waiting may be inevitable, but customer experience depends to a great deal on how queues are managed.[26] Customer satisfaction is affected by perceived waiting time, which is not directly proportional to the actual waiting time. Waiting time feels shorter if customers feel the queuing discipline is just, they are informed about their progress, the waiting area is amicable, and they have something to do while passing time.

Third, customers have a variable degree of bargaining power for how services are set up and how the value stream will run. If a manufacturer produces a defective product that causes harm to a user, the manufacturer can be held responsible and be subject to product liability lawsuits. If a service customer does not follow rules or keep his part of the setup, the responsibility is on the customer. From customer involvement follows that the service value stream is not necessarily under the full control of the producer. Services are produced in open systems that are subject to customer-introduced variability.

## Additive and Multiplicative Flows

Value streams can be additive and multiplicative. In manufacturing, each step, unless errors are made, is supposed to add value until the final touch. The value chain can be described as additions; this step assembles some components, and the next step adds some more. The value of the flow unit accumulates step-by-step. If something goes really bad, the flow unit can't be sold; however, it still may have a salvageable scrap value.

In services, it can't be assumed that value in terms of the service experience is monotonously added from event to event. A service encounter may add to or subtract from the accumulated value. A single service failure can destroy everything done so far and leave an embittered and litigious former customer. A failed service does not have scrap value. If you get stranded in the middle of nowhere, you are worse off than if you never embarked on the journey.

Thus, each step of a service process can be seen as a multiple. If it is larger than 1, value is added; if less, value is destroyed. Steps that attain the value zero destroy all

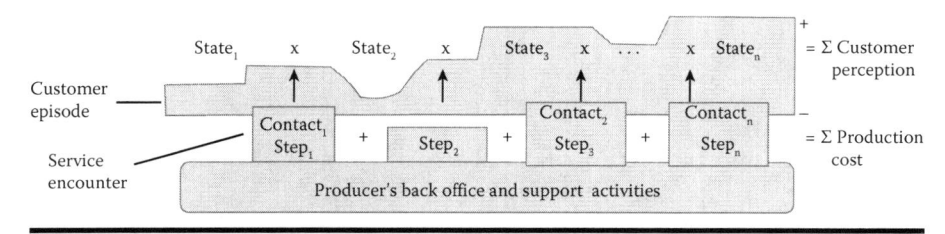

**Figure 4.12   Services as steps and flow.**

accumulated value; multiplication by zero is zero. These are mission-critical killer incidents. While customer perceptions can go up and down, the production costs add up monotonously, as illustrated in Figure 4.12.

Buildings, machines, and people are subject to the inevitability of life cycles, decay, deterioration, and obsolesce. Maintenance services produce value by bending the curve by preventing, arresting, or postponing the inevitable. Value, however, is not "added" in the conventional sense. Rather, maintenance ensures that less value is destroyed than otherwise would be the case. The value of prevention and maintenance is accounted for in negative numbers; what could have been –5 is now –3.

## 4.3.5 *Open and Closed Systems*

Variability is inevitable. Factories are production systems where the utmost is done to eliminate, reduce, or control variability. The most fully closed systems are semiconductor manufacturing and surgical theatres, where air is filtered, protective gear is the norm, and hands must be washed. Factories and surgical hospitals are, or strive to be, closed or at least semiclosed systems.

Like a manufacturing plant, services can be subject to unwelcome external impacts, such as bad weather and power failures. Weather can't be controlled, but it can be predicted and routines detailing what to do in case of a downpour can be developed. Service facilities can restrict entry and draw lines of visibility and interaction; there are closed doors for staff only. But the front office can't be closed. A resort hotel might want to reduce the variability that comes from rowdy behavior by closing the bar before midnight and installing a curfew. That would not be appreciated and defeat the very purpose of service. What a hotel could do, though, is to reduce the variability of customers by segmentation. Hotels that cater to pilgrims do not offer alcoholic beverages. Some hotels exclude families with small children, and others invite them.

If variability can't be eliminated and systems can't be closed, variability must be managed in open systems.

The sharp distinction between goods and services was blurred when it was recognized that many offerings employ both in various combinations. In a similar vein, a continuum can be applied to how service production systems deal with variability.

The end points of the continuum are akin to ideal types. At one end is a closed system, and at the other an open system. Some basic dimensions are summarized in Table 4.1.

Service systems can be open and closed to a variable degree. A service episode can have some phases or layers that are open and some others that are closed. A patient wheeled into surgery enters a very closed phase; when wheeled out to postanesthetic care, the system is slightly more open, and when going home with instructions of rehabilitation exercises, the system is thrown wide open. Open and closed systems follow different logics and are different parts of the service multiverse.

## 4.3.6  Capacity Management

Immaterial services cannot be stored in a finished goods inventory to be used as a buffer between supply and demand. Customers and their requirements are heterogeneous and cause quantitative and qualitative variability in demand.

The quantitative aspect, that is, the variability in the volume of similar service requests, is the easy part. The basic options are, first, the level capacity strategy.[27] A gatekeeper protects the service provider (server) by regulating the inflow of customer requests. Server capacity is kept constant and not used as a buffer. Waiting time and queues are the shock absorbers. Second, the chase capacity strategy can be applied when demand fluctuations are predictable. More capacity is added when demand is high, such as restaurants employing more help during the lunch rush. Third, demand management strives to segment, filter, direct, and route demand

**Table 4.1  Production Systems as Dimensions**

| *Closed Systems* | *Open Systems* |
| --- | --- |
| Production facility is closed; customers have no access | Production facility has front offices or service theatres for customers to enter |
| Variability is reduced by all means | Customer-introduced variability is accepted |
| Processing is deterministic and leads to predictable output | Processing is subject to perceptions and interpretations |
| Setup is standard or formatted | Setup is routine or explorative; bargaining is allowed |
| Make copies of a prototype | Individual setups and designs |
| Focus on what | Focus on how |
| Value chain is additive; each step adds value | Value stream includes multiples that create or destroy value |

through promotions and pricing. Variety at peak demand can be restricted; restaurants serve a limited menu at lunchtime.

After air traffic was deregulated in the 1970s and price controls were lifted, airlines became adept at demand management.[28] The hard facts are determined by architectural elements:

- Routes from Airport A to Airport B.
- Scheduled flights on routes.
- Schedules can be coordinated to allow connecting flights.
- Each aircraft has a given number of seats that puts a strict limit on the number of passengers (can't squeeze in more passengers as in a subway car).
- An empty seat will not bring revenue; when it is gone, it is gone forever.

Customer behavior can be predicted to react to price, departure time, and travel time; that is, direct flights at convenient hours are preferred.

From this follows a simple strategy called the cabin factor: fill all the seats. This, however, is not necessarily wise, given the observation that customers' willingness to pay is related to the time between decision and departure. Those who decide late usually have a pressing need to travel and are ready to pay more.

The consequent strategy is to shift focus from seats to revenue. Yield management is a method to maximize revenue per flight; sell as many seats as possible at a price as high as possible. To this end, airlines need to predict how different customer types will demand future flights. Seats must be reserved for late-coming high payers. This is a trade-off. If too much capacity is reserved, some of it may be left empty; if too little is reserved, high payers must be turned away. The trade-off can't be fully eliminated, but it can be amended by predictive analytics. Demand per flight can be estimated based on historical data and seasonal fluctuations; holidays bring leisure travelers, and trade fairs business travelers. Flight reservations are open months in advance. From the rate by which seats fill, airlines can estimate demand and develop algorithms that set prices accordingly. This is why the price for a flight posted on a reservation site can vary from hour to hour.

The qualitative aspect means that the service requests are different, and the service producer has limited means to segment and select. This is the situation in parts of healthcare, an issue that I will return to in Chapter 5.

# 4.4 Service Performance Measurement and Evaluation

In manufacturing, process performance appears to the customer only as quality, delivery time, and cost or price. In services, the same holds true for the back office. In the front office, processes are visible. Both the what (we take you safely to your destination) and how (we provide comfort and treat you respectfully) aspects can be spelled out as value propositions, promises of services. In services, conformance to specifications (small q) is to keep promises. They are not always as specific as the physical dimensions of a machine part.

## 4.4.1 Service Quality

SERVQUAL is a method to define and measure service quality, with quality here understood as the big Q aiming at customer satisfaction. It was developed by three American marketing scholars in 1988, Parsu Parasuraman, Valarie Zeithaml, and Leonard Berry[29] and has since been widely applied, revised, and elaborated.

The authors started by defining the attributes of good service. They initially came up with a list of 10 points, which eventually was boiled down to the core 5, known as RATER:

**R**eliability: Do what you promise
**A**ssurance: Convey trust and confidence
**T**angibles: The appearance of facilities, equipment, personnel, and materials
**E**mpathy: Caring, individualized attention
**R**esponsiveness: Adapt to changing situations

The distinction between small q and big Q is useful here. Of the RATER attributes, reliability is equal to small q. Assurance and empathy are how issues heavy on personal style. Tangibles are the grade to which the servicescape and the service process are designed and kept in shape. Responsiveness is to deal with variability. It resembles daily management in a factory. Was a service failure observed before a customer came around to complain? Did the observation prompt action? Did the person in charge know what to do and have the means to do it?

Service quality has some peculiarities that are not present in the production of goods. Small q is the relation between measurable specifications and measurable output. Big Q is the relation between expectations and experience, both subject to perceptions: what is perceived as real is real in its consequences.

The *service paradox* denotes a situation where the higher the expectations of service, the lower the customer satisfaction in general.[30] Consider this example. A couple with small children boards an intercontinental flight. The 4-year-old boy is restless and unruly and creates havoc by running around and making noise. The parents are struggling, as they feel the uncomfortable gazes of their annoyed fellow passengers. A flight attendant sees the situation and finds a remedy. The boy is invited to the cockpit to meet the pilots. The boy is all excited and, when back in his seat, immediately falls asleep. What a wonderful service experience! On the return flight, the same trouble resumes. Now, however, the plane is fully booked and the weather is turbulent. The flight attendants have no time to spare for 4-year-olds. The parents' expectations are not fulfilled, and they deplane dissatisfied. The negative feeling may be stronger than the initial positive, leaving the emotional balance below water. The lesson for service producers: do not create expectations that you are not able to fulfill.

The *service recovery paradox* denotes a situation in which a customer's perception of a service provider is better after a corrected service failure, compared with a situation of nonfaulty service. Successful recovery of a failure leads to an increased sense of assurance and empathy among customers. For example, a flight is canceled. The airline sends a text message where they apologize profoundly and offer another flight on the same day, plus a discount voucher. The airline has demonstrated they care and correct. The traveler may not be happy, but is now more loyal to the airline than before. Service recovery is especially important in services subject to external variability. Most customers can understand that sometimes error-free service is not possible.[31]

## Here and Now

Services as collaboration add a new time dimension to quality. For *small q*, the focus is *ex ante*, before the fact. How well are situations defined and activities specified before production? For big Q, the focus is *ex post*, after the fact, since the expectations–experience relation is difficult to predict in advance. In service production, part of quality is *ex nunc*, right now, in the setup and collaboration.

## 4.4.2 Gaps, Handovers, and Risks

Big Q is the relation between customer-perceived expectations and customer-perceived outcomes. A service setup results in three types of perceptions: what the provider understood, what the customer understood, and what they agreed to understand. This is the ontology; the epistemology deals with how to define and measure perceptions and their differences.

SERVQUAL is based on the GAP theory. It postulates that on occasion, the RATER attributes do not materialize, because there are gaps in the service flow. They appear in the front office, where providers and customers interact, and in the back office, where services are prepared and designed. This equals the problems with handovers in production processes. The original five GAPs are

1. Management does not understand what customers expect.
2. Management understanding of expectations (right or wrong) does not translate into a proper service design.

3. Services are not delivered as promised.
4. Details of the service content are not communicated to the customer with sufficient clarity.
5. Expected and experienced service do not match.

An expanded GAP model, combined with big Q, produces Figure 4.13. Gaps 1 and 2 are handover problems within the back office, where services are designed. Gap 3 refers to problems with the service design; frontline workers are not instructed properly and do not know what to do. Gap 6 is about the communication and interactions between the customer and provider that produce unrealistic expectations, the service paradox. Gap 5 is the small q of executing a service. Gap 7 is the big Q.

Quality management is about reducing variability. Risks should be identified and managed through quality assurance. The gaps of Figure 4.13 can be redefined as the five basic types of risks in the world of transformations and transactions,[32] as illustrated in Figure 4.14.

First, the designer's risk is that customer requirements are not understood properly. This is the "requirements capture" dilemma that is a continuous challenge for marketing. No matter how many surveys or focus groups are conducted, a product may still be a dud. People simply have difficulties in articulating what they have not experienced.

Second, a production risk is the possibility that something that has been designed cannot be produced as intended. A realized production risk may be quantitative

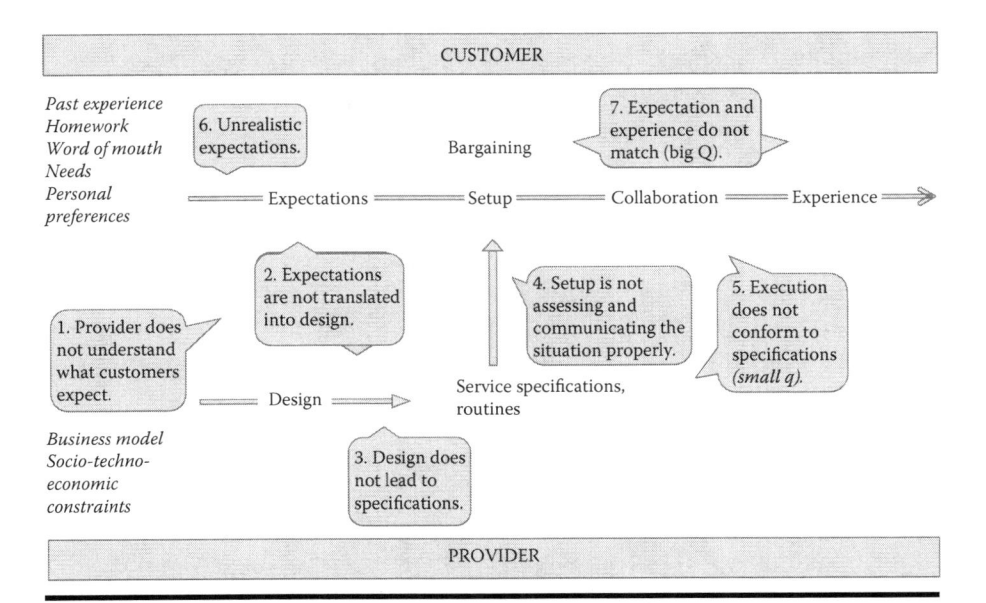

**Figure 4.13  GAP model of service quality.**

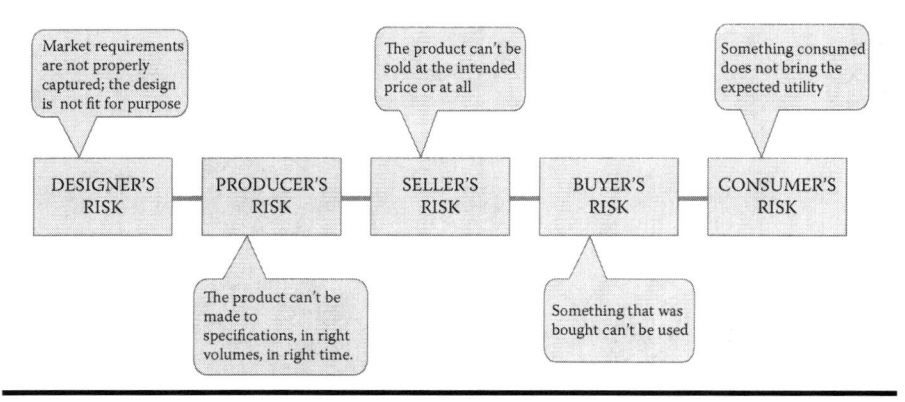

**Figure 4.14  Types of risk.**

(promised volume cannot be delivered), related to time (delivery cannot be made in time), or qualitative (output does not conform to specifications).

Third, a seller's risk refers to the possibility that something that has been designed and produced cannot be sold at the intended price or at all, or that reserved capacity cannot be utilized due to a lack of customers. As services cannot be stored, this is a major risk that requires capacity management.

Fourth, a buyer's risk means that something has been paid for but cannot be consumed as intended, such as when a customer buys a ticket but misses the plane.

Fourth, a consumption risk refers to the possibility that something that has been consumed does not carry the intended value-in-use, such as when a vacation is spoiled by bad weather. This is buyer's remorse; something purchased does not deliver the expected satisfaction.

### 4.4.3 Service Productivity

Service productivity increase, or the lack of it, has been a concern big enough to have a name. *Baumol's disease* is the macroeconomic equivalent of Alzheimer's disease. It got its name from the economist William Baumol.[33] In the 1960s, he observed that the perceived quality of some services seemed to deteriorate, despite the fact that the economy was growing and more money was spent.

In personal services, productivity is not increasing at the same rate as in manufacturing. While a factory can increase its volume, exploit economies of scale, and reduce prices, a hairdresser or a nurse cannot serve any more customers than before. Nevertheless, their salaries, and the price they ask, tend to follow the general income level in the economy, which in turn is driven by increased productivity in manufacturing. As a consequence, the relative price of services in contrast to manufactured goods is rising. Services simply became more expensive to produce. Until the 1950s, upper-middle-class families in the Western world considered it normal to employ a live-in maid. Such a service is no longer within their reach.

> In the 1950s, it cost a few cents to have a dress shirt laundered, pressed, and folded. The first home-use washing machines were introduced in 1948. The price was equal to the annual income of a qualified laborer. Services were relatively cheap compared with goods. These days, in northern Europe it costs about $5 to have a shirt laundered and pressed. To keep a gentleman properly coiffured for a year with 200 working days will cost $1000. For that sum, a high-performance washing machine–dryer combo can be purchased.

When services become relatively more expensive, several things happen. People consume less of them (no maids), self-service starts to proliferate (no help at the gas pump), routine services are outsourced to cheaper locations (call centers), a low-income service sector emerges (McJobs), and costly services are financed by the public sector (childcare in welfare societies).

Baumol noted that in services, productivity does not grow. New technologies have a marginal impact, if any, on how many customers a hairdresser can serve per day. A personal service can be produced only one at a time. Baumol's favorite example was the symphony orchestra. If it attempts to increase productivity by reducing cycle time and plays Beethoven's fifth symphony 10 minutes faster, or cuts costs by leaving out the wind instruments, it will destroy the music.

The ratio of services in the whole economy keeps growing. With such a large part of economic activity in a productivity trap, overall productivity growth slows down.

Baumol assumed that there were two causes to the disease. First, in services processing time can't be shortened too much with technological improvements in the production function. Second, a service producer can serve only one customer (hairdresser), or a limited number of them (concert audience), at a time. I may add a third. Each service requires an individual setup. A standard setup can't be applied to a batch of customers (at some barber shops, it feels like they are trying hard).

Baumol's disease is still influential in the macroeconomic debate on services. Fortunately, times have changed. Baumol's disease, like many management chunks of logic, is as true as ever, but its application area has shrunk. It is still at work in services where the production function is person intensive and time constrained; that is, the value of a service, such as physiotherapy, is directly proportional to its duration. Going from 60- to 40-minute appointments increases utilization but not productivity. Productivity improves with difficulty in services where setup requires personal attention and can't be formatted (complex diagnostics), and where flow units can't be collected in batches.

Where these constraints are not present, service volumes can increase, and with them productivity. Budget airlines have formatted setups and batch production. Internet banking fully automates processing. A special case of high-volume, high-productivity, and reasonably personal services is the franchise, such as McDonald's and Starbucks. Their service theatres are not huge installations. There is a limit to how big a restaurant can grow before it becomes impractical and unfriendly. Setups are handled individually and personally. The trick is to format the setup by offering limited menus and apply the assemble-to-order principle; components such as burger patties are precooked and kept under heat lamps, waiting for customer orders.

A franchise exploits division of labor, specialization, and economies of scale in administrative and managerial tasks. The service production site has a minimal back office. Volume-sensitive tasks subject to economies of scale, such as purchasing, service design, facilities management, accounting, and finance, are concentrated in the franchise head office. Central management functions can be seen as macrolevel setups, and each outlet is a near-identical replication of the concept. Thus, a Starbucks outfit is a very Lean operation compared with an independent mom-and-pop coffee shop, where the proprietor has to double as barista, rapid-order cook, accountant, marketer, and purchasing officer. Franchises are highly scalable in that they can add outlets as much as the market bears without having to expand headquarter functions and bureaucracy at a similar pace.

Baumol's disease has not been cured, but several services have developed immunity to it. Service productivity improvement has recently begun to show up at the macroeconomic level. A report by the Organisation for Economic Co-operation and Development (OECD) noted that productivity in leading service companies has increased faster than in manufacturing.[34] In both sectors, the difference between the frontier firms and the laggards is widening, more so in services. This indicates that productivity in service can indeed improve, but it does not happen across the sector, and not necessarily following the manufacturing model. Consider the music industry. The production function (composing and playing music) and the workstation (orchestra or band) can't improve their time-measured performance very much. But music can be recorded and then distributed in several ways. In some services, productivity improvement does not arise from transformations but from transactions. Trade and distribution matter.

## 4.5 Service Transactions

In manufacturing, the traditional view has been, as Paul Samuelson put it, you build the best mousetrap and the world will beat a path to your door. That may have been true at times when mousetraps were few and far between. Currently, very few products fly off the shelves. Services are state-changing collaborative processes where the customer is an adaptive agent. How are services bought and sold?

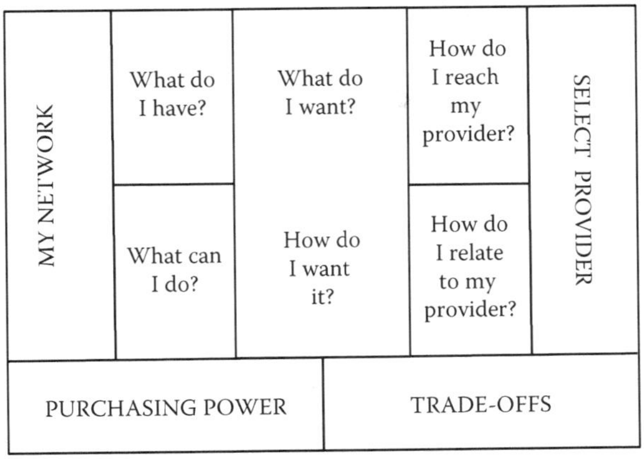

| | | | | | |
|---|---|---|---|---|---|
| MY NETWORK | What do I have? | What do I want? | How do I reach my provider? | SELECT PROVIDER |
| | What can I do? | How do I want it? | How do I relate to my provider? | |
| PURCHASING POWER | | | TRADE-OFFS | |

**Figure 4.15   The service customer's Business Model Canvas.**

Compared with manufacturing, services offer more degrees of freedom to design business models. Customers as collaborators can make up their own Business Model Canvas, as illustrated in Figure 4.15.

## 4.5.1 Service Customer

In a trade with manufactured products, the customer has three roles: chooser, payer, and user (Figure 3.16). In services, the roles are more complicated, as illustrated in Figure 4.16.

### The Chooser and the Payer

The customer chooses the service provider. This is a consumerist choice, a blend of availability, price, promotions, reputation, and calculative but bounded rationality.

The payer pays the price at the point of purchase. Depending on how far the payer's bounds of rationality reach, she may also calculate the terms of trade, financing, and timing, plus the cost of ownership, upkeep, maintenance, and disposal. The service customer pays both a price and the effort that comes with collaboration. Self-service offers a trade-off: pay less money but pay more effort. Individual setup is an effortful accomplishment.

If an agent is not in the position to choose, she can allocate choices to another party. Such an agent is called a client. Client relations are typical in professional services, such as law and healthcare. A client acts as a principal, who chooses an agent to serve his interests. The principal does not have the possibility or the expertise to get involved in all choices. The principal monitors the agent by looking at some performance criteria, such as whether the court case leads to victory, or the medical procedure accomplishes the expected outcome. The principal–agent relation has been subject to much academic inquiry.[35]

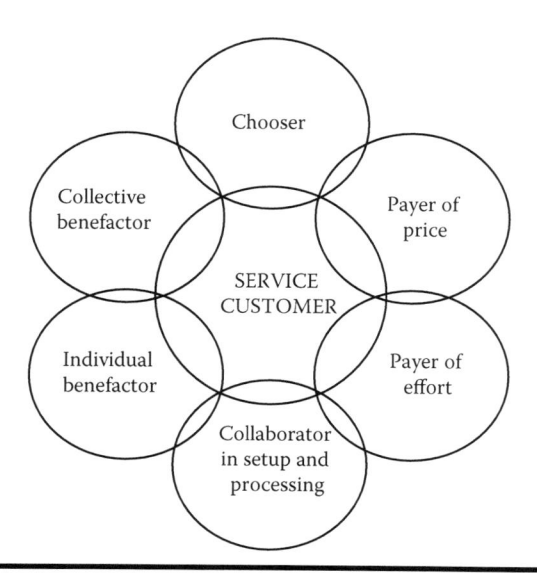

**Figure 4.16  Service customer.**

## The User and the Benefactor

In both products and services, you can choose and pay, and then let somebody else use and benefit. In public services, the customer is not always the benefactor. If the police stop you on the highway for speeding, there will be interactions that require collaboration on your part. But you can hardly say you are a customer and the police a service provider. This is not a voluntary trade; you are at the receiving end of administrative government power and would prefer to be somewhere else. There is no value for you that the state of your personal finances is altered by the amount on the ticket. You are a subject of the law, and you have no choice but to comply and pay. (Don't even think of offering a bribe if you are in Scandinavia.) The police officer may have the choice to look the other way, but essentially officials are supposed to enforce rules. Here the customer, or rather the benefactor, is the general public that benefits from laws being enforced, and especially road users in whose collective interest it is that traffic rules are followed. You are member of that collective, but right now it doesn't seem like much when you are a citizen with responsibilities.

Administrative actions are processed and set up like collaborative services. But there is no voluntary transaction and several parties benefit. Law enforcement and public administration, such as the tax office and the land authority, are rather clear cases of administrative action based on the legitimate powers of the central and local governments. There is, however, a complicated gray area of tax-financed and publicly administered services. There are situations where the agent pays, but not directly to the producer of a specific service. Taxpayers and insurance customers put their money into pools, where their individual contributions are anonymized. Somebody in authority decides when, how, and for what purpose the funds are used. If there are no markets with free choice, then there are no real customers. This is the situation in much of health and social services.

## Property Rights versus Rights and Responsibilities

A service trade is based on immaterial value propositions. The object of trade is not physically present at the time of the trade. Services require contractual trade arrangements that do not include change in ownership.[36]

If a customer is disappointed with a physical product, or is unable to pay for it, he can return it to the seller. An intangible service cannot be returned. If you, after having got your haircut, discover that you forgot you wallet, you can't undo the haircut and give it back to the barber. Spent resources cannot be recovered, services have no scrap value, and there is no secondhand market for used services. A service customer hit by buyer's remorse can refuse to pay. In such transactions, the risk is on the seller. Some commercial services deal with such risks by insisting on payment in advance.

When physical goods are sold and bought, there is a transfer of ownership and property rights. What was mine is now yours, and vice versa. Commercial services are sold and bought. Given that the offerings are intangible, property rights are difficult to assign. If you get a new haircut, can you say you own it? To an extent, yes; it is your hair on your head, but a coiffure is not the same as hair. It belongs to you, but you do not own it in the sense that you could sell it or, worse, that somebody could steal it from you. This becomes quite a complicated ethical issue in the parts of health services that deal with organ transplantations and care at the end of life. Do you own your kidneys so that you are free to give one away or sell it for a price? Do you own your life? Are you free to terminate it if death appears to be a state preferable to unbearable pain that will not go away?

In the material world, economic exchange is founded on property rights. In services, value-in-exchange is in a proposition, a promise to do something. Since providers and customers collaborate, an exchange involves an understanding of the rights and responsibilities of both parties. A right is a privilege earned through responsible action.[37] In the material world, a customer's only responsibility is to pay. In the immaterial world of service, the customer participates and thereby is partly responsible for the outcomes.

## 4.5.2 Service Revenue Models

The business model concept rose into prominence during the dotcom boom around the millennium shift. Before that, business models were simple and ignorable. If you manufactured widgets, you did so as cheaply as possible, put the price as high as the market would bear, and enjoyed the difference. If you produced services, you charged by the hour, billed by task, or collected a fee at the entrance to a facility. But how do you charge for an Internet service?

The emergence of the World Wide Web in the early 1990s opened a wide range of possible revenue models. A content producer can charge a subscription fee (most newspapers do), charge per item accessed (Amazon Kindle bookshop), offer a platform for free but charge for in-app extras (Pokémon Go), or offer the service free of charge, but collect eyeballs, clickstreams, and customer information to lure advertisers (Facebook). The revenue model tells where the price tag is attached; what is the billable item?

## Proof of Service

Services are promises of processes to be carried out, and therefore their quality cannot be confirmed at the point of purchase. Pricing is based on different revenue models built around *proofs of service*.[38] Examples include the following:

- *Access* to a facility, such as an entrance ticket to a museum. Once within the facility, customers can browse the items at their leisure.
- *Usage* of equipment or a resource, such as rental cars and temp staff. The buyer can use and manage the resource for a set time. The price is subject to type and duration.
- *Enactment* of a process, such as a trip to a beach resort or a surgical procedure. The producer gets paid for performing tasks at a fixed price, or following an algorithm, such as those in taxi meters that calculate the price from the elapsed time and traveled distance.
- *Outcomes* are results of transformations, that is, the achieved utility of a state change based on some preset criteria. When real estate agents close a sale, they get paid a percentage of the deal, irrespective of how much time and effort has been spent. This is the value-based revenue model.

Risks are shared differently in the revenue models. In the access and usage types, the customer carries the main risk. If the customer rents a car but leaves it idling on a parking lot, it has no transport value, but the rental company is paid anyway. In the process-based model, the risks are shared through various arrangements: if a taxi driver takes a customer to the wrong address, the fee is negotiable, but if the customer gives the wrong address or nobody is at home, the risk is on the customer. With the outcome-based model, the service provider carries the risk. If a house remains unsold, the real estate agent takes the risk.

In some services, several revenue models can be combined. Take a nightclub. It can decide to charge a high entrance fee, but offer drinks and entertainment cheaply. Alternatively, it may have free entrance, but charge dearly at the bar. Which works depends on the types of customers it attracts. A place where those on the go just have to show off before heading somewhere else obviously benefits from a high entrance fee. Places where customers tend to linger all night long do better getting their revenue from sales within the facility.

## Servitization

The development of revenue models has created a great deal of options and fluidity. Business can be done in various ways. A recent trend is servitization, to sell goods as services.[39]

A pioneer is Konecranes, a supplier of industrial lifting equipment. Traditionally, they sold and installed cranes, charged a price, and offered a maintenance contract on the side. Now the business is selling lifting as a service. Konecranes builds and installs a crane at the customer's premises. The equipment remains the property of the manufacturer. The crane has a device that reads all uses and movements. The customer agrees to pay a certain sum for each ton lifted. The benefits to both parties are significant. The customer does not pay for idle time, only for processing. As the manufacturer gets paid only when the crane moves, it has an interest to keep it in good repair, monitor its performance, and conduct preventive maintenance. The manufacturer assumes a big part of the risk and charges for it. A company that designs and builds cranes knows more about their anatomy and physiology than the user who has other worries. The manufacturer can leverage its knowledge and skills to manage risks more efficiently. The crane user, as virtually any customer, is willing to pay if somebody else carries the risk. Competence is monetized and leveraged through risk management.

## 4.5.3 Service Distribution and Time–Location Constraints

In traditional manufacturing, production and distribution are clearly separated. In services, production and distribution are intertwined in preparations, setups, and collaboration. Some services are facility based. The service workstation requires some equipment that is not easily moved. The customer and the service provider meet at the location. In field-based services, the workstation moves to the location of the customer. Fire engines have to rush to the fire, and repairmen and cleaners have to be at the customer's premises; home help, by definition, is services brought to the customer's home.

Facility-based services are constrained by time and location. As illustrated in Figure 4.17, there are four basic time–location combinations. If a service is both time and location dependent, a customer and a provider must meet face-to-face at a specific location at a specific time. The customer has to travel, which adds to the total cost of the service. If the location is fixed but time is not, a customer can enter the provider's facilities at any time during the opening hours and ask to be served. Some queuing may be required. If time is fixed but location is not, providers and customers can engage through real-time communication devices, such as telephones or data links. A service that is both time and location independent, that is,

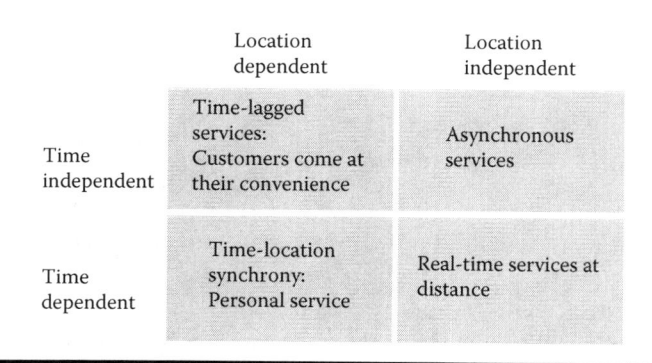

**Figure 4.17   Types of time–location dependency.**

a customer can engage the service any time from any location, is asynchronous. Web-based services, e-mails, and text messages are of this type.

Location-dependent facility-based services follow the general principles of goods distribution, the chunk of logic that connects catchment area, time–location access, variety, and specialization level, as discussed earlier. New communication devices carry the potential to amend the involved trade-offs. In some services, the setup and processing are separated by time and location. In healthcare, finding out a patient's problem, making a diagnosis and devising a care plan (setup), and administering a cure (processing) can in some situations be done at different locations. This is the promise of telemedicine.

# Notes

1. For overviews of the intellectual history of services, see Salvendy and Karwowski (2009), Rozenes and Cohen (2017), Grönroos (2000), and Johnston and Clark (2004).
2. For global statistics, see http://data.worldbank.org/indicator/NV.SRV.TETC.ZS.
3. Zeithaml et al. (2013).
4. Wemmerlöv (1991) and Fitzsimmons and Fitzsimmons, (2006).
5. Schmenner, R. W. 2004. Service Business and Productivity. *Decision Sciences,* 35:333–347.
6. The idea was originally presented in Shostack (1977) and elaborated in Kotler and Keller (2006).
7. The customer contact model was introduced in Chase (1978) and elaborated in Chase (1981).
8. The concept of customer contact lies at the core of many service classifications. For reviews, see Silvestro et al. (1992) and Cook et al. (1999).
9. Roels (2014).
10. Vargo and Lusch (2004) and Sampson and Froehle (2006).
11. The resource integration model has been developed in two papers by Sabine Moeller (2008, 2010).

12. The American Marketing Association defines marketing as "the activity, set of institutions, and processes for creating, communicating, delivering, and exchanging offerings that have value for customers, clients, partners, and society at large" (https://www.ama.org/Pages/default.aspx).

13. The idea of services as state changes was originally presented by T P Hill (1977). Unfortunately it did not get much traction in the service definitions debate.

14. Servicescape is a model developed to describe the impact of the physical environment in which a service process takes place. The service environment is usually the first aspect of the service that is perceived by the customer, and it is at this stage that consumers are likely to form impressions of the level of service they will receive (Bitner 1992).

15. The idea of customers as a source of variability was introduced by Frei (2006).

16. An earlier version of this conceptualization is Lillrank (2003b).

17. Pentland and Rueter (1994).

18. Davies and Brady (2000).

19. A special case of explorative processes is computationally irreducible problems. They have no mathematical shortcuts that could be exploited by simulations. The only way to determine the outcome is to go through every step. By contrast, a computationally reducible problem can be described by a mathematical formula that gives the outcome at any chosen instant of time without going through all the time steps. See Chapter 6 in Bookstaber (2017).

20. For a literature review on agility in healthcare, see Tolft et al. (2015).

21. Lillrank (2002).

22. Sharman (1984).

23. Miller et al. (2016).

24. Service blueprinting principles and methods are described in Bitner et al. (1997), Fliess and Kleinaltenkamp (2004), and Womack and Jones (1996).

25. Sarkar (2007).

26. Davis and Heineke (1998) and Baker and Cameron (1996).

27. Johnston and Clark (2004).

28. Kimes (1989).

29. Parasuraman, Zeithaml, and Berry (1990).

30. Grönroos (2011).

31. The service paradox and the service recovery paradox are ontologically real in the sense that this kind of thing happen. The dynamics between expectations and experiences makes sense. However, the epistemology is problematic. Empirical research has not been able to demonstrate that these phenomena are regularly present. That comes back to the difficulty of defining situations, that is, how context and instance interact. For a review on the literature, see de Matos et al. (2007).

32. Lillrank and Särkkä (2011).

33. Baumol (1967) and Baumol and Bowen (1967).

34. McGowan et al. (2017).

35. Eisenhardt (1989).

36. Gadrey (1988, 2000).

37. Spohrer and Maglio (2008).

38. Shostack (1982).

39. Baines and Lightfoot (2013).

# Chapter 5

# The Logic of Healthcare

## 5.1 Purposes and Products of Healthcare

Healthcare is a service industry. It delivers help in medical issues. As in any service, providers collaborate with customers to transform states to better ones. The difference between states is value. The logic of service meets the specifics of health, illness, and healing.

### 5.1.1 Health and Help

In economic activities, the typical line of logic starts with perceived needs. Needs turn into wants as customers become aware of how to fulfill them and get ideas of jobs to be done. Wants turn into demand with purchasing power. The supply side springs into action to meet demand and earn money. Neoclassical economics has it that people know their needs and wants to the extent that they show up as preferences that are rational in the sense that they seek to fulfill some general objective, such as welfare maximization.[1]

The health economics literature defines health as a utility, a primary good that enables functioning. The influential health economist Michael Grossman[2] used the theory of human capital to explain the demand for health and healthcare. Individuals invest in themselves through education, training, and health promotion to increase their earnings and enjoy leisure. In this sense, health is instrumental; it makes something else possible, while illness takes that possibility away. Health can be analyzed as an investment. People also desire health because it makes them feel better, like any consumption. The product of healthcare is health; health services are intermediate products.

In line with Grossman, Michael Porter[3] has claimed, "Patients do not care about care; they care about results." In a sense it is true. While being healthy in enjoyable, being subject to medical treatment is not. The less time, cost, and effort spent on therapies, the better. But it is not the whole truth. Consider this example. When John Lennon was tragically shot in New York in 1986, he was rushed to a hospital and pronounced dead on arrival. Nevertheless, a team of surgeons spent 20 minutes frenetically working on his body. They knew it was fruitless, but it had a meaning. The bereaved and the fans had to be left with the impression that everything possible was done.[4] Patients may not care about care, but others do.

The confessions of a doctor[5] literature is rife with stories of how relatives or superiors force a doctor to do things for critically ill patients that do more harm than good. There is another literature detailing how the medical establishment and pharmaceutical companies invent diseases to create demand for their offerings.[6] Some critics of Western medicine[7] have proclaimed that at times, it does more harm than good. But there is purpose in harm, as there is purpose in war. Medicine is sometimes allowed, even encouraged, to harm, since in the face of death and suffering, people demand something to be done, anything, whether effective or not. Healthcare is a purposeful activity with the tasks to cure illness, treat wounds, prevent diseases, and improve health, but also to provide for the existential questions of randomness, suffering, and death.

The utility and purpose of healthcare needs to be restated. Health services may or may not produce health. But in all cases, help is demanded, and help is what is delivered. The purpose of healthcare is to help people with problems that, for whatever reasons and justifications, are perceived to be medical conditions. Help is what healthcare delivers; health is a consequence that may or may not happen.

If this sounds cynical, so be it. I believe healthcare gets a lot of undue stress from unrealistic demand. On the supply side, there are con men who peddle snake oil as pharmaceuticals and keep their MRI machines spitting out useless images. But why should they be different from marketers in any consumer industry? All big companies have departments where the best and the brightest spend their days figuring out how to hook youngsters on games and create craving for brands and trinkets. Most of their efforts fail because customers are not easily tricked. Marketers have to hit a nerve to succeed. In healthcare, supply can create demand only if the demand side is responsive. Help is always in demand. Bundling it with health creates peculiar demand, not easily understood as rational calculations.

Health has been defined by the downside. If disease stays away, health is what remains. Recently, health has gained an upside, the enhanced, quantified, and purposefully sculpted mind and body. The emerging wellness industry lives on the upside. Health is not only to escape the flames of hell but also to enjoy the social status of the rightful. A conceptual pair similar to illness and health occupied the human mind for millennia. Sin was a deviation from the path of right living and thinking, as staked out by a divine being. Salvation was the solution and eternal bliss the expected outcome.

> Foucault[8] describes in *The Birth of the Clinic* how during the French Revolution there were attempts to establish twin institutions, the church and the hospital. The priest would cater for the soul and the doctor for the body. With secularization, the ideas of sin and salvation have been pushed into the margins of the popular mind. In the highly secular societies of northern Europe, established churches have, by and large, abandoned their task of discussing the afterlife and preparing people for death. Doctors have taken over, or rather have been forced reluctantly into the role of caretakers of the soul. The Swedish psychiatrist David Eberhart[9,10] argues that when the idea of an afterlife wanes, this one life is all there is—then nothingness. People cling to what they have at all cost. Consequently, the pursuit of longevity and avoidance of all health risks, real and imagined, starts to resemble addictive behavior.

Operations management assumes that external demand shows up when it pleases. It is like a force of nature that has to be tamed with segmentation, sorting, buffering, and scheduling and turned into neatly listed work orders. The demand for health services is different. Some demand for help is urgent and can't be rejected. Supply can't always deliver what is demanded. Diagnostics may reveal needs that were not perceived. Demand and supply get intertwined in myriad ways and cannot be easily separated. Figure 5.1 depicts the logic of demand and supply in healthcare.

The starting point is disease and/or a wound, the inevitable variability in the human condition. While external wounds are observable, the ontology of disease is sometimes not clear. Symptoms are both manifestations and interpretations of disease. They are observed, classified, and measured as clinical indicators, such as temperature, blood pressure, or the presence of microbes in the bloodstream. Clinical medicine is a scientific undertaking to establish theories about diseases (ontology) that explain observed symptoms (epistemology), and generate technologies for cures.

Symptoms are generally negative experiences perceived as deviation from the expected normal. As in all services, a discrepancy between the experienced and the expected states creates a need for a state change. Illness creates a need and a social justification to get help. A sick person gets the social status of patient and is not expected to show up at work. The first obligation of somebody ill is to get well and spend whatever resources available. Needs turn into wants and health-seeking behavior when a solution is thought to be available. The sick seek out a doctor. Wants turn into demand when backed up by purchasing power, cash, insurance coverage, or a citizen's right to care. The expectation of being paid, together with the availability of technologies, induces the supply side to invest in resources and capabilities. Demand and supply meet; production can start and help is produced.

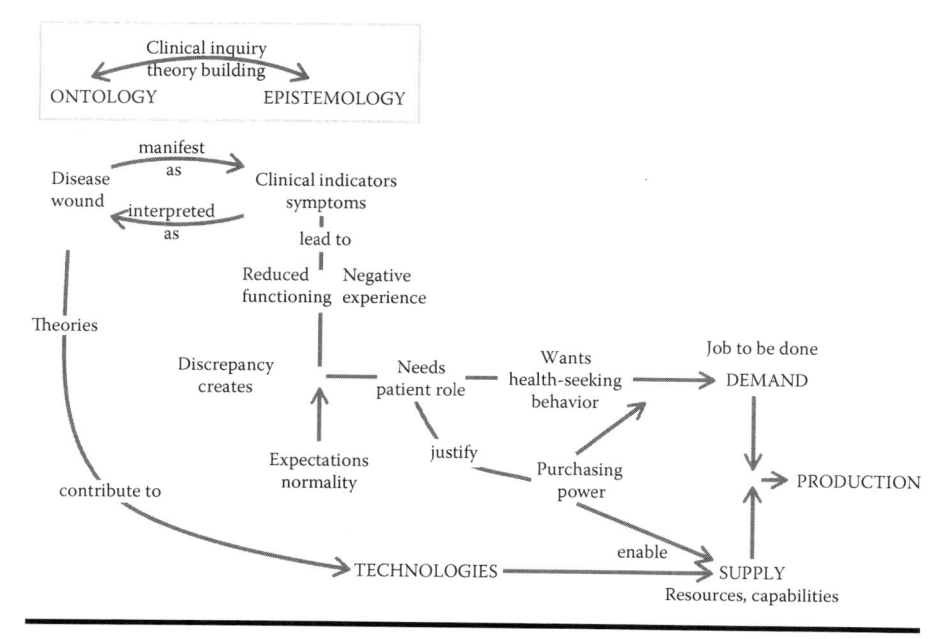

**Figure 5.1   Dynamics of demand and supply in healthcare.**

## 5.1.2  Ontology of Health

It is better to be healthy than ill; pleasure is preferable to pain; functioning beats disability. Common sense says that health is the absence of illness or wound. The simplicity of this definition is akin to the definition of economics. If there were no scarcity, there would be no need for allocative economic decisions. No illness, no health. Health is an issue because it is in short supply; diseases and wounds are unavoidable.

### Complete Health

The World Health Organization (WHO) defined health in its 1948 constitution as "a state of complete physical, mental, and social well-being and not merely the absence of disease or infirmity."[11]

The problem with the WHO definition lies in the word *complete*. It is next to impossible to determine exactly when something related to the human condition is 100% of its theoretical maxim. It implies complete elimination of variability, which, as I have discussed, is a futile task even in controlled factory environments. Complete health can be seen as a Weberian ideal type. Like another example, the perfect market, it does not exist in the real world. It can first be imagined and then used as a benchmark in relation to which the real-world situation is positioned. Replacing *complete* with *sufficient* would be more realistic, but equally difficult.

Complete as an ideal state suggests a maximizing strategy. But as Herbert Simon and his followers within behavioral economics have pointed out, people do not often single-mindedly maximize one utility. Rather, they satisfice, compromise, and optimize through various trade-offs. There are conflicting objectives: health versus the pleasure of gluttony, fitness versus the pain of exercise, and physical safety versus the thrill of adventure. Health and illness are subject to fate and providence, in more modern language, to risk and uncertainty. Best efforts can fail; some diseases are curable and others not. Every clinical intervention carries risks. Healthcare deals with a witches' brew of variability and decay, risk and uncertainty, where not much can be complete.

## Health as Adaptation

The WHO definition of health is no longer fit for purpose given the rise of chronic disease. These are conditions that are far from complete well-being, but to which there is no cure, and worse, to which the alternative would be death. Georges Canguilhem, a French physician, set this out in his 1943 book, *The Normal and the Pathological*.[12] Canguilhem rejected the idea that there were states of health that could be defined statistically or mechanistically. Rather, he saw health as the ability to adapt to one's environment. Health varies for every individual, depending on circumstances. The role of the doctor is to help individuals adapt to their unique prevailing conditions.[13] More recently, Machteld Huber and colleagues[14] have proposed a new definition. Health is the ability to adapt and self-manage in the face of social, physical, and emotional challenges. This is an agency and process-based definition of health.

The WHO definition is about a steady state; the agency-based definition is about state changes, value chains, and streams. It fits neatly with the service-dominant logic (SDL) and the resource integration model of services. SDL states as a foundational premise, "Value is always uniquely and phenomenologically determined by the beneficiary".[15] Operations management people see here an enormous amount of complicated setups.

## Illness as a Social Role

Health is part of the artificial world. Biological facts can't be denied; neither can social, technical, and economic considerations be ignored. Being sick is a social role. Illness is perceived to be involuntary, caused by external or unknown factors working against the sufferer's will. If alcoholism and obesity are defined as diseases, they are no longer consequences of choices. An alcoholic is not an agent but a victim of body chemistry, hereditary dispositions, or social circumstances. Illness can be faked for economic gain.

From man's capability to feel sympathy for others follows that the sick require pity and help. There is a universal legitimate right to do everything to get rid of disease and, to that end, receive help from others. This goes beyond calculative rationality; also, prisoners of war are provided healthcare. However, in welfare societies that believe resources are unlimited, boundless empathy turns into a destructive force. This can be observed in the Swedish paradox. On all measures, the Swedes are among the healthiest people on earth. However, in terms of paid sick leave, they are rampantly ill.[16] Social norms regulating the choice to report in sick have loosened as the system has become more generous and oversight more relaxed. As long as the economy grows and paid sick leave can be afforded, it is not necessarily a problem. If the economy tanks and austerity is in order, the ensuing political problems can be devastating.

## Disease and Trauma

While disease is subject to controversy, wounds are pretty clear. Trauma carries the physiological meaning of physical injury, as well as the psychological meaning of a deeply distressing experience, such as witnessing a mate being blown to pieces by a roadside bomb. Traumatology is the branch of surgery that deals with injured patients, usually on an emergency basis.

All the complex philosophical hand-wringing about ontology of disease, and the normal and the pathological, is absent from traumatology. Trauma victims can be in horrible shape; there is no end to what bizarre things can happen. But philosophically, it is clear. There was an incident. It was an outer force or event, intentional or unintentional. Somebody was shot or stabbed, was hit by a vehicle, was bitten by a snake, drowned, fell from a platform, touched a live wire, or was burn by fire. All wounds are not easily detected; exposure to radiation, for example, and the causes of an accident may remain mysterious. However, the ontology of a wound is no mystery. The machine is broken; it needs to be repaired. Even the most ardent critics of Western medicine, such as Ivan Illich and Michael Foucault, leave traumatology alone. Chinese herbalists turn to Western medicine when they are hurt. Trauma has a logic of its own.

## Mental and Somatic: Mind and Body

A particularly fuzzy issue is the questions of mind–body interactions and the question of mental and somatic illness. While bodily symptoms and wounds can be observed and measured, mental symptoms must be deduced from behavior or self-reporting. Behavioral deviations are more influenced by social norms than physiological ones. In tribal societies, a shaman is highly respected; in modern society, a person with such behaviors would be locked up. There are disturbing problems of the human lifeworld, such as loneliness, alienation, and old age, that could be seen as abnormalities. This blurs the boundaries of the unit of analysis. When it comes to psychiatric problems, the question has been put as follows: Is it proper to think only of the individual? Why can't a family, a community, or for that matter, the whole Western civilization be called sick?

## Units of Analysis

In all definitional endeavors, the unit of analysis must be clarified. For health, the unit of analysis, the basic instance, is an individual human being. An individual can be in various states due to her medical condition. A disease or wound can be located in a specific limb, an organ, or an organ system, such as the cardiovascular or neurological system. Those are relevant units of analysis for clinicians. Nursing has traditionally had the task of looking after the whole person. That is also the appropriate unit of analysis for healthcare operations management; the individual patient is the central flow unit. Families and significant others matter, but odd as it sounds, they can be seen as partners in a supply chain.

Individuals can be counted, summed up, and aggregated according to criteria, such as type and severity of problem, location, gender, and age. That is done in epidemiology, the study of the patterns, causes, and effects of health and disease conditions in defined populations. Thus, epidemiology, and its corresponding technologies, public health and health policy, deals with batches.[17]

There is a crucial difference between the individual and the population, a flow unit and a batch of them. A sick or wounded person needs help, no question about that. But a population should not generate diseases in the first place. This dilemma is accentuated in the debate about antibiotic prescriptions and the threat of superbugs. An individual would benefit from a shot of antibiotic to shorten the inconvenience of tourist diarrhea. For the doctor, the easy way out is to write a prescription. However, on the aggregate this creates an evolutionary opportunity for bacteria to evolve drug-resistant strands and thereby generate harm on the population level. The demand from an individual should under ordinary conditions not be refused. However, the aggregate demand from a population should be managed by all available means, prevention, health literacy, and proactive rather than reactive interventions.

For an individual, getting rid of a life-threatening illness is worth any cost and effort. However, on the population level, cost can't be ignored. Healthcare consumes resources that could be used for other noble purposes, such as education, culture, and security. Health maximization at any cost can't be the purpose of a society that cares about its overall functioning, now and in the future. In other walks of life, markets deal with such trade-offs. But as I will discuss in a moment, markets don't work in healthcare as they do elsewhere. Therefore, healthcare is under chronic economic distress.

The Institute for Healthcare Improvement (IHI) neatly captures the units of analysis as the Triple Aim: the care of individual patients, the aggregated health of populations, and the cost of it all.[18,19]

### 5.1.3 Epistemology of Health

The epistemological question is, how can we know about states? After the states have been defined, they should be measured. Then they can be evaluated by comparing them with an ideal and subjected to experimentation to find dynamics.

### The Normal

Health is like ownership or friendship. As long as you have them, you take them for granted and do not pay attention. Their value becomes painfully clear only after they have been lost. Normality does not prompt action; illness does. Health is considered normal; illness is a deviation from normal. Normal can mean two things. The first is the statistical normal, the modal type or the arithmetic average. Normal is what most people are. The second type is normative, that is, a social conception of what should be the ideal state, what is a good person, and what kind of life she should live. Abnormality is a deviation from something considered normal.

Normality is affected by social, technical, and economic factors. The statistical and the normative tend to go together; the more common a state, the more acceptable it is. Take lactose intolerance as an example. It is a condition where the body cannot easily digest lactose, a type of natural sugar found in milk and dairy products. In most parts of the world, lactose intolerance is normal. In some others, such as northern Europe, where dairy farming has historically been prominent, the majority tolerate lactose. Now, what is normal and what is abnormal? Imagine an isolated community where everybody is clubfooted. From within that community, it would be both statistically and normatively normal. Only an outsider would question the normative, while not being able to deny the statistical. The line between normal and abnormal is drawn differently in different cultures.[20]

Normality is subject to what is technically possible. Before modern medicine, it was considered normal that bad eyesight and stooped frame come with old age. With cataract and spinal surgery, the normal has become abnormal. Technology enhances the ability to observe and measure symptoms and indicators. As the power of microscopes increased, the amount of observable bugs increased as well.

### Deviations from Normal

Deviations from normality, whatever it is, manifest as symptoms. While health is an elusive concept, its opposite is observable. Illness, disease, infirmity, and pain can be experienced, observed, described, and recorded. Therefore, pathology has been easier to study than normality. Symptoms can be measured on three dimensions, clinical indicators, functioning, and experience, as illustrated in Figure 5.2.

The first perspective is *clinical indicators*. Clinical medicine has developed general and specific indicators to describe various states of the body. Some indicators can be established with precision. Blood pressure is measured as, say, 140/70.

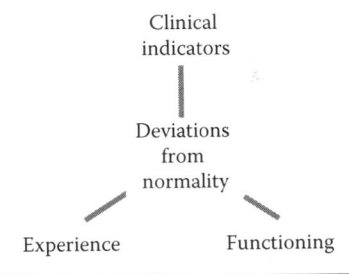

**Figure 5.2  Deviations from normality.**

Whether that means a life on medication, changes in dietary habits, or watchful waiting can be discussed. The numbers can be questioned only in terms of measurement error and bias. A central task in diagnostics is to define the relevant indicators and measure them through observation, anamnesis, or diagnostic devices, such as blood pressure meters, MRI images, or blood chemistry analysis. When the indicators have values, they are evaluated against past or normal values, and contrasted to what is known about the possible condition and its clinical picture.

A second perspective to deviations is functioning. It should not be confused with functionality, which, as I have discussed, is a property of goods and services. As Amartya Sen[21] puts it, functioning is how well people can do what they want and must, and reach for goals and purposes meaningful to them. Functioning depends on resources and capabilities. Health enables people to perform their social roles at work, in the family, and in the community without undue suffering and limitations. Societies develop explicit and implicit conceptions about what a healthy person should be able to do, adjusted for age, sex, and position in society.

A purely normative and instrumental view of health is not satisfactory. When I am down with the flu, my first concern is not the abnormality or that I am missing a day in the office. The experience is an overwhelming sensation of displeasure, discomfort, and pain—in philosophical terms, subjective disutility. The third perspective to health must be experience. It impacts indicators through various mind–body interactions and affects functioning.[22] There are standardized instruments for capturing patient experience, such as the patient-reported experience measures (PREMs).[23]

## Health Systems

These brief observations of a huge topic sum up a major argument of this book. The purpose of health services is to collaborate with patients to address deviations with the purpose of restoring a state back to or close to normal, improve a deteriorated state, arrest decay, help patients to adapt to the inevitable, and proactively prevent adverse events and developments.

Healthcare is a production system that is needed in all societies. It uses all available theories, and then some, to develop technologies, bundle them into production functions, and design production systems. The factory has served as an ideal type and role model. However, the mass production factory is an anomaly in the artificial world, a tiny rock of stability, predictability, and control in a sea of variability and decay. Even there, behind locked doors and air filters, variability can't be fully eliminated. In healthcare, variability is all over the place, even in the fundamental objectives and purposes. This is the human condition; healthcare has to deal with it.

## 5.2 Resources and Capabilities

Resources are not; they become. Resources are a set of assets that have the capability to transform a state into another. In healthcare, resources[24] are classified into three types:

- *Money spent*: Absolutely in total and per individual and as percentage of gross national product (GNP), that is, the ratio of all available means that are allocated to health services
- Staff, doctors, nurses, and others, counted as available labor hours per year
- Facilities, service provision points, hospitals, nursing homes, ward beds, and emergency departments (EDs), that is, capital invested in fixed assets

There are two sides to resources. The qualitative side is what they can do; the quantitative side is how much they can do when exploited to the fullest. These are the questions of outcome effectiveness of therapies, and the output efficiency of production systems.

### 5.2.1 Theory and Therapy

Technology is a purposeful action—to reach a goal using methods based on a conception of how the relevant phenomena work. Technologies are built on theories. New technology evolves from old. When a technology is used, new observations are made and insights found. Therapies, cures, and clinical procedures are technologies founded on biomedical and/or behavioral theories. The history of Western medicine is a story about the interplay of theory and therapy.

> The germ theory of disease got its first impetus from the microscopes built by Galileo and taken further by Leuwenhoek. For two centuries, nobody really knew what these buggers were and what they did. Pasteur and Koch laid the foundations of the theory of microbes as causes of disease. It took still a while before Thomas Lister developed the first technology based on the theory. He performed the first surgical operation

with antiseptics in Edinburgh in 1865. The positive outcomes were quickly recognized. The real breakthrough had to wait until the 1930s and the discovery of penicillin. As often told, the story is that Alexander Fleming forgot to clean some samples before going on vacation. When he got back, he discovered that some molds had feasted on some bacteria. The conclusion was not immediate. It took a while before this discovery was turned into a pharmaceutical. The germ theory did not straightforwardly lead to the invention, but it speeded up the process of seeing the value of this "gift of nature." Indeed, moldy spider webs had been used for centuries to help wounds heal. But without a theory of microorganisms, the ancients had no way to move beyond tinkering.

The limited theoretical base hampers the development of technologies that could be turned into therapies, that is, production functions, and organized into processes that would accomplish the jobs to be done. This is the fact of life in all industries; in healthcare, the discrepancy between what needs to be done and what can be done is larger than elsewhere.

## 5.2.2 Production Function in Healthcare

The production function denotes the mechanisms that cause or contribute to transformations. In manufacturing, the production function is a combination of the natural science–based technologies employed. If causal mechanisms are sufficiently known and the production system can reduce variability, things are under control and results are as expected. In services, the production function is the integration of producers' and customers' resources in collaborative efforts to create economic value by changing states. In healthcare, the production function is healing by applying therapies. It is only partly under control.

### Natural History of Disease

Every wound and disease has its natural history. Nature, when left to its own devices, heals, kills, or leaves a cripple. There are situations where the best course of action is to do nothing but watch. The natural history is the base case against which medical therapies are contrasted—what happens if nothing is done but providing rest, comfort, fresh air, sanitation, and nutrition to assist nature. The natural history of disease resembles the production function in agriculture. If organisms are provided a beneficial environment, they can heal themselves and grow.

### Placebo and Nocebo Effects

A second aspect of the production function is that healing can happen without a directly known or controllable reason that is not equal to the natural history. This is called the placebo effect. The word comes from Latin and literally means "I shall/I will please, soothe, or gratify." The placebo effect is a change in a patient's illness attributable to the symbolic import of the treatment rather than a specific pharmacologic or physiologic property.[25] Its opposite is the nocebo effect. A symbolic import, such as a look-alike doll penetrated by needles, can make a victim of voodoo lie down and die.[26]

The placebo effect is a great headache for the experimental method in medical sciences. Any possible therapeutic gain must be tested in order to isolate it from the placebo effect. In an unbiased experiment, the placebo effect equals the differences in outcome between a test group receiving the experimental treatment, a placebo-treated group that gets look-alike but ineffective treatment, and an untreated group. For a new cure to be considered effective, it must show significantly better results than the placebo.

The placebo and the nocebo effects are most likely mind–body interactions on a very miniscule level. They are within a black box that the gaze of biomedical sciences has not yet been able to penetrate. As with any black box, only inputs and outputs can be observed.

The greatest success in placebo occurs in the treatment of chronic painful conditions with no observable disease, such as headaches, backaches, and irritable bowel syndrome, where stress has a role and symptoms fluctuate. The effect is less prominent if outcomes are binary (yes or no) or objectively measurable indicators.

A placebo administered by a doctor appears to be more powerful than that by a nurse or a clerk. A placebo sent by mail devoid of human interaction is the least effective. The more frequently the patient visits the doctor, the greater the placebo effect. The more attention paid to symptoms during the first visit, the more satisfactory the result. An injection is more powerful than a pill; a large pill is more effective than a small pill, but a very small pill is better than a regular-sized one. Failure to take the placebo pill lessens the effect. While a placebo can reduce symptoms and make people feel better, there is little proof that it alters the disease process. People react differently in different situations. On any occasion, it is impossible to predict who is a placebo responder and who is not.

The placebo effect apparently resides in and is activated by the patient–healer interactions. The relationship must be considered an essential part of the production function. Because the mechanisms are not sufficiently known, there are no precise technologies. However, making a person feel better and helping her find meaning in the predicament are important accomplishments, even if the disease is unchecked.[27] Using the terminology of the SDL, it can be said that healing is cocreation where subtle social and mind–body interactions show up as value at the biological and experiential levels.

## Clinical Interventions: Theory-based Therapies

Clinical interventions are based on conceptions of the ontology of the problem, observations of symptoms and effects, and ideas of mechanisms and ways to manipulate them.

A basic type of intervention is pharmaceutical. Some substances are inserted in the human body for therapeutic effect. Before the advent of modern medicine, the ancients observed effects of various herbs on various conditions and developed remedies without knowledge of mechanisms. Modern pharmacology is based on the understanding of biochemical mechanisms involved in, for example, how cancer cells reproduce. If a molecule to interfere with such mechanisms can be developed, a therapeutic effect can be expected.

A second type is surgery. An opening is cut into the human body. Something is extracted, inserted, or repaired. A third type is physical or thermal manipulation, such as physiotherapy, massage, stretching, and hot and cold baths. A further type is radiation, where rays are concentrated on tumors with the intention to kill some cells.

Clinical interventions can have the intended effect, be without effect, or cause harm. A risk is taken when a scalpel penetrates human skin, or constructed molecules are inserted into the body. The good and the bad may be simultaneously present; the net effect can be on the upside or the downside.

## Functional Medicine

A stream of thinking called functional medicine has emerged from recent advances in genetics and understanding the role of gut microbes.[28] It is different enough to be considered a fourth aspect of the production function. The basic principles are, first, that genes do not predetermine health. Epigenetics is a research area that looks into how patterns of health and illness are determined by how families of genes are expressed.[29] Environmental factors, such as lifestyle, diet, exercise, stress, and pollutants, influence the expression. Second, chronic illness is a result of an imbalance in one or several physiological processes. The source does not reside in a single organ system but in interactions between several such systems. Therefore, attempts to treat them one by one will not necessary help. Imbalances derive from the interactions between genes and environment and alter functions, which lead to symptoms. Changes in diet and exercise can bring physiological processes back into balance. Third, each person's physiological response to lifestyle and dietary and environmental factors is unique to his or her genetic makeup and personal history.

Without delving any deeper, it is apparent that functional medicine is based on different theories, derives different technologies, and employs different production functions than mainstream medicine.

## The Production Function Is a Compound

The production function in healthcare is like a four-cylinder engine. The healing effect, or the treatment benefit, is a compound of the natural history of illness, the placebo effect, the therapeutic gain of clinical interventions and/or lifestyle changes. As illustrated in Figure 5.3, all four can be positive or negative, that is,

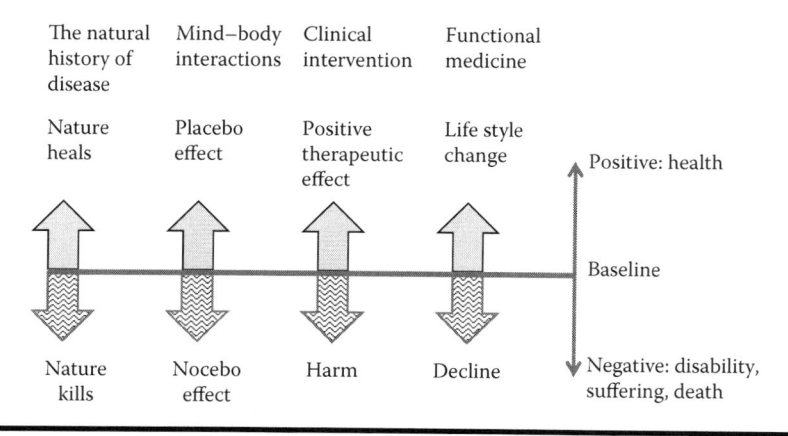

**Figure 5.3   Production functions of healthcare.**

lead to improvement or deterioration in relation to a baseline, the status before the onset of a medical issue. The production function of healthcare implies that the area under explicit control is limited. When there is no theory, intuition must rule. Intuition is a collection of chunks of logic that are not systematically connected under a master logic.

While the body and its interactions with the mind and other people are still mysteries, there is reason to believe that in due course, the scientific gaze will penetrate and illuminate the black box layer by layer. This has happened and will continue as evidence accumulates.

## Evidence-based Medicine

In contrast to intuitive medicine, evidence-based medicine means the conscious, explicit, and judicious use of the current best evidence from clinical research in making decisions about the care of individual patients.

Decades of research by John Vennberg[30] and others demonstrate that in the United States, about one-third of doctors' decisions are based on solid research evidence or are obvious, such as cleaning and stitching a wound. The second third is judgment based on patients' preferences, and the last third is supply-driven practice. If there is an MRI scanner, use it!

The evidence-based movement has given rise to calls that taxpayers' money should be directed only to cures that are supported by proof of efficacy, while those who want something else should pay out-of-pocket. Given the enormous waste associated with supply-driven medicine, there is some sense in it.[31] However, lack of proof of efficacy does not yet prove lack of efficacy. Limiting healthcare to clinical interventions supported by evidence collected by approved scientific methods would create myopia and complicate clinical decision-making. Evidence-based medicine is not necessarily precise on the individual level. Much of the evidence is gathered from sampled populations and results that are statistically significant with a margin of error. Even if the statistical evidence is clear, there can be no absolute certainty that an approved cure will be effective for an individual. Treatment is developed for the average person, with less consideration for the variability within patient populations.

Evidence-based medicine is developing in several directions. Precision medicine is an emerging approach for disease treatment and prevention that takes into account individual variability in genes, environment, and lifestyle.[32] Although the term *precision medicine* is relatively new, the concept has been a part of healthcare for many years. For example, a person who needs a blood transfusion is not given blood from a randomly selected donor; instead, the donor's blood type is matched to that of the recipient to reduce the risk of complications. While doctors have traditionally treated patients as individuals as to their personal and medical history and the ways they deal with their problems, advances in genetics turn the patient into a biological individual. While the practical applications are still years, if not decades, away, they carry the potential to significantly change the production function in healthcare.

Biomedicine is most successful in dealing with acute diseases with a known cause; that is, the phenomenon (ontology) is sufficiently understood, its existence and state can be known (epistemology), its effects and reactions are mapped (dynamics), and precise technologies can be deployed. The best examples are cataract and knee and hip joint replacement surgery. In these, the causes are the dimming of the eye lens with old age and the wear on joint cartilages resulting in painful bone-to-bone connects. Diagnosis is precise, and the procedure is routine. This is elective precision medicine.

Diagnostic and procedural precision plays out differently in areas where the intervention does not require anesthetics and a scalpel. If the setup can be formatted precisely, the diagnosis can be established with accuracy, and a patient can self-administer the cure, medicine turns into self-service or, more precisely, assisted self-care within supporting networks.

## Production Function and Processing

The fuzziness of the production function has profound implications on operations management approaches to healthcare. As I have discussed in Chapter 3, production management is founded on the premise that processing, the transformations done at a workstation, is stable and predictable due to the physics employed. Processing time is the variable that is expected to have the least variation, assuming that small quality is under control. Other issues, such as utilization, inventories, and cycle time, can vary and be subject to management action and trade-offs. Large parts of health service production lack the predictability of processing, the basic anchor of production systems.

The production function is a compound of the technologies used to accomplish transformations. The four types in healthcare require different production systems. The natural history of disease can be supported, like growing an apple tree. A placebo requires personal relationships. Interventions take tools and techniques. The patient enacts lifestyle changes as assisted self-service. The production functions and technologies overlap and are not clearly separable. Even when evidence-based precision procedures are performed, the natural history and the placebo effect are at work and some physiological processes have to be dealt with through lifestyle adjustments. Healthcare is a multiverse with many simultaneous things with fuzzy borders.

## 5.3 Production Systems in Healthcare

Production systems are founded on division of labor, specialization, and standardization to get the pieces right, then on integration and coordination to get them together. A production system is a spatiotemporal arrangement of the production function. Examinations, conversations, interventions, and relationship building happen at a location at a time. The time–location constraint can be amended by information and communication technologies (ICT). For now, focus is on the original type of care where a patient and a healer both must be at a specific place at a specific time for collaboration to take place.

Health services follow the basic logic of production. A workstation performs tasks that are set up to meet the requirements of a flow unit, which is processed and handed over to the next step to connect as a flow and accumulate inventories, eventually resulting in throughput. The flow can be organized in various architectures, projects, job shops, disconnected lines, connected lines, and continuous flows. Figure 3.3 is relabeled as Figure 5.4.

In health services, workstations are medical resources organized as stationary production units, such as doctor's offices, nursing stations, labs, and operating rooms (ORs), as well as mobile units, such as doctors making rounds checking on inpatients, the family doctor making house calls, or the ambulance providing help at a site of need. The patient is the flow unit, which can split into one or several cases. Diagnostics and the design of a patient journey through a clinical pathway are setup and routing. Processing is akin to that in services, a combination of steps and flows. Clinical interventions are discrete steps where interventions, such as medication, surgical procedures, and advice, are administered. The patient's medical condition is a continuous flow of the time it takes for wounds to heal and medication to take effect. Handovers require documentation, referrals, and prescriptions stored in patient information systems. A patient may spend time as inventory (patient in process [PIP]), which is managed as a buffer. Throughput is the volume of output, completed cases per a time unit, day, week, month, or year. Outputs result in outcomes in various ways.

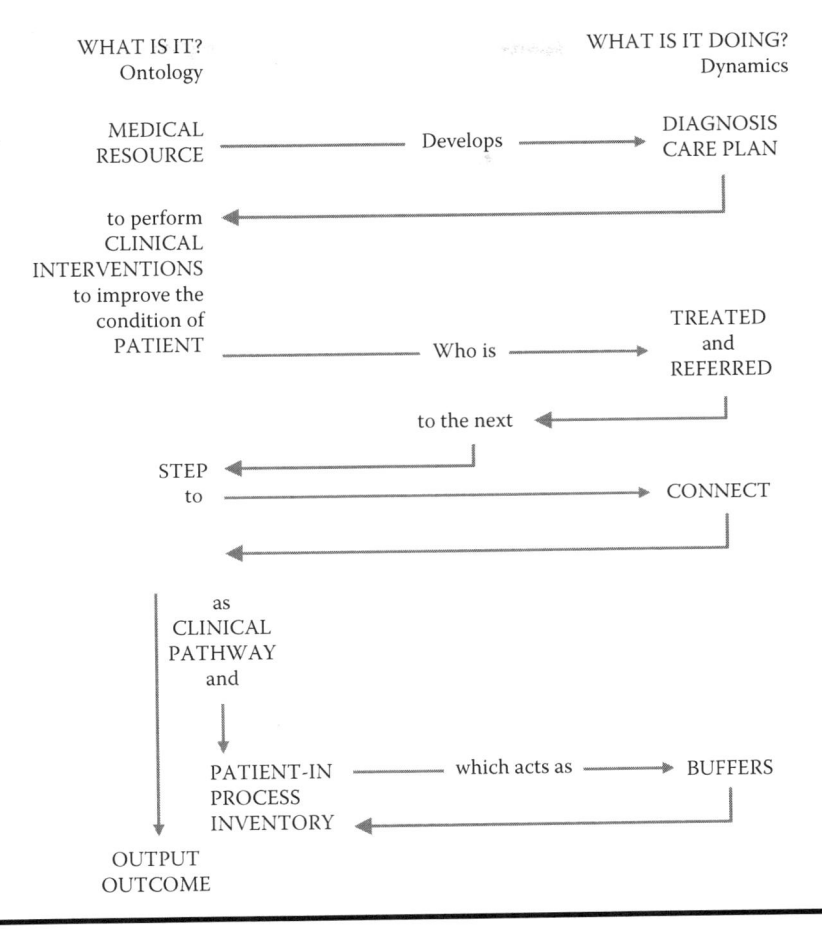

**Figure 5.4    Elements of health service production systems.**

## 5.3.1 Patient as Flow Unit

Healthcare processes are service processes where the flow unit is a person, her property, and/or her case.

### Person, Property, and Case

A patient is a person in an unpleasant state that is interpreted as medical. It manifests as deviations from normal clinical indicators, reduced functionality, and experiences of pain or anxiety. A healer can approach a patient in three ways. The patient can be seen as a person with "whole-person needs,"[33] a lifeworld that has been disrupted by adverse events. If the problem can be clearly located in an organ (heart), or an organ system (cardiovascular), the organ can be seen as the property of a person. The healer can then be like an auto mechanic: receive and order from the owner with indications of the problem, and then be left to work on the car as a piece of machinery. Radiologists and pathologists deal with information about the medical problem without meeting the person. For them, the patient is a case.

Would you like to be treated as a person or as a case? Patient-centric medicine[34] seeks to bring all relevant aspects into the healing relationship. Again, whether this is preferable depends on the situation. At one extreme is nursing home care at the end of life, which clearly calls for consideration of all relevant aspects. At the other extreme are minor nonurgent issues, such as dental cavities. Do it quickly, professionally, and with minimal pain; be polite and considerate, but treat me as a case and stay out of my life.

## Adherence

As a service customer, the patient is an adaptive agent. The patient may or may not follow instructions, or venture to do something that may disrupt the service. This is a phenomenon called compliance to care. More recently, the term *adherence* has come into use to reflect observations that the problem is broader than mere disobedience. Patients can have several reasons not to follow their doctor's orders. The WHO estimates that only about 50% of patients with chronic diseases follow treatment recommendations.[35] The reasons seem to be the complexity of modern medication regimes, the lack of perceivable treatment benefits, side effects, and the cost of prescription medicine. Efforts to improve adherence have been simplifying medication packaging, medication reminders, and patient education. It is still unclear how adherence can consistently be improved in order to promote clinically important effects.

## Patient Choice

Patients are not only "customers in careland"[36] who rationally choose, pay after running through cost–benefit calculations, and maximize economic value. Patients are also service customers who pay effort, collaborate with caregivers, and have to consider collective and long-term benefits. When suffering from diseases or risks, patients are physically and mentally fragile. Attractiveness is a central condition of choice. But health services as such are unattractive; they may cause pain and even harm. Choosing something unattractive where the best option may be that something that could happen does not happen is not easily associated with free choice in a free market.

Patients can make four types of choices[37]: choice of treatment (what), choice of individual health professional (who), choice of which provider (where), and choice of appointment time and date (when). Choosing who, where, and when in nonurgent situations can be assumed to fall under the same mental calculations as in any professional services. What treatment to choose is the tricky issue that runs into the problem of information asymmetry. I return to it later in this chapter.

Patient choice modeling has followed the rational choice theory,[38] amended by the notion of bounded rationality. The advances of behavioral economics have effectively punctuated the belief in the rational calculative capabilities of isolated individuals. Choices are affected not only by perceived benefits but also with contexts and situations, and moral considerations of justice, solidarity, and authority.[39] Consequently, a conceptual construct called shared decision-making (SDM) has gained popularity. Its essential elements are recognizing and acknowledging that a decision is required, knowing and understanding the best available evidence, and incorporating the patient's values and preferences into the decision.[40] In other words, SDM acknowledges that there are contexts in which patients enter as instances and bargaining ensues to create a shared understanding of the situation in terms of what needs to be done and what can be done.

SDM has led to the development of behavioral technologies known as patient decision aids (PtDAs).[41] They are standardized, evidence-based tools designed to provide information about the available options, empower patients to actively participate, assist patients in personalizing this information, help patients clarify their values and preferences, structure the decision process, and ultimately facilitate an informed, deliberate, values-based, preference-sensitive choice. The PtDAs, however, have problems dealing with the variability of multidimensional contexts and preferences.

## 5.3.2 Diagnosis as Setup

Standard processes where one setup is followed by identical repetition of steps are rarely used in personal services. Where they are, such as in the military, they are not services, but rather administrative acts that do not ask for collaboration, only compliance. In formatted and routine processes, the flow and each step require setups.

In healthcare, setup is done as in services, as illustrated earlier in Figure 4.6. A person seeking care (instance) is assessed to determine the initial demand–supply constellation: what needs to be done and what can be done. The architecture of the caregiving organization (context) determines what can be done. As discussed earlier, architectures are fixed allocations of resources and capabilities. An ED has the architecture for responding to emergencies; a dentist's office has the architecture to deal with dental problems. If demand does not fit the supply architecture, help must be sought elsewhere.

If the assessment produces a go, the person gets the social role of a patient. In obvious cases, such as bleeding accident victims, the assessment happens in a flash. If the patient is a repeat customer, the assessment is just about confirming identity and schedule. For others, the setup takes some effort.

In healthcare, setup is diagnosis and care plan. The word *diagnosis* comes from classical Greek. *Dia* means "through" or "transparent"; *gnosis* means "knowledge."

Diagnostics is to peek into a black box in order to acquire knowledge about states and their causes. Diagnosis is used in many engineering tasks, such as system analysis, complex event processing, and fault analysis. In healthcare, diagnosis is the identification of a medical condition by taking the anamnesis, that is, the patient's story; systematic analysis of the background; examination of signs and symptoms; and evaluation of test results and images. A diagnosis is typically formalized and given a code following the International Classification of Diseases, 10th revision (ICD-10) disease classification system. The code is the key to the accumulated body of medical knowledge. The patient case as a single instance is placed in the context of known and documented similar cases. Diagnosis is the basis of prognosis, *pro* meaning projecting forward to estimate a future state.

Diagnosis produces knowledge about what to do. With diagnosis and prognosis at hand, doctors consult memory, the knowledge base, colleagues, or computerized decision aids, and design care plans. Therapies (processing) are selected and arranged as steps that are supposed to connect as flows. A care plan is a master setup including routing, scheduling, and allocation. Each step requires a setup that considers both the master setup and the information that comes with the handover; what was done, did it go as planned, and are there any changes or new developments that require modifications? Once a care plan has been established, it equals a production schedule and the specifications of small quality. At times, the specifications are not correct, or the patient's status changes unexpectedly. The initial specifications are no longer valid and need to be adjusted.

Diagnosis is the cognitive foundation of care. It equals the product technology in manufacturing and services. Diagnoses can be clear or unclear, based on intuition or evidence, statistical or precise. A strep throat is identified, the cause is known to be a bacterial infection, and the cure is rest or antibiotics. At the other extreme, a diagnostic process can be explorative, a long struggle of unearthing information, setting up hypotheses to be confirmed or disconfirmed through experimentation. The plan that sets the patient out on a journey across workstations can follow a standard map and route that have been used many times before, or be a patient-specific exploration. In such cases, the map is not complete at the start. It has white spots, which like old navigational charts have the writing "sea monsters here"; risks and uncertainty are expected. In other words, each patient journey has a map depicting the logic flow of the case. The accuracy and precision of the map are variables that distinguish the predictable from the unpredictable.

## 5.3.3 Handovers

Much of the reported poor experiences with health services, including my own, come back to handovers. In production, a handover happens when a workstation hands over a partly processed flow unit to the next station, to a work-in-process (WIP) inventory, or to a finished goods inventory. Even when a flow unit is an identical copy of a prototype, it requires identification, at a minimum the batch to which it belongs. If flow units are individuals, handovers contain essential information for setups.

In health services, handovers come in two basic types. Internal handovers happen within an organization unit where doctors have the administrative power to ask juniors and nurses to dress a wound or administer medication. When working shifts at a hospital ward change, the outgoing team reports and hands over the ward to the incoming team. A referral is an external handover. A doctor determines that a patient needs something that she or her team can't provide. The referral is a request to another unit. A prescription for medication is a purchase order that authorizes a patient to buy pharmaceuticals that are not sold over the counter. A patient may receive advice and instructions. The case is handed over from the professionals to the patient or relatives for self-service.

The main tool for handover management is the patient health record. It is a document that details and accumulates all relevant medical information of a patient. As many medical issues are path dependent and history matters, the availability of medical records in a central issue. Documenting a patient's condition, indicators, and interventions in a medical record is akin to a handover with no specified recipient. There are several types of health information systems (HIOs), patient care information systems (PCISs), electronic health records (EHRs), and personal health records (PHRs). For details, see the literature on healthcare informatics.[42]

### 5.3.4 Patient in Inventory

A patient, as any flow unit, can be processed or wait to be processed. In healthcare, the equivalent of WIP is PIP.[43]

#### Patient in Process

In manufacturing, WIP is the inventory of flow units between the start and end points of a product routing. Cycle time is the time a flow unit spends as WIP. PIP shares characteristics with WIP, but some clarifications must be made.

First, in health services, the patient journey starts when a gatekeeper says go and a person is accepted as a patient. It ends when the case is closed and no further action is scheduled. The medical problem may have started much earlier and may continue after the case is closed. The episode of illness is thereby the broader context within which PIP resides. As long as a person is PIP, she is part of the health service system.

Second, a person may simultaneously have several medical problems and/ or be a patient at several caregivers. One person can have several PIP statuses simultaneously.

Third, in manufacturing WIP is primarily a cost driver. Inventory binds capital, there are costs associated with storage and retrieval, and high inventory levels clutter the production layout. In perishable products, there are additional costs of decay and obsolesce. In services, waiting time has an impact on customer experience. If queues are too long, customers will turn away. For a patient, the entire time spent in the healthcare system is a cost due to the loss of missed opportunity and potential earnings, as well as the cost of inconvenience and anxiety.

Fourth, in manufacturing a flow unit is either processed or waiting to be processed. In services, a customer's status is not black or white; she can be in several states, such as a hotel guest engaging with the front office in a service encounter, making use of hotel facilities on her own, or doing something that the service makes possible.

As I have discussed, the distinction between value-adding and non-value-adding time is not useful. The relevant distinction is between the time that is determined by the production function (processing) and the time that is subject to managerial arrangements. In healthcare, there is the distinction between tasks that are counted as output (what was done to a patient and billable items) and things that contribute, positively or negatively, to the outcome (what happened to a patient).

Fifth, in mass manufacturing setup time is considered a necessary evil that should be reduced. One setup should be followed by an optimal number of repetitions. In personal services, this approach works only in some subprocesses where resources are prepared or cases are processed. In healthcare, setup is the making of a diagnosis and a care plan. This equals engineering in manufacturing, the adjustment of a product design to the needs of a customer or a segment of them. In complex medical cases, setup is akin to research and development (R&D).

## Types of Time

A patient in process can spend time in many ways, as depicted in Figure 5.5. A distinction can be made between active time, when the service producer is engaging resources and accumulating costs, and passive time, when patients are

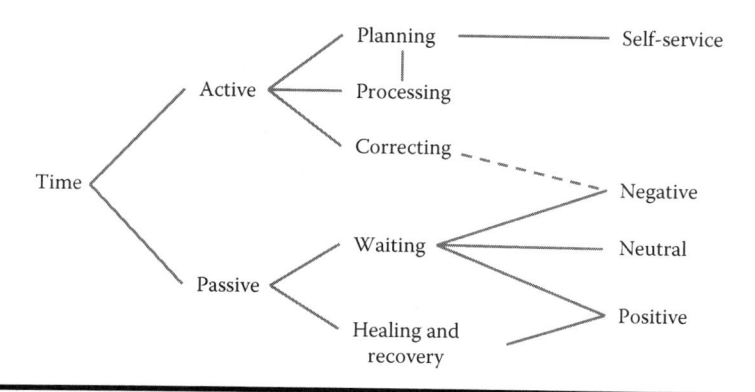

**Figure 5.5  PIP time types.**

waiting and biological processes have their course. Another distinction can be made between time that is related to the production function (active and passive processing) and time that is subject to managerial action, integration, and coordination.

The time related to the production function is

- Active planning, including collecting data and making diagnostics, and care planning (master setup, routing, and scheduling), including advice to patients for self-service.
- Active processing as clinical interventions (steps).
- Passive care time as a wound heals or medication takes effect under observation. This can also be time on life support in an intensive care unit (ICU) or recovery at a postanesthesia care unit (PACU).
- Self-service, such as taking medication, following an exercise regime or self-monitoring the condition.

A strict Lean approach would consider clinical interventions the only value-adding activity. The others would be waste. In services, this is a misleading. Diagnostics is service design; like product engineering and R&D, it can by no means be considered waste. The difference, as discussed before, is that processing is constrained by technology, while planning and coordination are managerial tasks that can be performed with variable efficacy.

The second type is time that is independent of the production function and manageable issues:

- Passive waiting time at home for a scheduled appointment
- Passive waiting time within a facility for a late appointment or procedure
- Passive waiting time within a facility as an unscheduled drop-in patient
- Time spent correcting avoidable errors, that is, the time cost of poor quality

Passive waiting is time when nothing happens; the caregiver is not engaged or in contact with the patient. It can overlap with passive care time, it can be neutral in terms of the medical condition, or it can be negative if the condition gets worse or if clinical information becomes obsolete and tests have to be redone.

## Queuing

Operations research has spent considerable effort in understanding the phenomenon of queuing. A queue is the result of demand–supply mismatch; the arrival rate of flow units is larger than the capacity of a process. Collaborative services can't be produced and placed in inventory. If a service provider can't maintain excess capacity, the only remaining buffer is time, a queue of customers waiting. Queue management is an optimization problem: patient waiting time should be minimized and staff utilization should be maximized.[44] The basic terms and principles are depicted in Figure 5.6.

The start is random, unsorted demand. It can be split into two types, appointments (on schedule, waiting list, and planned work) and walk-in demand (unplanned work). Before entering a caregiver's facilities, a patient is in an external queue and may pass that time as she pleases. At the caregiver, a walk-in patient first meets a gatekeeper. In EDs, the gatekeeper is a specially assigned person who performs the triage, that is, sorts the incoming patients in groups by urgency. In other settings, such as general practitioners' offices, there are no specific gatekeepers; the gatekeeping task is handled in many subtle ways.

The caregiver is described as one or several workstations, staff that can process a case. In processes with several steps, the queue problem appears between every step.

Once inside, the patient without an appointment is in an internal queue in a waiting area. The internal queue can be managed in many ways, known as queue discipline. A common example is first in, first out (FIFO); patients are served in their order of arrival. If the internal waiting time is too long, some patients may leave without being seen (LWBS).[45] Since patients are waiting, a server can pick patients from the queue without delay. The queue is thus a buffer inventory of flow units waiting to be processed.

The FIFO discipline can be disturbed by urgent arrivals. A way to deal with it is to assign all patients a priority number. The queue discipline would then be that patients are treated in the order of urgency. This would lead to very long waiting times for low or medium urgencies. This can be amended by the shortest service time (SST) queue discipline. Patients that can be expected to be processed quickly are seen first, while the longer cases wait. This, however, works only if the service times can be estimated and new entrants do not disturb the order. Another way is to reserve specific workstations or servers for the urgent cases, that is, have different

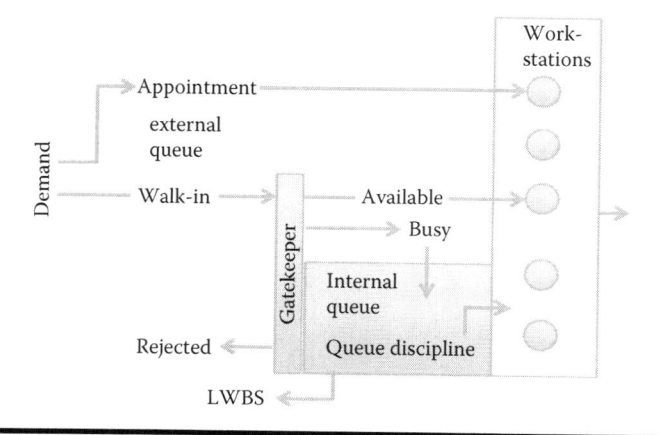

**Figure 5.6   Elements of queuing. Left without being seen (LWBS).**

flows to different levels of urgency. This in turn is possible only in large units where resources can be grouped.

Planned work is founded on appointments. Each patient is given a start time and a slot. This is akin to the takt time used in manufacturing; a production step has to be done within a given time limit. Appointments are scheduled for a set duration, say 20 minutes, so that a doctor can see about 20 patients during an 8-hour shift, given the need for scheduled breaks. Here variability is a problem. For some patients, 10 minutes is quite enough, and the workstation would be idling. For others, 30 minutes would suffice to ask, say, and do all that is needed. But there is a line of people behind the door anxiously insisting to be seen at the promised time. If the case is not urgent, the patient is asked to leave and come back another time, that is, sent to an external PIP inventory. If patient needs can be estimated, variable slot time, say 10, 20, or 30 minutes, can be used. Another way is to calculate the average time per patient, say 15 minutes. Then four patients can be scheduled per hour. Each is told to show up by the hour. The four are then processes following the FIFO discipline, and the variability is assumed to even out.

Planned and unplanned work can be mixed, but it requires vigilant daily management. If the appointment books are full and capacity utilization is high, emergencies have to go elsewhere or jump the queue, which creates variability and a continuous sense of disorder. A carve-out scheduling system, similar to the yield management system used by airlines, can be used. The average urgent demand is estimated and slots in the schedule are left open for them. If no emergencies show up, the workstation picks the next patient from the queue.

Whichever way is chosen, trade-offs must be made. If emergencies are not accepted at general-purpose clinics, choice is limited and demand concentrates to EDs, which will then have a lot of unsubstantiated demand. If times are allocated strictly by the minute, care events are fragmented to several visits or workstations are idle.

Queue management is a wicked problem with no silver bullet solution. Most generally, the solutions come in three forms.[46] First, the capacity and utilization of the servers can be increased; that is, reduce processing time and idle time. Second, the flow can be improved through scheduling, formatted setup, automatic handovers, and flexible slot times. Third, demand and arrivals can be managed in various ways to improve demand–supply matching. Patients can be directed to self-select into appropriate service channels, gatekeeping can be made more accurate, and supply can be adjusted to predictable fluctuations in demand.

### 5.3.5 Output and Outcome

A consequence of variability, decay, and the imperfections of production functions is that health services produce both outputs and outcomes. The former is the accomplished task; the latter is the result. Output signifies that help has been provided, outcome that health has been achieved. In systems with predictable production functions and statistical control, the two are virtually equal; in systems with significant variability, they drift apart.

## Output

Output signifies that something was done. Output is task accomplishment, the fact that a patient has been seen, given a diagnosis, and processed. Output is what the caregiver does. For a patient, output accumulates into the sum total of the things done during a care episode. For a provider, each output takes time and carries cost that add up to production cost. Outputs sum up as throughput volume, the number of patients processed during a period of time. Thereby, outputs can be analyzed as in any production system.

Outputs have several characteristics by which they can be identified, measured, and evaluated. Each output happens in time; it has a start point, an end point, and duration in between. It happens in a location with geospatial coordinates, unless it is in cyberspace. Costs are calculable as resource consumption per resource type, such as doctor's, nurse's, and facility time, as well as the supplies consumed. In health finance, an output is a billable item. Outputs typically, but not always, have *ex ante* specifications; they follow a template, script, or clinical practice. An output can be measured using the same variables used to specify it; did the syringe find the vein on the first attempt, were disinfectants applied properly, and were the readings from the lab analysis recorded properly? Outputs are classified and identified by codes. They are the equivalent to the stock-keeping unit (SKU) in logistics and inventory management.

## Outcome

Outcome is what happens to a patient's medical condition in terms of clinical indicators, functioning, and experience. It evolves step-by-step and constitutes the medical state when everything has been said and done: full recovery, death, or anything in between.

Outcomes are the results that matter. An ideal outcome, full recovery and continuous health, can be envisioned, but it is not always a realistic objective. Good enough may be all there is to go for. Thus, the experience part of outcome is subject to expectations; unrealistic goals produce disappointments and the service paradox.

The difference between output and outcome is a dry technical way to express the mysteries of health. Many things can lead to outcomes. The clinical intervention may or may not be the definitive change agent. It can also be nature following its course, the placebo effect, or a new lifestyle. Social circumstances can play a role. Outcomes are partly results of purposeful action, and partly they just happen. As Avensis Donabedian,[47] the first authority on healthcare quality, put it,

> Because a multitude of factors influence outcome, it is not possible to know for certain, even after extensive adjustments for differences in case mix are made, the extent to which an observed outcome is attributable to an antecedent process of care.

The difference between output and outcome is a fundamental chunk of logic in healthcare. Caregivers' varying resources, capabilities, skills, and morale explain part of the variation in outcomes. Beyond that, the problem lies at the very root of healthcare as a purposeful activity: the still insufficient theories about the human body and diseases, the lack of precision in technologies, the varieties in capabilities and collaboration, the risks and uncertainties in the human condition, and on the patient side, the variety in adherence and expectations. The differences in output and outcome are summarized in Table 5.1.

## Outcome Stream

The three concepts, patient as a flow unit, output as task accomplishment, and outcome as state change, combine into a conceptual construct, the outcome stream.

**Table 5.1  Outputs and Outcomes in Healthcare**

|  |  | *Output* | *Outcome* |
|---|---|---|---|
| Ontology |  | What is done to a patient (help) | What happens to a patient (health) |
|  |  | Tasks, processing | State |
|  |  | Steps | Outcome stream |
| Epistemology |  | Time, location, cost, type, *small q* | Clinical indicators, functioning, experience, *big Q* |
|  |  | Measurable after completion | Measurable at various time intervals |
|  |  | Measurable in positive numbers; outputs accumulate monotonously | Measurable in positive and negative numbers; outcomes can vary in time |
| Dynamics |  | Subject to caregivers' resources and capabilities | Subject to the production function, patient's medical history, collaboration, and expectations |

It is the healthcare equivalent of the value chain in manufacturing, and the value stream is services.

Processes in assembly manufacturing are describes as steps, flows, and inventories. The process modeling and improvement tools of Lean focus on what the provider is doing, with the assumption that the flow unit reacts in a predictable way following the laws of physics. The flow unit has no will of its own. Value is added step-by-step, less some *muda*.

In service processes, the production steps are equal to the service encounters or contact points where the customer and the producer meet and an output is accomplished. The provider has support and preparation processes going on in the back office behind the line of visibility. The value stream is the customer experience that runs in the background with varying intensity and turns into an experienced outcome.

Figure 5.7 is an elaboration of Figure 4.12. As all personal services, healthcare is a combination of steps and journeys, chains and streams. It aims at an outcome, a cure that ends the problem. The role of the flow is accentuated. For patients, the medical problem does not go away between visits. Anxiety is always there; pain may be getting worse as time passes. In chronic conditions, there is no end; therefore, the outcome is the development of the health status, to arrest a natural decline, relieve suffering, and assist functioning. In Figure 5.7, the outcome stream consists of the three epistemological layers: the observable and measurable clinical indicators, the ability to function, and the experiences of the patient. These layers can change together or separately.

> Anna feels fine but dutifully goes to her medical checkup. The doctor measures her blood pressure and finds it is elevated slightly above the norm. The indicator is recorded in her journal. To Anna, this is slightly disturbing; it affects the experience layer only momentarily. Otherwise, the only change is with a pair of numbers on her record.
>
> Bob wakes up with a blistering headache that does not go away. He finds it hard to concentrate and gets mightily irritated. The doc can't find anything that would indicate a problem; it is all in his head. Functioning is impaired and the experience is rotten, but nothing shows up at the indicator layer.
>
> Cecilia has a heart attack and is taken to the ED. All relevant indicators are red. She is incapacitated and feels really bad. All the layers shout the same message.

Figure 5.7 combines the elements. Starting from the bottom, the producer has a production process or, more exactly, the capability to activate steps as needed. There are back-office support and prepared resources on standby.

The patient episode describes health behavior, what a patient does for a health issue. That may include various things, such as resting, following an exercise regime,

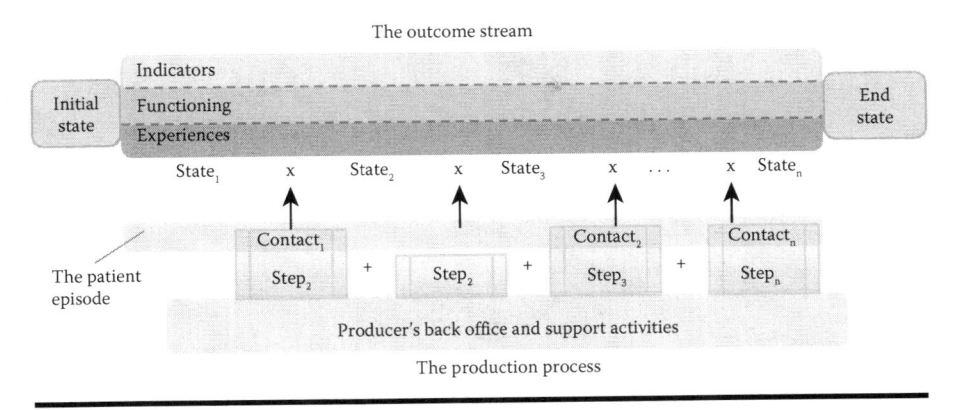

**Figure 5.7 Outcome stream and production process.**

taking medication, and self-monitoring. The outcome stream is a patient's health condition as a state that at any point in time can be described with indicators, functioning, and experience.

When the patient and the service provider meet, there is contact. From the producer's perspective, that is a step in a production process. There may be steps (Step 2 in Figure 5.7) where the patient is not physically present, but the doctor works on the case, for example, by checking x-rays or consulting decision support software. The producer's infrastructure, back-office resources, and support are activated.

The expectation is that a contact, a visit to the doctor with some advice, medication, or intervention, will change the state to the better. The patient's cumulative health, assuming that it could be given a numerical value, would increase by a multiplier effectuated by the step (×). If the multiplier gets a value above 1, health improves. If it is 1, there is no change. If it is less than 1, health gets worse. If it is 0, the patient dies and the stream comes to an end.

The steps in the production process consume resources. Adding one step always adds to the cumulative resource consumption, that is, to the medical bill. There is a profound difference between (×) and (+). If the healer gets paid for everything done, by either a fixed salary or a fee-for-service (F4S) remuneration, costs can accumulate while health deteriorates. That does not happen in manufacturing, unless there is a really mighty disaster at hand.

A producer can promptly plan and schedule processes; the service encounters can be managed by paying attention to interpersonal skills and bedside manners. The back office can be equipped with the best money can buy. But there is a line of visibility and a line of control beyond which purposeful action can't reach. The caregiver many not know what is going on, which biological processes are at work, or if the patient is following recommendations. It is the patient's back office, shrouded behind a line of visibility.

## 5.3.6 *Process Architectures*

Production processes are arrangements that coordinate flow units and workstations. As discussed earlier, there are five basic architectures. Which to use depends on the product and the production function, and whether the flow unit is stationary (project or job shop), moving (disconnected and connected lines), or instead of discrete pieces, a batch of divisible material (continuous flow). From this follows the product–process matrix (Figure 3.7) that combines certain product types with certain process architectures.

All the basic process architectures are easily recognized in healthcare. A patient can be a project. That happens if there are several diseases (comorbidity) or wounds (massive trauma) simultaneously present. The patient requires care from several specialized caregivers who may belong to different departments or organizations. The job shop is usually found in primary care where a general practitioner and his nurses and aides deal with a patient as a whole person. The disconnected line is at work where patients are waiting for the next step, a lab test, imaging, or their turn at the OR. Connected flows are typical in surgery, where patients with open chest cavities can't be put on hold in a buffer. Medication is akin to a continuous flow where pharmaceutical molecules do their job as uninterrupted incremental changes, like whisky maturing in a barrel.

In mass manufacturing, one setup is followed by several repetitions producing identical copies. In personal services, each customer requires an individual setup that can range from fully formatted to a series of bargaining and exploration.

The service–process matrix (Figure 4.9) uses as architectural elements demand variety, from "take all comers" to identical repetition, and setup type, from explorative to standard. The combinations are relevant for healthcare, although the lines are not as sharp. EDs accept all types of medically justified demand and have the capability of explorative setup when needed. Segmented demand typically employs routine setups. Similar problem types can apply formatted setups.

A dentist discovers a cavity in a tooth and then knows exactly what needs to be done step-by-step, how long it will take, and what it will cost. At the opposite end are explorations, cases that initially do not make sense, multiple vague symptoms in combinations that have never been seen before. In between come shades of gray, formatted and routine setups.

In a health services setup, diagnosis and the care plan are hampered by the limitations of the production functions, risk and uncertainty. At times there is not enough clinical clarity to plan a patient journey from end to end like a factory process. From this follows that many processes in healthcare are explorative, and the principles of factory management do not apply. I will return to process architectures in more detail in Chapter 6.

## 5.4 Performance Measurement and Evaluation in Healthcare

Measurement is to put numbers on things. Evaluation is to pass judgment on the numbers: How much is much; how little is little? How long can patients be kept waiting? How many errors can be tolerated?

In healthcare, the production function is not always precise. Output is not a straightforward predictor of outcome. A surgical procedure can be successful to the smallest detail of small q, but the patient nevertheless dies. How should the surgeon be evaluated? If help was given but health was not achieved, on what grounds can it be said that the producer did a good, or at least acceptable, job? The difference between output and outcome calls for different approaches to measurement and evaluation, as shown in Figure 5.8.

As discussed in Chapter 3, there are measures that are direct consequences of the production function, for example, processing time. It takes a given time to drill a hole in a piece of metal; a routine cardiac bypass operation always takes a certain amount of hours, with some variation, depending on the patient's chest and the surgeon's skill and form of the day. This type of performance can be changed only with technology and capital investment; new equipment, tools, and methods must be purchased, installed, and learned.

A different set of measures is needed for performance that is impacted by management. No new stuff is needed; just arrange what there is to make a better flow, ensure small q to reduce variability, and manage a portfolio of buffers to optimize cycle time, WIP inventory, and throughput. For example, in some medical practices it is assumed that length of stay (LOS), the number of days a patient spends in

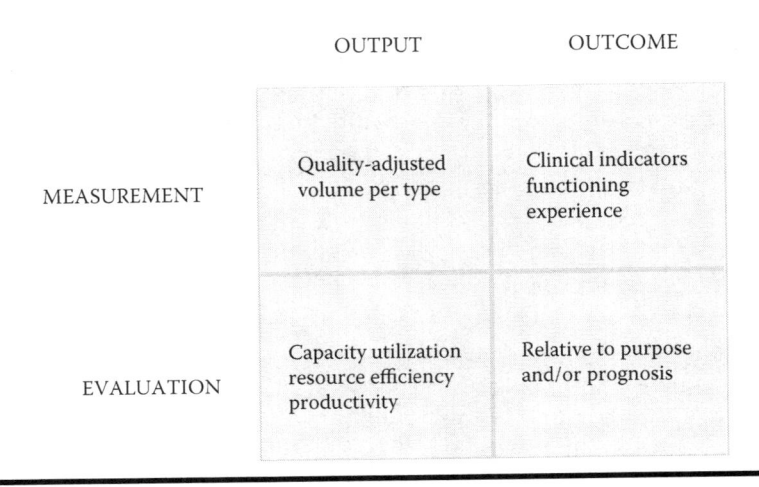

Figure 5.8  Measurement and evaluation of outputs and outcomes.

a hospital ward, depends on technology and a given progress of healing. However, research has shown significant variability in LOS in comparable patient cases.[48] In a study, discharges per weekday were examined (Ekelund et al. 2011). It was found that there was a surge of discharges on Mondays. Closer scrutiny revealed that many of those patients could have been sent home on Friday but for the want of the necessary paperwork. LOS is partly dependent on the production function and partly on management.

## *5.4.1 Output Measurement*

Outputs come in several basic types, such as a 20-minute visit to the doctor's office, a prescription written for antibiotics, a surgical procedure, or a number of days in a hospital bed. Output is task accomplishment. In healthcare, it has the same measurable properties as in other types of production:

- ■ Throughput, the volume of tasks accomplished in a time period
- ■ Processing time at the workstations
- ■ Capacity utilization
- ■ WIP inventory
- ■ Cycle time
- ■ Throughput time

In addition to these flow-related measures, outputs have differentiation and cost. Every output is meant to accomplish or contribute to something; thereby it has functionality and performance. An output can be administered in various ways and with more or less resources, it has the property of grade. When people are involved, every output has a style. The doctor can be respectful or rude; the "what was done" and "how it was done" distinction appears. To many, albeit not to all, outputs, there is a clinical standard, the right way to do it. Where such specifications exist, an output can be evaluated in terms of small q. If the output deviates from the standard, there is a quality problem. Outputs consume healers' time and attention, facilities, energy, supplies, and disposables. Everybody on the supply side must get paid. These can be calculated and expressed in a legal currency. As resource consumption correlates with time, cycle time and throughput time, including LOS, can be used as proxies.

Outputs can then be counted and summed up as raw production volume. Only outputs with acceptable quality should be included. Rework to correct errors should be counted separately.

## *5.4.2 Output Evaluation*

Evaluation is to pass judgment if something is good or bad, sufficient or insufficient, acceptable or not. Evaluation is the basis of improvement. Output evaluation thus requires that the produced volume be compared with something, the quantity of resources, labor hours and equipment used, or directly with the amount of money spent.[49] Productivity is the general measure of how resources are spent to produce output. It can be divided into more specific indicators, *production efficiency* and *economic efficiency* (Figure 5.9).

## Production Efficiency

Production efficiency use operative measures, the amount of output produced by a workstation with a set of resources. How many patients did a doctor see per day? How many surgical procedures did the team accomplish per week?

Capacity utilization is illustrated in Figure 5.10. Starting from the bottom, *theoretical capacity* is the sum of all resources expressed in working hours of staff and facilities. Under normal conditions, the theoretical maximum is not relevant, since people need breaks and equipment needs maintenance. Deducting these from the theoretical maximum gives the *operative capacity*. Unscheduled stoppages reduce the operative capacity into *usable capacity*. Some of it is not used, because there are no patients, or a critical piece of input, such as the results of a blood test, is late or missing. Bottlenecks cause idle capacity down the flow and reduce the actual *used capacity*. Finally, all the capacity working is not producing results. This is the core meaning of *muda*; work is done, resources are expended, but nothing worthwhile is accomplished.

The way capacity is utilized is an important diagnostic tool. Like statistical process control (SPC) and the distinction between common and specific causes discussed in Chapter 3, it reveals what needs to be done for each type of problem. If scheduled maintenance takes too much capacity, the problem lies with production planning. A typical case is that vacations or lunch breaks are taken simultaneously

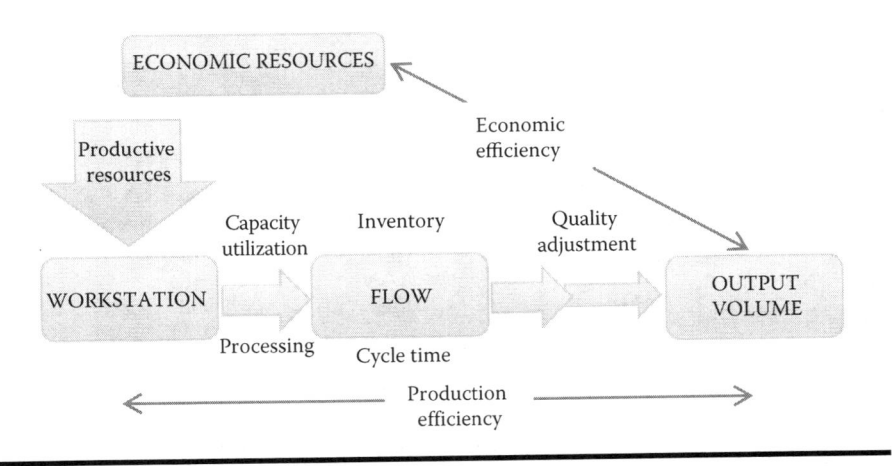

**Figure 5.9  Production efficiency and economic efficiency.**

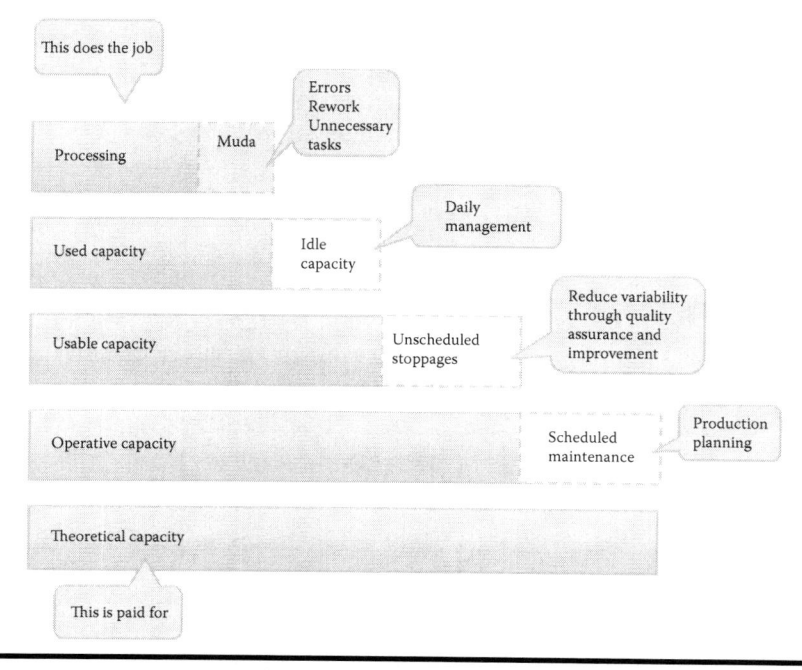

**Figure 5.10 How capacity can be used.**

and the whole operation grinds to a halt. If the operative capacity is hampered by unscheduled stoppages, disturbances, and sudden emergencies, it shows that the system is not in balance and operates at the mercy of variability. This calls for a Lean healthcare type of process improvement and stabilization. If capacity is idling, it is a symptom of scheduling problems, bottlenecks, and poor buffer management. It can also be simply lack of demand; that is, there is too much capacity. Finally, errors, rework, and unnecessary tasks call for close scrutiny of how work is done.

Capacity utilization is not regularly measured. In emergency services and other standby operations, short-term capacity utilization is not a problem. An idle ambulance crew simply shows that people are not getting sick. Capacity allocation must consider worst-case scenarios. In health systems with F4S remuneration, unused capacity is not paid for; therefore, doctors indulge in it at their own expense. In professional work, "scheduled maintenance" includes meetings and administrative tasks. Bureaucratic organizations on fixed budgets can increase such work with impunity.

## Economic Efficiency

Economic efficiency uses money as a measure. The quality-adjusted volume is contrasted to the amount of economic resources used (Figure 5.9). Economic efficiency can be calculated in two basic ways. The top-down method starts from the total cost of the production unit and divides it with the output volume. The perennial problem with this type of accounting is how to allocate fixed costs, such as buildings, equipment, and support staff, to outputs. If there are several types of outputs with varying demand for resources, the task becomes daunting, indeed. The bottom-up method is activity-based costing (ABC). Each output is decomposed to its parts, activities, and steps. The resource consumption of each, such as doctor time, nurse time, machine time, and pharmaceuticals used, is calculated and then aggregated.

Process improvement efforts often use the bottom-up calculation. If a process can be streamlined by taking out some steps that really are *muda*, the cost savings, let's say nurse time, can be recorded. However, there will be real savings only on two conditions. Nursing labor is reduced, which is to say that someone is fired. The alternative is that the saved labor is put into use elsewhere to increase throughput or provide better care.

Economic efficiency is subject to labor and capital substitution, and to resource intensity. Different resources have different costs; doctors and nurses are paid at different rates. If a job that is done by a doctor can be moved to a nurse, cheaper resources can substitute for expensive resources. Resource intensity means how much labor is used to perform a task. This is a staffing decision that varies considerably between production units.

> The resource intensity of six cataract surgery units was compared in a pilot study. In the worst-performing unit, there were three nurses and one surgeon in the OR. The average time per operation was 12:35, which multiplied with staff time (4) gives the total labor input as 50:20 per patient. For the best-performing unit, the corresponding figures were two nurses and one doctor, average time per operation of 5:38, and total labor time of 16:54 per patient. There were no significant differences in quality.
>
> When support and administration were included, the best unit had a total throughput of 8 patients per personnel per day, while the worst managed 1.2 patients per day per staff member. In the best-performing unit, 31% of personnel resources were spent on the operation, while the corresponding figure in the worst was 12%.[50]

## Output Dynamics

The road from measurement to evaluation continues to dynamics. Measures indicate certain phenomena (ontology) that are related in some ways. Such relations are chunks of logic. Many of them, such as Little's law (throughput, WIP, and cycle time), are universally true expressions of how the world works, but hampered by variability and imprecise data. The logic chunks are important, as their elements are subject to management action. Figure 5.11[51] illustrates a chunk of logic applied to the production efficiency of surgery. In surgery, assuming a constant processing time, input is determined by resource intensity, that is, the number of nurses, surgeons, and support staff allocated to a typical case. The associated managerial task is staffing.

Output is determined by two factors. Cycle time is the time a patient spends in an OR between wheel-in and wheel-out. It is a measure of the efficiency of a workstation, that is, the relation of the surgical intervention (connected flow) to setup and preparation (disconnected flow). Cycle time depends on the surgical methods and tools, the experience and dexterity of the surgeon, and collaboration within the surgical team. These are subject to clinical management and leadership.

Utilization means how many percent of the available time the OR is in use, that is, the used capacity of the facility versus the time it is idling. Scheduling is the responsibility of the management of the surgical clinic.

### Aggregated Measures

Productivity measurement and evaluation in healthcare run into a number of problems. The basic unit of analysis is the journey of a flow unit. In a single case, all relevant contingencies can be accounted for. But productivity is an aggregate measure that lumps together several teams into an OR, several ORs into a surgical clinic, and several clinics of different types into a general hospital. Various averages must be calculated. It becomes an exercise in comparing apples and oranges. That, however, is not impossible, if the right variables are chosen, as in Table 5.2.[52]

The point is to find indicators that go beyond the outer appearance and the visible differences between cases.

Even when patients have similar diagnoses and care plans, that is, they are of the same variety, they can differ in terms of severity, the point in the natural history of the condition, or individual idiosyncrasies. Within-variety differences can be dealt with by averages that can be weighted. Every instance is slightly different, but share some common characteristics. That is like evaluating a batch of apples.

> Patients are classified into groups having the same condition, based
> on principal and secondary diagnoses, procedures, age, complexity

**Table 5.2  How to Compare Apples and Oranges**

| Measure | Apple | Orange |
|---|---|---|
| Average mass | 160 g | 150 g |
| Carbohydrates/100 g | 8.3 g | 8.9 g |
| Energy/100 g | 41 kcal | 47 kcal |
| Fibers/100 g | 2 g | 2.1 g |
| C vitamins/100 g | 12 mg | 51 mg |

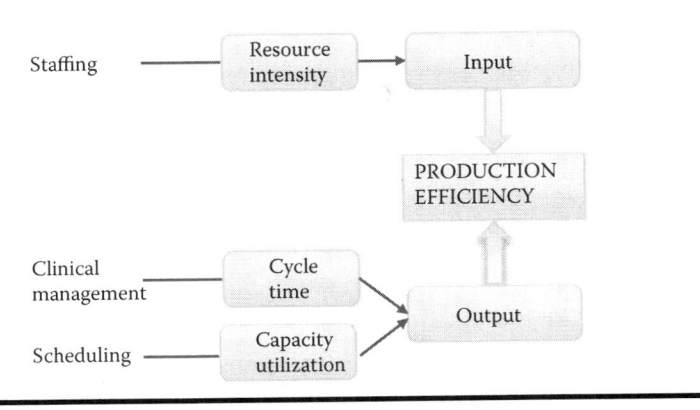

**Figure 5.11    Production efficiency of surgery.**

(comorbidities), and needs. Such are called diagnosis-related groups (DRGs) or medical severity diagnosis-related groups (MSDRGs). Each DRG has a relative average value assigned to it that indicates the amount of resources required to treat this group, as related to all other DRGs within the system. Each DRG has a numeric weight referring to the calculated average costs, which are used as the basis of billing. A case mix index (CMI) is a relative value assigned to a DRG of patients in a region. The CMI of a hospital reflects the diversity, clinical complexity, and need for resources in the population of all the patients in the hospital. It is used in determining the allocation of resources to care for and/or treat the patients in the group.[53] In operations management, the term *DRG* is akin to a product classification system, and CMI is a measure of the variability and expected costs associated with demand. The definition, calculation, refinement, and use of the DRG system is a mighty undertaking guided by national and international professional bodies.[54]

The efficiency model shown in Figure 5.11 can be used to compare apples and oranges. It doesn't matter that cataract and orthopedic surgery use different technologies on different patient groups. Both have inputs driven by resource intensity, and outputs determined by cycle time and capacity utilization. While the numbers, rations, and acceptable performance levels vary, in both cases the managerial tasks are staffing, clinical management, and scheduling.

## Benchmarking

In the discussion so far, evaluation has been an internal matter of a production system. Several measures are contrasted, linked, and compared to elicit relations between them. The question remains, what is an acceptable level of production efficiency or capacity utilization? If there are no absolute, physical measures to which performance could be anchored, it is hard to say how good is good, and how bad is bad. The solution is benchmarking (BM).

In factories, theoretical BM can be used. If the production function and processing time are known, a theoretical maximum efficiency level can be calculated as the sum of processing time. While it is akin to an ideal type, a state that does not exist in nature, it provides an idea of the distance between the current and the ideal state. As healthcare operates with fuzzy production functions and unclear objectives, theoretical BM is not practical.

Sensemaking by comparing oneself to others is a basic human capability to help one gain orientation in various environments. BM is a specific type of comparison, a real-to-real comparison of systems: my system in relation to other comparable systems. Comparing real to real implies that the object of comparison is documented performance. The better performer has arguably been able to achieve something that the worse has not. Therefore, catching up does not involve assuming the risks of innovations, given that the contexts are similar. BM is primarily a low-risk tool for catching up by learning from others. If something has already been done, it is doable.

Performance can be defined and comparisons can be made on different levels of abstraction. That calls for the selection of appropriate variables as key performance indicators (KPIs). As with apples and oranges, different procedures, such as hernia and knee arthroscopy surgery, can be compared using OR utilization rates, since utilization relates more to scheduling methods than to the particular procedures of each clinical subspecialty.

BM starts with defining the variables and collecting the data. For BM to be more than an exercise in nice-to-know information, performance measures should be linked to managerial tasks, as in Figure 5.11, where resource intensity is a staffing issue, cycle time is a clinical management issue, and utilization is a scheduling issue.

Combining performance and process BM turns BM into a development tool. It is used with the purpose of learning something that increases an organization's welfare. While organizations may lean from trial and error, or from casual observations, BM is a way to accelerate learning. If the other systems perform better on some performance criteria, something can be learned about the practices of the system in question. If it performs similarly but does things differently, it is still possible to learn something interesting. If it performs worse, it is useful to learn to avoid its mistakes. Therefore, BM does not require an up-front identification of best practices.

### 5.4.3 Outcome Measurement

Output measurement tells the amount of help that is administered with given resources. Outcome is what happens to a patient's health. It can be measured as clinical indicators, functioning, and experience.

Clinical indicators are specific to each medical condition. Operations management can't contribute to the definition of indicators; if the doctor says so, so be it.[55]

Functioning means what a person can do within her circumstances and personal objectives. There are, however, some universal functioning requirements, such as moving one's body, being able to see and orient oneself, and coordinating hand movements. Functioning can be measured by asking and observing which basic tasks a person can do: get out of bed, go shopping, and take care of personal hygiene. There are several standardized measurement instruments. For example, orthopedics use the Disabilities on the Arm, Shoulder and Hand (DASH) score, a composite of 30 questions put to the clinician and patient.[56] The 15D is a generic 15-dimensional instrument for measuring health-related quality of life and is used to determine how much help a person needs to get by with her daily life.[57]

Patient experience can be measured by asking and observing. Patient-reported outcome measures (PROMs) and PREMs are standard tools. PROMs capture personal perceptions of health, validate generic and disease-specific indicators, and elicit symptoms, distress, anxiety, and unmet needs. PREMs capture experiences with health services, such as time spent waiting, access to and ability to navigate services, and knowledge of care plans and pathways.[58,59]

Outcome measures are sensitive to the point in time when the measure is taken. In episodic cases, such as a surgery, outcomes can be measured at the end points of phases, such as after the last stitch, when the patient is wheeled out to the PACU, after waking up, at the point of discharge, a week later, or a year later. In chronic cases with no end, there is no obvious measurement point. The patient's condition should be monitored at given intervals.

## 5.4.4 Outcome Evaluation

Assume that outcomes are reliably measured. We have a set of numbers describing the condition of a patient at given points in time. However, without context and references a measure is just a number lost in space. Outcome evaluation asks, was it good in relation to expectations and prognosis, and was it good in relation to cost and effort?

### Outcomes and Prognosis

As illustrated in Figure 5.12, there are four basic types of outcome evaluation in relation to what is expected. The upper left panel describes the typical trauma victim. An accident happens and health status deteriorates quickly. Help is at hand and an effective technology can be applied to restore health. The patient is back to normal, good as new. The second type in the upper right panel comes in cases, such as stroke or heart attack, where the incident imposes damage and leaves the patient with reduced functioning. A person who once had a cancer incident is forever a cancer survivor. For the patient, it means a new normal, a life with watchful

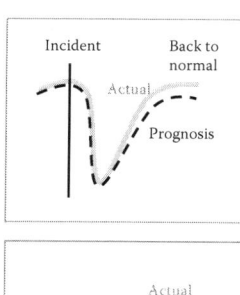
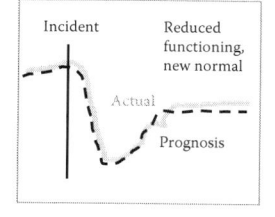
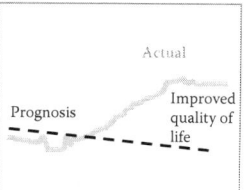
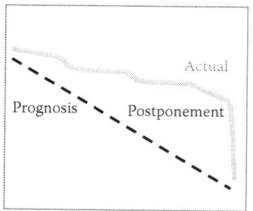

**Figure 5.12  Types of outcomes.**

waiting, reduced functioning, or permanent disability. These two situations, back to normal and back to new normal, have in common a sudden onset of the problem that allows a clear before–after comparison.

In the third and fourth types shown in the lower panels, there is no sudden incident. The patient's condition slowly deteriorates, as in a case with bad dental hygiene. Cavities expand, teeth rot away, and the overall condition decays. An intervention is done to repair damage and initiate a new lifestyle with an electric toothbrush and floss. The condition improves slowly but steadily. The fourth type is a chronic or terminal condition to which there is no cure. The disease can be managed to ensure a better quality of life. Brakes are applied and the inevitable is postponed.

In all four cases depicted in Figure 5.12, the outcome is evaluated by comparing the actual condition with a prognosis. The worth of an outcome depends on both what happens and what should and could have happened. Therefore, outcome evaluation is subject to the accuracy and reliability of prognosis in each case and condition. Making a prognosis is subject to variability, risk, and uncertainty. The way around it, as in much of medicine, is to use statistical aggregates, averages, and standard deviations. A stroke victim in her fifties with no preexisting conditions should on average recover in such and such way. But unless the prognosis can be made accurate on the individual level, outcome evaluation can't be an exact science.

## Outcome Related to Cost: Economic Value and Utility

The second problem is the relation between outcomes and resources spent per instance and in aggregate. The producers' resources are the fixed and variable costs, staff time, and money. These can be calculated. The monetary costs to the patient can be defined with some accuracy, although in third-party payer systems most costs are carried by taxes or insurance. A relevant cost measure is the trouble, time, anxiety, and pain the patient suffers, although this is difficult to express in numbers.

Finally, there is the question of utility, health benefits, and quality of life. It is to ask, what will a person do with her health? And whose problem is it? Operations management and health services can't really answer. There is a system boundary between professional services and people's lives. Healthcare can help, and at best restore health, but not ensure happiness.

## 5.5 Risk and Uncertainty in Healthcare

If something can go wrong, it will go wrong. To err is human. Variability is both the creative and the destructive force of nature. Purposeful activity requires control, reduction, or elimination of variability that hampers the purpose. Quality management, the small q, is the effort to secure that things go as they should.

In health service processes, production risks appear in many ways (Figure 5.13). Data can be bad or incomplete, causing errors in judgment and choice of procedure; that is, there is uncertainty about the setup. Resources may be occupied elsewhere when they would be needed right here. Adverse events happen and execution can go wrong.

In healthcare, there are specific risk points that are not simply producers' or sellers' risk. They resemble the buyer's and the consumer's risk and can be called collaboration risks. They appear in three relations, shown in Figure 5.13: (1) between output and outcome; (2) between outcome and experienced utility, benefit, quality of life, or however the purpose is described; and (3) between outcome and total resources spent.

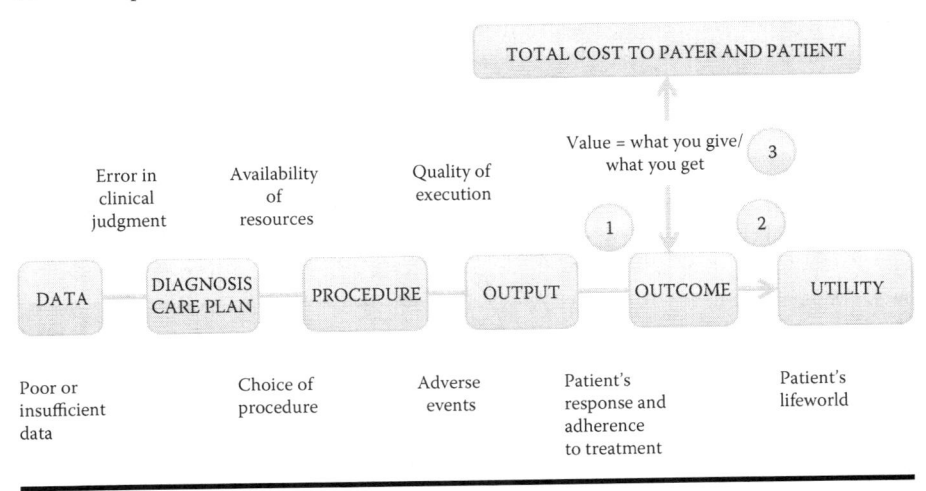

**Figure 5.13 Production risks in healthcare.**

## 5.5.1 Quality in Healthcare

*Quality* is a fuzzy word, a compound of two phenomena that differ significantly as to their ontology, epistemology, and dynamics. Big Q contains everything between expectations and experiences, including functionality, performance, grade, style, quality, and reliability. Quality in its core small q meaning is conformance to specifications. If the specifications can be described in sufficient detail, and the output is measurable using the same variables, small q can be known. The basic unit of analysis is an individual instance, the outcome stream as shown earlier in Figure 5.7.

### Small Quality in Healthcare

Quality in health services is based on the Hippocratic notion *primum non nocere*: at least, do no harm. This is akin to patient safety, a small q definition. While healers do not perform miracles, they should not intentionally put a patient in harm's way. An avoidable error is, per definition, something that was known before the fact but execution failed. Like in all small q issues, zero defect is a realistic performance target. There is no excuse to allow the preventable to happen.

Patient safety is a small q issue about executing tasks to which specifications exist *ex ante*, including standard procedures, waiting times, and information. There are exact requirements for hand hygiene, instrument control, and how a central line should be inserted. Much of the work of regulative bodies is about imposing quality standards on production, and screening pharmaceuticals and devices. It follows the industrial logic of the small q. Quality assurance systems can be built to monitor compliance; adverse events and near misses can be reported, counted, evaluated, and acted on through continuous improvement.

### Big Quality in Healthcare

The general discussion about quality in healthcare is about big Q. The WHO[60] defines six "areas or dimensions" of quality: safe, effective, patient centric, efficient, timely, and equitable. These, however, are more like a general mission statement that has a way to go before turning into actionable measures.

Given the difference between small and big quality, it is no surprise that there is no universally accepted gold standard for the definition of quality in healthcare.[61] That is not for lack of trying. There have been several attempts to establish sets of essential quality parameters for healthcare.[62] Azam and colleagues reviewed the literature and produced a list of hospital service quality parameters: tangibles, reliability, responsiveness, communication, credibility, security, competence, understanding, access, assurance, waiting time, physical appearance, support services, clinical quality, respect, religious needs, dignity, food, structure, atmosphere, personalization, security, and convenience.[63] Consequently, the aggregated to-do list includes tasks, such as professionalism, facility management, nurse satisfaction, change management knowledge, Total Quality Management projects, quality function deployment, integrated care pathways, infection control, value chains, information technology (IT) access, and doctor–patient relationships. There is no arguing that all these are relevant to the mission of healthcare, as they are to any service.

Small q is an essential element of big Q. If a design can't be implemented as planned or not at all, it is meaningless. But the remaining issues in big Q are the basic competitive differentiators, functionality, performance, grade, and style. Functionality here equals the cures that are available. Performance is outcome effectiveness. To which degree can it be assumed that diagnosis, the care plan, and its execution contribute to the expected outcome? Grade means the individual adjustments to a treatment scheme and the service level. Style is social relations and beside manners.

The simple big Q definition would be to take the outcome, measure it as clinical indicators, functioning, and experience, and compare it with expectations. From the patient perspective, it would be sufficient. For the professional and the manager, it would offer no more guidance than the tired old slogan, "Always do the right things right." Given the inherent variability in the relation between output and outcome, big Q in healthcare is not manageable in the same way as small q. The big Q question is how to make sure that diagnoses are as correct as possible and include all relevant data. This is, indeed, a matter of professional competence, to which operations management can't contribute much more than perhaps to design information processes. Big Q is product technology, clinical decisions, and design of care.

## Collaborative Quality

A care plan is a design of a process for the patient to follow. As any processes, it requires a setup. The patient, unless incapacitated, is supposed to collaborate. Quality in healthcare, small and big, faces the same dilemma as quality in services. The patient is a source of variability, and there are gaps in how the parties understand, communicate, and collaborate. The roles, rules, rights, and responsibilities of the involved parties must be settled for smooth collaboration.

From these principles, a conceptual model of quality management in healthcare can be summarized, as in Table 5.3. Quality applies to four distinct areas: diagnostics and care plan, the patient's role in collaboration, execution and patient safety, and patient experience. These can be examined in terms of their ontology, epistemology, relevant objectives, and principal methods for improvement.

Diagnostics and care plan are the healthcare equivalents of product and service design. In all but the simplest cases, they are explorative processes and require individual setup. Even though the process for diagnostics and clinical decision-making can't be specified in detail, there are nevertheless general guidelines and best practices embedded in professional competence. Because each patient is an

**Table 5.3  Quality in Healthcare**

|  | What It Is? Ontology | How It Is Known? Epistemology | Relevant Objectives | Principal Methods |
|---|---|---|---|---|
| Diagnostics and care plan (big Q) | How an individual patient care episode is designed | *Ex ante:* Best practice *Ex post:* Outcomes | Relative to benchmarks and past performance | Education, consultations, professionalism, decision aids |
| Patient's role in collaboration (service quality) | How a patient fulfills rights and responsibilities | Health behavior | Compliance, adherence | Advice, counseling, support |
| Execution of patient safety (small q) | How a care plan or task is executed, patient safety | Conformance to *ex ante* specifications | Zero defect | Quality assurance and improvement |
| Patient experience | A patient's subjective perception of a care episode | Interviews, surveys, observed behavior | Situational, style | Service culture and values, recruiting |

individual, and all aspects of the situation can't be known, relative measures must be used. Outcomes can be evaluated case by case, studied as historical trends, and benchmarked to others.

Services are collaborations; therefore, service quality should include both parties. On the patient side, the issues are compliance, adherence, and health behavior. On the provider side, small quality is how a care plan is executed, particularly in terms of patient safety. Patient experience can be seen as the overall summary measurement of outcomes that is not necessarily reducible to specific acts or events. Experiences are subjective perceptions; what is perceived as real is real in its consequences.

## 5.6 Volume–Variety in Healthcare

Donald Berwick,[64] the founder of the IHI, lamented, "The Craft of care has turned into the machinery of care." Many others have voiced similar concerns, longing back to the time of the family doctor, a fixture in all junctures of life.

Health systems in Continental Europe and Japan have institutional arrangements to support the family doctor. In Sweden and Finland, the family doctor has disappeared into municipal health centers. Everywhere the central hospital ED is competing for the attention of patients. The family doctor is like the mom-and-pop corner store. The concept is likeable, but when faced with real choice, the majority prefer variety, specialization, and low prices.

Volume in healthcare, as in travel and tourism, can be achieved by simply adding resources, bigger hospitals, denser networks of service providers, and more procedures. But would more volume trigger the mechanisms of economies of scale, the cornucopia principle that the more you make, the cheaper it gets?

## 5.6.1 Economies of Scale

Health policy makers are attracted to the idea of economies of scale. People demand more care, and more capacity must be built. It would be neat if the long-range average costs per unit of output would fall as a consequence. The research literature, however, does not give a clear answer. Some studies find moderate-scale effects, while others don't.[65] Economies of scale appears most clearly in production systems with single products and production lines. A hospital is usually a multiproduct, multiprocess system. Therefore, some parts may be sensitive to scale, while others are not and the aggregate effect remains unclear.

As discussed in Chapter 3, economies of scale exploits a basic chunk of logic: several products can share the fixed cost of technology, design, and setup. The more products, the smaller the cost burden placed on each. Setup in healthcare produces a diagnosis and a corresponding care plan. They have to be made separately for each individual patient. In some cases, formatted setups can be used. The core of the matter is the setup, its absolute cost, and its cost in relation to processing. The extent to which scale mechanisms can be used varies between different areas of healthcare, a subject to which I will return in Chapter 6.

Big hospitals can utilize the classical drivers of productivity, division of labor, specialization, and standardization. A big hospital has a lot of patients, which can be segmented by clinical specialty. With a steady supply of patients with narrowly defined ailments, doctors can build up specialized skills in processing. The learning curve depicts a phenomenon that the more you do, the better you get. A surgeon who specializes in, say, cardiac bypass or knee joint replacement surgery becomes faster and makes fewer errors than colleagues who operate on a wider range of cases. New members climb rapidly on the curve, while for seniors it tapers off; when it starts to decline, it is time to retire. A hospital with a large team of surgeons with a steady recruitment–retirement ratio will have a rather stable aggregated position on the learning curve.

Big hospitals have several attractors. As any large production facility, they become central in regional economies and can throw their weight around. They offer employment and career opportunities and can afford latest technologies.

University hospitals lure those interested in research. None of these, however, answers the basic question, will volume drive down cost?

## 5.6.2 Affordable Care to the Masses

The predicament of healthcare can be boiled down to the dilemma of volume and variety. Diagnosis and a care plan require integration at the patient level, that is, individual setup. Demand is for craft production, while supply has to strive for mass production in order to contain cost and make health service affordable. Division of labor leads to specialization; individual components perform better but are harder to integrate, which leads to fragmentation. Specialization also leads to standardization, which in turn reduces variety. The antidote is integration and coordination. The former is product technology, that is, clinical medicine; the latter is production technology, that is, management.

Manufacturing and commercial services have struggled with these problems for decades. The contours of the solutions are clear: modularization, mass customization, platform with apps, formatted setup, and franchising. All these can be used in healthcare. However, they are not general solutions that would apply to all health services equally. Healthcare needs a managerial typology to clarify which solutions apply where. This is the topic of Chapter 6, after considering the complexities of transactions in healthcare.

# 5.7 Healthcare Transactions

Transactions take place in markets. People engage in exchanges voluntarily to gain from trade. Buyers and sellers have to comply with the social rules of markets. In personal services, the relation between producer and customer is thicker than that with goods, as the parties need to collaborate. A great deal of risk is included, as services can be sold only as value propositions, promises to do something.

There is a great deal of risk involved in healthcare transformations. But there are even greater risks in life. Facing the prospect of death, suffering, or permanent injury, human beings ask for help, solutions, and explanations. Without health, everything else loses value; credit cards are not accepted on the other side. Something must be done. Therefore, even at great risks, people engage in transactions with healers.

Business models combine transformations and transactions. A generic Business Model Canvas (BMC) for healthcare is presented in Figure 5.14.

## 5.7.1 Healing Relationship

The patient–doctor relationship can be envisioned as a customer–provider relationship. However, a lot is lost if the healing relationship is seen as a purely commercial relation.

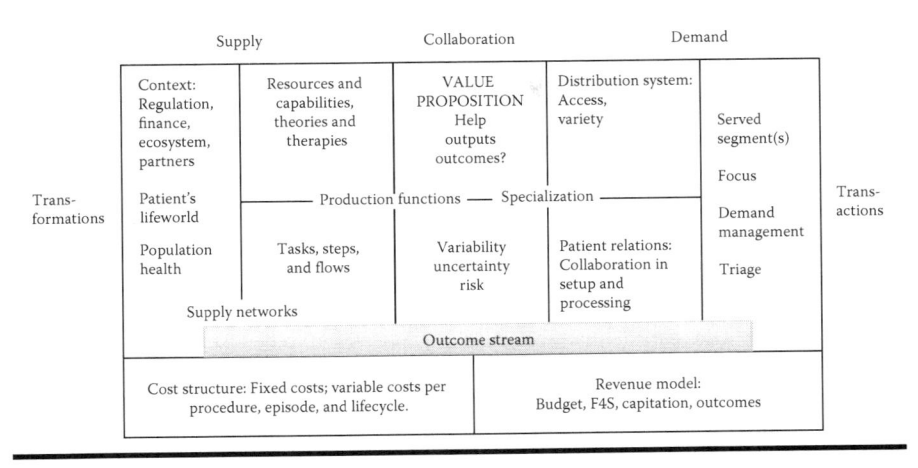

**Figure 5.14  BMC for healthcare.**

The healer–patient relationship is one of the oldest and most important human relations, together with the teacher–disciple, lord–samurai, and master–apprentice relationships. Deals and calculative rationality, loyalty and betrayal, rights and responsibilities are there, but to reduce them to market relations is an especially bad case of reductionism. Such relationships are not transactions between equals; neither are they coercive. Both parties benefit, but the relation is not symmetrical. The master has resources and capabilities that the apprentice wants to acquire and benefit from; the master's income and status depend on how well the apprentice is doing. Modern welfare societies seek to dilute and equalize traditional relationships. But when teachers strive to become buddies with their pupils, the purpose of schooling will be lost. Even with advancing health technologies, a substantial part of healthcare is, and will continue to revolve around, the social relationship. Even so, the economic layer can't be ignored. Inevitably, commercial concerns enter the healing relationship.

## 5.7.2 Patient–Doctor: The Commercial Relationship

### Effort or Outcomes

For analytic purposes, a patient and a healer can, for a moment, be considered economic agents. A person is sick, has a job to be done, seeks help, engages a healer, and assumes the role of a patient. The healer is a professional, who evidently can help, or is perceived to be in possession of some skill sets and facilities that can do what mere mortals can't, enable a transformation from sick to healthy, or lacking that, provide comfort and consolation with the notion that everything doable will be done. The healer does not gain skills without effort; facilities are not for free. Specialized professionals need to be remunerated to make a living. The patient is willing to pay to get the job done. This is an ordinary constellation for a market with a buyer and a seller. Both bring resources and expect to benefit from exchange.

So what's the problem? Let the market work its magic, as in other industries.

The service trade is immaterial. It cannot be but a value proposition and an agreement about rules of engagement. In healthcare, given the ever-present variability, decay, and fuzzy production function, the buyer can only buy hope; the seller can only sell promise.

In a situation where effort matters but cannot be directly observed, measured, and evaluated, economic theory raises the possibility of market failure. If patients cannot observe and judge a healer's effort and the effectiveness of therapies, a lazy healer has the option not to exert extraordinary effort on patients' behalf. Although patients are willing to pay and healers are available, markets could still fail to accomplish best possible outcomes.

The standard economic solution is to pay the provider for results. Salespersons are paid commissions and CEOs get stock options. Patients could try to make deals where the payment would be contingent on confirmed outcomes. Researchers at the U.S. National Bureau of Economic Research (NBER) seriously sought to find whether, anywhere in the world, there was a case of outcome-based health service markets where the healer was paid only if the patient got well.[66] They thought they found a case in Western African traditional healers. Closer inquiry, however, revealed that patients believed the healer would cast a spell on a deviant payer. Belief in magic served as a powerful enforcer of an orderly market.

An outcome-contingent trade would link pay with outcome. If health is fully restored, more is paid; if the outcome is a new normal with reduced functioning, less is paid. The transaction could be contractible; agreements about payments would be enforceable by a third party, a market arbiter such as a court of law or a professional community.

Linking pay with outcomes would open up the possibility of opportunistic cheating. The patient could simply lie about his condition, pretend to be sick despite all cures and claim that the healer did not act as promised and therefore refuse payment. The healer would find it hard or inconvenient to seek third-party confirmation. This is why healers in general refuse outcome-contingent deals. Given what has earlier been said about health services as collaboration, they have even more reasons to refuse. If a health outcome requires that the patient stops smoking and starts exercising, the healer's income is contingent on patient effort. If value propositions with certain outcomes can't be made, they are not offered. The patient is given the choice: take what is on offer or go home to die. Such lopsided trades can be actuated only in the extraordinary circumstances of life and death, pain and suffering. To get help matters more than health outcomes.

Outcomes can't be guaranteed, but outputs and the effort put into them can be monitored. That enables effort-contingent contracts. The healer is paid by observed output and effort. However, the necessity of each task will still elude the patient. If output is what you pay for, output you will get, whether you need it or not.

The value proposition in healthcare creates an opportunity for predation. Therefore, healers have been subject to rigorous moral codes and religious and ethical norms, such as the Hippocratic oath. The baker and the butcher need no such oaths; the markets discipline cheaters. Where markets won't work, governments step in.

## Information Asymmetry

When a buyer and a seller contemplate a transaction, both want the best price: the buyer the cheapest, the seller the dearest. For transactions to work smoothly, without too much buyer's remorse and seller's regret, both parties should have a transparent view of the object of trade. Then it is up to both to do their homework. There are, however, situations when some of the parties, typically the buyer, cannot get the transparent view. It can be that the value of the trade can't be known because it hasn't happened yet and can't be reliably predicted. There are also situations where the information is there, but it is in the seller's interests not to disclose it. This is called information asymmetry. It is a transaction where one party has more or better information than the other. This creates an imbalance, which can sometimes cause the transactions to go awry.

A classic example is the market of used cars.[67] Cars are sold in two ways: brand-new fresh from the factory and used. In the former case, a diligent buyer can do the homework, access technical specifications and independent test results. There is no principal reason why the customer couldn't be as well informed as the salesperson. The information available to them is symmetrical. The value of a used car is more difficult to determine. Generally, it is a function of time and mileage. But importantly, maintenance and repair of possible damage impact value. Some damages can be painted over and hidden. An honest seller will, for moral reasons, tell everything, but as he has a disincentive to do so, it frequently happens that the damaging information remains untold.

Information asymmetry leaves the buyer in a structurally weaker position. If such experiences are common, markets will not function smoothly, particularly in high-price items, such as cars and housing. Buyers become reluctant because of an overriding fear of being cheated. The market-based solution is to use independent, third-party evaluators, such as car doctors and building inspectors, as well as money-back guarantees. If this is not sufficient, regulators step in. In some countries, the sellers of prefabricated homes have a 20-year product liability.

Information asymmetry is also present in labor markets, especially that for chief executives. An owner-manager runs her business for her own benefit, as ownership and executive control are aligned. When businesses grow and founders retire, professional managers are called in. How can the owners be sure that the chief executive is not running the show for his own benefit, or putting in less than the maximum effort? This is the principal–agent constellation.

The owner is the principal, who hires an agent to work on his behalf. But the principal has limited vision into the activities of the agent. To deal with the issue, various result-based executive compensation systems have been developed. The owner wants to create a situation where his interests and those of the manager are aligned.

The patient–healer relation is clouded by both information asymmetry and the principal–agent predicament. Doctors usually know more about diseases and cures than patients do. That is the very reason a patient seeks a doctor, and why doctors spend years at Medical school and put in incredible hours as interns. Patients are principals who employ doctors to help them with medical issues that are beyond their own comprehension and skill. But they have limited vision into the efforts, and into the likely outcomes.[68]

Information asymmetry and the possibility of monitoring in principal–agent relationships are, as so many other things, variables. There are situations where the patient knows more. A patient who for the umpteenth time seeks relief for a strep throat knows pretty well what needs to be done, and which of the pills and potions work and which do not. Vigilant parents of children with rare diseases can inform themselves of the condition far beyond the average general practitioner. For the parents, this one case takes 100% of their attention; for the doctor, it is just one of many.

The difficulties with outcome-contingent contracts and information asymmetry are not ill will or capitalist conspiracy; they are just the logic of healthcare. Information asymmetry is a chunk of logic that predicts how actors with different information endowments behave. The asymmetry can be changed by more and better information to patients. This is the promise of ICT: to alter the very core of the relationship that is the core of healthcare.

## 5.7.3 Health Finance: Third-party Payers

Health finance systems have two parts. There is a collection system that siphons off money from the public, and aggregates and pools it in various ways. There is a distribution system that channels money to providers. The system is akin to manufacturing: a supply networks that brings in the materials for processing, and a distribution system that delivers the goods to the public.

Everywhere in the developed world, healthcare is financed through arrangements that include a third party, insurers, and/or the state. The logic is clear. Health incidents are like accidents, fire, and burglary. Paying for them out-of-pocket can be devastating. Because all accidents can't be foreseen or prevented, the way to manage the consequences is to have insurance. Several players with similar risk conditions pool their resources in an insurance fund. When something happens, the fund pays. The unfortunates get paid, while the fortunate keep contributing, because they know others' misfortune could someday be their own—there but for the grace of God go I.

The one who pays the piper calls the tune. Payers have an interest to watch where the money goes. Quacks and unscrupulous players can't be allowed. Therefore, healthcare is a highly regulated activity. Third-party finance and public regulation are necessary solutions, which create new problems, to which there is no obvious solution.

## Health Is a Public Good

An individual's health is an individual issue. Your health is your business. As long as you do not harm others, nobody will stop your unhealthy habits that will take you to an early grave. But many diseases have externalities; they inconvenience others. The extreme case is virulent, contagious disease, such as Ebola, tuberculosis, and smallpox. To contain the carriers is in the public interest, which is acknowledged by even the most extreme libertine defenders of individual freedoms. Health, when aggregated over populations, is a public good, and therefore subject to legitimate public interest.

Public health became a political concern in twentieth-century Europe, where the imperial powers struggled for dominance. The principal tool was the mass army. That required a steady supply of healthy youngsters who could take grueling marches and endure combat.[69] In the postwar world, the militaristic argument has lost power. Now the story is that you need your health to serve the economy and pay your taxes to support the welfare state.

The social contract between people and government is founded on the principle that the government has the power to rule and collect taxes, but in return, it must provide external security and internal safety to the people. Getting help in medical need is an essential part of internal safety.

## Catastrophic Healthcare Costs

Disaster seldom announces its approach. Suddenly it happens—the heart attack, the automobile accident, ice sliding down a roof and hitting a hapless pedestrian in the head. In a fraction of a second, a state has irrevocably changed. Most health problems in the modern world, particularly for the basically healthy adult population, are trivial in their economic consequences. Some are, or have the potential to become, personal financial catastrophes. In the developing world, this is a pressing public problem. In India, millions of households are annually pushed to the wrong side of the poverty line because a family member becomes seriously ill.[70] Paying the doctor out-of-pocket drives many into the hands of moneylenders, and all the evils that follow thereof.

Being ill is bad enough, becoming a pauper on top of it is unbearable. It is in the public interest that the financial consequences of health catastrophes are contained. Since this is not easily done within the patient–doctor commercial relation and out-of-pocket payments, third parties must step in.

## Third Parties

The basic logic of health finance is illustrated in Figure 5.15. The lower part with dotted lines is the Singaporean system with self-insurance.

The parties are the patient, the third-party financier, and the service provider. The patient also doubles as a payer, directly to the provider: premiums to insurers or taxes to governments. The third party can be private insurers under various degrees of regulatory control, a single national health insurer, or a government. The third party financier has, or is associated with, regulatory power. The service providers are public or private charities, not-for profit or for-profit players, arranged as hospitals, clinics, and doctor's offices.

The constellation allows the five basic financial architectures: out-of-pocket private insurance, regulated insurance, national insurance, public care, and self-insurance. Most countries have their own combinations of solutions.

## Hazards of Insurance

Insurance, like market and marriage, is a social institution. As such, it is prone to variability, decay, abuse, and failure. The two most prominent are adverse selection and moral hazards.

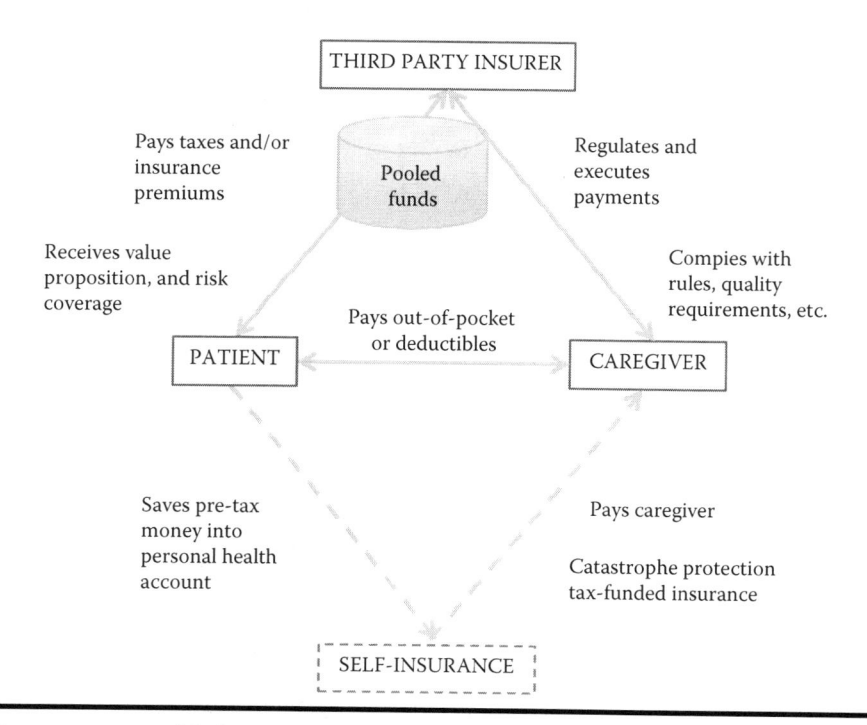

**Figure 5.15   Health finance.**

Adverse selection is a case of information asymmetry. Assume that there are two sets of people in a population. The one is the worried well, who watch their diets and exercise regularly; the others indulge in risky behavior, such as tobacco and fatty food. Suppose a low-risk and a high-risk individual both seek to buy insurance. The insurance company cannot easily differentiate between them. Questionnaires can be administered, but the high-risk person has no incentive to answer truthfully, and the insurer can't monitor it effectively and is in a disadvantaged position. Adverse selection happens when the company charges both the same premium. The insurance is more valuable to the high-risk individual, who has more to gain from it.

From this follows that insurers have an interest to identify and lure customers who are low risk, while restricting coverage for those with preexisting conditions that imply high risks. If only the sick buy insurance, the system will collapse.

Moral hazard occurs when a person's behavior changes after an insurance deal has been struck. The person feels safe and covered, and pays less attention to potential risks than before. The insurance company is now covering risks that are higher than before.

The young and healthy tend to believe they are immortal. As they often are short on cash, they do not buy insurance. If an accident happens, they have to beg for charity or be a burden for EDs that are not allowed to refuse anybody in dire need. Free riders strain the moral order of social systems. Why should I be a good citizen and pay my premiums promptly when the irresponsible still get care when in need, and at my expense?

## Deductibles and Co-payment

Insurers have developed ways to manage adverse selection and moral hazards. Insurance plans are segmented as different grades according to what they cost and what they cover. From this follows inequality, which flies in the face of health as an essential public good.

A deductible is a fixed amount you pay each year before your health insurance kicks in fully. Once you've paid your deductible, your health plan begins to pick up its share of your healthcare bills.[71] Co-payment is a fixed amount to be paid for every service encounter. The insurer covers the rest of the bill.[72]

Plans, deductibles, and co-payment make a mess out of healthcare. An episode of illness is a struggle not only against disease but also against a tight-fisted insurer who may or may not pay. Private insurance implies that for each health event, there must be a financial setup. In the U.S. private insurance sector, such dealings cost up to 15% of the health expenditure.[73]

## Mandatory Insurance

The problems with voluntary health insurance have several solutions. The one applied in central Europe is called the Bismarck model, in honor of its founder, the German chancellor. Insurers are private companies. However, insurance is mandatory; everybody must be covered. For those without means, the state pays the premium. Insurers are considered tools of public policy and therefore strictly regulated. They are not allowed to deny coverage to anybody, even with preexisting conditions. In some countries, they are not allowed to make a profit. Insurers compete primarily on the kind of packages they offer and the ease of use. While every citizen is covered at a base level, people are allowed to top up their coverage with voluntary insurance or out-of-pocket payments.

## Governments as Insurers

For governments, dealing with several insurers can at times be messy. The solution is to have one institution, a national health insurer, do the job. It is a public organization operated as a bureaucracy with no profit motive and tight accountability. Everybody pays and is covered. If there is not enough money, the populace is asked to contribute more. Service production can be private, with for-profit and nonprofit players, and public, with governments, states, and municipalities operating hospitals. The national health insurance (NHI) system is in use in Canada and Taiwan.

When Taiwan ceded military rule and started on the road to democracy, many institutions, healthcare among them, were overhauled. The Taiwanese government asked a prominent health economist, William Hsiao of Harvard University, to review the options and propose a solution. That he did, and came up with the NHI system, modeled after the system in Canada.[74]

## Governments as Financiers and Service Providers

A further way is to have a fully national, tax-funded system with public providers. This is the Beveridge model, named in honor of Lord Beveridge, who drew up plans for the UK National Health Service (NHS) in 1943. The whole population is covered. There are no deductibles or co-payments of office charges at the point of care. While the NHS is much loved by the British public, it has its shortcomings. Essentially, it is a socialist planned economy. It builds on normative, rather than economic, incentives to providers. As in any planned economy, supply finds it difficult to meet demand, queues are long, and the quality of care varies significantly within the system.

The Nordic countries have by and large adapted the Beveridge model. But each has made some twists to the original. In Sweden, more than half of primary care is operated by private, for-profit health enterprises. Specialist care is the responsibility of regions, county councils, that finance their activities through taxes. In Finland, patients pay a co-pay for every visit; out-of-pocket payments cover about a fifth of the total budget. Primary care is organized in large municipal health centers, typically with about a dozen doctors each. In Denmark, the family doctor is an individual private practitioner. In Norway, the central government operates hospitals, but not primary care.

For patients, the Beveridge model and its variants provide a trade-off. There are no, or only nominal, fees to be paid at the point of care. There is no hassle with insurers. On the other hand, there are the typical problems of public production, shortages that manifest as long waiting times and queues. Patients have limited choice, particularly in sparsely populated areas, and therefore not much bargaining power.

The major problem with the Beveridge model is that health finance is part of all other public finance. People pay taxes, but the portion that goes to healthcare is not earmarked as in the NHI system. With no financial gatekeeping, the public never seems to get enough care, demand increases, and so does cost.

A rare and special solution is the Singaporean system with individual health accounts. No medical service is provided free of charge to reduce the overutilization of healthcare services. Singapore uses a combination of compulsory savings from payroll deductions within a national system known as Medisave. Each citizen accumulates funds in a personal health account. Contributions are individually tracked and can be pooled within an extended family. Funds from Medisave accounts are used to pay service providers, who in turn comply with public price regulation. Medishield is a low-cost insurance scheme intended for those whose savings are insufficient to meet their medical expenses. Premiums can be paid out of Medisave accounts. Medifund is a safety net for those who are unable to meet their assessed contribution.[75]

## All Systems Have Problems

Health finance is a triangle drama with trade-off relations. Therefore, a universal best solution has not been found. All systems have their strengths and weaknesses. All systems have heavy, path-dependent legacies not easily changed. If there was an opportunity to start from a blank slate, I believe many countries would follow the example of Taiwan.

As a curiosity, the United States does not have a health system. It employs variants of all the general models. Several million people lack insurance and pay out-of-pocket. Many are under voluntary insurance with or without their employer's help. Medicare and Medicaid are national insurance schemes for the old and the poor. Similar arrangements exist for federal employees. The Veterans Health Administration (VHA) is pure-blood Beveridge.

## Gatekeepers

When third parties, insurers, or governments mediate transactions in healthcare, the basic commercial relationship is diluted. There is no value-in-exchange. People pay a fixed sum per year in deductibles, insurances, or taxes, and nominal fees that have no relation to production cost. Economic value can't be used as a yardstick. Moral hazard appears when people have no economic incentive to reduce their consumption of service. Production systems come under strain when demand is not induced to self-select or self-sort. If money is not the gatekeeper, it has to be something else.

The typical gatekeeping arrangement used in the Nordic countries is the rule that the route to specialist care goes through primary care. In nonemergency cases, you go to the hospital only with a referral from a general practitioner. A cheaper asset regulates access to a more expensive asset. The trouble is that primary care can't offer service on demand. You can't just walk into a health center and expect to see a doctor. An appointment is required, which puts you in a queue that can be up to 6 weeks. The obvious consequence is that people go to EDs, where at least a triage nurse will see them. From this, it follows that EDs are chronically overcrowded with trivial cases. Triage, the gatekeeping function in EDs, is notoriously difficult to maintain.

### 5.7.4 Paying the Provider

When the health finance collection part has done its job, providers are remunerated. This is a core issue of both health policy and service science: How are the revenue models constructed? Who gets paid for what? If we believe in the REMM model (resourceful, evaluative, maximizing model) of human behavior, incentives matter. There are other incentives than money, obviously. Many people honestly get into healthcare to serve humankind. But economic incentive is the great equalizer. If you don't pay heed, your economy is going to get ruined. All your good intentions and high morale come to nothing.

The revenue models have to skate the thin ice between two hazards: undercare and overcare, doing too little or doing too much in relation to the resources available and the desired health outcomes.

A third-party financier can pay a provider, be it a hospital, a general practice, or a larger supply network, in three ways: global budget, F4S, and capitation. These are ideal types as solutions to trade-offs; one problem solved creates a new one.

### Global Budget

The global budget is also known as cost plus. The cost of operating a hospital for a year is estimated, and it gets a lump sum of money. Here are your resources, go and do the good work!

What happens is easy to predict. There are no economic incentives to make extra effort. Whatever you do, the pay is the same. If, on top of that, patients don't pay at all or only token sums, economically unconstrained demand meets incentive-constrained supply. There will be rationing through queues and the ever-present temptation to accept bribes.

A system with global budgets will try to manage itself with the classical tools of planned economies. There will be posters and slogans, appeals to professional morale and the nobility of public service. There will be production quotas. In the Nordic countries, governments have stipulated minimum waiting times for first contacts and elective procedures. Penalties apply if the waiting time is too long. The effects are predictable. If the maximum waiting time for a knee operation is 3 months, the average waiting time is a day or two below that. The maximum becomes the norm. Producers manage queues with stopgap measures to avoid penalties. Using penalties and bonuses to fine-tune a global budget system is to accept defeat. Incentives are not supposed to matter in a planned economy, but now they are used to rescue it from failure and public wrath.

## Fee-for-Service

The capitalist alternative to a global budget is the classical industrial piece-rate system to pay for output. This is called the F4S system. The payer, government, or insurer pays for documented output. The payer will not accept any invoice. It applies price controls and set remuneration for each and every procedure. Again, the results are predictable. The more you do, the more you earn. Effort pays, regardless of results. Given information asymmetry, overcare comes as no surprise. Those who get paid also decide what is to be done.

In F4S, the proof of service is a production step. Flow management, integration, and coordination are not billable items. Neither is setup, unless it can be itemized as diagnostics, such as MRI scans or lab tests. The logic of pure F4S inevitably drives fragmentation and poor processes. This is why Lean initiatives fight an uphill battle in F4S environments.

The adverse effects of F4S have been amended in many ways. The most common is the system of DRGs. The idea is to prevent the fragmentation of billable items by bundling them together as packages wrapped around major diagnoses. A diagnosis is a codified description of an illness and its cause. It can be linked to typical procedures, surgery, and medication. The average cost can be estimated from historical data. Each DRG is weighted and given points. The financier now gets an intermediate currency of DRG points, to which real money can be attached. The price of a DRG point is so many dollars. The provider now gets paid for diagnosis–procedure bundles. There is no incentive to overcare within the bundle. Some bundles may be doable with less than average effort, others may require more. The assumption is that over time and volume, this averages out.

DRGs are applicable only to episodic cases where there is a diagnosis and a known care plan. Metaphorically speaking, the DRG has the same problem as the connected line in a factory. It can't manage too much variability.

Pay-for-performance (P4P) is another attempt to tweak both the global budget, and the F4S systems. The financier establishes some performance objectives, such as patient-reported satisfaction, patient safety, average LOS, and waiting time. If performance targets are met, bonuses are paid.

## Capitation

A third major payment type is capitation. It is akin to the members' fee used in country clubs. For a fixed annual fee, a member can make use of a given set of services with no or negligible additional charges. In health services, the financier pays the fees per capita, hence the term *capitation*. In rural areas with limited choice and given catchment areas, a service provider is paid to care for a given population. In densely populated areas, choice of caregiver is possible and capitation is connected with choice. Each person registers with a primary-level caregiver. Money follows the patient to the caregiver, together with the responsibility to provide for all or a defined set of needs.

Capitation differs from global budgets in that the caregiver has a defined responsibility for a defined population. Capitation with choice carries an element of competition. Reputable caregivers will get more members and more fees. Like in bundles, there is a disincentive to overcare.

Capitation, as any system, solves some problems but creates some new ones. A service provider in the capitation system has the same incentive as an insurance company to attract low-risk customers and keep the high-risk people away. This is called skimming. A worst-case scenario is that a provider intentionally gives bad care to expensive patients to prompt them to take their troubles elsewhere, preferably to the competition, and with them the money that doesn't cover their expenses anyway. Even in less drastic cases, a caregiver is tempted to undercare. A patient that is under-cared for at the early stage of an episode of illness frequently turns into an expensive case later on. If the caregiver is stuck with the patient, this should put brakes on the temptation to undercare. However, not everybody has the long time horizon and the capability to estimate future scenarios. This is particularly so if the financial and legislative environment is not stable—which tends to be the case in countries with budget deficits and aging populations. Further, capitation models have problems defining which services are included. If only minor ailments are included and specialist care is somebody else's responsibility under a different payment regime, a provider has little incentive to look at the long-term health of patients.

Capitation is not a stable solution like a self-regulating market. It requires meat-fisted regulation from financiers and government. Since pay is not linked to outputs but to membership, the average health status, or outcome of the member population, is a natural performance indicator. This calls for general, valid, and accurate outcome measurements, which must allow BM, that is, comparison of all service providers. Measures must have teeth. Outcome levels must be enforced. Providers must get penalties for underperformance; those continuously under the mark must close. This is not easy, if the loser happens to be a public organization; civil servants are not customarily sacked for poor performance. Bonuses may be used, but they are not really necessary. A provider who can achieve good outcomes with effective processes will reap the benefits as honest profit.

While DRG is usable in hospital-based episodic specialist care, capitation is suited for primary care with ongoing customer relations and long-term community care.

## Value-based Care

The Holy Grail of health finance is value-based healthcare (VBHC). It would be a modern version of the Chinese tale, where doctors get paid for health, not for procedures. The implementation of VBHC faces several technical problems of definitions and measurements. As I have discussed, health outcomes are not easily turned into reliable numbers with relevant and context-specific meanings. It will face the classical resistance to outcome-contingent contracts, which tend to load most of the inherent risk on the provider.[76]

A further dilemma lies in the definition of value as outcome per dollar spent. Providers would in some cases have to be rewarded for doing less. This requires a solution akin to capitation, and the accompanying problems. VBHC is still work in progress, with significant potential for clever IT solutions. It may not work in a pure form in all of healthcare, but rather in some niches and in combination with other revenue models.

# 5.8 Distribution in Healthcare

Separating production and distribution of health services leads to the following conceptualization:

1. The need for service arises at a time and location where a person, or a significant other, becomes aware of the need for medical help, that is, the *point of need* (PN).
2. Services are prepared; resources are acquired and kept in back offices that have little or no customer contact. These are called *resource units* (RUs).
3. Services are distributed, that is, made available to the population through distribution units, *contact points* (CPs)—the location, facility, phone number, or website where patients contact providers for appointments or advice.
4. Services are delivered at front offices, *service provision points* (SPPs), where service events and encounters take place.

In practice, RUs, CPs, and SPPs can be located at the same facility and operate in an integrated way. Therefore, they are easily lumped together. Analytically, however, it is important to keep them separate, since there are instances where a physical or operational separation may be beneficial. For example, call centers can be arranged to answer telephone inquiries and provide advice in real time but do not have to be colocated with a physical care unit, that is, the CPs and SPPs can be separated. A centralized RU, such as a pathology laboratory or a blood center, can serve several SPPs. Various e-health solutions can realign RUs, CPs, and SPPs to amend, twist, or break the constraints of time and location.

Economic constraints arise from the fact that most of healthcare is time and location dependent. The healer and the patient must be at the same physical location at the same time. Even if resources exist and can be afforded, they might not be at the location where they would be needed at the time when needed. This is the problem of access, the distance between a PN and an SPP, that shows up dramatically with health and rescue services, ambulatory care, medical transports, and flying doctors.

At a care unit, demand can be highly variable in terms of case mix, severity, urgency, and arrival time. The logic of services dictates that service procedures cannot be produced to inventory; therefore, capacity must be managed according to fluctuations in demand. Sometimes capacity may hit the ceiling and patients will have to wait, or LWBS. Supply may be temporary constrained by daily or seasonal variance and an ensuing shortage of critical equipment or labor.

From this follows two basic arrangements. Facility-based service means that the patient comes to the healer. Field-based service means that the healer comes to the patient. In both cases, there are issues of transport and travel time. If a field-based doctor needs to see several patients during the same day, she will face the classical traveling salesman's problem.[77] What would be the best order to visit the patients so as to minimize the distance and/or time of travel? For the patient, there is the decision of where to go and how to get there. This is the time–location access problem.[78]

As with physical distribution, discussed in Chapter 3, access is not all there is. The variety available at an SPP and the level of specialization must be considered. As illustrated in Figure 5.16, access, variety, and specialization form a trilemma, a three-factor problem with no obvious solution. There is no natural equilibrium that would optimize all three.

When a patient reaches the destination, the next question is, what is available at this location? This is the question of variation of supply. It has two dimensions. First, there is the variation of nonsubstitutes. That means the range of different services at one location that are not alternatives (substitutes) to one patient at one time. If the patient has a dental problem but the doctor does only internal medicine, service variety does not meet the need. The health policy issue that follows is the

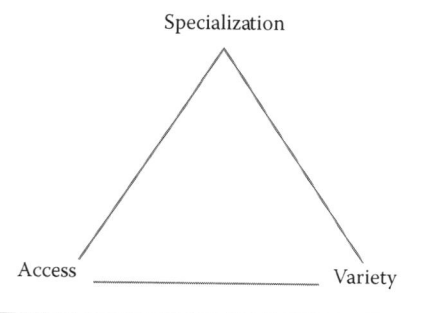

**Figure 5.16   Access, variety, and specialization trilemma.**

question of what should be the variety of service at the first CP. In the tax-financed Nordic systems, the solution is to build full-range primary care centers with at least a dozen doctors with various specialties, supported by diagnostics and the capability to do minor interventions. But patients who get prescriptions for medication still have to travel to the nearest pharmacy, which may be miles away. In Japan, a lone general practitioner typically does primary care, but also sells the most common pharmaceuticals. The Nordic solution has its merits. Like somebody living within the catchment area of a superstore, a patient does not have to spend effort figuring out where to go. However, if the population is spread out over large areas, as it is in the northern parts of the region, the nearest point of care may offer great variety but be a hundred miles away. In urban areas, there can be the combination of easy access and limited variety with a doctor's office at every block.

The second dimension of variety is that of substitutes at different levels of specialty. The same problem, say a wrist wounded in a bicycle accident, can be treated by a paramedic, a nurse, a general practitioner, a trauma specialist, an orthopedic, or a super-specialized hand surgeon. The higher the level of specialization, the more costly is the resource. From this follows the dilemma, how and who should determine the appropriate level of care. If there are no economic or other gatekeepers, there will be immense pressure for the higher levels of specialization.

If the expensive specialized resources are to be used only for those who really need them and to maximum efficiency, there should be a sufficient flow of screened and selected patients to keep the expert profitably busy. As demand appears randomly, this means large catchment areas, longer distances, and worse access.

## 5.9 The Problem

The discussion so far has treated health services as one entity. But the story is frequently punctuated with modifiers: some patients seek help, others pursue health; some but not all ailments are life-and-death issues; some therapies rely on technologies, others on intuition; sometimes there is information asymmetry, other times not that much. There is a multitude of demand types, production functions, processes, and revenue models in a jumbled multiverse.

In industry, companies tend to center around one or a few technologies, production types, distribution arrangements, or market demand. Very few firms are spread as wide and thin as healthcare.

Operations management will not be able to come up with helpful and widely applicable models and methods if everything that is said must be followed by a caveat; this applies here but not there. There is a need to segment activities into meaningful parts, something like the product–process matrix that specifies which types of products are produced with which types of processes. The question for the rest of this book is, is healthcare one or several production systems? Could it be segmented into managerially meaningful parts?

# Notes

1. The transitive nature of preferences in one more logic chunk. It makes sense to assume that if a person likes coffee more than tea, and likes tea more than cocoa, that person would prefer coffee over cocoa. But again, variability and epistemology confuse the real world. Preference can be situation dependent, coffee in the morning and tea in the afternoon. Coffee, tea, and cocoa may vary in their perceived quality in different settings. The variability of the real world beats the logic.
2. Grossman (1972).
3. Porter (2006).
4. Price (1994).
5. See, for example, Gawande (2002, 2007), Mukherjee (2015), and Kalanithi (2016).
6. Rosenthal (2017), Cutler (2004), and Mahar (2006).
7. Illich (1974).
8. Foucault (1973).
9. Eberhart (2006).
10. For general perceptions of risk, see Gardner (2008).
11. The bibliographic citation for this definition is the preamble to the constitution of the WHO as adopted by the International Health Conference, New York, June 19–July 22, 1946; it was signed on July 22, 1946, by the representatives of 61 states (Official Records of WHO No. 2, p. 100) and entered into force on April 7, 1948. The definition has not been amended since 1948.
12. The English translation is Canguilhem (1991).
13. *Lancet*, Editorial, Vol. 373, March 7, 2009.
14. Huber et al. (2011).
15. Lush and Vargo (2014).
16. Sick leave in Sweden has been characterized by high levels and extreme fluctuations. Following a clear decline between 2003 and 2010, sick leave is now once again on the increase. The government anticipates that expenditure on sickness benefits will total approximately SEK 50 billion in 2018, which represents an increase of 150% since 2010 (Hägglund and Johansson 2016). For an English summary, see http://eso.expertgrupp.se/wp-content/uploads/2016/02/Summary-till-webben1.pdf.
17. For an introduction, see Berridge (2016) and Bodenheimer and Grumbach (2016).
18. Whittington et al. (2015).
19. http://www.ihi.org/engage/initiatives/tripleaim/pages/default.aspx.
20. Womack (2009).
21. Sen (2001).
22. Doyle et al. (2013).
23. Faraz et al. (2014).
24. The Organisation for Economic Co-operation and Development provides a comprehensive set of data on health resources in its member countries. See https://stats.oecd.org/Index.aspx?DataSetCode=HEALTH_REAC.
25. For a review and discussion on the placebo and nocebo effects, see Thompson (2005).
26. Benedetti et al. (2007).
27. The unease with the placebo effect in healthcare is unnecessary. Similar phenomena are frequent in industry and trade. Marketers and sales administrators have long been aware of the effect a confident and attentive salesperson has on getting deals closed.

Some people simply feel bad for disappointing a friendly person. The social logic is important. The Hawthorne effect caused a sea change in organization theory. In the 1920s, researchers at the Western Electric Hawthorne assembly plant sought to find the best work environment through a set of experiments. Various factors, such as heat and lighting, were varied and their effect on labor productivity examined. Surprisingly, productivity increased and kept doing so regardless of changes in the variables. In the end, the assemblers produced top results in semidarkness. It was concluded that the mere fact of being observed by curious researchers created an effect on productivity. The observation led to the birth of the human relations school of thought and the sociotechnical systems theory. People do not react only to the physical environment. The mere situation of being seen and placed at the center of attention creates measurable results. There, indeed, is a large and growing sector of complementary and alternative medicine (CAM) and spiritual healing that can be assumed to exploit the placebo effect to these ends.

28. Bland (2014).
29. Moore (2015).
30. Vennberg (2010).
31. The best-known example of prioritizing evidence-based cures is the Oregon Health Plan, which has generated a list of prioritized cures. http://www.oregon.gov/oha/healthplan/Pages/priorlist.aspx.
32. National Institutes of Health U.S. National Library of Medicine, https://ghr.nlm.nih.gov/primer/precisionmedicine/definition.
33. "Whole-person needs" is an expression made popular by Berry and Bendapudi (2007).
34. Patients want patient-centered care that (1) explores the patient's main reason for the visit, concerns, and need for information; (2) seeks an integrated understanding of the patient's world—that is, their whole person, emotional needs, and life issues; (3) finds common ground on what the problem is and mutually agrees on management; (4) enhances prevention and health promotion; and (5) enhances the continuing relationship between the patient and the doctor (Little et al. 2001).
35. World Health Organization (WHO) (2003).
36. Mol (2008).
37. Dixon et al. (2010).
38. Rational choice theory postulates that people are logical and rational decision makers who are motivated by goals, have consistent values and preferences, possess complete information, weigh the various options with good computation skills, and choose something that they believe will maximize benefits and minimize risk. The foundation of the rational choice model is Von Neumann and Morgenstern's (2007) expected utility (EU) theory, the major paradigm of individual rational decision-making under uncertainty since the Second World War.
39. Haidt (2012).
40. Légaré and Witteman (2013).
41. Stacey et al. (2017).
42. Wager et al. (2017).
43. The term *patient in process* was developed in Kujala et al. (2006).
44. For a compact introduction to the queuing problem, see Chapter 18 in Ben-Tovim (2017). Also see Griffin et al. (2016).

45. An Australian study found an ED LWBS rate of 10.7% (Crilly et al. 2013). A study of 262 California hospitals revealed a range of LWBS from 0% to 20.3%, with a median percentage of 2.6% (Ash et al. 2011). LWBS patients are generally at no greater risk of mortality, but are at a higher risk of representing to an ED than patients who complete treatment and are discharged home.
46. Hall (2013).
47. Donabedian (1988).
48. Pearson et al. (2001) and Miani et al. (2014).
49. The difference between money and resources is the cost factor, most significantly the cost of labor. In international comparisons, this becomes a problem, as labor rates vary significantly. Labor time per labor type can be used as a universal measure.
50. For a description of cataract surgery management, see Mikola and Lillrank (2015). The numbers are from an unpublished study by the authors.
51. An earlier version of this model is published in Lillrank et al. (2015).
52. I owe this insight to my former student, Dr. Paulus Torkki.
53. For example, if Hospital A has an average cost per patient of $1000 and a CMI of 0.80 for a given year, its adjusted cost per patient is $1000/0.80 = $1250. Likewise, if Hospital B has an average cost per patient of $1500 and a CMI of 1.25, its adjusted cost per patient is $1500/1.25 = $1200. Therefore, if a hospital has a CMI greater than 1.00, its adjusted cost per patient or per day will be lowered, and conversely if a hospital has a CMI less than 1.00, its adjusted cost will be higher (http://www.healthand-hospitalcommission.com/docs/May26Meeting/CasemixIndexDefintion.pdf).
54. For an overview of the DRG systems in Europe, see Busse et al. (2011).
55. Standard methods and manuals for disease-specific indicators are developed by professional bodies. See, for example, the Joint Commission, http://www.jointcommissioninternational.org/.
56. http://www.orthopaedicscore.com/.
57. http://www.15d-instrument.net/15d/.
58. Weldring and Smith (2013).
59. For applications, see Kenney (2010).
60. WHO (2006).
61. Blozik et al. (2014).
62. Rashid and Jussof (2009) and Mosadegrad (2013).
63. Azam et al. (2012).
64. Berwick (2014).
65. For a literature review on the relation between hospital size and productivity, see Lillrank et al. (2015).
66. Leonard (2001) and Leonard and Zivin (2003).
67. Akerlof (1970).
68. Arrow (1963).
69. It is no coincidence that in Finland, the Mannerheim League for Child Welfare, a major nongovernmental organization, takes its name from General Mannerheim, the commander of the armed forces during the First and Second World Wars.
70. Health shocks are the single biggest cause of impoverishment in India. Roughly 6% of the urban population, or about 18 million people, face impoverishment entirely due to out-of-pocket medical expenses (Chowdhury 2015; Bhandari et al. 2010).

71. You have a $2000 deductible. You get the flu in January and see your doctor. The doctor's bill is $200. You are responsible for the entire bill since you haven't paid your deductible yet this year. After paying the $200 doctor's bill, you have $1800 left to go on your yearly deductible. In March, you fall and break your arm. The bill is $3000. You pay $1800 of that bill and you have met your yearly deductible of $2000. Now, your health insurance kicks in and helps you pay the rest of the bill. In April, you get your cast removed. The bill is $500. Since you've already met your deductible for the year, you don't have to pay any more. Your health insurance pays its full share of this bill.

72. Your health insurance may require a co-payment of $30 each time you see your primary care physician (PCP), $50 each time you see a specialist physician, and $20 each time you fill a generic prescription. When you see your PCP, you pay the physician $30 that day. Your health plan picks up the rest of the bill for that visit. When you go back a few days later, you have to pay another $30, and your health plan pays the rest. Your PCP sends you to a specialist. When you see the specialist, you pay a $50 co-payment. Your health insurance pays the remainder of the specialist's bill.

73. Jiwani et al. (2014).

74. Hsiao (1995).

75. Britnell (2015).

76. Moriates et al. (2016).

77. Applegate et al. (2006).

78. In health policy, access usually means economic access, that is, insurance coverage or ability to pay. Time–location access is independent of that.

# Chapter 6

# The Demand and Supply–Based Operating Logic of Healthcare

## 6.1 Segmentation beyond the Obvious

The predicament of healthcare is captured in dilemmas: craft versus mass production, health versus help, output versus outcome, specialization versus integration, and jumbled versus coordinated flows. Healthcare is more an institution that an organization; there is no command center where all strings can be pulled just right. Healthcare is a multiverse of overlapping and at times contradicting logics.

### 6.1.1 Overlapping Logics

The American sociologist Elliot Freidson[1] has developed a typology of logics found in organizations, the professional, the administrative, and the commercial.

A profession is a work group that reserves to itself the right to judge the quality of its own work. Society cedes this authority to a profession because of three beliefs. It is assumed that professionals are altruistic and will work to the best interest of those they serve. Professionals are in command of expertise, knowledge, and technologies not readily accessible to the public. Professionals will self-regulate and police each other. They have the power to determine who is allowed to join their ranks and is qualified to perform certain tasks.

The administrative logic is centered on order and predictability in the ceaseless battle against variability and decay. Administrators are expected to ensure quality and see to it that promises are kept and rules followed. Mass manufacturing and governments in rule-based societies take the administrative logic to its extreme.

The commercial logic focuses on value, choice, preferences, needs, wants, and demand. The customer with money in hand is always right. The supplier is supposed to produce whatever makes customers happy.

The three logics are ideal types that rarely exist in pure form in the real world. A system view will have to consider all of them. At the intersection is the managerial logic, a combination of administration and leadership. Practical managers deal with going concerns. Leaders articulate vision, define strategy, set policy, and design systems. Managers depend on professionals to tend the production functions, on administrators to maintain order, and on customers to bring in revenue. Managers need to attend to all key constituencies, paying customers, rulemaking regulators, financiers, personnel, and supply chain partners.

All logics need to make sense of their respective domains by segmenting them into meaningful and internally homogeneous parts. Segmentation becomes necessary when the variety of offerings expands; needs become more specific and one size does not fit all. Within a segment, variability can be reduced and action focused.

The administrative logic is segmented by organizational architectures, as exemplified by the product–process matrix. The commercial logic uses demographic groupings, needs, wants, and lifestyles to identify demand types to which products are matched in terms of functionality, performance, grade, style, and price. Professionals need to segment their world by categories of knowledge and technology. The history of medicine is a story of empirical discovery and the development of conceptual tools to identify, group, analyze, and connect elements of the human body and its pathologies.

## 6.1.2 Segmenting the Human Body

### The Whole and Parts

Hippocrates (460–370 BC), the patron saint of Western medicine, insisted that every patient is a unique individual. There was no point in classifying symptoms and arranging them into categories.[2] Religious norms forbade doctors from looking under the skin. The human body was a black box with unknown innards. External observations about health and illness could only lead to learned speculation about humors and body fluids.

Andreas Vesalius (1514–1564) was one of the first to look inside the black box. This entailed some difficulties, such as finding bodies to dissect by sneaking corpses from cemeteries. His *De humani corporis fabrica* was for a long time the most influential book on anatomy. It showed in minutia detail the parts of the human body and how they come together as a structure. Vesalius developed the epistemology (dissection) and laid bare the ontology (anatomy) of the human body. The organs, such as the heart and kidneys, are boxes within the box.

## Organs Are Made of Tissue

From the discovery of organs, scientific inquiry led to micro and macro: What are organs made of and how do they connect? Marie Francois Xavier Bihart (1771–1802) applied a segmentation principle based on structures comparable in texture but present in different organs. Bihart described 21 such tissues, distinguished by appearance and vital qualities, for example, cellular tissues, nerves, arteries, veins, and absorbent and exhalant vessels. Tissues were for Bihart the analytical building blocks of anatomy, physiology, and pathology. He set out to delineate their structure, vital properties, responsiveness, and abnormalities. Bihart famously noted the power of epistemology: "You may take notes for twenty years from morning to night at the bedside of the sick, and all will be to you only a confusion of symptoms, a train of incoherent phenomena. But start cutting bodies open and, at a stroke, this obscurity will soon disappear".[3]

The discovery of tissues called for more detailed scrutiny. The science of optics and advances in lenses produced the microscope. It was an epistemological device that allowed the collection of observations not visible to the naked eye. Antonie van Leeuwenhoek (1632–1723) is usually credited with developing the first workable version. Microbes and cells were found. In 1839, Matthias Schleiden and Theodor Schwann finally connected the dots as the cell theory. Explorations deeper into the cell eventually led to the discovery of the gene and the development of molecular genetics and DNA sequencing.

## Organs Connect as Systems

William Harvey (1578–1657) studied how different organs are connected. His major discovery was blood circulation. Minuscule capillaries, not visible to the naked eye, connect arteries and veins, solving the mysteries of the pulse and the heart that had puzzled premodern science.

As the dynamic connections between different organs emerged, anatomy as the study of components, materials, and structures was joined by physiology, the study of the dynamics of organ systems.[4] The heart, veins, and arteries combine as the circulatory system, which in turn links to the respiratory system for the supply and circulation of oxygen, combining as the cardiovascular system. The renal system consists of kidneys that filter blood and extracts substances through the urinary system. The organ systems are connected with boundaries and interfaces. The system view led to the invention of anesthetics, the methods to shut down parts of the neural system to eliminate the sense of pain. Another was the heart–lung machine, a necessary enabler of open-heart surgery. The cardiovascular system could be stopped and its function replaced by an artificial device.

Physiology led to improved understanding of pathologies, diseases, and abnormalities. Infections are causes of illness that reflect the existence and spread of microorganisms, such as bacteria, viruses, and fungus. Cancer is caused by tumors formed by cells that go crazy and start to multiple uncontrollably. Clinical genetics looks into problems that have a root in the genome.

Functional medicine has developed a segmentation principle based on physiological processes that extend across organ systems.[5] It is based on advances in genetics that reveal hither to unknown dynamics. Genome–environment interactions cause imbalances, chronic ailments that appear not to have a seat in any singular organ system. Each process has its own logic of health, illness, and cure. Changing the perspective, and the unit of analysis, from organ systems to physiological processes opens new insights.

The study of the human body and its dynamics has led to several overlapping perspectives with distinct theories and therapies. Production functions require processes and organizations. The professional logic runs into the administrative and commercial logics in the quest for how healthcare should be organized.

## 6.1.3 Segmenting Healthcare

As the understanding of the human body expanded, the principles of division of labor and specialization got in motion. Each organ, tissue, organ system, and pathology got its own specialty of science, clinical practice, and professional communities, such as ophthalmology for eyes; neurology for brains and nerves; orthopedics for bones, joints, and tendons; and oncology for cancer. The division between internal medicine that uses pharmaceuticals and surgery that uses cutting and stitching has long historical roots. Other methods are radiation used to kill tumors, physical manipulations used in physiotherapy, and various counseling and coaching methods applied to support healthy lifestyles.

### Urgency, Severity, and Specialization

In healthcare, the historically oldest and still profound segmentation principle is that which separates the urgent from what can wait, the severe from the mild. Urgency demands immediate, or fastest possible, access to resources. Resources and capabilities have to be arranged in specific architectures to allow rapid action meeting random demand.

The severity of a medical condition is associated with specialization level, that is, substitutable variety. The association is not perfect; severe bleeding can be stopped with simple means; cosmetic surgery takes a great deal of specialized skill. Specialization, however, is linked with the cost of education, which in turn defines the remuneration of doctors, nurses, and paramedics. Expensive resources should not be used for tasks where cheaper is good enough. From this follows segmentation into primary, secondary, and tertiary care. Primary care is the base layer, the first contact points of unsorted demand. It is like mass retailing: broad variety, large volumes, easy access, and low level of specialization. Secondary care, also known as general specialist care, typically employs doctors with specialization in a clinical field. While primary care is mostly outpatient visits, secondary care has diagnostic equipment, operating rooms, wards, and beds for patients who recover from surgery or need special monitoring. Tertiary care is in the hands of the super-specialists with deep and narrow diagnostic capabilities and therapeutic skills. They are typically affiliated with medical schools.

Specialization is a supply-based segmentation principle. Combined with the urgency principle, it produces the basic organizational architecture of health services in many countries (Figure 6.1).

## Phases

A further segmentation principle is the phases of illness and cure. Screening is done to find subclinical symptoms, that is, signs of illness before they are perceivable by natural means. Diagnostics is the phase where causes and states are investigated making use of imagining (radiology) and laboratory tests (pathology) on tissues and fluids. Clinical decision-making takes the diagnostic data, combines it with other observations and sources of information, and designs care plans to be implemented by various production units. These correspond to the industrial separation of marketing, design, engineering, and production.

## Overlapping Segments

The organization chart of a general hospital is an overlap of several segmentation principles. For example, a cancerous tumor (cause) affects the large intestine (gastrointestinal organ system) and needs to be removed surgically (method). The required skill set calls for specialization. Three specialized professionals can form a team, or some individuals may want to acquire mastery in two or all three. Professionals tend to want positions, recognition, and organizational units of their own. As specialization goes on, the number of possible combinations increases exponentially. Organizations and the patient journeys through them become truly

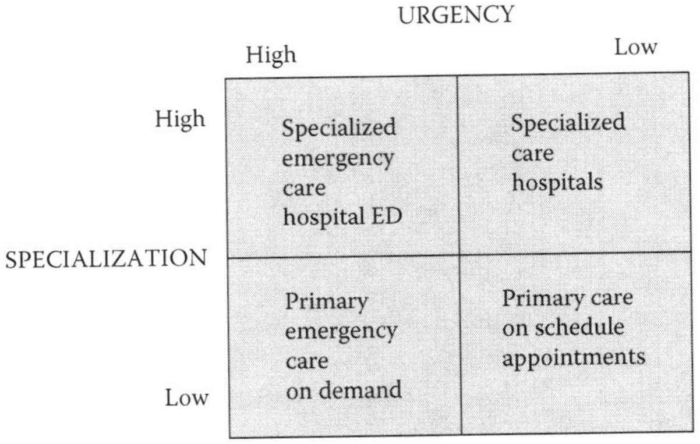

**Figure 6.1    Structure of care based on specialization and urgency.**

complex cross-functional processes, disconnected flows with complicated handovers and time buffers between professional silos.[6]

The upside of specialization is accuracy, precision, and efficiency. It greatly benefits patients who have a problem that matches with a narrow specialty. Division of labor, specialization, and standardization should be counteracted with integration and coordination. Indeed, there is an arms race between specialization and integration, where the latter tends to be the perennial loser.

The volume–variety dilemma becomes an issue. Specialized organizational units can build clinical pathways with dedicated resources to match specific needs profiles. However, resources can be dedicated only if there is enough demand for a particular profile. That can be only if the catchment area is large enough. Specialization drives centralization into large production units.

The clinical segmentation principles do not provide an obvious, universal guide to how service production should be organized, beyond the classical distinction between emergencies and schedulable cases. There is no natural hierarchy of principles, nor a universally accepted dominant design for health service production. Consequently, there is a great deal of variety between care organizations.

Clinical segmentation is a sensible technology-based and supply-side way of thinking. It focuses on what the medical professions want, know, and can do. As other industries, healthcare is under pressure to align supply with demand.

## Segmentation by Needs

A traditional demand-side segmentation principle follows demographics, categories of people that are easily recognized and correspond to specific needs profiles. Segmentation can be by gender; hospitals for women have been around for some time. Age group is a convenient segment, as infants, children, adolescents, and the elderly require different services. There are also segments by status, such as military and corporate hospitals, and activity-based segments, such as sports and occupational medicine.

Lynn and colleagues have developed a construct that comes closest to what can be called segmentation by the needs of people.[7] The model divides the population into eight groups: people in good health, maternal and infant situations, acute illnesses, stable chronic conditions, serious but stable disability, failing health near death, advanced organ system failure, and long-term frailty. Each group has its own definitions of optimal health, priorities, targets, and corresponding services.

Garfield has suggested that organizational architecture should follow a segmentation scheme that divides patients into the well, the worried well, the early sick, and the sick.[8] The corresponding organizational units would be a health testing and referral center, a healthcare center, a preventive maintenance center, and a sick care center.[9]

## Managerial Segmentation

The very brief history of medical discovery highlights the methodological principles of analysis and synthesis. A similar but not identical intellectual endeavor is needed for the understanding of health service production. A basic premise of operations management is that tasks with similar coordination and control requirements should be performed in similar organizations. Different production functions, time perspectives, goals, performance criteria, and metrics require different process architectures and management practices. Producing standard products together with custom-engineered goods on the same production line creates confusion. Connected lines can't be used if variability is high. The product–process matrix is the classical operations management segmentation device.

The need for managerial segmentation in healthcare has been recognized, but so far not developed into practice. Glouberman and Mintzberg (2001) have proposed a model that divides healthcare into four different worlds: cure (physicians), care (nurses), control (administrators), and community (boards).[10] The four worlds operate on different logics, and therefore exhibit communication problems.

In their book *Hospital Operations*, Hopp and Lovejoy divide the hospital into four functional units: emergency department (ED), nursing units, operating rooms, and diagnostic services.[11]

Bohmer and Lawrence suggest that care platforms should be defined by identifying families of health conditions and interventions that may cross disease or organ system boundaries if the work is identical.[12] A production system for each family should be designed to integrate the elements into an end-to-end process, a patient journey, or a clinical pathway.

Christensen et al.,[13] followed by Hopp and Lovejoy,[14] build on the insight that the fundamental dividing lines run between intuitive, evidence-based, and precision medicine, that is, the accuracy of production functions. Intuitive medicine relies on clinical judgment and heuristics in the face of uncertainty. Evidence-based medicine builds on statistically confirmed outcomes of treatment schemes on patient groups. Precision medicine allows exact diagnosis and the application of known or predictable treatment schemes. Intuitive medicine requires job shops, labeled "solution shops," where the uncertainties and risks are managed within the doctor–patient relationship. Where evidence-based medicine is applicable, flow lines can be used and "value-adding processes" can be configured. Precision medicine leads to two production types. Individual medicine develops precise diagnoses and care plans based on genetic and personal profiles, which take a job shop arrangement. Where setups can be accurately formatted, interventions can be standardized and foolproofed, and self-service can be used with the assistance of "supported networks."

Managerial segmentation resembles Bihart's approach to anatomy by focusing on tissues. Management should identify task combinations that are organized similarly across organ systems, methods, causes, and demographic groups.

# 6.2 Demand and Supply–based Operating Logic

## 6.2.1 The Healer Operates in Modes

Medical professionals tend to look at healthcare through clinical categories. That is what they have trained for. A naïve observer may look at it through a veil of ignorance. Like a kid who asks his dad, the country doc, why do these people come here? What are you doing for them? What is the demand and what is the supply?

### The Doctor's Bag

My father was a country doc and worked like a craftsman in a job shop. At the time, in the early 1960s, in the sticks there was very little division of labor and specialization. A community nurse and a midwife looked after expectant mothers and babies. A dentist from a nearby town visited once a fortnight and set up shop in the nurse's office. This little team looked after a population of 5000.

Every weekday morning, people lined up in the doctor's office, patiently waiting to be seen. There was quite some variety. Elderly lumberjacks showed up complaining about severe cough. Not much was to be done, except the sensible advice to quit smoking. Bad dental hygiene was endemic. Rotten teeth were unceremoniously pulled out, and that was it. Occasionally, trauma patients with open wounds from woodworking tools came with the village's only taxi, a beaten-up Chevrolet. Urgencies were allowed to jump the line. People with sharp abdominal pain indicating appendicitis could not be operated on at the premises. The Chevy was summoned to take the patient to the nearest hospital some 120 km away. Then there was the endless stream of people with chronic conditions, frail elderly, war veterans curing posttraumatic stress disorders with vodka, malnourished children—you name it. Sometimes a call came and the doc had to leave a waiting room full of people and rush to the site of an accident, turning from a facility-based to a field-based service provider. The country doctor had the bag and some skills, as illustrated in Figure 6.2.

Without knowing anything about clinical medicine, the naïve observer can see that what the doc does is a function of what is asked for and what can be done in a situation with limited resources at hand. Demand is what needs to be done; supply is what can be done, given the circumstances. Together, they produce an understanding of the job to be done. It may take some bargaining before the setup is clear. Demand may have to accept that everything requested is not available or cannot be had. Supply may have to bend backwards to find an unorthodox solution. The demand–supply constellation is set up in different operating modes.

### Operating Mode

The operating mode is not part of the standard management vocabulary. It takes a bit of explanation. In criminal investigations, it is known that serial killers have

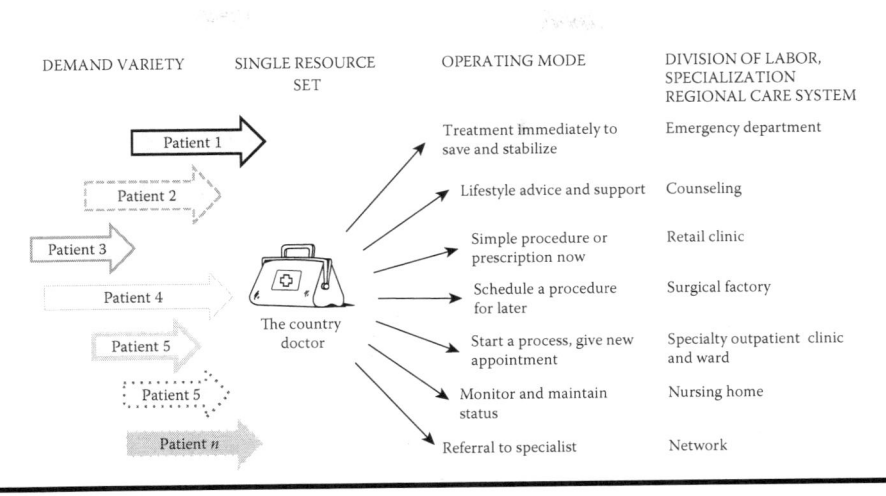

**Figure 6.2  A single resource responds to demand variety through different operating modes.**

a *modus operandi*, an operational fingerprint, a certain distinctive way of doing things that may give them away. Cameras have program mode and manual mode. Animals respond to threats by fight-or-flight modes. SUVs can be driven in four-wheel or front-wheel modes. The country doctor switches modes to respond when demand comes calling.

Technically speaking, mode means the different states in which a production system can operate with a given set of resources. In terms of resources and capabilities, it is a closed system; new supplies and skills are not instantly available. In terms of demand, it is an open system; a large array of demand must be considered. The same resources are set up and put into different uses in different ways, because the situation so demands. An operating mode is the result of a setup.

> Think of a soccer team as a production system. One team starts off playing aggressively and scores an early goal. To protect the lead and secure victory, the manager decides to change the mode from offensive to defensive. The team, the field, the rules, and every resource remain the same, but the mode of play changes. If the manager decides to change the setup of the team by replacing attackers with defenders, the mode change is amplified by a change in resource configuration.

A multipurpose tool, such as a knife, can be used in several modes. A single-purpose tool, such as a potato peeler, is built for one type of job. That is, the potato peeler is high in asset specificity, while the knife, with its multiple modes, is low. A multimode organization is akin to self-sufficiency; everything is done, but nothing very proficiently. Help is offered, but not necessarily health.

## A Mode Stabilizes and Specializes

Shifting between operating modes is necessary when resources are scarce. With abundance, there can be division of labor, specialization, and standardization of best practices. Setups can command the resources of a whole hospital. Patients can be directed to the appropriate care unit. As the process continues, labor is divided into smaller parts with increasingly deep expertise. What started as single-resource multimode operation turns into a facility with several specialized skill sets, assets, buildings, and permanent structures, the general hospital. It deals with maximal demand variety with maximal supply variety.

The naïve observer loses sight of operating modes behind sorted and selected flows. However, the logic of illness and cure, problem and solution remains as demand and supply-based operating logic (DSO).[15]

## 6.2.2 Demand Side

Demand appears when a customer shows up in a store, money in hand and ready to buy. Needs and wants turn into demand when backed by purchasing power, insurance cover, or citizens' rights. The dynamics of demand is at the root of the predicament of health service systems. Needs that do not turn into demand mean undercare. Wants that elude the gatekeepers lead to overcare and cost inflation. The ontology, epistemology, and dynamics of needs, wants, and demand are summarized in Table 6.1.

### Needs and Wants

Standard marketing models assume that people have needs that are expressed as wants, which, combined with purchasing power, constitute effective demand.[16] In healthcare, this sequence is not obvious. Patients may want what cannot be provided and ignore what is available. Patients are often reluctant, scared, and confused and have difficulty articulating their needs.

True need is an ancient question with no definite answer in sight. Abraham Maslow (1943) became famous for his conceptual construct of the hierarchy of needs.[17] Survival is the base. Five minutes without oxygen, and we are all dead. A human being can go 3 days without water and 30 without food. When survival is secured, people look for safety. Then come belonging and love, social esteem, and finally, self-actualization, the higher-level spiritual purposes. When one layer is satisfied, it turns off as a motive force and the next one is activated. When basic needs are fulfilled, people desire status, fashion, and experiences.

While the Maslovian chunk of logic makes sense, the ontology and epistemology of need are clear only at the base levels. Higher-level needs can be satisfied in innumerable ways. Need has a connotation of objectivity. It takes a third-party observer to confirm it. Wants are easier. Wants are articulated, expressed, and communicated. Want is known when somebody expresses intention to acquire, do, or be something.

**Table 6.1 Ontology, Epistemology, and Dynamics of Needs, Wants, and Demand**

|  | *Ontology* | *Epistemology* | *Dynamics* |
|---|---|---|---|
| Need | Something necessary for survival or well-being | Third-party assessment against some legitimate criteria Urgency and severity | Hierarchy of needs Priorities |
| Want | Expressed desire to have, do, or be something | Articulated by words or deeds Help and health | Proclamation of intent, or claim on others |
| Demand | Want backed by purchasing power or justified claim of service | Arrival volume, timing, and primary complaint | Activates supply |

In third-party financed care, the distinction between need and want becomes a pressing matter. An old man with an enlarged prostate may want surgery, but does he really need it? If resources are constrained, all wants cannot be fulfilled and all needs are not legitimate. A gatekeeper approves needs and wants and turns them into demand.

## Demand

Want brings the needy to the store; money turns desire into demand. Demand requires purchasing power or its equivalents. Where these are lacking, access is blocked.

All health systems struggle under resource constraints. Third-party payers face moral hazards and insist on gatekeeping. Access can be denied or restricted in many ways. Money is the easiest bouncer. Insurance policies post co-payments and deductibles. A triage nurse can send a patient home if she determines that no urgent or severe need is present.

In commercial services, demand is associated with revenue, and therefore welcome. In health services, that is not always the case. To for-profit providers, demand means revenue; for third-party financiers, it means cost. For public providers on global budgets and monthly salaries, more demand means more work for constant pay.

## Demand for Help and Health

Health episodes can start in a flash, such as being hit by a car, a cardiac attack, or a stroke. In such cases, the need for help is obvious; wants are clearly articulated and accepted as legitimate. A central feature in health services is the occasional urgency and severity of medical conditions. Severity implies loss of life or permanent damage. Urgency implies a time-elastic loss function. The longer the elapsed time between onset and help, the more damage there will be.

Where urgency and severity are perceived, they are articulated as wants. There are, however, cases with needs but not (yet) perceived wants. A person may run a risk of becoming seriously ill without knowing it. The causes can be hereditary or lifestyle issues, such as substance abuse or obesity. Some episodes of illness can start slowly as unease at the periphery of perception, unusual sensations, and worries. Eventually, there is a tipping point; a decision is made to contact a caregiver. As the case is not urgent, patients have the time to articulate their needs and express their wants. Knowledgeable patients can choose the type of care they request and what kinds of health outcomes they expect.

In factories, demand is divided into external and internal. External demand comes from the market; internal demand from sales, engineering, or a supply chain partner. External demand reflects what happens out there; internal demand is sorted, selected, and scheduled. Health services meet external demand for help in cases that are obviously urgent and severe and something needs to be done right away. In other cases, demand is sorted and a diagnostic process is started to find out what should and could be done.

## Arrival Characteristics

The arrival of demand has two basic attributes. Arrival time means the point in time when demand materializes. Arrival rate means the number of contacts within a period, hour, day, month, or year. Time and volume together show demand surges and fluctuations.

> In a classical study from the early 1950s, Charles Enid (1953) observed a curious empirical fact in the maternity ward at a Birmingham hospital.[18] In more than 40% of the cases, the onset of labor came between 10:00 p.m. and 4:00 a.m.; 5.2% started at the midnight hour versus 2.7% at noon.

The larger the volume, the more predictable the fluctuations. Demand for health services is a consequence of variability in the human condition and in the environment. Traffic systems produce injuries and fatalities at predictable rates. Influenza epidemics come and go in seasonal patterns. Even in cities that never sleep, emergency rooms are quiet between 2:00 and 5:00 a.m.

People arrive at the health service provider's doorstep, or use whatever electronic communication devices, for reasons. Arrival reasons can be visually obvious, such as an open wound or a limb out of joint. If not, patients are asked to state a reason.

According to a study by the Mayo Clinic,[19] covering more than 140,000 patients, the top 10 primary complaints were

1. Skin disorders
2. Osteoarthritis and joint disorders
3. Back problems
4. Cholesterol problems
5. Upper respiratory conditions, excluding asthma
6. Anxiety, depression, and bipolar disorder
7. Chronic neurologic disorders
8. High blood pressure
9. Headaches and migraines
10. Diabetes

A further generic arrival characteristic is first-timers versus repeaters.[20] A first-timer is a patient who makes the first contact related to an episode of illness. Such a patient is a blank slate without a medical history related to the current complaint. Repeaters have a continuing episode of illness. There is a medical history; what has happened and been done before matters to what will be done next. A diabetic under a disease management regime creates highly predictable demand. It is all in the calendar.

Arrivals are initiated in two ways. On demand means that a patient, or somebody in the vicinity, contacts a caregiver with a request for immediate action. On schedule means appointments. On-demand arrivals are of two types, walk-ins and wheel-ins. The latter obviously tend to be more severe.

Arrival channel is a key issue in hospital design. Some places have one entrance for all comers, while large modern hospitals typically have special ambulance entrances and special entry points for pregnancies, and for those with appointments, to keep them separate from the unsorted arrivals. With the development of information and communication technologies (ICT), much innovative effort has been invested in attempts to replace foot traffic with electronic media.

For operations management, demand actualizes when somebody places an order or makes a justified claim. The arrival of demand activates the supply side.

## 6.2.3 Demand Meets Constrained Supply

When demand has arrived and knocks on the door, supply must do the setup and run through the familiar set of questions:

- What is it? Does it belong here? Is it our case? Do we want to work on it?
- Do we know what to do, or can we find out? What will work? Do we have a design for it?
- What can be done? Do we have the resources and capabilities?

In the orderly world, five loaves of bread and two fishes can't feed a multitude. Scarcity is real, and allocative decisions must be made. The supply side in healthcare struggles under several constraints, as do all purposeful activities in the artificial world. Social constraints refer to patients' resources and capabilities, including understanding and articulating their condition, collaboration, compliance with instructions, motivation to self-service, and the support they can expect from their social networks. Technical constraints are present in the production function, the clarity of diagnosis, and the efficacy of therapies. Economic constraints refer to the availability of resources, both in general and at the particular time–location coordinates of the point of need. Production constraints follow technology and economy; processes must be designed in certain ways.

## DSO Construct

Demand is what needs to be done; supply is what can be done. Together, they define the job to be done. The demand–supply constellation is like the cell from which the tissues and structures of service production systems are built. The constellations come in seven ideal types. The DSO construct is built by running through a set of questions that produce the algorithm depicted in Figure 6.3.

Imagine you are the gatekeeper at a caregiver. You are not a medical professional; you are not supposed to make diagnoses and administer therapies. You know the supply situation and have a general idea of what can be done. Demand comes your way, and you meet a number of patients that ask to be helped. Your task is to sort and direct the patients into certain types of activities that include diagnostics, care plans, and therapies.

Starting in the upper left corner of Figure 6.3, you ask the first question: *Are you really sick?* If the person definitely looks sick or is bleeding, you do not have to voice the question. If the answer is not obvious, you continue with a follow-up. It appears that you are not acutely ill, but everything is not all right. *Are you at risk of becoming ill?* If that is the case, the patient is assigned to the DSO category prevention.

If the patient is clearly ill, you ask, *Do you need urgent help?* If the answer is not clear, you may get some help from a triage nurse. If the situation is found to be urgent and severe, the patient goes to the DSO category emergency.

If the case is not urgent to the extent that the resources of emergency are needed, you consider other options. Some resources are at hand. You ask, *Is your problem such that we can do all that is needed here and now?* Assume that the problem is a dental cavity and a dentist is available, or it is a minor wound that a nurse can patch up. The patient goes into the one-visit DSO. The problem is solved as a connected flow—case closed without further ado.

Emergency and one visit face external, unsorted demand. For the others, gatekeeping and setup have been done at least to some extent; demand is internal.

If there is a resource constraint and help is not immediately available, or the problem is not treatable right away, there must be a process like the disconnected flow.

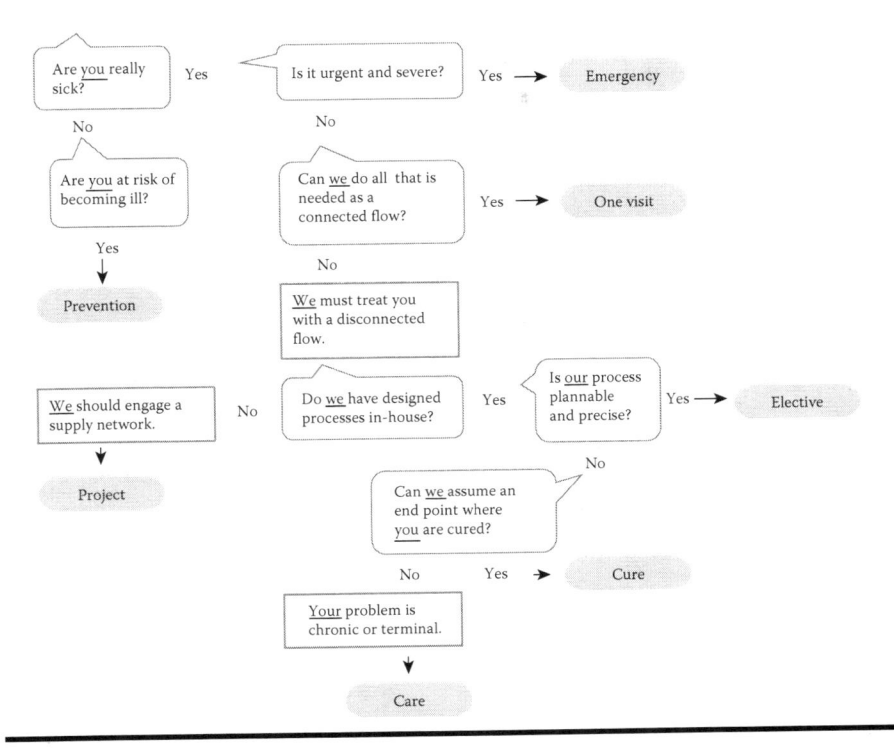

**Figure 6.3  DSO algorithm.**

Something is done now, say an initial examination, and a follow-up is scheduled. The patient goes home and is placed in inventory to wait for the next step.

As for the next steps, you must check whether similar cases have been treated before. *Is there an in-house repository of resources, capabilities, and process designs that can be selected and activated?* If not, the patient is referred to another caregiver. A service supply network is activated. If the primary caregiver is a family doctor, she may remain the case manager. If the case is complicated, a project coordinator should be engaged. The patient goes into the DSO category project.

If processes are available, the question becomes, is the situation sufficiently clear, with one problem and one possible solution? *Can a reasonably well-formatted setup be done to select a procedure that can be executed on schedule?* If that is the case, the patient goes into the DSO category electives.

If the clinical picture is not clear and a care plan cannot be established, there is a need for more diagnostics and explorative sensemaking. *What should be found out so that an appropriate therapy can be selected and implemented?* If it appears that the ailment can be cured and there is a reasonable prognosis for a happy ending, the patient goes into the DSO category cure.

The unfortunates who have a chronic or terminal condition that available therapies can't cure go into the DSO category care.

Now let's look at the decisions and categories in more detail. Please keep in mind that DSOs are Weberian ideal types, conceptual artifacts that elicit the most central features of a phenomenon. They provide benchmarks, mental anchors with which the messy real world can be compared.

## Emergency DSO: Minimally Constrained Supply

True emergencies are, and have always been, special cases. The time-elastic loss function means that no time should be wasted, and all means should be used. Emergencies come in many shapes; therefore, the supply side must be equipped with a variety of resources and capabilities to deal with trauma, cardiac events, drowning, poisoning, electrocution, sudden allergic reaction—whatever the variability of life brings up. The production function concentrates on active therapies, and the placebo effect is a bonus, while the slow-motion natural history and lifestyle changes are not relevant at the moment. The primary organizations are emergency and rescue services, that is, ambulances and EDs.

On aggregate, demand is predictable, but from day to day and workstation to workstation, it hits randomly. EDs are open 24/7 and should have slack resources. Capacity utilization can't be a performance indicator on the microlevel. Emergency is the DSO category that pushes against constraints and strains resources the most. A person in need obviously wants to use the best-available resources. A lot of unsorted demand pushes against the ED.

Emergency as an ideal type is confused because the level of urgency and severity is not necessarily apparent. A severe toothache is painful and prompts urgent action, although the problem is unlikely to lead to loss of life. Only a small fraction of ED arrivals are urgent in the sense that immediate action is required to save a life. However, if a patient perceives a need to be urgent, he behaves as if it is urgent and asks for all possible resources to be activated. A caregiver may not agree. Barring the obvious cases, urgency and severity are a matter of bargaining in a situational asymmetry. For the patient, the issue is personal, perhaps a once-in-a-lifetime event that may be the game changer for the future. For the caregiver, this is just one more among the many that arrive during a shift.

Urgency and severity are variables with ranges from the most urgent to those that can wait, or eventually do not need emergency services at all. Triage thus has to deal with a two-variable combination, as illustrated in Figure 6.4. There are several triage scales, usually with six levels from A to E, or color codes.[21]

1. Black/expectant: Patients are so severely injured that they will die of their injuries, possibly in hours or days (large-area burns, severe trauma, or lethal radiation dose), or are in a life-threatening medical crisis that they are unlikely to survive given the care available (cardiac arrest, septic shock, or severe head or chest wounds); their treatment is usually palliative, such as being given painkillers.

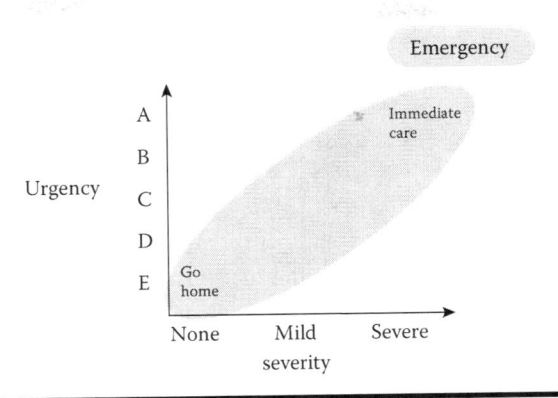

**Figure 6.4  Arrival characteristics at the ED.**

2. Red/immediate: Patients require immediate surgery or other lifesaving intervention, and have first priority for surgical teams or transport to advanced facilities; they cannot wait but are likely to survive with immediate treatment.
3. Yellow/observation: A patient's condition is stable for the moment but requires watching by trained persons and frequent retriage; it will need hospital care and will receive immediate priority care if resources are available.
4. Green/wait (walking wounded): The patient will require a doctor's care in several hours or days but not immediately; he may wait for a number of hours or be told to go home and come back the next day (broken bones without compound fractures and many soft tissue injuries).
5. White/dismiss: The patient has minor injuries; first aid and home care are sufficient, and a doctor's care is not required (cuts and scrapes and minor burns).

## Social Constraints: The Motivation to Prevent

Some patients do not have a current ailment, but an elevated risk level. Problems in the future are predictable. This calls for risk management, where the condition is monitored and treated in order to avoid getting ill.

The prevention DSO is determined by the medical problem being a state with known risk. The production function is typically medication, lifestyle changes, and/or watchful waiting. In some rare cases, such as hereditary disposition to cancer, preventive surgery can be used. In most cases, the service provider can provide assistance, advice, and regular monitoring, but the patient has to do the job. A nurse can't stop smoking on behalf of his patient; a doctor can't hit the treadmill to lose the weight of another person. Prevention is the DSO category where self-service dominates. Patient motivation and compliance are issues in all types of care; in prevention, they are mission critical.

Self-service is affected by social constraints, the limits of human understanding, and capability. For the patient, healing is an effortful accomplishment. The required capabilities, competences, and motivation are not equally distributed in a population. If a patient does not cooperate, there is not much a service producer can do.

## Technical Constraints

*Technical constraints* are the limits of theory and therapy. For reasons that lie with the imperfections of science and the human condition, clinical medicine cannot always produce the expected outcomes. Sometimes diagnoses cannot be set with sufficient accuracy; for some medical conditions, there is no known cure. The healer may not know what the problem is, where it comes from, what consequences it may bring, and what to do. The technical constraints come down to diagnostic clarity (theory), knowledge about what should be done (therapy), and the ability and possibility to do it (can do). The theory–therapy constellation creates the four combinations illustrated in Figure 6.5.

In the ideal case, labeled 1, established theory supports a clear diagnosis, from which follows a precise, schedulable, and predictable intervention that can be assumed to lead to expected outcomes. The diagnostic phase creates internal demand for services.

In situation 2, there is a diagnosis and a known therapy, but it can't be done. The reasons may be economic access, availability of required equipment or capabilities, the patient's general condition, or advanced age.

In situation 3, a diagnosis exists, but there is no known therapy. Such is the case with diabetes, Alzheimer's disease, and many other chronic conditions. Before the advent of modern medicine, most diseases fell into this category.

Situation 4 is when there is an ailment with symptoms, but no diagnosis. It may be an ill-defined condition, such as irritable bowel syndrome and chronic fatigue, which drive many patients to alternative medicine.

In situations 2–4, the options are to continue searching for a solution, or to live with the problem within a regime of disease management and continuous care.

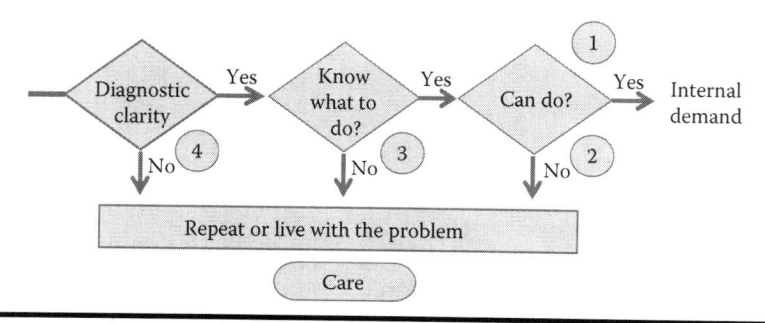

**Figure 6.5   Diagnostic clarity.**

Monitoring, supportive action, and occasional remedies arrest the inevitable decline. Maintaining a reasonable quality of life despite the condition is the central outcome target. Care is the DSO category that takes all those who can't be cured.

## Economic Constraints

Economic constraints are associated with the allocation and use of resources. A situation at the opulent extreme can be envisioned. A wealthy ruler could have a full-service hospital on standby 24/7, ready to jump into action any time he or his family needed help. Every ailment would be treated as if it were urgent and severe and arranged as a connected flow. The other extreme is common in developing countries. A cure exists, but this patient can't afford it. In tax-financed universal access systems, sometimes patients die while waiting for a lifesaving procedure.

Economic constraints come in four types. First, medical resources do not exist at all within a region or for a patient population. Second, resources are there, but a patient can't afford them. Third, the patient may be in a location where help can't be reached in time. The fourth type is related to opportunity costs and prioritization under scarcity. Resources are available, but they are denied to a patient because a decision maker determines that they should be used for somebody else for better effects. As long as resources are finite, priorities must be established.

> Health economics has developed methods to help decision makers deal with economic constraints. The best known is a measure known as quality-adjusted life years (QUALY). The effect of a medical procedure is established based on historical data, or for new therapies, estimated based on the expected therapeutic effects. The quality of life is measured on a scale from zero to one, from death to full recovery. A procedure would extend a patient's life by, say, 4 years. If it would leave the patient with some problems and the quality of life would be 0.5; the QUALY of the procedure would be 0.5 × 4 = 2. The cost of the procedure can now be compared with the prospective QUALYs. In the United Kingdom, the National Institute for Health and Care Excellence (NICE) uses the rule-of-thumb formula that more than 30,000 pounds of taxpayers' money should not be spent per QUALY.[22]

Under ordinary conditions in wealthy societies, economic constraints turn into production constraints. In cases that are not urgent and severe, health services must strive for mass production efficiency and employ division of labor, specialization, and standardization. From this follow care arrangements that are not ideal for the patient, but nevertheless must be undertaken.

## Production Constraints

Production constraints limit the ways in which nonurgent care can be produced and administered. The ideal situation is a connected flow within a job shop. A skilled team would fully focus on one patient at a time. Everything needful would be done swiftly with no interruptions, delays, or unnecessary waiting. Throughput time would be the sum of the processing time. The patient as a flow unit would not spend passive time in a patient-in-process (PIP) inventory.

As discussed in Chapter 5, PIP can be divided into time related to the production function, clinical interventions, and natural healing, and passive time when at best nothing happens and at worst the condition deteriorates. In healthcare, the outcome stream is not identical to production. Healing takes place between steps; it takes time for medication to take effect and wounds to heal. The production constraints are related to both healing time and waiting time, the clinical and the managerial constraints.

The production constraints are illustrated in Figure 6.6. The output of Figure 6.5 is the input to Figure 6.6: internal demand, a patient case with reasonable diagnostic clarity. Designing a care process, the clinician has to ask, do we have a process for this? Do we have all the required resources, skills, and equipment at hand under our authority and budget? If the answer is no, the caregiver may conclude that this patient does not belong here at all, the case is closed, and the patient is asked to go elsewhere. If the patient belongs to a caregiver, overall responsibility is taken but some parts and components of the patient journey are outsourced to a supply network. That makes the case a project DSO. In the ideal world of integrated and coordinated care, the principal caregiver appoints a case manager to run the supply network. In the real world of fragmented care, the case is kicked between different actors and the patient has to become her own case manager.

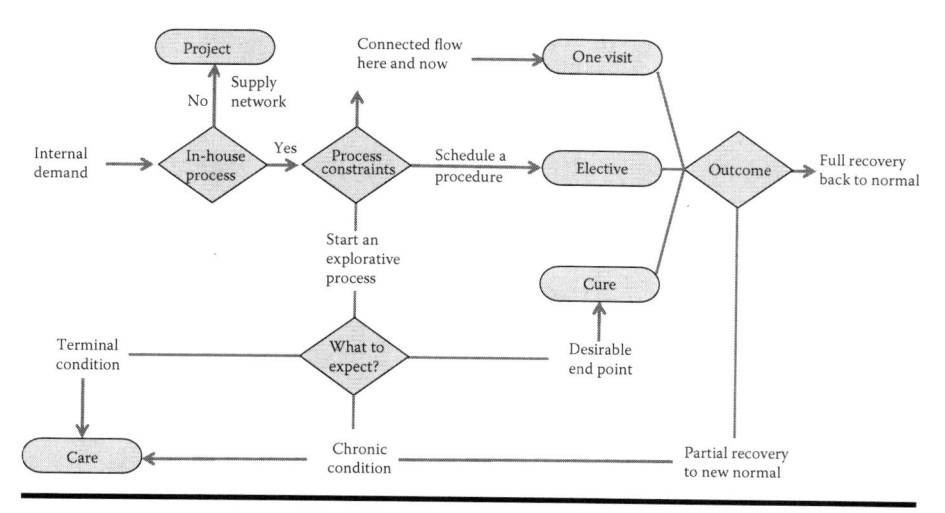

**Figure 6.6   Production constraints.**

If a process is available, the question is, what constraints are there? If the medical problem is not severe, the clinical picture is clear, the procedure is routine, all the required resources are at hand, and no specific preparations are needed, the patient can be treated as a one visit. Everything that needs to be done is done as a connected flow. Health kiosks, retail clinics, and dentists' offices work like this, with either appointments or walk-ins with minimal waiting time. EDs have nursing stations where patients with minor ailments can be directed for patch-up and then sent home.

If the procedure requires preparations, a connected flow can't be used. The case is split into steps, and the process is disconnected. Some inconvenience is inevitable. Medication may take time to kick in, so there must be waiting and seeing. Laboratory analysis requires that the patient go without food and drink for some hours before a sample is taken. As the case is not urgent, the patient may want to choose a time and a location of her convenience. The caregiver can allocate and schedule resources for optimal capacity utilization. This is the elective DSO.

The one-visit and elective DSOs are appropriate when there is one problem and one solution. They can't be used if there are several problems with unknown interactions, or the solution and the steps to reach it can't be known at the beginning of the care episode. This is typical for cancer. The process can be started after the initial diagnosis, but it can't be planned with precision from end to end. How the patient reacts to medication needs to be found out. The process is explorative and iterative; it is planned a few steps ahead, outcomes are observed, and further steps are decided and scheduled. There is a reasonable expectation that a positive outcome can be achieved. This is the cure DSO.

Any process can fail and turn into an emergency. Expectations can be ruined. If it turns out that a preferable end point is not achievable, the only remaining thing is care.

## DSO and Processes

Emergency is historically and logically the mother of all DSOs. It takes all types of urgent demand and runs a job shop. As shown in Figure 6.7, one visit and electives both have plannable processes that are expected to lead to stepwise improvement; a rotten tooth or an infected appendix is removed and the patient is expected to recover. The difference is that one visit employs a connected flow, while electives are disconnected flows with preparations and require some planning and scheduling.

Cure and project both have expected end points, but not care plans, that can be accurately scheduled from beginning to end. Processes are explorative and proceed step-by-step as new information is gathered and plans are adjusted. The difference between cure and project is akin to the make or buy decision in industry. Cure is "make"; a patient case is managed by administrative fiat in one organization under one administrative and budgetary regime. Project is "buy" and involves several caregivers and a supply chain with contractual

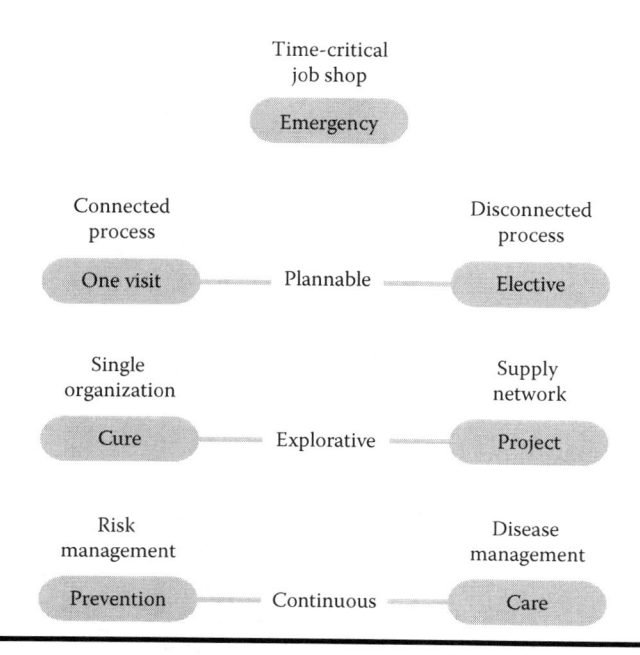

**Figure 6.7 DSO typology of processes.**

relationships and bargaining between parties. A similar patient case could be cure in the well-equipped general hospital, while it would be project in a smaller establishment.

Prevention and care are never-ending stories of continuous outcome streams. Both lack a fixed end point. A smoker who quits needs to fight the urge continuously. Weight needs to be watched even when it has come down nicely. Patients leave care only feet first. The difference is that those in care do have a diagnosis and a debilitating condition, while those in prevention only run a risk. The difference between prevention and care hinges on the question, say, is hypertension a symptom or a disease? To the extent that this is debatable, the boundary between prevention and care remains fuzzy.

## DSO Matrix

The DSO construct builds on the product–process matrix presented in Chapter 3, and the service–process matrix introduced in Chapter 4. In manufacturing, the classifying variable for products is complexity; for processes, the movements of the flow unit. In services, they are variability of demand and setup type.

The DSO matrix for healthcare is depicted in Figure 6.8. The vertical axis combines external and internal demand into five types: random and urgent, plannable procedures with a logic flow that can be known at the start, complex cases with an

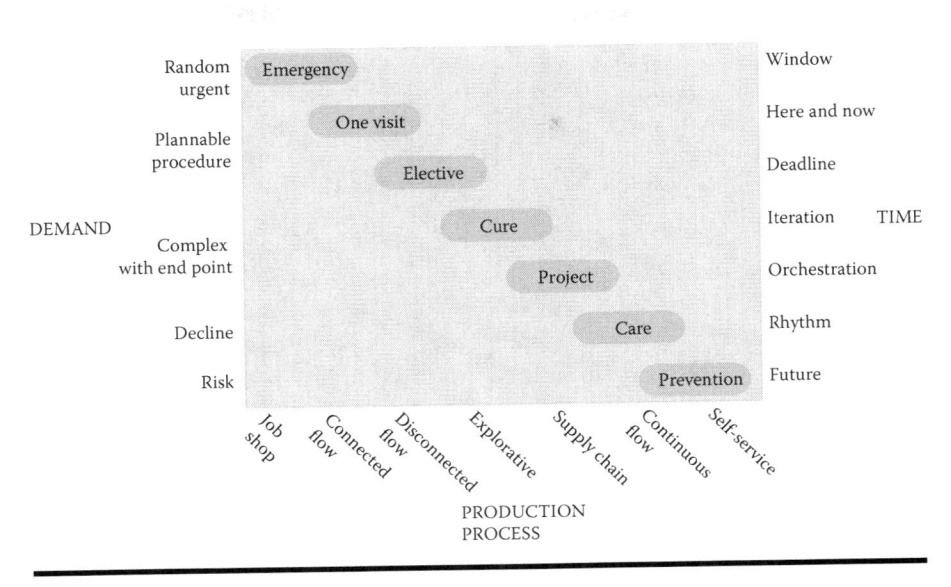

**Figure 6.8  DSO matrix.**

expected end point, the management of decline associated with chronic conditions, and risk reduction. The horizontal axis consists of the service production process architectures: job shop, connected flow, disconnected flow, explorative processes, supply chains, continuous flow, and self-service.

The vertical axis on the right adds a time perspective. In urgent emergencies, there is a time window within which care must be initiated and the patient stabilized. One visit is here and now, minimal waiting, and a connected flow. Electives are planned and scheduled procedures with a deadline; all preparations must be completed before the procedure can start. Cure employs explorative processes that require foresight and may include iterations. If a step does not produce the expected results, the logical process must be rewound some steps back and a new route is selected. Projects are orchestrated in the sense that there may be several things going on simultaneously. Care runs with a rhythm; measurements, controls, and therapies are administered following a regular schedule. Finally, prevention is about the future, the relationship between current sacrifices and future gains.

## DSO as a Construct

Conceptual constructs are by definition not true or false, but rather more or less useful. Do they illuminate something that is not obvious or visible to the unstructured naked eye? Do they clearly separate meaningful categories with little overlaps, gray zones, and ragged seams? Is a construct exhaustive, or does it leave something essential beyond its borders?

Each DSO is a chunk of logic and an ideal type. It confronts the variability of the real world that shows up in the accuracy of the questions and answers of the DSO algorithm (Figure 6.3). They are not exactly measurable physical properties, but rather estimates or perceptions on both the demand and the supply side. The patient may perceive something as extremely urgent, while the experienced triage nurse begs to disagree. A doctor may conclude that smoking two packs of cigarettes a day implies an elevated risk, while the patient is sure it is negligible. A problem that appears minor, say a cavity in a tooth, may hide a complicated problem in the root canal. A procedure that was expected to be routine runs into a complication and becomes explorative. Each of the variables is subject to clinical knowledge, information asymmetry, availability of measurable indicators, and perceptions of reality. As a chunk of logic, each DSO is ontologically real, but in practice, it is only as true as the data that defines it. The range of variables are given in Table 6.2.

A further question is about the exhaustivity of the construct. Is everything covered? Are there some areas of healthcare that can't be described as one of a few overlapping DSOs? This question is left for further research and practice.

A divide that can be considered is that between voluntary and forced care. The latter refers to cases where a patient is taken into involuntary custody because he is dangerous to himself, that is, suicidal, or dangerous to others, such as violent psychiatric patients or those with a contagious disease. In democratic societies, the use of force is strictly limited to public authorities. Medical professionals will occasionally have to rely on the authority of government. The same applies to

**Table 6.2   Variables That Define DSOs**

| *Scale Variable* | | | | |
|---|---|---|---|---|
| **Urgency** Time–loss function | Urgent Immediate action | Schedule at earliest | Schedule at convenience | Not urgent Wait and see |
| **Severity** Max loss | Loss of life | Permanent injury | Harm | None |
| **Risk** Probability | Actualized | Elevated | Significant | Negligible |
| **Clinical clarity** Knowledge | Precision | Statistical | Intuitive | None |
| **End point** | Expected | Probable | Possible | None |
| **Production** | Connected flow | Plannable disconnected process | Explorative process | Continuous monitoring Regular therapies |

forensic medicine. As these are specific and volume-wise rather minor issues, I have chosen not to include them in order to keep the construct simple.

The exhaustivity issue should not be confused with characteristics that are logically independent and apply to all DSOs. One example is the question of new versus repeat patients. This is, indeed, a practically meaningful distinction. First-timers are blank slates, while repeaters have a medical history. The same or a different ailment can bring a person repeatedly to the ED, one visit, electives, cures, and projects because all treatments that end can start again. Care is the only DSO where there are no repeaters, since patients are not expected to leave care alive. Thus, repeat does not constitute an independent DSO. The same can be said for the distinction between primary and secondary care, the intensity of collaboration, and the closed–open systems dimension of service systems. All DSOs can be managed at any level of specialization and collaboration intensity. The degree of system closure can vary in all DSOs.

## 6.3 Ontology of DSO

The DSO is a conceptual construct that describes the relation between demand and supply. Many management concepts are similarly relations. Quality (small q) is the relation between *ex ante* requirements and the actual output. Productivity is the relation between input and output. DSO is the relation between what needs to be done and what can be done. Strictly speaking, the DSO is not a model that would allow prediction and tell managers what to do. It is rather like a set of lenses through which health service systems can be observed and some regularity can be found.

> The DSO construct resembles other management constructs. The Boston matrix[23] was developed for executives of multibusiness conglomerates as a tool to manage their portfolios of companies. It is built on two variables, growth (high–low), and market share (high–low). They produce four combinations, the cash cow, the dog, the question mark, and the star. It asks executives to put each business in its proper place in the matrix, and then decide what to do.
>
> The balanced scorecard (Kaplan and Norton 1996) was developed for managers who need to know the state of their business and where it is going.[24] It uses two variables, future versus past and external versus internal. It tells managers what conventional accounting tells about the past; there also need to be measures that look into the future. It says businesses depend on their customers for revenue, so pay attention to what customers think. Likewise, companies are dependent on their employees, so managers need to know about their satisfaction and motivation.

The DSO construct applies to two units of analysis. A care organization can operate under one or several DSO logics. A patient case can be treated in one DSO or in several, concurrently or simultaneously.

Like the proverbial elephant approached by blind men, the DSO construct can be seen from many perspectives. It can be an operations management classification based on process types and time perspective, as in the DSO matrix. Each DSO category can be seen as a business model. As DSOs overlap, they can be seen as layers of an organizational multiverse, platforms with apps, and delivery channels of a core competence.

## 6.3.1 DSO as Setup, Design, and Architecture

On the microlevel of the country doctor, the DSOs appear as modes of operation, the results of setups in situations with given resources. At the level of designs, DSO appears as how processes and production lines are configured. Electives require the mobilization of several resources for a deadline, and checklists to make sure that everything is ready before the scalpel cuts flesh. One-visit dental offices must see to it that dentists, nurses, and chairs are available in synchrony. Cure requires flexibility, as the patient's status may unexpectedly change, new information may make old diagnoses obsolete, and care plans have to be adjusted.

DSO is visible in architectures, organizations dedicated to operate with only one DSO logic. The ED, as we have seen, is the classical one-DSO operation. Nursing homes do mostly care. Others, more recent, are health kiosks and minute clinics that do only one visits. Surgical factories focus on a narrow range of elective procedures.[25] There are project operators who do only complex diagnostics, care planning, and monitoring, while procedures and therapies are outsourced to supply networks.[26] Indeed, many of the most interesting care innovations tend to be one-DSO organizations.

> Megaklinikka is a dental care organization established in Helsinki in 2010 as a pure-play one-visit organization. It offers a limited range of services, the 16 most common procedures including filling cavities, examinations, and dental hygiene, and only for adults. It promises low prices, easy access, and the possibility to do all procedures in one visit.
>
> Prices are fixed to 1 euro below the lowest-cost competition, municipal dental clinics. There, however, access is poor and nonurgent patients will have to wait for several weeks. The process is cut into steps, and patients will have to schedule several appointments to deal with one problem.
>
> Megaklinikka has a web-based appointment system that is modeled along those used by airlines. Appointments are available within days. The system keeps track of open time slots. If it appears in the morning that times are available, the system offers discounts for fast takers to

maintain high-capacity utilization. Patients will have to pay a fixed fee when they make a reservation to minimize no-show.

The starting times of appointments are not fixed; neither is the duration. Patients are given a time and a promise to get into a chair within an hour. An SMS message will alert a patient 15 minutes before her procedure will start. Once the condition is assessed, patients have the choice to do everything needed in one session, or split it up into several visits. Some people are willing to sit up to 4 hours rather than book another appointment. The flexibility is accomplished by a sophisticated scheduling system. The dentist chair and a nurse are fixed locations, while dentists move from room to room and perform only the tasks to which a dentist is needed. The variability of processing time is absorbed. This, however, requires, at minimum, more than a dozen chairs and dentists to average out.

## 6.3.2 DSO as Business Model

The seven DSO types have the characteristic of distinct business models. In Table 6.3, the categories of the Business Model Canvas (BMC)[27] are applied to each DSO.

### Emergency

The emergency DSO is a business organized to save and stabilize patients with urgent and severe conditions. Each case has a time window, within which activities are coordinated and capacity allocated. The goal is preventing death or permanent injury by shortening the response time from the point of entry to the point at which the patient's condition is stable enough for discharge or admission to the next care step. In practice, EDs have to accept demand that is not strictly urgent and severe,[28] which, when it happens, compromises the business model. External demand is random in both arrival rates and primary causes. As cases are urgent, there is seldom room for excessive bargaining about setups; therefore, the provider–patient relationship is professional paternalism. The key resources are triage to do the initial assessment, and flexible, multiskilled teams operating like a job shop. To manage fluctuations in demand, some excess capacity has to be allowed as buffers. Emergency services are in many countries seen as part of government's responsibility of internal safety. The variability of demand and the need to maintain overcapacity call for budget-based financial arrangements.

### Prevention

Prevention is to take action to reduce or eliminate predictable risks. Prevention as a public health issue targets populations. It uses vaccination programs to reduce

**Table 6.3   DSOs as Business Models**

|  | Value Proposition | Segment | Customer Relation | Customer Channel | Key Resources | Key Activities Process | Key Partners | Primary Revenue Model |
|---|---|---|---|---|---|---|---|---|
| Emergency | Save and stabilize | Urgent and severe condition | Paternalistic | Random arrival Call center Wheel-in Walk-in | Flexible multiskilled teams | Job shop | Ambulances Hospital wards | Global budget |
| Prevention | Something that could happen does not happen | Elevated risk | Supported self-service | Screening Health promotion | Risk evaluation Monitoring Advice | Outcome stream with service encounters | Public health | Outcome based |
| One visit | Solve minor problem at convenience | Mild, not urgent | Discrete event | Retail location Booking system | Modularized offerings Flow management | Connected flow Queue management | Specialists | Out-of-pocket |
| Elective | Procedure with stepwise improvement | Prescreened, precise diagnosis | Consultative Patient choice | Referrals Reputation | Clinical skill sets | Disconnected flow | General practitioner Rehabilitation | Bundles |

(Continued)

**Table 6.3 (Continued)   DSOs as Business Models**

| | Value Proposition | Segment | Customer Relation | Customer Channel | Key Resources | Key Activities Process | Key Partners | Primary Revenue Model |
|---|---|---|---|---|---|---|---|---|
| Cure | Solution to complex problem | Difficult diagnosis | Ongoing collaboration | Referrals Reputation | Diagnostics and therapies | Explorative | Clinical specialties | Fee-for-service |
| Care | Arrest Decline Disease management | Chronic and terminal conditions | Ongoing collaboration | Referrals | Continuous care | Monitoring Rehabilitation | Housing Social services | Regular fee |
| Project | Orchestration | Complex Multimorbidity | Case manager | Referrals | Integration and coordination | Case management | Supply chain partners | Fee-for-service |

the risk of contagious diseases, health education, and regulatory measures to ban hazardous substances and improve road and workplace safety. The prevention DSO is about situations where risk is revealed through screening or monitoring and preventive services are offered to individuals. The patient is not yet acutely ill, but there is a risk that can be inferred from symptoms, such as high blood pressure (hypertension), or obesity that might lead to cardiac conditions or diabetes if allowed to continue unabatedly. Elevated risk is typically not yet causing harm or inconvenience, but prevention requires sacrifices from the patient, such as regular monitoring, medication, and lifestyle changes. Prevention differs from other DSOs in that patient motivation is based on knowledge rather than experience. It is therefore highly sensitive to health literacy and general awareness of health risks.

Recent advances in sensors, wearable technologies, and mobile devices carry a great deal of promise for the management of prevention.[29] Timely and precise data and instant feedback allow earlier identification of risk and more precise monitoring.

Some prevention issues, such as hypertension and high cholesterol level, can be managed by medication. For issues that require lifestyle changes, the production function is weak and processes rely on supported self-service. Given the current status of behavioral medicine and clinical psychology, there are no technologies for behavioral change that could be compared with those in other areas of medicine.[30] From the provider perspective, the general output–outcome connection is weak; which types of counseling and advice with what intensity will work for which person can't be reliably known in advance. For patients, prevention is an effortful accomplishment in maintaining vigilance and routines, a continuous flow with occasional health events and service encounters. Prevention, like organizational change management, wrestles with denial, resistance, and motivation. Prevention is like financial investments; resources must be committed now, while payback comes in the future. Like insurance, successful prevention does not register as events, but rather as nonevents; something that could have happened does not happen. There must be predictive models and worst-case scenarios to which actual outcomes are compared. If such measurements can be developed, prevention is well suited for outcome-based financial arrangements. A service provider specialized in prevention could assume the responsibility of all individuals within a population who have, say, the metabolic syndrome that predicts diabetes. The provider and the financier, an insurer or a municipality, would agree on a base case scenario is a commonly used term for the most likely scenario. It typically lies between the best case and the worst case. The actual outcomes would be compared with the scenario, and the eventual savings would be split between the provider and the financier according to a set formula. Such arrangements are social impact bonds (SIBs),[31] launched in the United Kingdom in 2010.

## One Visit

One visit is a business that deals with demand that is mild and not urgent; problems can be addressed at earliest convenience. The conditions are typically discrete issues and clinically clear, say a tooth cavity or strep throat. One visit is here and now; patients' medical histories are not highly relevant, and extensive integration of knowledge beyond the current situation is not necessary. Patients know what they need and can self-segment. Formatted setups can be used.

Demand can be structured as drop-in or by appointment. The required therapy is a well-known routine, not particularly drastic or risky. Convenience calls for good time–location access, appointment systems, short or no queues, connected flows, and case closure without further delay. The coordination issues are proper scheduling, staffing, and buffer management to keep cycle times short. Expensive equipment and highly specialized skills are not needed. Prices and the financial return per patient must remain low. Dedicated one-visit outfits require large volumes.

One visits resemble small-item retailing, kiosks, and fast food. Franchising can be used. Since price and cost are reasonable, out-of-pocket and capitation can be used as revenue models.

## Elective

Electives, as the term suggests, are based on choice. A diagnosis is made with reasonable accuracy, and the care plan suggests an intervention, typically surgery, but it can also be intensive medication and physiotherapy. The process can be planned and scheduled from start to end. However, due to technical and economic process constraints, it can't be done right away as a one-visit connected flow. The case will require several steps of preparations with corresponding scheduling. Electives have adopted the checklist methodology from airlines.[32] All systems must be a go before the procedure can start. It is expected to result in a step change in the patient's health condition. There are observable before–after differences that can be used to evaluate outcomes. The process is planned, setups are formatted or routine, and the intervention, especially in surgery, is a connected flow. Adherence to protocol and small q quality makes elective the DSO that most resembles manufacturing.

Electives can be organized as surgical factories that accept referrals. In such a case, the referring general practitioners are key partners who feed demand to the factory, and also take care of rehabilitation and follow-up. Electives can also be organized as clinics that do both diagnostics and procedures. Electives are founded in clear diagnoses; therefore, bundled payment, such as diagnosis-related groups (DRGs), can be used.

## Cure

In the cure DSO, demand is not urgent, but the case is too complex for one visit and does not suggest a single solution as in electives. The diagnostic picture is not clear at the start. The process can be planned only a few steps at a time, as the results of the previous step influence the next. There may be several possible treatment schemes that can be evaluated only by trying. But there is reason to believe that there will be an end point. The patient can recover, either fully to the old normal or to an acceptable new normal.

Cure employs explorative processes that may include phases of various types and cross-functional processes involving several clinical specialties. This makes cure the DSO that is most difficult to manage. Indeed, in manufacturing undertakings that involve explorative processes, such as new product development and innovation, are notorious managerial challenges.

Coordination requires accurate and up-to-date patient information systems and referral routines. In order to maintain a steady flow, the handovers between steps should be fast and seamless.

As cure is explorative, the total cost of an episode of treatment can't be known at the start. Therefore, fee-for-service is the appropriate revenue model, combined with bundles for phases that can be defined as DRGs.

## Care

There are instances where there is no realistic hope for recovery. This can be because of lack of theory or therapy, such as with diabetes, Alzheimer's disease, Parkinson's disease, or frailty that comes with old age. Care is to manage the condition, arrest decline, improve quality of life, reduce pain, and support functionality. There is no expected end point other than death.

The demand is to maintain an optimal quality of life. Various perspectives need to be integrated to produce a balance of care. Care should be provided up to a certain level, below which there is a risk of complications and beyond which additional care has only a marginal impact. Patients are monitored and receive care or therapy following a coordinated daily, weekly, or monthly schedule. Care patients' outpatient visits should not be confused with the one-visit DSO, as each step is part of a continuous outcome stream and based on the condition. Many of the control issues pertinent to elective or cure processes are irrelevant, since therapy does not accumulate value toward an end result. As there is no end point, there is no inventory, cycle time, or throughput. The care patient is continuously part of the process. Control is concerned with monitoring the patient's health condition against set standards. Like in prevention, care outcomes must be gauged against a prognosis.

Care is a long-term and predictable process; therefore, the revenue model can be based on regular monthly fees gauged to the grade of service.

## Project

In the project DSO, demand refers to complex, resource-intensive, multispecialty cases that have no predefined treatment process. Unlike cure, projects call for resources that by tradition and convention are in different organizations. Such cases are typical in child and juvenile psychiatry, in which several clinical specialties and external stakeholders, such as school, police, family courts, child protection, and social services, are involved. If managed badly, patients may be referred back and forth to different specialists and may repeatedly undergo the same tests if handovers are not done properly. Coordination pertains to synchronizing several parallel examinations and procedures. Each patient is a project with case-specific objectives and control items, to which a particular case manager should be assigned. Thus, projects, more than other DSOs, require managerial resources to integrate and coordinate a supply network. As with cure, revenue models are founded on fee-for-service.

### 6.3.3 DSO as a Managerial Multiverse

#### Overlapping DSOs

Metaphorically speaking, organizations with only one DSO are like the organs of the human body. They have a physical manifestation and clear system borders. DSOs can also appear like tissues and cells in various organs and organ systems. One organization may have to deal with several DSOs.

EDs have the architecture and design to deal with urgent and severe cases. EDs are commonly perceived to be problematic with long waiting times, overcrowding, and stressful environments. A major part of the problem is that EDs in practice are multi-DSO operations swamped with demand that is neither urgent nor severe. There is a large body of research on ED management.[33] The central concern is how to manage demand by gatekeeping and triage, and offer fast-track lines to patients who essentially should go to a one-visit unit or be treated within a care regime.

Maternity care and birthing is by necessity a four-DSO operation. Pregnancy is not a disease. However, it is a state during which there are known risks for both the expectant mother and the unborn baby. Maternity care, also known as prenatal care or antenatal care, provides regular checkups that allow doctors and midwives to identify and treat potential health problems throughout the pregnancy. Expectant mothers will receive medical information of physiological and psychological changes and advice on prenatal nutrition and healthy lifestyles. Maternity care is prevention.

A baby can be born in basically three ways. It can be an uncomplicated routine vaginal delivery with the assistance of a midwife. After delivery, the baby's and the mother's conditions are checked. If nothing abnormal appears, they will be discharged from the birthing unit to a maternity ward or a patient hotel for further observation and then sent home. Uncomplicated birth is one visit.

In some instances, complications can be predicted during the pregnancy. In such cases, the decision is often to do a scheduled C-section, which is elective.

Deliveries that start normal can turn into complications requiring immediate emergency care. The time window is short. If a fetus is deprived of oxygen, brain damage sets in within minutes. Scheduled C-sections can take unexpected turns. Birthing can become an emergency.

From a management perspective, the question is, how should an activity with four DSOs be organized? The integrated solution is an organization that has all the required resources and capabilities. When situations change, the operating mode changes quickly and easily.

Such a multimode solution, however, runs into the problem that not all DSOs are equal. A rapid-response birthing team is expensive. It requires a gynecological surgeon, an *anesthesiologist*, nurses, and perhaps a pediatrician. As demand for their services can't be predicted, they need to be on standby 24/7. The emergency logic is justified by the risk of complications, damage, and death. The crucial indicator is perinatal mortality, the number of stillbirths and deaths in the first week of life per 1000 total births.[34] These are partly related to how birthing is organized.[35]

The numbers are small, a few incidents per year per a medium-sized unit. However, as the number of cases falls, the attention paid to the remaining increases, bringing media coverage and malpractice suits.

Hospital managers prefer to have each birthing unit equipped with a full standby emergency capacity. From the low incidence ratio follows that such an expensive resource must be justified by a large number of cases, from which follows that the size of birthing units must grow. The organization runs into the access, variety, and specialization trilemma. The emergency DSO as the leading principle means both long distances to travel and the impersonality of mass production. This conflicts with the expected service experience of the one-visit DSO. The process should be calm, nice, and personalized, preferably managed by the same midwife that the mother has learned to know during the pregnancy. The father or other significant others should be allowed to be present.

When the unit can't be everything to everybody, trade-offs must be faced. Should focus be on safety, which implies centralization, or on experience, which implies risk? Policy makers are not keen on letting patients decide. Which DSO should take the lead?

In most of Europe, the emergency logic dominates. A curious exception has been the Netherlands,[36] where prevention and one visit have been the leading principles. About 15% of births happen at home, while the ratio in other comparable countries is virtually zero. Some 10% of Dutch babies are born in specific birthing centers following the one-visit logic. Maternity care makes rigorous screening and all cases with the slightest risk go to hospitals. Nevertheless, perinatal mortality is 3.3, significantly higher than in comparable countries. While the debate in the country has been intense,[37] it appears that this is the price the Dutch have been willing to pay for preferring one visit over emergency.

## DSO as a Phase in a Flow

A patient as a flow unit can be simultaneously under several DSOs, or cross over from one DSO to another during an episode of care. Typical examples are illustrated in Figure 6.9.

Stroke is a blockage of the blood supply to the brain. A blood vessel may clog or rupture. Brain tissue dies, causing severe damage. A stroke is a medical emergency requiring treatment within a tight time window. Stroke is the fifth leading cause of death in the United States, with one person dying every 4 minutes.[38] It is a leading cause of adult disability. A typical stroke victim loses functionality in one or several limbs, which requires continuous care.

The prevalence and the grave consequences of stroke have led to the establishment of specialized stroke units within EDs. After the intensive save and stabilize phase, many stroke patients face a lengthy cure process that, when successful, leads to recovery. A stroke survivor has an elevated risk of recurrent incidents; prevention is recommended. If the patient does not recover fully, permanent disability and care follow.

There are handovers from emergency to cure, and from cure to prevention or care.[39] The emergency part is heroic medicine that attracts attention and funding, while the rest is low-intensity medicine. The handovers have to cross administrative boundaries. If they are not managed properly, a stroke patient coming for rehabilitation is akin to random demand, which puts undue stress on cure units.[40]

A similar DSO phase change is frequent with elderly people suffering from frailty and some chronic conditions. An incident happens, at home or at a nursing facility, the ambulance is called, the emergency is treated at an ED, and an elective procedure may be scheduled. Nursing home patients tend to clog EDs and contribute to congestion. During these events, patients remain in the care DSO and their

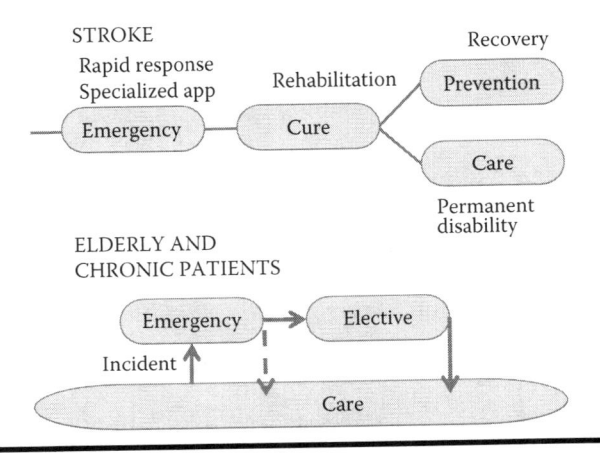

**Figure 6.9  Patient processes with several DSO phases.**

overall condition is known. Therefore, the question arises, could not a care unit have a tailored emergency mode?

> Doctagon is a Finnish private care provider.[41] It offers primary and occupational care services and specialist geriatric care to nursing homes. Each patient is thoroughly reviewed and a care plan is established. Typical emergency situations for each patient are estimated, and an appropriate response is documented for the nurses to use. Geriatric consultations are available through a telemedicine link 24/7. As a consequence, the use of ambulances and ED services has been drastically reduced. During its first year of operation, the system saved about a quarter of the total cost, while perceived care quality improved.

Cross-functional processes and interorganizational handovers are difficult to handle even under the best circumstances. If the handover, on top of this, is between different operating logics, trouble can be expected. The first take-home message is that cross-DSO handovers should be handled with care.

## 6.3.4 DSO as a Managerial Platform with Clinical Apps

The general hospital is the result of specialization based on several segmentation principles. The ED caters to urgent cases. There are organ system, cause, and method-based clinical specialties. Polyclinics and day surgery centers are designed to do one visits and electives. There are counseling units for prevention and palliative care units for the terminally ill. Tension appears between different principles. It resembles the tension in the software industry between operating systems and specialized application programs, the issue that Apple solved with platforms and apps.

A platform or operating system is the low-level software that supports a computer's basic functions, such as scheduling tasks and controlling peripherals. For hardware functions, such as input and output and memory allocation, the operating system acts as an intermediary between application programs and the computer hardware.

A DSO can be seen as a managerial platform on which several clinical specialties attach, like apps. Figure 6.10 illustrates a situation with emergency as a managerial platform. EDs are designed to deal with a specific type of demand, the urgent and severe that arrive randomly. Some social, technical, and economic constraints have to be bent. Triage requires behaviors that would be considered rude elsewhere. Technologies must be organized following agile principles, and the economics must adapt to the necessity of slack resources and round-the-clock staffing.

The tasks are performed by various clinical specialties and skill sets after triage has established the urgency priorities. If the case is a cardiac arrest, a specific cardiac app is activated. The specialist knowledge is applied under the rules of emergency. If there are no emergency cases, the cardiac resources may return to

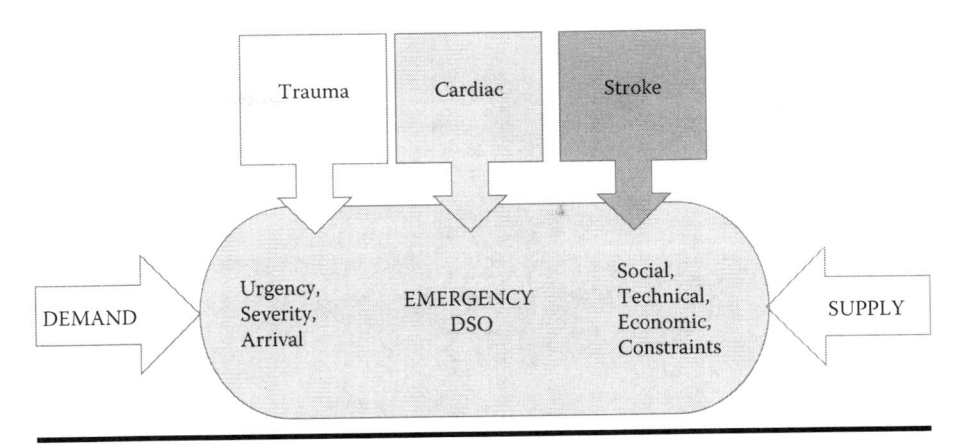

**Figure 6.10  DSO as a platform with apps.**

their clinics and wards to apply their skills on elective or cure DSO platforms, like a smartphone app is modified to work on both iOS and Android platforms.

Prevention is a managerial platform. It is based on the logics of risk management and supported self-service. Maternity care is a clinical app that attaches to a prevention platform. The same managerial platform is used to monitor elderly gentlemen with subclinical prostrate problems. The platform defines the type of collaboration and the rules of engagement. The apps build on respective clinical specialties.

When one DSO combines with one technology, the result is a super-specialty unit that deals only with certain demand using certain technologies. Such ED subunits that deal only with stroke, and surgical factories that do only orthopedic electives on knee and hip joints.

## DSO as a Way to Deliver Core Competence

The platform and app perspective can be turned on its head. Clinical skill sets are resources and capabilities that can respond to different demand types in ways that can be described as DSO types. A case in point is orthopedics (Figure 6.11).

Orthopedics is the branch of medicine dealing with conditions involving the musculoskeletal system, the biomechanics of bones, joints, and tendons. Orthopedics is mainly surgery, but it also uses noninvasive methods, medication, and physiotherapy. The orthopedic skill set can be organized on several DSO platforms. Serious bodily injuries require emergency, followed by cure aiming at full or partial recovery. Slow degenerative conditions, such as severe hip and knee arthritis, are treated with joint replacement surgery, done as an elective, often in specialized surgical factories. Minor fractures or dislocated joints can be dealt with as one visits. Osteoporosis is a weakening of bone. It can, to an extent, be prevented; when severe and irreparable, it requires continuous care.

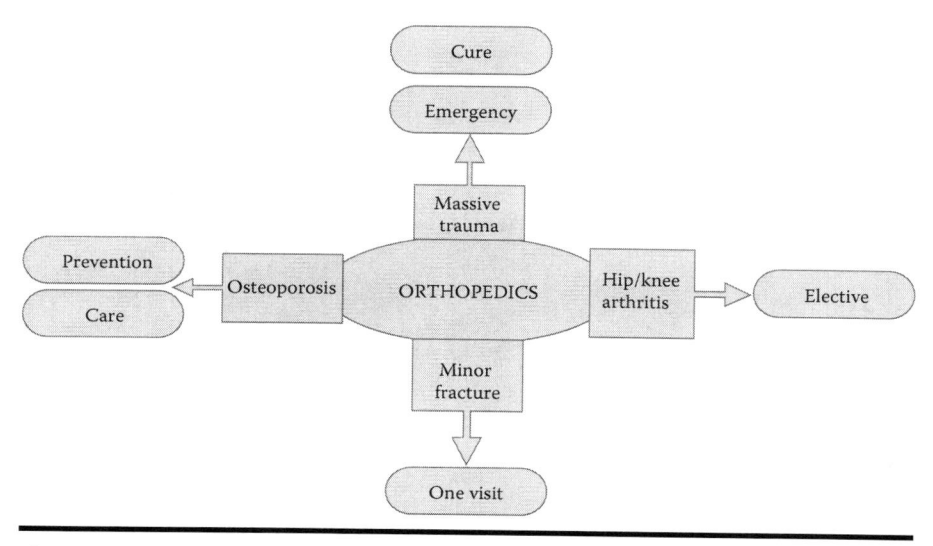

**Figure 6.11  DSO types of orthopedics.**

# Notes

1. Freidson (1988, 2001).
2. This section draws on Wootton (2006) and Porter (2002).
3. Porter (2002, pp. 72–74).
4. The main systems of the human body are as follows:
   ■ *Cardiovascular/circulatory system*: Circulates blood around the body via the heart, arteries, and veins, delivering oxygen and nutrients to organs and cells and carrying their waste products away.
   ■ *Digestive/excretory system*: Mechanical and chemical processes that provide nutrients via the mouth, esophagus, stomach, and intestines. Eliminates waste from the body.
   ■ *Endocrine system*: Provides chemical communications within the body using hormones.
   ■ *Integumentary/exocrine system*: Skin, hair, nails, sweat, and other exocrine glands.
   ■ *Lymphatic/immune system*: A network of lymphatic vessels that carry a clear fluid called lymph. Defends the body against disease-causing agents.
   ■ *Muscular/skeletal system*: Enables the body to move using muscles. Bones supporting the body and its organs.
   ■ *Nervous system*: Collects and processes information from the senses via nerves and the brain and tells the muscles to contract to cause physical actions.
   ■ *Renal/urinary system*: Where the kidneys filter blood.
   ■ *Reproductive system*: The sex organs required for the production of offspring.
   ■ *Respiratory system*: The lungs and the trachea that bring air into the body.
5. The physiological processes are as follows (Bland 2014): Assimilation and elimination are the processes involved in digesting, absorbing, and using nutrients and then excreting the waste products. Big food molecules are broken down so the body can make proper use of them. The process begins in the mouth and continues in the stomach and the small and large intestines. Detoxification processes occur primarily in the liver to convert toxic substances into nontoxic by-products, and eliminate them via the

kidneys and intestines, which have some additional detoxification abilities. Defense means the various processes that stand guard to protect the body from infection and cellular injury. The immune system acts as a cellular defender seeking and destroying uninvited guests whose presence could create infections or give rise to chronic illnesses. Defense is also needed to recognize and eliminate old and dead cells within the body to prevent debris from accumulating. Cellular communications sense and respond to the environment and send physiological messages back and forth from one region of the body to another. These are the nervous system that connects the brain to all regions of the body, hormones, neurotransmitters, and a range of special-purpose messengers that bind themselves to a specific receptor on the surface of cells. Within each cell, there are specific communication systems that carry messages from outside the cell to the genes within the cell. Cellular transport carries the nutrition that the digestive system has assimilated to the cells. That works through the circulatory system pumped by the heart through the lungs and via the lymphatic system. Energy, or bioenergetics, is the process that converts food to energy and manages the use of it within cells. Structure refers to the skeleton and connective tissues. The skeleton is remodeled every 5–7 years. Connective tissues constantly affect function, posture, muscle tone, and skeletal health.

6. Tett (2015).
7. Lynn et al. (2007).
8. Garfield (2006; see also Calkins and Sviokla 2007).
9. The hilarious medical novel by Samuel Sheen, *The House of God*, chronicles how interns fresh from medical school become real doctors. A part of their practical education is to segment patients into gomers and those who die young. The former (get out of my emergency room) is an elderly patient with multimorbidities who just refuses to die. The best way to treat them, the interns learn, is not to do too much, and vigorously turf them to other departments or the nursing home where they belong. The latter are the real challenges, of which the interns have to learn that the patient is the one with the illness, not them.
10. Glouberman and Mintzberg (2001).
11. Hopp and Lovejoy (2012).
12. Bohmer and Lawrence (2008) and Bohmer (2009).
13. Christensen et al. (2009).
14. Hopp and Lovejoy (2012).
15. Lillrank et al. (2010).
16. Kotler and Keller (2006) and Kotler et al. (2008).
17. Maslow (1943).
18. Enid (1953).
19. St. Sauver et al. (2013).
20. In manufacturing, runners are products or parts that are produced frequently, such as every week. Repeaters are products or parts that, although being produced regularly, are manufactured at longer time intervals. Strangers are products or parts that are produced at long, irregular, and possibly unpredictable intervals.
21. For a review of triage scales, see Christ et al. (2010).
22. Weinstein et al. (2009).
23. The Boston matrix, also known as the growth-share matrix and the BCG matrix, was originally developed by Bruce Henderson at the Boston Consulting Group in the early 1970s.
24. Kaplan and Norton (1996).
25. One of the best-known surgical factories is Shouldice Hospital in Canada, which focuses on hernia repair (http://www.shouldice.com/). For a case study, see Herzlinger (1997).

The Aravind Eye Hospital in Tamil Nadu, India, is focused on cataract surgery and renowned for its high quality and productivity in service of the poor (see Mikola and Lillrank 2015, pp. 189–196; Mehta and Shenoy 2011). Coxa is a hospital in Tampere, Finland, that is exclusively focused on knee and hip joint replacement surgery (http://www.placidway.com/profile/2155/Coxa-Excellence-Hospital-for-Joint-Replacement, https://www.coxa.fi/en/).

26. The MD Anderson Cancer Center at the University of Texas is focused on complex cancer and runs a network of specialists (https://www.mdanderson.org/). Docrates is a private cancer clinic in Helsinki that is doing only diagnostics and case management and outsourcing procedures to university hospitals (https://www.docrates.com/en/).

27. The BMC category cost structure is not included. In rich countries, the cost structure is typically up to three-quarters of personnel expenses. Therefore, cost structure does not provide a meaningful distinction between the DSOs. Revenue models are discussed in Chapter 7.

28. Americans seek a large amount of nonemergency care in EDs, where they often encounter long waits to be seen. Urgent care centers and retail clinics have emerged as alternatives to the ED for nonemergency care. We estimate that 13.7%–27.1% of all ED visits could take place at one of these alternative sites, with a potential cost savings of approximately $4.4 billion annually. The primary conditions that could be treated at these sites include minor acute illnesses, strains, and fractures (Weinick et al. 2010).

29. Oram (2014).

30. Little et al. (2017).

31 SIBs known as pay-for-success projects in the United States and social benefit bonds in Australia. See http://www.socialfinance.org.uk/database/.

32. Gawande (2011).

33. For an overview, see Strauss and Mayer (2013).

34. WHO definition: http://www.who.int/maternal_child_adolescent/topics/maternal/maternal_perinatal/en/. The term *early neonatal death* is used by the European Health Observatory. The principal causes of neonatal death in high-income countries are congenital anomalies and complications related to very preterm birth. Babies from multiple pregnancies have neonatal mortality rates that are four to six times higher than those of singletons. Suboptimal care is also associated with neonatal deaths at term, and these factors contribute to an explanation of the variation in mortality rates between European countries. European Perinatal Health Report, C2, http://www.europeristat.com/images/doc/Peristat%202013%20V2.pdf.

35. European Perinatal Health Report, C2, Figure 7.5, http://www.europeristat.com/images/doc/Peristat%202013%20V2.pdf. In Europe, the incidents of perinatal mortality have declined. In 2010, Iceland had the lowest perinatal mortality at 1.2; Finland was the second with 1.5. The worst European performer was Romania at 5.5; the corresponding figure for the United States was 6.2. For the U.S. figure, see the National Center for Health Statistics, https://www.cdc.gov/nchs/products/databriefs/db169.htm.

36. European Perinatal Health Report 2014, Figure 5.8, http://www.europeristat.com/images/doc/Peristat%202013%20V2.pdf.

37. Wiegers et al. (1998).

38. National Stroke Association, http://www.stroke.org/understand-stroke/what-stroke.

39. Teasell et al. (2003).

40. MacIntosh-Murray and Choo (2006).

41. https://www.doctagon.fi/en/.

# Chapter 7

# Summary, Conclusions, and Challenges

## 7.1 Tools for Thinking

In the previous chapters, I presented some tools for thinking. Ask, what is it? What can be known about it? How does it work? What can be done to and with it? The artificial world is a socio-techno-economic system founded on both evolution and agency. Purposeful action is constrained by knowledge (know what to do), capabilities and resources (can do), and motivation (want to do). There is no single logic to rule it all. What works in one context will not work in another; prediction and control have limits, subject to variability and decay. Chunks of logic can be used to make sense of things. As parts of managerial and clinical intuition, they help us to make sense of the world and act accordingly.

Transformations (production) and transactions (trade) are purposeful activities to improve the human condition using technologies with knowledge bases. Technologies are bundled into production functions that transform flow units. The production function is organized into tasks that are grouped and sequenced as processes. They come in a few architectural types, constellations of product and process technologies. Processes are artificial creations that need management and maintenance to counteract variability and decay. Processes and outputs have to be measured and evaluated in order to improve quality and productivity.

Commercial and professional services follow the basic logic of production. The value of service is a changed state of people and things achieved through collaborations between customers and producers. Personal services require personal interaction, from which follows that each process has to be set up individually. Setup involves bargaining, which, however, can be formatted to achieve high volumes at affordable cost. Some service processes are explorative; they do not have material embodiments and no detailed plans from beginning to end.

Health service production is purposeful action within the artificial world. It follows the logic of production processes, setups, steps, handovers, inventory, and cycle time. It struggles with the same issues as any services, immaterial state changes, individual setups, collaboration, and time–location constraints. A hospital resembles a factory only in part. Processes that are explorative and can't be planned in advance are more like R&D labs, design studios, and shopping malls. Healthcare, however, has peculiar characteristics that make it special. The product is a value proposition to offer help and health. They are achieved by production functions, the natural history of disease, placebo, theory-based therapies, and lifestyle changes that do not have the precision and predictability one would wish. From this follows demand that will not saturate, individual healing relationships that need to be produced in large volumes, the decoupling of output and outcome, information asymmetry, and third-party finance.

The general logic of healthcare offers diagnostic tools for innovators. If you think you have a great idea about a new therapy, device, pharmaceutical, or information technology (IT) gizmo, ask what or which part of the logic your innovation will hit and in which way. Run through the following checklist:

- Will it affect the production function somehow? Will it provide a way to narrow the gap between outputs and outcomes? Will it lead to better evidence, more individualized and precise medicine?
- What will it do to variability? Could it reduce variability to the extent that different process architectures could be used? Self-service, perhaps, or going from disconnected to connected flows?
- Will it affect the healing relationship, the commercial relationship, and information asymmetry? Will it empower patients?
- Will it improve the accuracy and/or reduce the time and cost of setups?
- Will it help manage handovers and supply chains?

Affordable care requires the tools of mass production. The classical drivers of production are division of labor, specialization, and standardization. While creating plenty, they have the nasty side effects of fragmenting whole jobs and reducing variability of offerings. The managerial antidote is integration of diagnoses and coordination of processes. Industry has come a long way with product integration, modularization, mass customization, and complexity management. Healthcare could and should benefit more than it has so far. My main argument in this book is that healthcare is a multiverse of different logics. There can be no one-size-fits-all solution. Improvement must focus on the managerially homogeneous demand and supply–based operating logics (DSOs) one by one. They cross over segments based on organ systems, clinical methods, and demographic groups to ask the most managerially relevant questions: What needs to be done, and what can be done?

# 7.2 DSO Lens

With the DSO construct, I have aimed to fulfill the mission of this book, which goes back to Stuart Kauffman: only what is clearly separated can be properly joined.

Research on various aspects of healthcare has emphasized the need to put things in context. Contextualism and contingency theory are major streams of thought within social sciences. Few dare to postulate universal truths that would apply similarly across all conceivable contexts. However, contexts are difficult to define, leading to lame statements such as "It depends on the situation."

DSO is a conceptual lens that defines contexts. Like a kaleidoscope, it separates healthcare into seven parts. Each can be described as distinct business models with value offerings, patient segments, relations and channels, key resources and activities, process types, a position in a broader partner network, and financial models. The DSO construct can be said to be useful if it provides a sharper and better understanding of the predicament of healthcare, when compared with the conventional view of healthcare as one industry.

In the following, I run through a few thought experiments by looking at various problems through the DSO lens. Does it provide clear contexts that may take the lame "It depends on the situation" contingency theory to a new level of precision? Do issues look different when studied separately for each DSO? All thought experiments need to, in due course, be scrutinized by empirical data and practical experimentation.

## 7.2.1 Processes and Process Improvement

Lean is attractive to healthcare, as it proclaims some universally valid principles, such as waste reduction, teamwork, and continuous improvement. As for process improvement, Lean thinking applies to some, but not all, aspects of healthcare. It has little to say to job shops, other than that they should be abolished and turned into processes. It has a lot to say for one-visit, high-volume production, although the automobile assembly plant is not the obvious role model here. The humble coffee shop and hamburger joint are better benchmarks. Lean healthcare is at its best in electives and care, as well as in back-office preparations, with plannable and schedulable processes where the production function can be assumed to be reasonably stable, variability can be controlled, and the logic of connected and disconnected processes is clearly manifest. Where processes can't be planned in advance and must be explorative, as in cure and projects, Lean management is in the same tar pit with the management of knowledge work, content production, research and development, and innovation. These are areas where the administrative logic is at its weakest; managers have to yield to professionals, and professionals, lacking clear-cut, one-best-way theories and therapies, have to engage in shared decision-making (SDM) with patients.

## 7.2.2 *Patient Choice and Information Asymmetry*

Patient choice is about what, where, who, and when. Free choice is constrained by information asymmetry. Much of the literature on patient choice is anchored in the emergency and cure DSOs. When medical misfortune hits suddenly, a human being is fragile, not in a position to choose location, bargain about setups, and pick between therapies. For emergency patients, urgency determines everything; there is no real choice but the fastest. Patients want to be in good hands; paternalism is justified. In every other DSO, the view is different.

Excluding vaccinations and other population-based programs, prevention is all about patient choice. The caregiver can at best advise and support; the execution of the production function is in the hands of the patient. The information asymmetry is the other way around: the caregiver can't know what goes on in the mind and body of the patient.

One visit and electives are consumerist choices. Since the issues are neither urgent nor severe, and the what issue has been settled, the choice is between where, who, and when. Patients can take their time to choose, ask friends, find out track records, consider the reputation of doctors, and ponder the how. Patients can behave like any service customer.

Cure indicates lack of diagnostic clarity and explorative processes. There is no one best way. There are trade-offs under risk and uncertainty, like the prostate cancer patient who has to choose between probabilities of dying prematurely and living the rest of his years in diapers. Here SDM and patient decision aids (PtDAs) are truly needed. Care is somewhat similar, but the scope of choice is broader. It includes not only therapies and adherence to them but also issues of the daily life of physically or mentally incapacitated people.

Projects deal with multiprovider and multimorbidity cases. Here patients, even those well informed and active, run into bounded rationality. Projects require project managers to act as agents on behalf of principals.

The DSO lens neatly slices patient choice and information asymmetry into distinct contexts and problems.[1]

## 7.2.3 *Professional, Administrative, and Consumerist Logics*

In healthcare, as in all professional services, managers have to deal with a chronic conflict between the professional, the administrative, and the consumerist views. The relative balance varies between DSOs.

Emergency and sophisticated electives, such as brain and open-heart surgery, are heavy on professionalism. Administrators should leave the professionals alone, establish broad-based output and outcome-based performance criteria, and organize flows, scheduling, and staffing but otherwise not micromanage. Prevention, one visit, and care are tilted toward the consumerist logic. Patients can and will choose. Cure requires a workable overlap of the professional and the consumerist logics. Projects are very much the playing field of administrators managing supply chains and complex patient journeys.

## 7.2.4 Integration

High-volume production systems rely on division of labor, specialization, and standardization. These lead to fragmentation that should be counteracted with integration and coordination. Integration applies to products and services, and coordination to production processes.

In emergencies, integration pertains to performing quick and accurate triage that allows a patient to be pointed to the right clinical flow. When emergency patients with severe conditions have been stabilized, they are handed over to cure.

Prevention needs to integrate across current sacrifices and future gains, as well as clinical and behavioral medicine.

In one visits, integration needs to consider what can be done during one visit to complete the case, without needlessly asking the patient to come again.

Elective procedures are based on precise diagnoses and schedulable interventions. Integration is primarily done at the diagnostic and care planning phases.

In cure, integration is focused longitudinally on iterations of the process with learn-as-you-go loops.

Care processes last until the end of life and typically affect large areas of a patient's lifeworld. Several aspects need to be integrated into a comprehensive understanding of patient needs and the development of a continuous care scheme that is integrated with nonmedical issues, such as housing, mobility, and daily routines.

Projects require the deep integration of various types of specialized knowledge and stakeholder perspectives.

Various types of integration should be developed and organized based on the dividing lines across which integration should reach: the time frame (here and now vs. rest of life), plannable versus explorative processes, and the number and types of relevant contributors both within and beyond the medical community.

## 7.2.5 Coordination and Time

Coordination is seeing that the right things are done at the right time, in the right order, at the right place, and with the right tools and instructions. In management parlance, it is routing, scheduling, staffing, and supply management. Coordination happens in time; each DSO has a distinct time perspective.

Urgent emergencies work against a time window, within which the patient must be saved and stabilized. Waiting is harmful to emergency patients; the viable buffer is excess capacity. Emergency is ideally job shop production with a multifunctional team focusing on a patient. The perennial problem with emergency departments is that when arrival rates are high, the job shop breaks down into disconnected flows.

Prevention is future oriented. Something must be done now, or something bad will happen in the future. Focus is on the outcome stream, the progress of a patient's risk profile and its development. Prevention is akin to a continuous flow process, where status is monitored and interventions and service encounters are used as needed.

One visit is here and now. It requires connected flows. Convenience is paramount; patients should not be kept waiting.

Electives can be planned and properly scheduled. They have deadlines, when all preparatory flows must be completed, and all resources must be in time–location synchrony before the procedure can start.

Cure is explorative processes that can't be planned from end to end. If a therapy does not produce expected results, the setup must be redone. Coordination is an ongoing task.

Projects imply several things going on simultaneously. A project manager should orchestrate the tasks of several providers.

Care runs with a rhythmic steady beat following a regular schedule.

## 7.2.6 Benchmarks

Keeping in mind how apples and oranges can be compared (Table 5.2), industries can learn from each other. The automobile assembly plant is not the only excellent operation in this world.

Emergency departments can benchmark other operations with random demand and narrow time windows, such as the military and police. Industrial services and the maintenance of critical components require emergency procedures. A telecommunications operator can't sit on his hand if a mobile network is down. There have to be repair crews out there with the speed of an ambulance.

Prevention has to live with the unfortunate limitations of behavioral technologies and the difficulties that impact people's minds and behavior. Thereby it resembles both consumer marketing and political propaganda. Further, prevention deals with the relation between current sacrifices and future gains. So do investment bankers.

One visits resemble small-item retailing, kiosks, and fast food. Franchising can be used.

Elective is the DSO with the most resemblance to the automobile plant. It has planned processes, given schedules, connected and disconnected lines, a struggle against variability, and a relentless focus on the small q. Elective surgeries have preparation phases that must come together at a deadline, when the operation is supposed to start. In this respect, electives resemble all deadline-constrained production systems, such as news media and airlines. Like a pilot, a surgeon does well in checking that all systems are a go before takeoff.

Cure is in many ways similar to research, development, and content production, that is, music, literature, films, and games. While there is an idea, or a vision of the preferable outcome, the process is not plannable in advance.

Care is about managing inevitable decline. The maintenance of industrial machines and buildings shares the same problems and tackles them with means, such as regular monitoring, risk assessment, and predictive maintenance, which in healthcare would be called rehabilitation.

Projects can draw on the accumulated experience of project-based businesses, such as shipbuilding, software development, and construction. Supply chain management has developed into a sophisticated tool for managing multisupplier networks.

## 7.2.7 Volume, Variety, and Economies of Scale

Economies of scale is the cornucopia principle: the more you do, the cheaper it gets. It should not be confused with mere volume expansion: the more you do, the more you get. The primary mechanism is the dynamic relation between setup and processing, the possibility to divide fixed costs over a large volume of repetition. The necessity of individual setup defeats economies of scale. However, this applies to the service front office; the back office can operate like a factory. The question hinges on setup. To what extent can explorative setups be routinized, routines formatted, and formats standardized?

Economies of scale is applicable for plannable processes, that is, one visit and electives. Both can select demand, match it to supply, and use formatted setups. They can also exploit the franchising principle with a centralized back office and decentralized front offices with optimal time–location access. For the other DSOs, economies of scale remains a pipe dream. A more relevant issue is the distribution trilemma. How should time–location access, variety at one service provision point, and specialization be optimized?

## 7.2.8 Health Finance and Revenue Models

Health finance has two parts, how funds are collected and how they are distributed to caregivers. The collection methods are out-of-pocket, insurance, and taxes. Third-party financiers can distribute money as global budgets, fee-for-service, and capitation, and by outcomes. These are ideal models that appear in various combinations with several adjustments, such as bonuses and penalties. The question thus is, what should be the leading financial principle for each DSO?

Emergency medical services, here understood strictly as those dealing with urgent and severe cases, can be seen as a part of the social compact between taxpayers and governments, akin to the institutions of external security and internal safety. Therefore, it stands to reason that emergency departments should be financed, while not necessarily managed, by governments or other national bodies with the authority to impose and maintain triage rules. The qualitative and quantitative randomness of demand supports global budgets based on estimates of long-range average demand and required service levels. Due to random demand, excess capacity is needed as a buffer, and short-term capacity utilization is not a relevant measure.

Prevention has a weak production function with a lot of risk and uncertainty. It is patient centric, relationship intensive, and employs continuous processes with an element of exploration. Elevated risk is not necessarily physically inconvenient; motivational issues are central. This suggests the application of outcome-based finance that would include carrots and sticks to both parties.

One visits are cheap and could be left to out-of-pocket finance. For patients who may accrue significant costs, the proper cover is insurance with deductibles; that is, patients pay out-of-pocket to a certain dollar amount per year, and the rest is insured. One visits can also be covered with capitation; that is, a financier pays a membership fee for each patient that entitles him to a certain range of services at a chosen caregiver.

Electives can be financed like one visits; however, as they tend to be more costly, out-of-pocket is not a viable option. As electives typically are procedures anchored in a diagnosis, bundled payments, such as the DRG system, are appropriate.

Care means ongoing relationships and reasonably predictable expenses. Monthly fixed fees and personal global budgets can be used.

Cure and project are the financial problem children. Expenses over the patient journey are not easily predicted and can accumulate to significant levels. I will not attempt to solve these problems here. It is wise to notice, however, that as with patient choice, the difficult and the dramatic should not be allowed to dominate the health policy debate.

### 7.2.9 Heroic Medicine—and the Rest

This brief thinking experiment with the DSO lens leads to a significant conclusion. The debate on healthcare has been misaligned, romanticized, and bedeviled by the dramatics of emergency and the complexity of care.

There are valid reasons why citizens, markets, and policy makers focus on heroic medicine. But as in many other walks of life, the dramatic may obscure the significant, and the urgent push out the important. Emergency and care imply serious management problems to which there are no ready-made panaceas on offer. But for the others, there is a lot that can be done by applying known and proven management methods. A task for future research emerges: how to define, separate, and manage the different demand and supply logics in the real world.

## 7.3 Take It from Here

What do you do now when you have a lens that produces a view of healthcare as seven managerial segments? This book is not a how-to manual on what you should do differently next Monday. Rather, the aim is to implant some chunks of logic to impact your thinking and intuition. Let me close with a few suggestions.

Whatever your problem is, make it a habit to run it through the DSO lens. If your issue looks different per DSO, you can start to cut it into manageable pieces, find contexts, and dig deeper.

If you are an innovator and entrepreneur pondering a new way to deliver healthcare, check if it belongs to one or several DSOs. If it is one, or close to one, consider making it a pure play.

If you have an organization that by architecture is one DSO, but in practice is clogged with several types of demand and supply constellations, see if you can separate them to distinct streams or competence centers.

If you are running an operation that by necessity must have several DSOs, pay attention to handovers. Do you need to have fixed designs, or can you apply a flexible multimode logic?

If you are a researcher within health systems science and your data gives inconclusive results, see if you can elaborate your material per DSO and get more clear-cut findings. While you are it, look to see if you can find other, alternative, or complementary managerial segmentation principles. If you do, drop me a note.

## Note

1. For an application of the DSO construct to the choices associated with maternity care and prenatal screening, see Chen (2017).

# References

Abel-Smith, B. 1992. The Beveridge report: Its origins and outcomes. *International Social Security Review* 45:1–2, pp. 5–16.

Acemoglu, D., and Robinson, J.A. 2012. *Why Nations Fail: The Origins of Power, Prosperity, and Poverty*. New York: Crown.

Aherne, J., and Whelton, A. 2010. *Applying Lean in Healthcare: A Collection of International Case Studies*. Boca Raton, FL: CRC Press/Taylor & Francis Group.

Akerlof, G.A. 1970. The market for 'lemons': Quality uncertainty and the market mechanism. *Quarterly Journal of Economics* 84:3, pp. 488–500.

Albanese, C., Aaby, D., and Platchek, T.S. 2014. *Advanced Lean in Healthcare*. North Charleston, SC: CreateSpace Independent Publishing Platform.

Applegate, D.L., Bixby, R.M., Chvátal, V., and Cook, W.J. 2006. *The Traveling Salesman Problem: A Computational Study*. Princeton, NJ: Princeton University Press.

Ariely, D. 2008. *Predictably Irrational*. New York: Harper Collins.

Arlbjørn, J.S., and Freytag, P.V. 2013. Evidence of Lean: A review of international peer-reviewed journal articles. *European Business Review* 25:2, pp. 174–205.

Arrow, K. 1963. Uncertainty and the welfare economics of medical care. *American Economic Review* 53:5, pp. 141–149.

Arthur, B. 2009. *The Nature of Technology—What It Is and How It Evolves*. London: Allen Lane.

Ash, S.A, Weiss, R.E., Zigmond, D., et al. 2011. Hospital determinants of emergency department left without being seen rates. *Annals of Emergency Medicine* 58:1, pp. 24–32.

Ashby, W.R. 1956. *An Introduction to Cybernetics*. London: Methuen.

Axelrod, R. 1997. *The Complexity of Cooperation: Agent-Based Models of Competition and Collaboration*. Princeton, NJ: Princeton University Press.

Azam, M., Rahman, Z., Talib, F., and Singh, J.K. 2012. A critical study of quality parameters in health care establishment, developing and integrated quality model. *International Journal of Health Care Quality Assurance* 25:5, pp. 387–402.

Baines, T., and Lightfoot, H. 2013. *Made to Serve: How Manufacturers Can Compete through Servitization and Product Service Systems*. New York: Wiley.

Baker, J., and Cameron, M. 1996. The effects of the service environment on affect and consumer perception of waiting time: An integrative review and research propositions. *Journal of the Academy of Marketing Science* 24:4, pp. 338–349.

Baldwin, R. 2017. *The Great Convergence—Information Technology and the New Globalization*. Cambridge, MA: Belknap Press.

Banerjee, A., and Duflo, E. 2011. *Poor Economics: A Radical Rethinking of the Way to Fight Global Poverty*. Philadelphia: Public Affairs.

Baumol, W.J. 1967. Macroeconomics of unbalanced growth: The anatomy of urban crisis. *American Economic Review* 57:3, pp. 415–426.

Baumol, W.J. 2012. *The Cost Disease—Why Computers Get Cheaper and Health Care Doesn't.* New Haven, CT: Yale University Press.

Baumol, W.J., and Bowen, W.G. 1967. On the performing arts: The anatomy of their economic problems. *American Economic Review* 55:1–2, pp. 495–502.

Beinhocker, E. 2007. *The Origin of Wealth—Evolution, Complexity, and the Radical Remaking of Economics.* Cambridge, MA: Harvard Business Review Press.

Benedetti, F., Lanotte, M., Lopiano, L., and Colloca, L. 2007. When words are painful: Unraveling the mechanisms of the nocebo effect. *Neuroscience* 147:2, pp. 260–271.

Ben-Tovim, D.I. 2017. *Process Redesign for Health Care Using Lean Thinking—A Guide for Improving Patient Flow and the Quality and Safety of Care.* Boca Raton, FL: CRC Press/Taylor & Francis Group.

Berger, P.L., and Luckman, T. 1966. *The Social Construction of Reality.* New York: Random House.

Berridge, V. 2016. *Public Health—A Very Short Introduction.* Oxford: Oxford University Press.

Berry, L.L., and Bendapudi, N. 2007. Health care: A fertile field for service research. *Journal of Service Research* 10: pp. 111–122.

Berwick, D.M. 2014. *Promising Care—How We Can Rescue Health Care by Improving It.* San Francisco: Jossey-Bass.

Bhandari, L., Berman, P., and Ahuja, R. 2010. The impoverishing effect of healthcare payments in India: New methodology and findings. *Economic & Political Weekly* 45:16, pp. 65–71.

Bitner, M.J. 1992. Servicescapes: The impact of physical surroundings on customers and employees. *Journal of Marketing* 56:2, pp. 57–71.

Bitner, M.J., Farada, W.T., Hubbert, A.R., and Zeithaml, V.A. 1997. Customers contributions and roles in service delivery. *International Journal of Service Industry Management* 8:3, pp. 193–205.

Bland, J.S. 2014. *The Disease Delusion—Conquering the Causes of Chronic Illness for a Healthier, Longer and Happier Life.* New York: Harper-Collins.

Blozik, E., Nothacker, M., Bunk, T., Szecsenyi, J., Ollenschläger, G., and Scherer, M. 2014. Simultaneous development of guidelines and quality indicators—How do guideline groups act? A worldwide survey. *International Journal of Health Care Quality Assurance* 25:8, pp. 712–729.

Bodenheimer, T., and Grumbach, K. 2016. *Understanding Health Policy—A Clinical Approach.* New York: McGraw-Hill.

Bohmer, R.M.J. 2009. *Designing Care: Aligning the Nature and Management of Health Care.* Boston: Harvard Business School Press.

Bohmer, R.M.J., and Lawrence, D.M. 2008. Care platforms: A basic building block for care delivery. *Health Affairs* 27:5, pp. 1336–1340.

Bookstaber, R. 2017. *The End of Theory—Financial Crises, the Failure of Economics, and the Sweep of Human Interaction.* Princeton, NJ: Princeton University Press.

Bowles, S., and Gintis, H. 2011. *A Cooperative Species—Human Reciprocity and Its Evolution.* Princeton, NJ: Princeton University Press.

Brawley, O.W. 2011. *How We Do Harm: A Doctor Breaks Ranks about Being Sick in America.* New York: St. Martin's Press.

Britnell, M. 2015. *In Search of the Perfect Health System.* London: Palgrave.

Brownlee, S. 2007. *Overtreated: Why Too Much Medicine Is Making Us Sicker and Poorer.* New York: Bloomsbury.

Busse, R., Geissler, A., Quentin, W., and Wiley, M., eds. 2011. Diagnosis-related groups in Europe. *European Observatory on Health Systems and Policies Series.* Berkshire, UK: McGraw-Hill Open University Press.

Calkins, C., and Sviokla, J. 2007. What health consumers want. *Harvard Business Review* 85:12, pp. 14–15 (December).

Canguilhem, G. 1991. *The Normal and the Pathological.* New York: Zone Books.

Chase, R.B. 1978. Where does the customer fit in a service operation? *Harvard Business Review* 56:6, pp. 137–142 (November–December).

Chase, R.B. 1981. The customer contact approach to services: Theoretical bases and practical extensions. *Operations Research* 29:4, pp. 698–706.

Chen, A. 2017. Understanding patient choice—A study of women's choices in prenatal screening and testing. Doctoral dissertation, Aalto University School of Science, Department of Industrial Engineering and Management. https://aaltodoc.aalto.fi/.

Chowdhury, S. 2015. Public retreat, private expenses, and penury—A study of illness induced impoverishment in urban India. *Journal of Developing Societies* 31:2, pp.153–183.

Christ, M., Grossmann, F.M., Winter, D., Bingisser, R., and Platz, E. 2010. Modern triage in the emergency department. *Deutzsche Ärtzeblatt International* 107:50, pp. 892–898.

Christensen, C.M., Grossman, J.H., and Hwang, J. 2009. *The Innovators Prescription—A Disruptive Solution for Health Care.* New York: McGraw Hill.

Christensen, C.M., Hall, T., Dillon, K., and Duncan, D.D. 2016. *Competing against Luck: The Story about Innovation and Customer Choice.* New York: HarperCollins.

Clark, G. 2007. *A Farewell to Alms: A Brief Economic History of the World.* Princeton, NJ: Princeton University Press.

Clarke, S. 1981. *The Foundations of Structuralism.* Brighton, UK: Harvester Press.

Coase, R. 1937. The nature of the firm. *Economica* 4:16, pp. 386–405.

Cohen, S.B. 2014. The concentration of health care expenditures and related expenses for costly medical conditions, 2012. Statistical Brief 455. Rockville, MD: Agency for Healthcare Research and Quality, U.S. Department of Health and Human Services.

Cook, D.P., Goh, C.-H., and Chung, C.H. 1999. Service typologies: A state of the art survey. *Production and Operations Management* 8:3, pp. 318–338.

Cooper, R., and Kaplan, R.S. 1991. Profit priorities from activity-based costing. *Harvard Business Review* 69:3, pp. 130–135 (May–June).

Cowen, T. 2010. *The Great Stagnation—How America Ate All the Low-Hanging Fruit of Modern History, Got Sick, and Will (Eventually) Feel Better.* London: Penguin Books.

Crilly, J., Bost, N., Thalib, L., Timms, J., and Gleeson, H. 2013. Patients who present to the emergency department and leave without being seen: Prevalence, predictors and outcomes. *European Journal of Emergency Medicine* 20:4, pp. 248–255.

Cusumano, M. 1990. *The Japanese Software Factory.* New York: Free Press.

Cutler, D.M. 2004. *Your Money or Your Life—Strong Medicine for America's Healthcare System.* Oxford: Oxford University Press.

Cyert, R.M., and March, J.G. 1963. *A Behavioral Theory of the Firm.* New York: Wiley-Blackwell.

Davenport, T.H. 1993. *Process Innovation—Reengineering Work through Information Technology.* Cambridge, MA: Harvard Business School Press.

Davies, A., and Brady, T. 2000. Organizational capabilities and learning in complex product systems: Towards repeatable solutions. *Research Policy* 29:7–8, pp. 931–953.

Davis, M.M., and Heineke, J. 1998. How disconfirmation, perception and actual waiting times impact customer satisfaction. *International Journal of Service Industry Management* 9:1, pp. 64–73.

Davis, S.M., and Lawrence, P.R. 1978. Problems of matrix organizations. *Harvard Business Review* 56:3, pp. 39–50 (May–June).

De Grauwe, P. 2017. *The Limits of the Market.* Oxford: Oxford University Press.

de Matos, C., Henrique, J., and Rossi, C.A.V. 2007. Service recovery paradox: A meta-analysis. *Journal of Service Research* 10:1, pp. 60–77.

Deming, W.E. 1993. *The New Economics for Industry, Government, Education.* 2nd ed. Cambridge, MA: MIT Press.

Deming, W.E. 1986. *Out of the Crisis.* Cambridge, MA: MIT Press.

Dennet, D. 2017. *From Bacteria to Bach and Back—The Evolution of Minds.* New York: W.W. Norton.

de Souza, L.B. 2009. Trends and approaches in Lean healthcare. *Leadership in Health Services* 22:2, pp. 121–139.

DiMaggio, P.J., and Powell, W. 1983. The iron cage revisited: Institutional isomorphism and collective rationality in organizational fields. *American Sociological Review* 48, pp. 147–160.

Dixon, A., Robertson, R., Appleby, R., et al. 2010. *Patient Choice: How Patients Choose and How Providers Respond?* London: King's Fund.

Donabedian, A. 1988. The quality of care. How can it be assessed? *JAMA* 260, pp. 1743–1748.

Douma, S., and Schreuder, H. 2008. *Economic Approaches to Organizations.* 4th ed. London: Prentice Hall.

Doyle, C., Lennox, L., and Bell, D. 2013. A systematic review of evidence on the links between patient experience and clinical safety and effectiveness. *BMJ Open* 3:1.

Eberhart, D. 2006. *I trygghetsnarkomanernas land: Sverige och det nationella paniksyndromet* [In the Land of Safety Junkies: Sweden and the National Panic Syndrome]. Stockholm: Nordstedts.

Eisenhardt, K. 1989. Agency theory: An assessment and review. *Academy of Management Review* 14:1, pp. 57–74.

Ekelund, U., Kurlands, L., Eklund, F., Torkki, P., Letterståls, A., Lindmarker, P., and Castén, M. 2011. Patient throughput times and inflow patterns in Swedish emergency departments. A basis for Answer, A National Swedish Emergency Registry. Scandinavian Journal of Trauma, Resuscitation and Emergency Medicine, 19:37.

Enid, C. 1953. The hour of birth. A study of the distribution of times of onset of labour and of delivery throughout the 24-hour period. *British Journal of Preventive Social Medicine* 7, pp. 43–59.

Faraz, A., Burt, J., and Roland, M. 2014. Measuring patient experience: Concepts and methods. *Patient* 7, pp. 235–241.

Fitzsimmons, J.A., and Fitzsimmons, M.J. 2006. *Service Management—Operations, Strategy, Information Technology.* 5th ed. New York: McGraw-Hill.

Fliess, S., and Kleinaltenkamp, M. 2004. Blueprinting the service company. *Journal of Business Research* 57, pp. 392–404.

Florida, R. 2002. *The Rise of the Creative Class.* New York: Basic Books.

Fogel, R.W. 2004. *The Escape from Hunger and Premature Death 1700–2100: Europe, America, and the Third World*. Cambridge: Cambridge University Press.

Foucault, M. 1973. *The Birth of the Clinic*. London: Routledge.

Frei, F.X. 2006. Breaking the trade-off between efficiency and service. *Harvard Business Review* 84:11, pp. 93–101 (November).

Freidson, E. 1988. *The Profession of Medicine—A Study of the Sociology of Applied Knowledge*. Chicago: Chicago University Press.

Freidson, E. 2001. *Professionalism—The Third Logic*. Cambridge, UK: Polity Press.

Fukuyama, F. 1992. *The End of History and the Last Man*. New York: Free Press.

Gadrey, J. 1988. Rethinking output in services. *Service Industries Journal* 8, pp. 67–76.

Gadrey, J. 2000. The characterization of goods and services: An alternative approach. *Review of Income and Wealth* 46, pp. 369–387.

Gardner, D. 2008. *Risk: The Science and Politics of Fear*. New York: Virgin Digital.

Garfield, S.R. 2006. The delivery of medical care. *Permanente Journal* 2:10, pp. 46–55.

Garvin, D. 1986. *Managing Quality*. New York: Free Press.

Gawande, A. 2002. *Complications: A Surgeon's Notes on an Imperfect Science*. London: Picador.

Gawande, A. 2007. *Better: A Surgeon's Notes on Performance*. London: Picador.

Gawande, A. 2011. *The Checklist Manifesto*. London: Picador.

Gawande, A. 2014. *Being Mortal—Medicine and What Matters in the End*. London: Profile Books.

Gerring, J. 2012. *Social Science Methodology—A Unified Framework*. Cambridge: Cambridge University Press.

Giddens, A. 1984. *The Constitution of Society*. Cambridge, UK: Polity Press.

Gilbreth, F. 1912. *Primer of Scientific Management*. Easton, PA: Hive (reprint 1985).

Gilbreth, F.B. and Carey, E.G. 1948. Cheaper by the Dozen. New York: Thomas Y. Crowell.

Gleeson-White, J. 2011. *Double Entry—How the Merchants of Venice Shaped the Modern World—and How Their Invention Could Make or Break the Planet*. Sydney: Allen & Unwin.

Global Burden of Disease Report. 2010. *Lancet Special Report* 380:9859.

Glouberman, S., and Mintzberg, H. 2001. Managing the care of health and the cure of disease, part I: Differentiation. *Health Care Management Review* 26:1, pp. 56–92.

Goffman, E. 1955. *The Presentation of Self in Everyday Life*. New York: Random House.

Goldratt, E., and Cox, J. 1984. *The Goal: A Process of Ongoing Improvement*. Great Barrington, MA: North River Press.

Goodman, J.C., Villarreal, P., and Jones, B. 2011. The social cost of adverse medical events, and what we can do about it. *Health Affairs* 30:4, pp. 590–595.

Gordon, R.J. 2016. *The Rise and Fall of American Growth: The U.S. Standard of Living since the Civil War*. Princeton, NJ: Princeton University Press.

Gottlieb, A. 2016. *The Dream of Enlightenment—The Rise of Modern Philosophy*. New York: W.W. Norton.

Grant Thompson, W. 2005. *The Placebo Effect and Health—Combining Science & Compassionate Care*. New York: Prometheus Books.

Greenberg, G. 2010. *Manufacturing Depression—The Secret History of a Modern Disease*. New York: Simon & Schuster.

Griffin, P.M., Nembhart, H.B., DeFlitch, C.J., et al. 2016. *Healthcare Systems Engineering*. New York: Wiley & Sons.

Grönroos, C. 2000. *Service Management and Marketing—A Customer Relationship Management Approach.* 2nd ed. New York: Wiley.

Grönroos, C. 2011. *Service Management and Marketing: Customer Management in Service Competition.* 3rd ed. New York: Wiley.

Grossman, M. 1972. On the concept of health capital and the demand for health. *Journal of Political Economy* 80:2, pp. 223–255.

Hackman, J.R., and Oldham, G.R. 1980. *Work Redesign.* Reading, MA: Addison-Wesley.

Hägglund, P., and Johansson, P. 2016. Sjukskrivningarnas anatomi. Rapport till Expertgruppen för studier i offentlig ekonomi 2016:2. Stockholm: Government of Sweden.

Haidt, J. 2012. *The Righteous Mind: Why Good People Are Divided by Politics and Religion.* New York: Penguin Books.

Hall, R., ed. 2013. *Patient Flow—Reducing Delay in Healthcare Delivery.* New York: Springer.

Hammer, M., and Champy, J. 1993. *Reengineering the Corporation—A Manifesto for Business Revolution.* London: Nicholas Breadley.

Harrington, H.J. 1991. *Business Process Improvement—The Breakthrough Strategy for Total Quality, Productivity, and Competitiveness.* New York: McGraw-Hill.

Hauser, J.D., and Clausing, J. 1988. The house of quality. *Harvard Business Review* 66:3, pp. 63–73 (May–June).

Hayes, R., and Wheelwright, S.C. 1979a. Link manufacturing process and product life cycles. *Harvard Business Review* 57:1, pp. 133–140 (January–February).

Hayes, R., and Wheelwright, S.C. 1979b. The dynamics of process-product life cycles. *Harvard Business Review* 57:2, pp. 127–136 (March–April).

Hayes, R.H., Wheelwright, S.C., and Clark, K.B. 1988. *Dynamic Manufacturing.* New York: Free Press.

Herzlinger, R. 1997. *Market Driven Health Care—Who Wins, Who Loses in the Transformation of America's Largest Service Industry.* New York: Perseus Books Group.

Hill, T.P. 1977. On goods and services. *Review of Income and Wealth* 23:4, pp. 315–338.

Hopp, W. 2011. *Supply Chain Science.* Long Grove, IL: Waveland Press.

Hopp, W.J., and Lovejoy, W.S. 2012. *Hospital Operations: Principles of High Efficiency Health Care.* Upper Saddle River, NJ: FT Press.

Hopp, W.J., and Spearman, M.L. 2011. *Factory Physics.* 3rd ed. Long Grove, IL: Waveland Press.

Hsiao, W. 1995. Abnormal economics in the health sector. *Health Policy* 32, pp. 125–139.

Huber, M., Green, L., van der Horst, H., et al. 2011. How should we define health? *BMJ* 343, p. d4163.

Illich, I. 1974. *Medical Nemesis.* London: Calder & Boyars.

Institute of Medicine. 1999. *To Err Is Human: Building a Safer Health System.* Washington, DC: National Academies Press.

Institute of Medicine. 2001. *Crossing the Quality Chasm: A New Health System for the 21st Century.* Washington, DC: National Academies Press.

Isaacson, W. 2014. *The Innovators: How a Group of Inventors, Hackers, Geniuses, and Geeks Created the Digital Revolution.* New York: Simon & Schuster.

Ishikawa, K. 1985. *What Is Total Quality Control? The Japanese Way.* Englewood Cliffs, NJ: Prentice Hall.

Jackson, M.C. 2000. *Systems Approaches to Management.* New York: Kluwer.

Jackson, T.L. 2011. *Standard Work for Lean Healthcare*. Boca Raton, FL: CRC Press/Taylor & Francis Group.

Jensen, M.C. 1998. *Foundations of Organizational Strategy*. Cambridge, MA: Harvard University Press.

Jiwani, A., Himmelstein, D., Woolhandler, S., and Kahn, J.G. 2014. Billing and insurance-related administrative costs in United States' health care: Synthesis of micro-costing evidence. *BMC Health Service Research* 14, p. 556.

Johnson, S. 2014. *How We Got to Now: Six Innovations That Made the Modern World*. New York: Penguin Books.

Johnston, R., and Clark, G. 2004. *Service Operations Management*. Englewood Cliffs, NJ: Prentice Hall.

Jolly, R. 2015. *Systems Thinking for Business—Capitalize on Structures Hidden in Plain Sight*. Portland, OR: Systems Solutions Press.

Juran, J.M. 1988. *Juran on Planning for Quality*. New York: Free Press.

Kahneman, D. 2011. *Thinking, Fast and Slow*. London: Allen Lane.

Kahneman, D., and Tversky, A. 1979. Prospect theory: An analysis of decision under risk. *Econometrica* 47, pp. 263–291.

Kalanithi, P. 2016. *When Breath Becomes Air*. New York: Random House.

Kaplan, R.S., and Norton, D.P. 1996. *The Balanced Scorecard: Translating Strategy into Action*. Boston: Harvard Business School Press.

Kaufman, S.A. 2008. *Reinventing the Sacred—A New View of Science, Reason, and Religion*. New York: Basic Books.

Kenney, C. 2010. *Transforming Health Care: Virginia Mason Medical Center's Pursuit of the Perfect Patient Experience*. Boca Raton, FL: CRC Press/Taylor & Francis Group.

Keynes, J.M. 1963. *Essays in Persuasion*. New York: W.W. Norton & Co.

Kimes, S.E. 1989. Yield management: A tool for capacity-considered service firms. *Journal of Operations Management* 8:4, pp. 348–363.

Knight, A. 2014. *Pride and Joy*. London: Never Say I Know.

Kolker, A. 2012. *Healthcare Management Engineering: What Does This Fancy Term Really Mean? The Use of Operations Management Methodology for Quantitative Decision Making in Healthcare Settings*. New York: Springer.

Kotler, P., and Keller, K.L. 2006. *Marketing Management*.12th ed. Upper Saddle River, NJ: Pearson Prentice Hall.

Kotler, P., Shalowitz, J., and Stevens, R. 2008. *Strategic Marketing for Health Care Organizations: Building a Customer-Driven Health System*. San Francisco: Jossey-Bass.

Kujala, J., Lillrank, P., Kronström, V., and Peltokorpi, A. 2006. Time-based management of patient processes. *Journal of Health Organization and Management* 20:6, pp. 512–524.

Laffer, A. 2004. The Laffer curve: Past, present, and future. Washington, DC: Heritage Foundation. http://www.heritage.org/taxes/report/the-laffer-curve-past-present-and-future (accessed April 7, 2017).

Lambert, D.M. 2012. *Supply Chain Management: Processes, Partnerships, Performance*. 4th ed. Ponte Vedra Beach, FL: Supply Chain Management Institute.

Landes, D. 1999. *The Wealth and Poverty of Nations*. New York: Norton & Co.

Landes, D. 2003. *The Unbound Prometheus—Technological Change and Industrial Development in Western Europe from 1750 to the Present*. 2nd ed. Cambridge: Cambridge University Press.

Lawrence, P.R., and Lorsch, J.W. 1967. *Organization and Environment: Managing Differentiation and Integration.* Boston: Harvard University Press.

Le Fanu, J. 2011. *The Rise and Fall of Modern Medicine.* 2nd ed. London: Hachette Digital.

Légaré, F., and Witteman, H.O. 2013. Shared decision making: Examining key elements and barriers to adoption into routine clinical practice. *Health Affairs* 32:2, pp. 276–284.

LeGrand, J. 2003. *Motivation, Agency, and Public Policy—Of Knights & Knaves, Pawns & Queens.* Oxford: Oxford University Press.

Leonard, K.L. 2001. African traditional healers: The economics of healing. Indigenous Knowledge (IK) Notes No. 32. Washington, DC: World Bank. http://documents. worldbank.org/curated/en/628471468210597088/African-traditional-healers-the-economics-of-healing.

Leonard, K.L., and Zivin, J.G. 2003. Outcome versus service based payments in health care: Lessons from African traditional healers. Working Paper 9797. Cambridge, MA: National Bureau of Economic Research. http://www.nber.org/papers/w9797.

Levinson, M. 2016. *An Extraordinary Time—The End of the Postwar Boom and the Return of the Ordinary Economy.* New York: Random House.

Lillrank, P. 2002. The broom and nonroutine processes—A metaphor for understanding variability in organizations. *Knowledge and Process Management* 9:3, pp. 1–6.

Lillrank, P. 2003a. The quality of information. *International Journal of Quality and Reliability Management* 20:6, pp. 691–703.

Lillrank, P. 2003b. The quality of standard, routine, and nonroutine processes. *Organization Studies* 24:2, pp. 215–233.

Lillrank, P. 2012. Integration and coordination in healthcare: An operations management view. *Journal of Integrated Care* 20:1, pp. 6–13.

Lillrank, P. 2015. The anatomy of managerial panaceas: Ontology, epistemology and technology. In Ortenblad, A., ed., *Handbook of Research on Management Ideas and Panaceas.* Cheltenham, UK: Edward Elgar, chap. 2.

Lillrank, P., Chaudhuri, A., and Torkki, P. 2015. Economies of scale in cardiac surgery. *Journal of Hospital Administration* 4:2, pp. 1–9.

Lillrank, P., Groop, J., and Malmström, T. 2010. Demand and supply–based operating modes—A framework for analyzing health care service production. *Milbank Quarterly* 88:4, pp. 595–615.

Lillrank, P., and Kano, N. 1989. *Continuous Improvement—Quality Control Circles in Japanese Industry.* Ann Arbor: University of Michigan Center for Japanese Studies Publications.

Lillrank, P., and Kostama, H. 2001. Product/process cultures and change management in complex organizations. *International Journal of Technology Management* 22:1–3, pp. 73–82.

Lillrank, P., and Särkkä, M. 2011. The service machine as a service operation framework. *Strategic Outsourcing: An International Journal* 4:3, pp. 274–293.

Little, J.D.C. 1961. A proof for the queuing formula: $L = \lambda W$. *Operations Research* 9:3, pp. 383–387.

Little, L., Sillence, E., and Joinson, A. 2017. *Behavior Change Research and Theory: Psychological and Technological Perspectives.* London: Elsevier.

Little, P., Everitt, H., Williamson, I., et al. 2001. Preferences of patients for patient centered approach to consultation in primary care: Observational study. *BMJ* 322, pp. 468–472.

Lupton, D. 2012. *Medicine as Culture: Illness, Disease and the Body.* London: Sage Publications.

Lush, R., and Vargo, S. 2014. *Service-Dominant Logic: Premises, Perspectives, Possibilities.* Cambridge: Cambridge University Press.

Lynn, J., Straube, B.M., Bell, K.M., Jencks, S.F., and Kambic, R.T. 2007. Using population segmentation to provide better health care for all: The 'bridges to health' model. *Milbank Quarterly* 85:2, pp. 185–208.

MacIntosh-Murray, A., and Choo, C.W. 2006. Information failures in health care. *Annual Review of Information Science and Technology* 40, pp. 357–391.

Maddison, A. 2007. *Contours of the World Economy 1–230 A.D.—Essays in Macroeconomic History.* Oxford: Oxford University Press.

Mahar, M. 2006. *Money-Driven Medicine—The Real Reason Health Care Costs So Much.* New York: Harper-Collins.

Makari, G. 2015. *The Soul Machine: The Invention of the Modern Mind.* New York: W.W. Norton.

March, S.T., and Smith, G.F. 1995. Design and natural science research on information technology. *Decision Support Systems* 15:4, pp. 251–266.

Marsh, H. 2014. *Do No Harm—Stories of Life, Death and Brain Surgery.* London: Weidenfeld & Nicholson.

Maslow, A. 1943. A theory of human motivation. *Psychological Review* 50, pp. 370–396.

Matsushita, K. 1986. *Not for Bread Alone—A Business Ethos, a Management Ethic.* Tokyo: PHP Institute.

Mazzocato, P., Savage, C., Brommels, M., et al. 2010. Lean thinking in healthcare: A realist review of the literature. *BMJ Quality & Safety* 19, pp. 376–382.

McCloskey, D. 2010. *Bourgeois Dignity—Why Economics Can't Explain the Modern World.* Chicago: University of Chicago Press.

McGowan, M.A., Andrews, D., and Millot, V. 2017. The walking dead? Zombie firms and productivity performance in OECD countries. OECD Economic Department Working Paper No. 1372. Paris: Organisation for Economic Co-operation and Development. www.oecd.org/eco/workingpapers.

Mehta, P., and Shenoy, S. 2011. *Infinite Vision: How Aravind Became the World's Greatest Case for Business Compassion.* Oakland, CA: Berrett-Koehler.

Miani, C., Ball, S., Pitchforth, E., et al. 2014. Organisational interventions to reduce length of stay in hospital: A rapid evidence assessment. *Health Service Delivery Research* 2:52.

Mikola, A., and Lillrank, P. 2015. Process efficiency by innovation. In Singh, V.K., and Lillrank, P., eds., *Innovations in Healthcare Management—Cost-Effective and Sustainable Solutions.* Boca Raton, FL: CRC Press/Taylor & Francis Group, pp. 189–196.

Miller, S., Abalos, E., Chamillard, M., et al. 2016. Beyond too little, too late and too much, too soon: A pathway towards evidence-based, respectful maternity care worldwide. *Lancet* 388:10056, pp. 2176–2192.

Mitra, A. 2016. *Fundamentals of Quality Control and Improvement.* New York: Wiley & Sons.

Modig, N., and Ålström, P. 2012. *This Is Lean—Solving the Efficiency Paradox.* Stockholm: Rheologica Publishing.

Moeller, S. 2008. Customer integration—A key to an implementation perspective on service provision. *Journal of Service Research* 11:2, p. 197.

Moeller, S. 2010. Characteristics of services—A new approach uncovers their value. *Journal of Service Marketing* 24:5, pp. 359–368.

Mokyr, J. 2016. *A Culture of Growth: The Origins of the Modern Economy*. Princeton, NJ: Princeton University Press.

Mol, A. 2008. *The Logic of Care: Health and the Problem of Patient Choice*. New York: Routledge.

Monden, Y. 1998. *Toyota Production System—An Integrated Approach to Just-in-Time*. 3rd ed. London: Chapman & Hall.

Moore, D.S. 2015. *The Developing Genome: An Introduction to Behavioral Epigenetics*. Oxford: Oxford University Press.

Morgan, G. 2007. *Images of Organization*. Thousand Oaks, CA: Sage.

Moriates, C., Arora, V., and Shah, N. 2016. *Understanding Value-Based Healthcare*. New York: McGraw-Hill.

Mosadegrad, A.M. 2013. Health care service quality: Towards a broad definition. *International Journal of Health Care Quality Assurance* 23:3, pp. 203–219.

Mukherjee, S. 2015. *The Laws of Medicine: Field Notes from an Uncertain Science*. New York: Simon & Schuster.

Murray, C. 2013. *Coming Apart—The State of White America, 1960–2010*. New York: Random House.

Nelson, H.G., and Stolterman, E. 2012. *The Design Way—Intentional Change in an Unpredictable World*. Cambridge, MA: MIT Press.

Niemietz, K. 2016. *Universal Healthcare without the NHS*. London: London Publishing Partnership.

Niiniluoto, I. 2002. *Critical Scientific Realism*. Oxford: Oxford University Press.

Nonaka, I., and Takeuchi, H. 1995. *The Knowledge-Creating Company*. Oxford: Oxford University Press.

North, D.C. 1992. *Transaction Costs, Institutions, and Economic Performance*. San Francisco: ICS Press.

Novignon, J., Olakojo, S.O., and Novignon, J. 2012. The effects of public and private health care expenditure on health status in sub-Saharan Africa: New evidence from panel data analysis. *Health Economic Review* 2:22, pp. 1–8.

Oakland, J. 1999. *Statistical Process Control*. London: Butterworth Heinemann.

OECD (Organisation for Economic Co-operation and Development). 2010. Health care systems: Getting more value for money. OECD Economics Department Policy Notes No. 2. Paris: OECD. https://www.oecd.org/eco/growth/46508904.pdf.

OECD (Organisation for Economic Co-operation and Development). 2015. Fiscal sustainability of health systems—Bridging health and finance perspectives. Paris: OECD.

OECD (Organisation for Economic Co-operation and Development). 2016. OECD Health at a glance 2016. Paris: OECD.

Offer, A. 2007. *The Challenge of Affluence—Self-Control and Wellbeing in United States and Britain since 1950*. Oxford: Oxford University Press.

Ohno, T. 1988. *Toyota Production System: Beyond Large-Scale Production*. Cambridge, MA: Productivity Press.

Olson, M. 1971. *The Logic of Collective Action: Public Goods and the Theory of Groups*. Cambridge, MA: Harvard University Press.

Olson, M. 1984. *The Rise and Fall of Nations*. New Haven, CT: Yale University Press.

Olson, M. 2000. *Power and Prosperity: Outgrowing Communist and Capitalist Dictatorship.* New York: Basic Books.

Oram, A. 2014. *The Information Technology Fix for Health.* Sebastopol, CA: O'Reilly Media.

Orlov, D. 2013. *The Five Stages of Collapse.* Gabriola Island, BC: New Society Publishers.

Osterwalder, A. 2004. The business model ontology—A proposition in a design science approach. PhD thesis, University of Lausanne.

Osterwalder, A., Pigneur, Y., Smith, A., and 470 practitioners from 45 countries. 2010. *Business Model Generation.* New York: Wiley.

Parasuraman, A., Zeithaml, V.A., and Berry, L. 1990. *Delivering Quality Service—Balancing Customer Perceptions and Expectations.* New York: Free Press.

Pava, C. 1983. *Managing New Office Technology.* New York: Free Press.

Pearson, S.D., Kleefield, S.F., Soukop, J.R., Cook, E.F., and Lee, T.H. 2001. Critical pathways intervention to reduce length of hospital stay. *American Journal of Medicine* 110:3, pp. 175–180.

Pentland, B.T., and Rueter, H.H. 1994. Organizational routines as grammars of action. *Administrative Science Quarterly* 39, pp. 484–510.

Perrow, C. 1999. *Normal Accidents: Living with High-Risk Technologies.* Princeton, NJ: Princeton University Press.

Phelps, E. 2011. *Mass Flourishing—How Grassroots Innovation Created Jobs, Challenge, and Change.* Princeton, NJ: Princeton University Press.

Piketty, T. 2015. *Capital in the Twenty-First Century.* Cambridge, MA: Harvard University Press.

Pirsig, R.M. 1974. *Zen and the Art of Motorcycle Maintenance.* London: Corgi.

Pirsig, R.M. 1991. *Lila—An Inquiry into Morals.* London: Corgi.

Porter, M.E., and Teisberg, E.O. 2006. *Redefining Healthcare—Creating Value-Based Competition for Results.* Boston: Harvard Business School Press.

Porter, M.E. 1980. *Competitive Strategy—Techniques for Analyzing Industries and Competitors.* New York: Free Press.

Porter, M.E., and Guth, C. 2012. *Redefining German Healthcare—Moving to a Value-Based System.* Heidelberg: Springer-Verlag.

Porter, R. 2002. *Blood and Guts: A Short History of Medicine.* London: Penguin Books.

Pound, E.S., Bell, J.H., and Spearman, M.L. 2014. *Factory Physics for Managers.* New York: McGraw-Hill.

Price, E. 1994. *Health Outcomes—A New Way of Defining and Managing Health.* Sydney: Tully Press.

Pwc. Medical cost trend: Behind the numbers 2017. https://www.pwc.com/us/en/health-care/publications/pdf/pwc-hri-medical-cost-trend-2017.pdf.

Rashid, W.E.W., and Jussof, K. 2009. Service quality in health care settings. *International Journal of Health Care Quality Assurance* 22:5, pp. 471–482.

Reid, T.R. 2016. *The Healing of America: A Global Quest for Better, Cheaper, and Fairer Healthcare.* New York: Penguin Books.

Roels, G. 2014. Optimal design of coproductive services: Interaction and work allocation. *Manufacturing & Service Operations Management* 16:4, pp. 578–594.

Rodrick, D. 2015. *Economic Rules: The Right and Wrongs of the Dismal Science.* New York: W.W. Norton.

Ronen, B., and Pliskin, J.S. 2006. *Focused Operations Management for Health Service Organizations.* New York: Wiley & Sons.

Rosenthal, E. 2017. *The American Sickness: How Health Became Big Business and How You Can Take It Back*. New York: Penguin Press.

Ross, L., and Nisbett, R.E. 2011. *The Person and the Situation: Perspectives of Social Psychology*. London: Pinter & Martin.

Roth, A.E. 2015. *Who Gets What—and Why? The New Economics of Matchmaking and Market Design*. Boston: Houghton Mifflin Harcourt.

Rozenes, S., and Cohen, Y., eds. 2017. *Handbook of Research on Strategic Alliances and Value Co-Creation in the Service Industry*. Hershey, PA: IGI Global.

Salvendy, G., and Karwowski, W., eds. 2009. *Introduction to Service Engineering*. New York: Wiley & Sons.

Sampson, S., and Froehle, C. 2006. Foundations and implications of a proposed unified services theory. *Production and Operations Management* 15:2, pp. 329–343.

Sandori, P. 1982. *The Logic of Machines and Structures*. Mineola, NY: Dover Publications.

Sarkar, D. 2007. *Lean for Service Organizations and Offices—A Holistic Approach for Operational Excellence*. Milwaukee, WI: ASQ Press.

Schmenner, R.W. 2004. Service business and productivity. *Decision Sciences* 35, pp. 333–347.

Schmenner, R.W., and Swink, M.L. 1998. On theory in operations management. *Journal of Operations Management* 17:1, pp. 97–113.

Sen, A. 1982. *Poverty and Famines: An Essay on Entitlement and Deprivation*. Oxford: Clarendon Press.

Sen, A. 2001. *Development as Freedom*. 2nd ed. Oxford: Oxford University Press.

Sharman, G. 1984. The rediscovery of logistics. *Harvard Business Review* 62:5, pp. 65–77 (September–October).

Shelling, T.C. 2006. *Micromotives and Macrobehavior*. New York: W.W. Norton.

Shem, S. 1978. *The House of God*. New York: Random House.

Shewhart, W. 1931. *Economic Control of Quality of Manufactured Product*. New York: Van Nostrand.

Shingo, S. 1988. *Non-Stock Production—The Shingo System for Continuous Improvement*. Cambridge, MA: Productivity Press.

Shostack, G.L. 1977. Breaking free from product marketing. *Journal of Marketing*, Vol. 41, April, pp. 73–80.

Shostack, G.L. 1982. How to design a service. *European Journal of Marketing* 16:1, pp. 49–63.

Shriver, L. 2016. *The Mandibles—A Family 2029–2047*. New York: Harper-Collins.

Silvestro, R., Fitzgerald, L., Johnston, R., and Voss, C. 1992. Towards a classification of service processes. *International Journal of Service Industry Management* 3:3, pp. 62–75.

Simon, H.A. 1947. *Administrative Behavior: A Study of Decision-Making Processes in Administrative Organization*. New York: MacMillan.

Simon, H.A. 1982. *Models of Bounded Rationality*. Cambridge, MA: MIT Press.

Simon, H. 1996. *The Sciences of the Artificial*. 3rd ed. Cambridge, MA: MIT Press.

Simonet, D. 2011. The new public management theory and the reform of European health care systems: An international comparative perspective. *International Journal of Public Administration* 34:12, pp. 815–826.

Skochelak, S.E., and Hawkings, R.E., eds. 2017. *Health Systems Science*. AMA Education Consortium. St. Louis, MO: Elsevier.

Sloman, J., Hinde, K., and Garrat, D. 2013. *Economics for Business*. 6th ed. London: Pearson.

Smith, A. 1776. *An Inquiry into the Nature and Causes of the Wealth of Nations*. London: W. Strahan & T. Cadell.

Spearman, C.E. 1904. General intelligence objectively determined and measured. *American Journal of Psychology* 15, pp. 201–293.

Spohrer, J., and Maglio, P.P. 2008. The emergence of service science: Toward systematic service innovations to accelerate co-creation of value. *Journal of Operations and Production Management* 17:3, pp. 238–246.

Stacey, D.F., Légaré, K., Lewis, M.J., et al. 2017. Decision aids for people facing health treatment or screening decisions. *Cochrane Database of Systematic Reviews* 4:CD001431.

Strauss, R.W., and Mayer, T.A. 2013. *Strauss and Mayer's Emergency Department Management*. New York: McGraw-Hill.

St. Sauver, J.L., Warner, D.O., Yawn, B.P., et al. 2013. Why patients visit their doctors: Assessing the most prevalent conditions in a defined American population. *Mayo Clinic Proceedings* 88:1, pp. 56–68.

Stuckler, D., and Basu, S. 2013. *The Body Economic: Why Austerity Kills*. New York: Basic Books.

Taylor, F.W. 1911. *The Principles of Scientific Management*. New York: W.W. Norton (reprint 1967).

Teasell, R.W., Foley, N.C., Bhogal, S.K., and Speechley, M.R. 2003. An evidence-based review of stroke rehabilitation. *Topics in Stroke Rehabilitation* 10:1, pp. 29–58.

Tett, G. 2015. *The Silo Effect: Why Putting Everything in Its Place Isn't Such a Bright Idea*. London: Little Brown.

Thaler, R.H. 2015. *Misbehaving: The Making of Behavioral Economics*. London: Allen Lane.

Thomas, W.I., and Thomas, D.S. 1928. *The Child in America: Behavior Problems and Programs*. New York: Knopf.

Tolft, S., Nyström, M.E., Tischelman, C. Brommels, M., and Hansson, J. 2015. Agile, a guiding principle for health care improvement? *International Journal of Health Care Quality Assurance* 28:5, pp. 468–493.

Topol, E. 2015. *The Patient Will See You Now—The Future of Medicine Is in Your Hands*. New York: Basic Books.

Torinus, J. 2014. *The Grassroots Health Care Revolution—How Companies across America are Dramatically Cutting Their Health Care Costs While Improving Care*. Dallas, TX: Benbella Books.

Toyama, K. 2015. *Geek Heresy: Rescuing Social Change from the Cult of Technology*. New York: Public Affairs.

Ulwick, A. 2005. *What Customers Want—Using Outcome-Driven Innovation to Create Breakthrough Products and Services*. New York: McGraw-Hill.

Vargo, S., and Lusch, R. 2004. Evolving to a new dominant logic for marketing. *Journal of Marketing* 68, pp. 1–17.

Vennberg, J. 2010. *Tracking Medicine—A Researcher's Quest to Understand Health Care*. Oxford: Oxford University Press.

Vissers, J., and Beech, R., eds. 2005. *Health Operations Management—Patient Flow Logistics in Health Care*. New York: Routledge.

Vogel, E. 1979. *Japan as Number One—Lessons for America*. New York: Harper & Row.

von Bertalanffy, L. 2015. *General System Theory: Foundations, Development, Applications*. New York: George Braziller.

Von Neumann, J., and Morgenstern, O. 2007. *Theory of Games and Economic Behavior*. Princeton, NJ: Princeton University Press.

Wager, K.A., Lee, F.W., and Glaser, J.P. 2017. *Health Care Information Systems: A Practical Approach for Health Care Management*. 4th ed. San Francisco: Jossey-Bass.

Warnecke, H.J. 1993. *The Fractal Company*. Berlin: Springer.

Weber, M. 1949. *The Methodology of the Social Sciences*. New York: Free Press.

Weber, M. 1978. *Economy and Society*. Los Angeles: University of California Press.

Weick, K.E., and Sutcliffe, K.M. 2007. *Managing the Unexpected: Resilient Performance in and Age of Uncertainty*. 2nd ed. San Francisco: Jossey-Bass.

Weinick, R.M., Burns, R.M., and Mehrotra, A. 2010. Many emergency department visits could be managed at urgent care centers and retail clinics. *Health Affairs* 29:9, pp. 1630–1636.

Weinstein, M.C., Torrance, G., and McGuire, A. 2009. QALYs: The basics. *Value in Health* 12, pp. 5–9.

Welch, G.H., Schwartz, L., and Woloshin, S. 2011. *Overdiagnosed: Making People Sick in the Pursuit of Health*. Boston: Beacon Press.

Weldring, T., and Smith, S.M. 2013. Patient-reported outcomes (PROs) and patient-reported outcome measures (PROMs). *Health Service Insights* 6, pp. 61–68.

Wemmerlöv, U. 1991. A taxonomy for service processes and its implications for system design. *International Journal of Service Industry Management* 1:3, pp. 20–40.

Westaby, S. 2017. *Fragile Lives—A Heart Surgeon's Stories of Life and Death on the Operating Table*. London: HarperCollins.

Whittington, J.W., Nolan, K., Ninon Lewis, N., and Torres, T. 2015. Pursuing the triple aim: The first 7 years. *Milbank Quarterly* 93:2, pp. 263–300.

Wiegers, T.A., Van Der Zee, J., and Keirse, M.J.N.C. 1998. Maternity care in the Netherlands: The changing home birth rate. *Birth* 25, pp. 190–197.

Williamson, O.E. 1985. *The Economic Institutions of Capitalism—Firms, Markets, Relational Contracting*. New York: Free Press.

Womack, J.P., Jones, D.T., and Roos, D. 1990. *The Machine That Changed the World*. New York: Rawson Associates.

Womack, J.P., and Jones, D.T. 1996. *Lean Thinking—Banish Waste and Create Wealth in Your Corporation*. New York: Simon & Schuster.

Womack, M. 2009. *The Anthropology of Health and Healing*. Lanham, MD: Altamira Press.

Wootton, D. 2006. *Bad Medicine—Doctors Doing Harm since Hippocrates*. Oxford: Oxford University Press.

World Health Organization. 2003. *Adherence to Long-Term Therapies: Evidence for Action*. Geneva: World Health Organization.

World Health Organization. 2006. Quality of care: A process for making strategic choices in health systems. Geneva: World Health Organization. http://www.who.int/management/quality/assurance/QualityCare_B.Def.pdf.

World Health Organization. 2008. World health report 2008: Primary health care, now more than ever. Geneva: World Health Organization. http://www.who.int/whr/2008/en/.

Zeithaml, V.A. 1988. Consumer perceptions of price, quality, and value: A means-end model and synthesis of evidence. *Journal of Marketing* 52, pp. 2–22.

Zeithaml, V.A., Bittner, M.J., and Gremler, D.D. 2013. *Services Marketing*. 6th ed. New York: McGraw-Hill.

# Index